EIGHTEENTH CENTU

EIGHTEENTH CENTURY SCOTLAND: NEW PERSPECTIVES

Edited by

T.M. Devine and J.R. Young

TUCKWELL PRESS

First published in Great Britain in 1999 by
Tuckwell Press
The Mill House
Phantassie
East Linton
East Lothian EH40 3DG
Scotland

ISBN 1 86232 051 9

British Library Cataloguing in Publication Data
A catalogue record for this book is available
on request from the British Library

Typeset by Hewer Text Ltd, Edinburgh
Printed and bound by Cromwell Press, Trowbridge, Wiltshire

For

Margaret Hastie

in appreciation of her outstanding service to the
Research Centre in Scottish History, University of Strathclyde

Contents

List of Contributors

Bernard Aspinwall Honorary Research Fellow, Research Centre in Scottish History, University of Strathclyde

T.M. Devine University Research Professor in Scottish History and Director of the Research Institute of Irish and Scottish Studies, University of Aberdeen

R.J.Finlay Senior Lecturer in Scottish History and Director of the Research Centre in Scottish History, University of Strathclyde

Michael Fry Independent Scholar

A. Mackillop Lecturer in Scottish and Imperial History, University of Aberdeen

Alexander Murdoch Senior Lecturer in Scottish History, University of Edinburgh

Allan I. Macinnes Burnett-Fletcher Professor of History, University of Aberdeen

James F. McMillan Professor of European History, University of Strathclyde

Elaine W. McFarland Senior Lecturer in History, Glasgow Caledonian University

Jane Rendall Senior Lecturer in History, University of York

Richard Saville Lecturer in Modern History, University of St. Andrews

T.C. Smout Director of the Institute of Environmental History, University of St. Andrews and H.M. Historiographer Royal in Scotland

R.E.Tyson Senior Lecturer in Economic History, University of Aberdeen

Christopher A. Whatley Professor of History, University of Dundee

I.D. Whyte Professor of Geography, University of Lancaster

John R. Young Lecturer in Scottish History, University of Strathclyde and Assistant Director of the Research Centre in Scottish History, University of Strathclyde and Assistant Director of the Research Centre in Scottish History, University of Strathclyde

One

Preface

T.M. DEVINE

FEW PERIODS CONTAIN as much interest and significance for the historian of Scotland as the eighteenth century. This was the time when the Union was forged with England and its longer-term political and economic effects started to become apparent. In the later decades of the century there were the first signs of the major industrial and agrarian changes which were soon to transform the way of life of the Scottish people. It was a time too of remarkable intellectual and cultural vitality which has come to be known as the Scottish Enlightenment, a period when Scots philosophers, historians and scientists were at the very cutting edge of European thought. Nearly thirty years ago, in their introduction to *Scotland in the Age of Improvement* (Edinburgh, 1970), still a valuable survey of key aspects of the eighteenth century, Rosalind Mitchison and Nicholas Phillipson lamented the absence of serious study of so many of the factors which helped to shape Scottish development in this seminal period. The same pessimistic verdict would not be as convincing in 1998. As part of the wider surge of interest in Scottish historical studies, major works have appeared on subjects as varied as the Union, Jacobitism, the Highlands, industrialisation, rural transformation and political radicalism. The Enlightenment itself has become a veritable cottage industry, attracting scholarly attention from Europe and North America as well as from students in Scottish universities.

This boom in research has inevitably produced revised views on old themes, new perspectives and fresh controversy. To encourage debate further on important issues the Research Centre in Scottish History at Strathclyde University organised a seminar in 1996–7 on Eighteenth Century Scotland to which many of the most influential researchers in the field were invited. This book is the edited proceedings of the seminar and is produced with the help of the participants. The volume is not to be seen as a textbook of eighteenth century Scottish history. Some key issues, such as education, are omitted and in other cases, such as the Enlightenment, the examination is confined to specialist aspects of a much broader and more complex subject. But a significant number of the classic themes of the eighteenth century, such as the Union of 1707, Jacobitism, Scottish Identity, Emigration, Radicalism, the Origins of Scottish Modernisation, the Highlands, the Improvers and

Urbanisation are given treatment at length. It is intended, therefore, that the book should prove useful to undergraduate students and a general audience as well as to professional scholars working in the subject areas who wish an up-to-date critical coverage of important aspects of Scotland in the eighteenth century.

What general issues emerge from the collection? A concern of several writers was to place the Union in perspective by stressing that the Scottish economic miracle of the later eighteenth century, demonstrated in I.D. Whyte's chapter on the extraordinary pace of urbanisation, did not depend exclusively on the benefits of 1707. The Union did not, in Michael Fry's phrase, 'change almost everything about Scotland as it raised her from primitive darkness into the light of modernity'. As Fry argues, to accept such a Whig conclusion would be to ignore the advances made before 1707 and the difficulties in the Anglo-Scottish relationship at least two decades after that date. Both Fry and Richard Saville trace Scottish imperial expansion and a national strategy of economic improvement to the later seventeenth century. Saville stresses that insufficient attention has been given to the Revolution of 1688–9 which proved a decisive break in economic policy and inaugurated, according to him, a new age of 'economic politics'. The ill-starred Darien Scheme, usually accounted an unmitigated disaster, fits into this new emphasis on national economic aggrandisement. The attempt to establish a Scottish settlement on the isthmus of Panama may have failed but the strategy to establish a commercial emporium was an original and visionary idea which collapsed because of incompetent planning and inefficient implementation.

Nevertheless, debate on the nature of the pre-Union economy and Scotland's capacity 'to go it alone' without inclusion in England's markets remains unresolved. While arguing that 1688–9 might have been a new start, Saville concludes that Scotland in 1707 was still a country 'with exceptional economic problems' induced by the bad harvests of the 1690s and the impact of war and mercantilism on Scottish trade. T.C. Smout's analysis in this volume also suggests Scotland remained poor and the economy balanced precariously between sufficiency and severe shortage. When dearth did come in the last decade of the seventeenth century it triggered massive emigration to Ulster, increased mortality and an estimated 13 per cent fall in population. Smout concludes: 'Revisionist historians and others who seek to put the brightening days of Scottish economic history decisively back to the seventeenth century need to come up with a better supported case'. In a sense, then, the balance between progress, stagnation and crisis in the years immediately before the Union remains an enigma and a question which deserves more research. Official policy was changing before 1705. Indeed, the turning can be pushed back further than Saville's 1688 to the launching of colonial schemes to South Carolina and New Jersey in the reign of James VII and II during the 1680s. But the new 'economic politics' may have been temporarily aborted by the sheer magnitude of the crisis at the very end of the century.

The older historiography argued that these disasters had a decisive effect on the passage of the Parliamentary Union of 1707. The Scots were locked, so it was suggested, in a contracting economic vice while at the same time they had come to depend on English markets for the vital trades of cattle, wool, sheep, linen and coal. They, therefore, had little choice but to accept the terms of a closer association with Westminster. John Young shows that this deterministic interpretation is misleading because it fails to take account of the angry surge of protest against Union throughout both towns and rural localities in the Lowlands which alarmed the governing party in Scotland and the Westminster authority. This in turn resulted in a new emphasis on political management to ensure the progress of the Treaty through the Scottish Parliament and military preparations to protect English security in the event that popular unrest became uncontrollable.

The Union long remained unpopular and one of the most dramatic manifestations of dissent was Jacobitism which spawned major risings in 1715–6 and 1745–6 and minor ones in 1708 and 1719 in support of the exiled House of Stewart. Allan Macinnes demonstrates that Jacobitism is not only to be associated with Highland clanship as by no means all clans were Jacobite and among the most fervent supporters of the Stewarts were non-juring Episcopalians from the Lowland counties north of the Tay. Nevertheless, as Macinnes concedes, the clans bore 'the brunt of the fighting and dying in the front lines during the major risings'. James McMillan's study of Scottish Catholics, whose small numbers were mainly concentrated in the western Highlands and Islands, stresses their strong sympathy for the cause. Missionaries were 'Jacobites to a man' and Catholic priests were appointed chaplains to Bonnie Prince Charlie's forces in the '45 with the rank of captain. Ultimately, however, this intimate relationship between Jacobitism and Catholicism and the refusal of the Stewarts to renounce the old faith until after 1750 were key factors in their failure to effectively exploit Scottish disaffection with the Union. The presbyterian Church of Scotland, which brought majority Lowland opinion behind it, remained resolutely hostile throughout.

However, the death of Jacobitism as a political force soon led to its resurrection in another form. By the 1750s growing prosperity was consolidating the Union relationship. The historical debate in this later period concerns the development of Scotland's identity as a stateless nation which had entered a politico-economic union with the most advanced society in Europe and feared for its sense of historic and cultural identity. A few decades after it had been ruthlessly crushed in 1746 Jacobitism started to develop 'an emotional response for a stateless nation' and by the early nineteenth century Jacobite song had become second only to love song in the popular canon. Bonnie Prince Charles was transformed into a national icon and the gallant clansmen who had fought and died at Culloden were now seen to have been heroic Scottish warriors rather than as heretical supports of the Catholic House of Stewart. Jacobitism's most enduring impact was on the national psyche long after its political relevance had disappeared.

The sentimental appeal of Jacobitism was the manifestation of Scotland's developing identity within the Union. But debate still rages on the timing and extent of Scottish acceptance of 'Britishness' in the eighteenth century. The chapters by Alexander Murdoch and Richard Finlay demonstrate how far we are from any consensus on this important issue. Both would probably agree that what emerged in the decades after c.1750 was a system of concurrent identities in which a continued sense of 'Scottishness' could coexist and interact with the growing influence of 'Britishness'. What is more at issue, however, is the balance between the two identities and the extent to which the mass of the population as well as the elite had been affected. Finlay argues that ideas of North Britain were mainly confined to a small group and that more attention might be paid to the rampant Scottaphobia which existed in elite circles in 'South Britain'. The common Protestantism of both England and Scotland should not be overemphasised as a force for unity. Protestantism can also be seen as a force for division given the presbyterian inheritance in Scotland and its traditional role in the formation of Scottish national identity.

However, in one important respect both England and Scotland were travelling the same route though at a somewhat different pace. By 1800 industrialisation was fashioning a new social order in both countries but economic growth, as evidenced by Iain Whyte's statistics on comparative urban development, was considerably faster in Scotland. R.E. Tyson also notes that though population was rising in both countries one crucial factor, age at marriage, was demonstrably lower in England because of significant differences in the agricultural labour market and welfare provision in each country. The nature of rural change in each society also stands out. England had no 'Highlands', a regional society which was transformed from feudalism/clanship to capitalism over less than two generations. The nature of and response to these cataclysmic changes is explored in two revisionist chapters by Andrew Mackillop and T.M. Devine which critically evaluate some of the most enduring beliefs in eighteenth century Highland history. Throughout these discussions and the chapters by T.C. Smout on the Improvers and Christopher Whatley on collier serfdom the vital influence of ideas in giving momentum to economic change is stressed. The Scottish

Enlightenment, aspects of which receive special treatment in this volume by Jane Rendall and Bernard Aspinwall, was also at the heart of the economic revolution and by no means confined to the lecture room and the salon.

It was a revolution, however, that was remarkably peaceful. In the 1790s considerable discontent was manifested, most obviously in the development of the Scottish Friends of the People Societies and the United Scotsmen. Elaine McFarland demonstrates how in the aftermath of the stimulus of the French Revolution ideas, organisation models and radicals moved from Ireland to Scotland. Nevertheless, political protest in Scotland remained united and there was nothing to compare with the disturbances which culminated in the carnage of the 1798 rebellion in Ireland. In Scotland, by the turn of the century the forces of conservatism held the whip-hand, the old regime seemed rock solid and such political dissent as survived had had to adopt clandestine methods and go underground. In Scotland the old order was buttressed, despite the manifest venality of the political system, because it was delivering for those who mattered in society. The economic revolution created a veritable material bonanza for landowners, merchants, manufacturers and professionals. This was not simply in Scotland itself. In the period after c.1750, as Michael Fry shows in his chapter, landed and bourgeois Scots penetrated the British Empire in increasing numbers as to the same extent soldiers, planters, teachers, doctors, merchants, officials and government servants. Ireland did not have such a safety-valve to the same extent for its 'restless spirits'. In Ireland too, both the vast Catholic majority and the presbyterian minority faced legal exclusion in varying degrees. After 1707 the Scots retained control over their Church and their laws and so avoided the kind of large-scale discrimination which not only scarred Irish society but also stored up the kind of deep-seated bitterness which was finally unleashed with a vengeance in 1798. In Scotland, on the other hand, the hereditary governing class who held control at the beginning of the eighteenth century were still well-entrenched in 1800, despite the tensions and stresses of industrialisation. There could be no better illustration of change and continuity in the complex period considered in this volume.

Two

Scottish Modernisation Prior to the Industrial Revolution, 1688–1763

RICHARD SAVILLE

THIS CHAPTER ADDRESSES economic aspects of the modernisation of Scotland from the late seventeenth century, down to the industrial revolution.[1] This was an awkward era in Scottish history, beginning with the intense inheritance of internal divisions, ambiguities and political rivalries. About these enough has been written to question any suggestion of a smooth progression to a more enlightened world. Moreover, contemporaries were only too aware of the apparently intractable economic fault lines in the early eighteenth century to display much confidence about employment and incomes. By 1763, in contrast, we have a clear picture of Whiggish processes built into Scotland's economic and political life, now shorn of the old-style obstacles of earlier decades. The questions long addressed by historians remain valid: how and why did this relatively impoverished and socially backward country manage to catch up with England and enjoy the benefits of the industrial revolution and foreign trade? How much of the catching up was due to indigenous sources, and how much to imported men, ideas and machines, and further, alongside the economic fault-lines, how did the positive processes work, which, eventually, made the result inevitable? While Scotland was not, at the later date, on a par with England in respect of incomes, and its middle classes were disproportionately smaller, the country was able to accumulate capital, generate new incomes, and grow new businesses. There were also advantages in banking and the organisation of enterprise which England did not enjoy, and by 1763 the overall growth rate was similar on both sides of the border.

The study of this 'old modernisation' in Scotland has broadened in recent years, as a range of interesting questions have elbowed their way into view: we now consider education and training as more relevant, especially so for artisans and the middle classes; there were subtle changes in the position of women, in the range of ideas that made up the 'common weal', including changes in religious attitudes, and the significance of the middle class family in raising expertise from one generation to another. For the more peaceful times after 1688 the Scots generated new ways of conducting business, and gradually altered the way social life fitted together. By the middle decades of the eighteenth century this was a cohesive society, in which the underlying attitudes focused on work-discipline and progress, together with a determination to increase the number of economic opportunities. The circulation of new ideas, many drawn from abroad, confirm the outward-looking nature of the middle-class, and the openness of the leading institutions. This was an expanding universe, and, by the onset of industrialisation, Scottish social life was much more diverse and sophisticated. The way progress was understood by contemporaries also changed: at the revolution politics and the military were the main avenues through which economic advance, and family well-being, could be guaranteed. While these still loomed large by the close of the Seven Years War, the earlier views were less appropriate. This shift in understanding was one of the key benefits of modernisation, and is why some thought must be given to the change in government ushered in with William and Mary, and also to its limitations.

The revolution foreshadowed a decisive break in economic policy and the direction of government in Scotland. The overthrow of the old regime was a joint English-Scottish-Dutch enterprise, was well-planned, and conducted with huge popular support. There was close co-operation between Whigs on both sides of the border, and from the time William landed in England (November 1688), Scots remained close to the highest ranks of Government and Army. There was a new potential for economic change in Scotland, which imparted a sharper edge to economic debate than had been possible before, and a more deliberate effort on the part of the leaders of society to modernise. This allowed possibilities, latent prior to the arrival of William and Mary, to emerge in the freer conditions. While some of the political elites, perhaps the majority, may not have fathomed all aspects of economic debate, it is striking how many nobles and landowners were determined to make the new times an economic as well as a political divide. What is so interesting is that these conclusions were reached on both sides of the border. In particular, property rights, industrial growth, and political power would run together, although, in practice, Scots adopted some very different methods for this new 'economic politics' and, in their enthusiasm, made serious mistakes which a richer country would have absorbed more easily than Scotland did.

The new settlement ushered in a range of opportunities suppressed, or unavailable, under the regimes of Charles II and James VII, two of the most hated monarchs ever to rule Scotland. Just how wide-ranging became clear from the debates in Parliament, at the Privy Council, before the Court of Session (which dealt with most civil and business cases), and in the larger of the royal burghs. These institutions, through their openness and by their inclusion of substantial property owners, were able to fashion a model system of aristocratic and business decision-making, based on the idea that 'inclusive' politics would augment economic wellbeing, and government administration should work for all property-owners. This 'economic politics' thus linked the owners of landed and commercial property, and aimed to strengthen their wealth by utilising the restoration of political powers rusty from nearly three decades of subservience to royal despotism.

From the time when the Convention Parliament of 1689 considered the pleadings of James VII, and William and Mary, few among the nobility, and the more economically significant of the lairds, could doubt the renewal of the landowners' role as the natural leaders of Scottish society, and as the years passed their interests and connections grew stronger. But the story was more complicated than it seemed at first: the years before the Union of 1707 witnessed severe economic and climatic obstacles which emphasised the limitations of the new 'economic politics' and impeded efforts to improve the condition of the country. Scotland was to remain poor, relatively backward, and geographically fragmented, with the many disadvantages of a semi-autonomous commercial and trading position within a union of crowns, where the more powerful partner vigorously protected its own trading and colonial interests. It was to take much longer for Scots landowners and business people to reach the economic security and wellbeing that seemed so close in 1688.

After the revolution there was a clear sequence of events: the supporters of William and Mary, including many who returned from exile, were determined to secure the military situation, and to right the wrongs inflicted on their families and recover estates seized by the Crown. The security situation was stable by 1692, apart from the rumours and speculation of wartime, and the military and personal processes merged into the programme of national rejuvenation. The speed of the repossessions of forfeited estates encouraged a swift transition to the 'national' phase of recovery. The reason was clear: virtually every family who recovered estates by Parliamentary legislation, found their inheritance mired in seemingly intractable legal disputes in which the central problem was a mismatch between credit and debt, together with a thin cash flow. Indebtedness had been a way of surviving the ravages of the previous regime, as it made estates less attractive to royal predators, although it was often unavoidable for straightforward business reasons. Initially, there were few routes to debt repayment: the rapacious, cut-throat, attitude to public office informs one answer, but there were limits to the extent of income available. This left cash flow from rents, sales of agricultural produce, trade and commerce, thus encouraging landowners to consider ways the institutions of state could encourage new incomes, without penalising anyone for merely political and religious beliefs.

It is not a simple matter to typecast the range of economic and financial ideas and decisions which emerged from the institutions of state and law, and it should be reiterated that the basic framework rested on the enlargement of the body politic, sweeping away the narrowly-based, capricious power of the royal stranglehold, and the ill-thought out attempt to borrow ideas from the absolutist tradition of royal power. The new system sought the in-bringing of the whole of the landowning class who supported, or acquiesced, in the new constitutional settlement, and allowed a new awareness of, and a positive attitude towards, the regulation of financial and economic affairs. The system also required the removal of James' supporters from the courts of session and justiciary, and their replacement by judges who supported the political settlement, and the new economic organisation which came with the politics. This was the underpinning of the new 'economic politics'.

The income problem encouraged a severe inquiry, as to how national progress in trade and industry could be achieved so as to cut the burdens of interest payments on estates and the costs of legal dispute; it also focused the minds of legislators on the sheer scale of the effort required to catch up with the English economy. In the sessions of 1693 and 1695, the Parliamentary Commissioners, as members of Parliament were termed, opened up the joint-stock company procedure with important trading innovations, large-scale joint-stocks were established, including the Bank of Scotland, founded in July 1695, and the Company of Scotland trading to Africa and the Indies in the previous month. Scots law was supportive of partnerships forming joint-stocks, and thus business and landed wealth could easily co-operate through existing legal structures: 47 such companies were formed by 1695, now secure from asset seizures by courtiers or licensed-to-plunder Highland clans.[2] Also passed in 1695 was the 'Act anent lands lying run-rig' which gave landowners the right to change, arbitrarily, existing land systems, including run-rigs. A month later, another Act overrode parts of the land laws, in respect of common rights, and thus reduced potential costs of estate re-organisation. These were important devices for improvers, and firmly shifted the legal process in favour of a market economy, away from customary rights and obligations which might have impeded a single-minded focus on increasing rents.[3]

There was a fiscal aspect to government deliberations: few landlords could afford to burden their estates with the additional costs of the European war: defeating the Scots Jacobites had been expensive, though involved such widespread voluntary and clan commitment that costs for most families were contained. But war overseas was a different matter, and the English Whigs realised that the Scots could not match their resolution with cash. The level of taxes on land (the cess) remained low, at under 1/40 of the English level of land tax, and the income was re-cycled within Scotland. Thus the majority of Scots lowland landowners, and the Highland clans who opposed James VII, including the many houses of Clan Campbell, were able to rely on the new English financial revolution, and Dutch finance, for their ultimate security. Most landowners realised that with France supporting James VII, war was likely for the foreseeable future and the main Scots contribution to this was the supply of troops. Dozens of landed families had members in the Scots brigade paid for by the States General, or in the Scots regiments in Flanders funded by the English: their numbers far exceeded those Scotsmen in arms for Louis XIV, both in the war which ended with the Treaty of Ryswick in 1697, and the subsequent war of the Spanish Succession, 1702–1713.

The memory of the old regime long remained an aspect of the Scots thought and contributed to a new, historical, tradition.[4] It focused on the distress of the restoration, the abuse of state powers, the favouritism shown to courtiers, and the transient nature of decision-making, which, all too often, had looked to the short-term income of government, at the expense, for example, of the integrity of the coinage, or expenditure on social overhead capital. There were numerous illustrations of Restoration government canvassed by historians in the olden days, and one of the valuable aspects of the recently published history of Glasgow has been to remind a modern audience of these bleak years. The burgh suffered at the hands of Highland looting expeditions, and the effects of the laying waste parts of the west of Scotland, including the seizure and destruction of much of value on the Campbell estates from 1685 to 1688. It seems extraordinary to the modern world that in June 1679, following the defeat of the Covenanters at Bothwell Bridge, senior military officers, including John Graham of Claverhouse, wished to 'plunder the west' and destroy Glasgow, Hamilton and Strathaven. In the years 1660–88 the population of Glasgow, the most important burgh in the west, fell by 2700.[5] This new Scots memory notwithstanding, we should notice that the 'persecution' focus of Scots Calvinism altered. In lowland Scotland the pre-1688 church policy was tainted with a lethargy on economic matters, but, with the removal of the bishops from the Presbyterian church, and at ease with the new politics, it focused on economic wellbeing, and in the long-term became less tolerant of persecution.[6] Some of this did not obviously favour economic progress as we understand it, though, on questions of traditional social and wage costs the Church worked to support progress and its effects on the national psychology should be emphasised.

This view of exceptional Scottish, literary and intellectual advantage may be strengthened: there was abundant commentary, on both sides of the border, about how modernisation might proceed, and the choices which legislators could make. Ideas which had hung around the exiles in the coffee houses in Amsterdam and Rotterdam, and common to the many who engaged in business overseas, were soon in print, and there was a considerable interchange of manuscripts. All sorts of schemes, many, no doubt, exaggerating the rewards to be reaped from their plans were put before the public. Leslie Stephen noticed this drawback: many of these tracts involved the contemplation of the planet as a whole, coupled with the vision from the horizon of a shop window.[7] Yet, individual trades always involved special pleading, which was not necessarily a bad thing, given the increase in business opportunities based on new trades in the seventeenth century, which helped, for example, to alter the ambivalent attitude to what was, and was not, a luxury trade.[8] Eventually, later in the eighteenth century in Scotland than in England, questions appropriate to a static and unsure society disappear from economic literature. In fact, most schemes faded from view, unless they enjoyed backing from business, or landed wealth. This was the fate, for example, of no fewer than four 'land-bank' schemes put forward in Edinburgh by Hugh Chamberlain; the first, in 1693, was rejected by a committee of the Scots Parliament, the last in a much diluted form went down in the aftermath of the economic and financial crisis of December 1704.[9] These, and other projects possessed a touching faith in the possibility of apparently endless cheap credit spun out of land, Parliamentary edict, or share-dealing, and the sceptical reception of these ideas, and the arguments over company formation and tax-raising, confirm the effectiveness of Parliamentary mediation of trade and business ideas. Further, we should remember that the Scots legislators, their English counterparts, and the rapidly expanding personnel of the departments of state, understood business and land at first hand. This was then an intellectual process, augmenting the knowledge within the governing classes: and for which Archdeacon Cunningham observed in the English context, was perceived as affording subsidiary help to the statecraft of the epoch he designated 'Parliamentary Colbertism'.[10] In the more limited Scottish context, historians and other intellectuals, assisted in the remarkable shift to a broadly based 'economic politics' by posing questions about Government, regulation and law, which were in abeyance in the cautious times preceding 1688.

Whilst one may contend that the intentions of the new Scottish 'economic politics' were sound in 1695, the argument fails to take into account that England's 'Parliamentary Colbertism' was built on a much richer economy, and a more robust credit base. The English East India Company had almost a century of trading, the Levant Company also went back to the sixteenth century, and the English shipbuilding and shipowning industries were among the largest in the world. Their colonial empire was long-established, their slave trades were growing, and the royal navy by 1695 contained over 100 vessels from first to sixth rates. There was a real breadth to the English industrial base. The new government policies thus augmented a strong position. Contrasts can be drawn at some length, and the Scottish position, which was always difficult, was aggravated by the de-facto declaration of war against Spain with the first expedition of the Company of Scotland trading to Africa and the Indies in 1698. Scotland was a minor, peripheral, country, with no colonies, little trading base in the Americas, and no navy; yet it intended to invade and seize territory in central America which had been under Spanish control for nearly two centuries. Moreover, the high costs of the Company were exacerbated because much of the equipment for the two expeditions to the Darien peninsula had to be purchased abroad, as they were not made in Scotland. Coinciding with this aggressive military endeavour came the dreadful dearth of 1695–1700. This was no ordinary famine, purchasing power in town and country collapsed, highland bands resumed their marauding, barter became common, tax-collecting was especially fraught, and merchants exported much of the good coin to buy food.[11] The results were etched on the memory of several generations of Scots. In contrast, the English economy surged ahead in the interval between the Peace of Ryswick, 1697, and the resumption of war in 1702.

Balance of payments studies for the Scots Parliament showed a dire situation by 1704.[12] Although these exaggerated the trade gap (the more detailed study gave a gap of almost 50 per cent), and omitted invisibles, such as soldiers' pay, they appear to confirm that there was a deterioration on the foreign exchanges compared with the early 1690s: each year the Scots had to send out gold and silver to meet the trade imbalance between low exports and high imports, although a certain, varying amount of overseas debt was accumulated in balances in the main trading burghs. A Glasgow merchant, knowledgeable in the cattle, linen and wool trades, put the trade gap somewhat lower, at 20 per cent, or £31,000 Scots sterling, after allowing for payments by nobles in London.[13] To ordinary Scots these imbalances were obscure; what was noted was the shortage of good silver coin, compared with the middle 1690s, and Government edicts trying to force worn and clipped silver failed to convince.[14] This problem was grappled with by the Duke of Argyll in 1705, as part of a concerted attempt to seize the assets of the Bank of Scotland, and the Duke's chief propagandist, the soon to be famous John Law, tried to blame the Bank's £1 Scots sterling notes, introduced in late 1700, for driving out silver. The problem was more subtle and embraced England as well as Scotland: the exodus followed a temporary demand (and hence higher price) for silver in Holland for export to the East Indies, and for their renewed war efforts against Louis XIV.[15] But ordinary folk could only see less silver, and that of poorer quality, and this doubtless contributed to the lowering of morale in Scotland which was evident in the pamphlets of this time. The struggle over credit, and the attempted seizure of Bank of Scotland, thwarted by politicians worried about the rise of Campbell power, marks the close of the unity forged in the Parliament sessions of the 1690s: independent 'economic politics' had run its course, replaced by faction-fighting, special pleading, and the run-up to the Union of Parliaments.

With the dearth of the 1690s came an exodus of skilled workers. Emigration was a long established route for impecunious, though employable, artisans.[16] Some writers now realised the significance of the loss of these skills: 'great numbers of people, after the expense bestowed on their education, being yearly forced out'.[17] Few skilled Protestant immigrants came in, the bulk of the thousands of Huguenots driven out by Louis XIV after 1685 moved to England, Holland and the colonies. This undoubtedly improved the quality of English and Dutch textiles, and may have been the occasion for the many adverse comparisons on quality, between Scots and others' textiles. There may have been some deterioration in the quality of other manufactures although this was more likely as a comparative problem, with foreign products improving faster, and widening the existing gap with the Scottish product. The evidence also suggests that there remained pockets of high quality textiles, especially in the linen trades in the Glasgow area, and in the north-east, though this was the preserve of a limited number of families and particularly women, including the 'many young gentlewomen that have little or no portions'; alongside, inevitably, the 'poor women who have no way to live', involved in large numbers in the coarser linen and stocking trades.[18] There were also unfounded worries over the droving trade, which had suffered during the dearth due to a shortage of stock. Our interest in this economic commentary in early 1700s Scotland is in the shift from confidence to worry, in particular the concern over the potential for erosion of the fine textile markets, and the other export planks of the economy.

The true core of Scottish exports was captured in the drafting of the Aliens Act of February 1705: Scotland's Parliament, by Christmas of that year had to agree to the constitutional position insisted on by England, (i.e., when Queen Anne died the succession would go to Sophia, Electress of Hanover, or her heirs), otherwise linen, wool, coal, cattle and sheep would be banned. The evidence suggests that little else could compete on international markets. While in Glasgow, Aberdeen, Dundee and Edinburgh, and a range of smaller manufacturing burghs, there were numerous skilled artisans, they rarely made goods to foreign standards. The acerbic comments of those who had occasion to travel and live abroad, needs qualification, but was accurate for a wide range of everyday wood-based and iron goods, pottery wares, and coarse textiles. The Scots market accepted a poorer, shabbier, product than the English. The problem was multi-faceted, low incomes, a stagnant population and a restricted demand for luxury goods largely met by imports which Scots artisans could not match. There was little expectation of change: burgh guilds served to maintain the traditional incomes of members and tended to discourage incomers, innovation and competition.[19] Many opposed 'fancy' work on religious and moral grounds. The gradual dissolution of guild control came relatively late; for Edinburgh tailors in the 1730s, for cabinet making and printing later still. So Scotland for several decades after the Union of Parliaments, produced cheap goods, but with little vent abroad, with artisan wages much below English levels. The failure to raise quality and wages, the partner of low consumer expectations, saw a continued skills drain from the country.

Although we have a country in 1707 with exceptional economic problems Scotland enjoyed several advantages which studies of modernisation now give more credit for than past generations did. The intellectual and literary culture was sophisticated, the re-invigorated religious ether was remarkably resilient and forward-looking, and the legal establishment effective in distancing itself from English control and mores. The military and political framework ensured that pro-government clans were slowly moving into the eighteenth century, leaving behind some, and then most, of their old-fashioned communal attitudes. The Campbells have been cited in this respect, and there were other clans on the Highland fringes moving in similar directions.[20] Scots everyday culture reflected the hard living and climatic uncertainty; for the majority of the population in the lowlands, culture was broadly based, a fact indicated in both religious and enlightenment writings. Scotland was both matriarchal and patriarchal, in the Highlands as well as the Lowlands, and women enjoyed property rights typical of northern Europe, including the right to work, market goods and negotiate sales. There were numerous cases in the pre-1688 era, of families and estates held together by women, as their menfolk were executed or in exile, and this undoubtedly strengthened the position of women in Scots society. One does not have to look far in most archives to find women running estates and businesses.

The legal framework was essential in protecting Scottish producers after 1707. While Scots law could be tedious, and ill-conform to international merchant law, it was flexible enough to fit in with a poverty-stricken and heavily indebted country. The court of session and the legal profession, provided a sophisticated array of decisions and advice, which enabled this backward and impecunious country to take the best advantage of the post-1707 constitutional framework. That is to say, the lawyers normally thought in terms of the existing common practices, only moving Scots law alongside England and France when Scotland could compete. This was especially important for the overriding basis of the cost of goods production, food prices, for which long-standing arrangements continued for the annual fiars' prices. It was also relevant to wages for traditional goods, and for supporting Scots business endeavour where English legislation might have proved onerous. The Court of Session refused to give way over important principles; Scots law was upheld over the joint-stock company where English statute law restricting non-statute companies to six partners was seen as a restraint on trade, and in the case of Scottish banknotes, the Court always supported this credit as legal tender, against a variety of English threats.[21]

In the crucial area of enforcement of payments across national boundaries the international merchant law on foreign exchange transactions clashed with out-of-date, though legally viable, views on payment of debts in Scotland. Yet it was to be many years into the new century before the European law on exchange, codified by Louis XIV's lawyers in an *Edict de Commerce*, 1673, was accepted in pleadings on exchange before the Court of Session. The Scots legal world kept to the unity of the 'common weal', and judges favoured solutions which avoided bankruptcy and social dislocation. Moreover, there were a series of fascinating decisions by the Court of Session which drew a distinction between the traditional supervision of markets, food prices, and wages, all applicable to the necessities of life, where custom and regulation continued, and newer forms of economic activity, including the sale of luxury goods, which their Lordships felt could be left to market forces. Far from preserving ancient forms for their own sake, the retention of controls should be seen as positive because these allowed Scots consumers and artisans to operate with lower levels of monetary activity and longer credit compared with England.

Before 1707 money in Scotland differed in several ways from that in England, the main being that the intrinsic silver value of £12 Scots no longer equalled the intrinsic silver value of £1 sterling set down in 1604. Because of a pressing need for cash, the Scots government of James VI, and subsequent governments, devalued this Scots standard, i.e., £1 sterling now bought more than £12 Scots. Before 1707 there is a lively and interesting history of the movements of the exchange rates between the two countries, which gave a great deal of work to goldsmiths who regularly assayed the exact up-to-date ratio. Further, when payments were made in Edinburgh and London the final rate would involve a charge for interest, profit for the exchanger, and would reflect supply and demand; if, as was increasingly the case by 1700, more money was needed in London than in Edinburgh, the discount on London would grow. Yet most businessmen continued to account in the ratio 12:1, and conduct wage and price negotiations in Scotland in these values, just as they had done since 1604. They also used a range of non-British currencies, as these tended to have a more uniform precious metal content. In 1695 when Bank of Scotland was established, the proprietors were given the right to issue bank notes. These the bank issued, from 1696, in sterling denominations at 12:1. This meant, therefore, that Bank of Scotland 'sterling' stood at a discount to English sterling. This rate comprised whatever happened to be the current exchange, described as before, plus the discount to allow for the different intrinsic values. For example, when in late 1700 Bank of Scotland issued the first ever one pound sterling note, at the nominal 12:1, its true worth was only 13 2/45:1, i.e., it would buy a little above 18sh 6d of English sterling full-weight coin, less the additional exchange costs, which could push the market value to 14:1 and above.

This may be shown in another way. In 1704 the London banker, John Campbell, borrowed £600 in Bank of Scotland sterling at Edinburgh, repayable in six months with 4 per cent interest, but if this debt was to be repaid in London, his liability was £528 sterling which represented a discount of 12 per cent, or an equivalent with the Scots sterling of around 17sh 7d. There was also the four per cent interest to add on. Prior to the Union the Edinburgh-London exchange transactions suggest a fluctuating discount from the exact intrinsic par, c. 8.5 per cent, though for a few drovers' bills only, up to 17.5 per cent. The trend was worse for the three years from end-1704, compared with earlier in Anne's reign. This undoubtedly contributed to the lowering of morale in Scotland, a result often observed with market-driven devaluations, while, of course, such a devaluation would be expected to benefit the producers of export goods.

The Union replaced the Scots currency with English sterling. Therefore, in theory, English buyers of Scottish goods would no longer benefit from the pre-1707 purchasing power, as they faced the revaluation of the Scots prices. This was made worse because England had opted, in 1696, for a gold standard which slightly undervalued silver, which was in greater use, and more precisely valued, in many export markets. The problem of revaluation, and of the gold standard, was understood (although more clearly in the former case). It meant that people with coin would benefit from the one for one translation at the recoinage of 1707, they would enjoy the extra value of 8.5 per cent rise in their asset values, but employers would suffer a potential disadvantage from wages and prices, where they would be selling to England. To cope with this businessmen had to depress wages, for example, by persuading their workforce to accept the intrinsic level of precious metals of their old wages; or by continuing to circulate the old Scots currency. This explains the continued use, after 1707, of this old currency, both as a unit of account, and in wage and price bargaining. This probably contributed to a higher level of employment after 1707 than would have occurred had the Scots wage rates been converted to English sterling equivalents. Furthermore, the evidence collected on wages suggests a continued 'wage gap' for similar work between the two countries, which lasted well into the eighteenth century.[22] Whatever the additional reasons for this 'gap', and cultural inertia and over-supply of labour, together with falling food prices before the 1740s, along with effective controls in the labour market, are the more likely, holding to the old currency for traditional payments should be seen as a strength.[23] The advantages, to business, of a locally acceptable paper currency, undervalued against sterling, was one of the reasons for the success of the Glasgow banks from 1749, although this lasted only sixteen years, and in 1765 the British state was persuaded, in large part by arguments from the Edinburgh banks, to enact punitive sanctions against these undervalued 'sterling' equivalent notes.

The question of wage rates and employment can be taken further. Wages remained below English levels, and only approached these later in the century, in the newer industries of the industrial revolution. Holding wages down, both in urban areas, and in the rapidly expanding rural industries, kept prices lower than otherwise, and thus helped sales, and owners of capital could increase their share of income with product improvements.[24] A variety of indications from several trades, including building, suggest rising incomes for capital by the mid-century. In an economy where labour was the chief input, and machinery and plant of lesser importance, controlling wages would help savings, and investment. It should be added that there is evidence of productivity growth in the first half of the eighteenth century. In the case of coal, which supplied the larger share of Scotland's energy requirements, Duckham suggested a variety of ways in which total output, and total factor productivity, rose, along with the huge increase in overall investment.[25] The cultivation of flax became more professional, in the context of the vast increase in acreage, with machines allowing an increase in productivity in processing and spinning of yarn.[26] Not all industries could compete effectively, the woollen trades were badly affected in the aftermath of 1707 and Scots salt was unable by 1750 to compete with the English rock-salt industry.[27] But the overall effect of wages and prices was to ensure that modernisation generated sufficient incomes for capital to maintain the process of industrialisation, and the marginalisation of uncompetitive and backward trades freed up labour and capital for more productive uses.

The incorporation of a poor and backward country into the dynamic trading empire of England, on equal terms for all citizens, has long been seen as an essential part of the explanation for the pace of growth in the Scottish economy; in particular, why Scotland was able to catch up during the eighteenth century, and why such a wide range of extra 'new' incomes for impecunious lairds, younger sons, merchants and lawyers were available, which had not been significant sources of family income, pre-1707.[28] Scotland joined a system with consistent ends in view for economic expansion and employment of labour, in particular it encouraged exports and the restriction of imports. Within the British market, home-based production was substituted for foreign, wherever feasible. The sharp rise of the Glasgow tobacco trades, the widely based linen trades, and the growth of the general trade of ship-owning, would have been much more difficult had Scotland remained outside the navigation system.[29] As entrepot, ship-owning, and employment opportunities were generated for British citizens, to the exclusion of foreigners, a huge range of ancillary services and financial incomes, not legislated for by Parliament, followed in the wake of the main thrust. The rate of growth of British exports to the colonies and Ireland, and later to India and China, outstripped that to Europe and Scandinavia, Scotland's traditional pre-1707 export markets.[30] The enforcement of this protectionist system was a major concern of the state service: piracy was virtually eliminated in the Caribbean by the late 1720s, and indigenous opposition to slavery in Jamaica defeated by 1736 and by 1760 the conquest of Quebec, and the expansion of power in India, saw new sources of incomes. Although the protectionist system has been criticised as inefficient, the consistency and transparency of the system, for well over a century, were of critical importance in helping Scots. Planning an investment in a plantation was much less risky than, for example, it would have been under free trade. The system delivered a gradual rise in Scots exports, and a wide range of historians, from the nineteenth century to today, have associated this with the timing of industrialisation, the growth of the middle classes, and the stimulation of a consumer society.

What happened within the agrarian sector in all countries undergoing modernisation was always going to be crucial in determining how much labour may be transferred, part or full-time, from food production, and moreover, how much food surplus could be generated for the market, and at what prices; and how the income surpluses of the property-owners were used and how swiftly they could be converted into credits available for rural industry, or the financial markets. Central to this process in Scotland was the high degree of concentration of land ownership. According to the exhaustive work of Loretta Timperley, land ownership in Scotland was compressed, by the onset of the industrial revolution, with only 2.5 per cent of the adult population owning land, some 7,838 in 1770.[31] The rest of the agricultural population were tenants or workers. These tenants sometimes accumulated a degree of wealth, but they did not enjoy the rights of ownership. This had several results. Large surpluses in rents were available to a small number of landlords, and these were then passed on to the banking system for use elsewhere. The size of landholding enabled the Bank of Scotland to lend long-term, against land, as early as 1696, and many borrowed to reduce interest charges on debts, and to invest. This move by the bank ensured that the very high levels of real interest payments of the pre-1695 era, came down, making it easier to have interest rates close to those of England after 1707, and to join the new, legal, maximum of 5 per cent APR in 1714. As in England, where landowning was also restricted to the few, landowners were a significant force in investment in infrastructure; including roads, ports, canals, wharfs, river improvements and planned villages, and linked up with merchants for joint-stocks, or, as in the provincial banks, in financial schemes. It is with these activities that modernisation linked land, banking and the nuts-and-bolts of enterprise.

This process was never quite as smooth as it appears with hindsight; there were numerous cases of bad management and over-enthusiastic investment, but double-entry book-keeping systems allowed the manipulation of long-term debts, and tight financial controls.[32] Thus in the central lowlands, with coal, iron, limestone, and high-quality stone on their lands, these landlords were able to realise extra profits from land ownership based on long-run investment and bank loans. Right across Scotland, by 1763, this improving movement eroded the traditional patterns of agricultural behaviour: prices were rising slowly, and the terms of trade were moving in favour of agriculture, a remarkable situation, in step with England, and important in so many ways to family fortunes and development.

By European standards the years before the industrial revolution saw an exceptional progress in industrial and commercial banking. There were, however, a series of severe disruptions, both from straightforward economic crises, and in several political upheavals, which included the above-mentioned crisis of 1704. The details of these assaults need not detain us, important illustrations though they are of the way Scotland's establishment operated, except to say that in every case Bank of Scotland rallied considerable business and landed support. By 1740, Bank of Scotland, and the Royal Bank of Scotland, founded in 1727, co-operated through discussions, later known as the agreements and understandings. The response of the banks in every crisis from 1740 was to hold existing credits firm and expand where they thought parts of the economy needed help. The accounting systems within the banks allowed a long view to be taken of debts difficult to recall in crises, and supplemented the views taken by the Court of Session.[33] At the risk of compressing a great deal of evidence in the pre-1763 era, and passing over the considerable inter-bank disputes, the fact remained that Scotland at the end of the Seven Years War possessed a memorable system of banking. At the pinnacle came Bank of Scotland, and the Royal Bank of Scotland, with a whole range of second-tier banks in the burghs, and private banks in Edinburgh. There was still a decade to go before the fully-fledged, hierarchical, regulated, and state-supported system of Scottish banking emerged after the collapse of Douglas, Heron & Co, (the Ayr Bank) in 1772, but the main elements, and the ideas and knowledge of what to do in time of crisis, existed earlier. The banking institutions in Scotland were augmented by the rapid expansion of the London-Scottish bill of exchange market, a small, though interesting, aspect of the eighteenth century bill on London phenomenon. The London market was a valuable partner, as so many new ideas, and employment opportunities for Scots, were generated in London.

This chapter has dwelt, disproportionately, upon the years 1688 to 1707. Preceded by a most difficult, intractable situation, the new, inclusive, political and legal formation proceeded to adopt sweeping changes in economic affairs, in administration and via legal reforms, which attempted to bring Scotland alongside, if not often equal to, contemporary European practices. The times also witnessed a new historical cognizance which enabled legislators to appreciate the scale of their task, in particular as to why economic improvement was so vital. In these few years there were some successes, in the case of Bank of Scotland for example, though rather too many failures.

All these changes were put through by an establishment which was sophisticated and probably more entrenched in 1707 than in the 1690s, and which negotiated a union which brought many of the economic and institutional benefits sought for in the earlier decade. The Scots aristocracy and lairds entered the new Britain in a strong political position, and eventually learnt how to exploit their Westminster connections. Factions were able to derive significant benefits for their members, families and clan connections, alongside the inevitable market-led changes which brought ever-increasing advantages to Scottish business life. In particular, joining the English state gave the modernisers a stronger hand to control backwardness, and to encourage economic growth and diversity. At the same time, business people continued to benefit from the Scottish legal framework and its wage and price advantages.

It may be invidious to suggest any causal ranking of the changes of the eighteenth century; new business techniques, the acquisitive role of landowners, the incorporation within the British colonial system, the operation of the new banking system, and the dynamic role of merchants in the larger burghs, and, of course, the dramatic changes in a whole range of ideas, and the overall discipline within the country. Historians will have their own preferences. The key point is that all these matters relate, in a variety of ways, to encouraging the productive over the unproductive, and making the former a sharper and continuous process. Yet, it does not quite follow that the industrial revolution was the obvious next step, although the establishment of modern plant, and a rapid expansion of coal mines, and a thorough search for textile machinery were inevitable parts of this change, together with a burgeoning interest in new processes and investment across the industrial spectrum. This modernisation of Scotland, most of which was generated by her own resources and skills, enabled the country to benefit from the connection with England and the empire, and, crucially, to continue to generate most of the needed capital from her own resources. Thus many of the entrepreneurs who moved north in the late eighteenth century were absorbed into Scottish business and financial life and there was, therefore, no question of a subordination to English business. In fact, by the later eighteenth century, the evidence shows a determined, forward-looking, Scottish business world, long able to move into English markets. For this success, the early phase of the industrial revolution, owed much to the vital, though compressed modernisation which occurred in earlier years, and the decisive political results which followed 1688.

REFERENCES

1. There is a huge literature on the industrial revolution R.A. Church & E.A. Wrigley (eds.), 11 vols. (Economic History Society, Oxford, 1994), which collects a range of articles in convenient form; H.J. Habbakkuk & M. Postan, *The Cambridge Economic History of Europe* vol. 6 'The Industrial Revolutions and After' (Cambridge, 1965). For Scotland, R.H. Campbell, *Scotland since* 1707 (Oxford, 1965); H. Hamilton, *An Economic History of Scotland in the Eighteenth Century* (Oxford, 1963); there is a bibliography in C. Whatley, *The Industrial Revolution in Scotland* (Cambridge, 1997).
2. W.R. Scott, *The Constitution and Finance of English, Irish and Scottish Joint-stock companies to* 1720 (Cambridge, 1917), 3 vols. A joint-stock in Scots law existed when the partners, who could be of any number, signed an agreement, endorsed by an Advocate. The usual practice was to lodge a summary of the agreement with the local burgh. Acts of Parliament could give powers not available to ordinary joint-stocks.
3. H. Hamilton, *An Economic History of Scotland in the Eighteenth Century* (Oxford, 1963), ch.3.
4. The whig pamphlet, *The reducing of Scotland by Arms and annexing it to England as a province considered* (London, 1705) carried a detailed record of royal actions during the restoration, and was followed by many similar writings.
5. G. Jackson, 'Glasgow in transition, c.1660 to c.1740' in T.M. Devine & G. Jackson, (eds.), *Glasgow vol.*1, Beginnings to 1830 (Manchester, 1995), pp.65–7, noting, also, C. Eyre-Todd, *History of Glasgow* (Glasgow, 1931) vol. 2, chapter 31. For a discussion of the battle as it fitted into the politics of the era, J. Willcock, *A Scots Earl in covenanting times: being Life and Times of Archibald 9th Earl of Argyll* (1629–1685) (Edinburgh, 1907), chs. 13, 14; Andrew Lang, *A History of Scotland from the Roman Occupation* 4 vols, (Edinburgh, 2nd edn., 1909), ch.12.
6. G. Marshall, *Presbyteries and Profits: Calvinism and the Development of Capitalism in Scotland,* 1560–1707 (Oxford, 1980). This new attitude only developed after the imposition of a more rigid puritanism in the 1690s.
7. L. Stephen, *History of English Thought in the Eighteenth Century* (London, 1902) Vol.2, p.297. His comment derived from reading the English literature, though the point has a general relevance.
8. There was considerable hostility to excesses, not just for material possessions, in protestant theology, including Scottish Calvinism; for an overview, W. Sombart *Luxury and Capitalism* (intro: P. Siegelman) (Michigan, 1967).
9. Hugh Chamberlain's proposal for a Scots land bank of 1693 was circulated by the Scots Parliament committee, NLS, Advocates Mss, 31.1.7 ff 30–8. rep. comm., Richard Saville, *Bank of Scotland A history* 1695–1995 (Edinburgh, 1996), Appendix 5, pp.854–60.
10. W. Cunningham, D.D. *The Growth of English Industry and Commerce in Modern Times* (Cambridge, 1919), Vol.2, part 3.
11. In a pamphlet of May 1705 John Law cited the effects of the wars, the Darien Scheme, and the famine as the determining causes of the financial situation, *The Circumstances of Scotland considered with respect to the present scarcity of money together with some proposals for supplying the defect thereof and rectifying the balance of trade* (May, 1705).

12. Saville, *Bank of Scotland*, ch.4.
13. GL 4137. *An Accompt Current betwixt Scotland and England ballanced* (25 July 1705).
14. GL 3821. Proclamation anent 14 shilling pieces (1701).
15. To be fair to John Law, his ideas could make sense if the assumption is made that merchants used Bank of Scotland credits to replace silver, which was then exported, with the eventual profit kept abroad, or in London. There is some evidence that this did occur, but it would have ensued, using gold or bills, had there been no bank credit.
16. T.C. Smout, N.C. Landsmen & T.M. Devine, 'Scottish Emigration in the Seventeenth and Eighteenth Centuries' in, N. Canny (ed.), *Europeans on the Move: Studies on European Migration*, 1500–1800 (Oxford, 1994); T. Burnard, 'European Migration to Jamaica, 1655–1780', *William & Mary Quarterly* 3rd series, vol. 53, no. 4. (October, 1996).
17. GL 3954 *A Letter from Mr Hodges at London to a member of the Parliament of Scotland* (Edinburgh, 1703). It should be noted that in the royal burghs there was little understanding of the overall problem, as emigration removed a source of competition for established tradespeople.
18. GL 4137 *An Accompt Current betwixt Scotland and England ballanced* (25 July 1705). For the linen trade at this time, A. Durie, *The Scottish Linen Industry in the Eighteenth Century* (Edinburgh, 1979).
19. W. Hamish Fraser, *Conflict and Class, Scottish Workers* 1700–1838 (Edinburgh, 1988), contains valuable information on this subject.
20. E. Cregeen, 'The changing role of the house of Argyll in the Scottish Highlands' in N.T. Phillipson & R.M. Mitchison, (eds.), *Scotland in the Age of Improvement* (Edinburgh, 1970); T.M. Devine, *Clanship to Crofters' War: the social transformation of the Scottish Highlands* (Manchester, 1994); A. Macinnes, *Clanship, Commerce and the House of Stuart* 1603–1788 (East Linton, 1996).
21. On the importance of the legal world in post-1707 Scotland, N.T. Phillipson, 'Lawyers, Landowners and the Civic Leadership of Post Union Scotland: An Essay on the Social Role of the Faculty of Advocates 1661–1830 in 18th century Scottish Society' *Juridical Review* 21 (1976), pp.97–120.
22. For evidence from the nineteenth century, see R.H. Campbell, *The Rise and Fall of Scottish Industry* 1707–1939 (Edinburgh, 1980).
23. A.J.S. Gibson and T.C. Smout, *Prices, Food and Wages in Scotland* 1550–1780 (Cambridge, 1995), while there are regional differences, the data collected in this fascinating study suggest little upward movement before the 1740s in fiars' prices.
24. There is a lengthy discussion of this in Fraser, *Conflict and Class*, chs.3, 4.
25. Baron F. Duckham, *A History of the Scottish Coal Industry* Vol.1, 1700–1815 (Newton Abbott, 1970).
26. A.J. Warden, *The Linen Trade, Ancient and Modern* (Dundee, 1892).
27. C.A. Whatley, *The Scottish Salt Industry* 1570–1850 (Aberdeen, 1987) ch.2.
28. Not all these were honest trades, the London career of William Patterson was rife with suggestions of fraud, and *see*, A.J.G. Cummings, 'The Business Affairs of an Eighteenth Century Lowland Laird: Sir Archibald Grant of Monymusk, 1696–1778', in T.M. Devine (ed.), *Scottish Elites* (Edinburgh, 1994).
29. In this respect, T.M. Devine, 'The Golden Age of Tobacco' in Devine and Jackson (eds.), *Glasgow*, pp.142–5. The only way round this question is to suppose that an independent Scotland would have had the power to break into the English colonies, and into India, or negotiate bilateral deals with other powers, and England.
30. R. Davis, *The Industrial Revolution and British Overseas Trade* (Leicester, 1979).
31. L. Timperley, *A Directory of Landownership in Scotland, c.*1770 (Scottish Record Society, new series, 5) (1976); and *see*, T.M. Devine, *The Transformation of Rural Scotland: Social Change and the Agrarian Economy*, 1660–1815 (Edinburgh, 1994).
32. William Forbes, *A Methodical Treatise concerning bills of exchange* (Edinburgh, 1703) p.1. Forbes was an Edinburgh lawyer, and published a second edition of his *Treatise* in 1718.

He was a supporter of Bank of Scotland during various disputes in the early years of the century.

33. For the case of the British Linen Bank, S.G. Checkland, *Scottish Banking A History* 1695–1973 (Glasgow, 1975), pp.92–7; A.J. Durie, *The British Linen Company* 1745–1775 (Edinburgh, 1996) Scottish History Society, 5th series, vol. 9. for the burgh banks, C. Munn, *The Scottish Provincial Banking Companies*, 1747–1927 (Edinburgh, 1981).

Three

The Parliamentary Incorporating Union of 1707: Political Management, Anti-Unionism and Foreign Policy

JOHN R. YOUNG

> The Whig Lords indulge themselves mightily in vilifying the Scottish Nobility or their part in the Union. My Lord Wharton owned yesterday, in the House, that he doubted much he could have been prevailed on to have parted with his birthright, had he been a Scotch Lord; and indeed, such are the times we live in, that I can scarcely persuade anybody that some have done it out of love for their country.[1]

Such were the comments of James Johnston[2], a leading figure in the Squadrone Volante and a former Secretary of State in Scotland, in correspondence with his Squadrone counterpart George Baillie of Jerviswood, one of the Members of Parliament for Lanarkshire in the last Scottish Parliament of 1703–1707. Johnston informed Jerviswood of the glee in Whitehall following the securing of an incorporating union between Scotland and England in 1707. A public thanksgiving was appointed by Queen Anne to celebrate the Union[3] and it was noted by Sidney, 1st Earl of Godolphin, one of the key architects of the Union, that 'the streets were fuller of people than I have seen them upon any occassion of that kind. The Bishop of Oxford preached a very fine sermon'.[4] The securing of an incorporating union in terms of the operation and nature of English politics marked 'one of the great accomplishments'[5] of the political triumvirate of Lord Treasurer Godolphin, Secretary of State Robert Harley, and John Churchill, 1st Duke of Marlborough, Commander-in-Chief of the British forces in the War of Spanish Succession (1702–1713) against Louis XIV of France. Such an achievement is perhaps ironic, yet no less statesmanlike, given Harley's speech in the House of Commons in 1704 when he said that 'he was ready to take his oath on it, that he knew no more of Scotch business than of Jappan, and that he avoided even the conversation of that country'.[6] The outlook of Marlborough, one of the most famous English generals of the eighteenth century, in his attitude towards the independence of Scotland and the Scottish Parliament as a political institution, was recorded in the winter of 1706; 'the true state of the matter was, whether Scotland should continue subject to an English Ministry without trade, or be subject to an English Parliament with trade'.[7]

Scotland in Crisis

The reasoning behind and explanations for the incorporating union between Scotland and England have been subjected to intense historical debate and interpretation, especially among historians of Scottish history.[8] Economic motives, skills of political management, and outright bribery have all been advanced as reasons for explaining why Scottish Members of Parliament voted in favour of an incorporating union with England. Fifteen of the 25 articles of the Treaty of Union were concerned with economic issues, yet this does not imply that the Treaty was primarily economic in nature. Certainly Scotland faced major financial and economic problems by the early eighteenth century. The failure of the Darien Scheme and the attempt to establish a Scottish colonial empire had resulted in the loss of circa 25% of Scotland's liquid capital, whilst a series of major famines, the Lean Years of the 1690s, had inflicted significant damage to the Scottish economy. Scottish trade links had become increasingly dependent on the English market, especially in terms of the export of linen and black cattle, at a time when there was a major political and constitutional crisis between Scotland and England. The Lean Years of the 1690s in many respects were an aberration after circa 35 years of abundant food supplies and low prices and over the period 1600–1700 there were only two significant harvest failures and shortages in 1674 and 1693–97.[9] Total linen exports to England amounted to between 1.2 and 1.8 million ells by 1700 and circa 30,000 black cattle were being exported to England by 1707 (cattle amounted to 40% of Scottish exports to England by 1703).[10] Nevertheless, the incorporating union did not provide an economic utopia in the short-term and it was only in the period after the 1740s that the direct economic benefits of union came to fruition.[11] Furthermore, eventual Scottish economic growth from the mid-seventeenth century onwards can be traced to structural developments and improvements in Scottish society and economy in the pre-1707 period.[12] The Treaty of Union, in this sense, constituted no clear-cut economic watershed.

National instability in the form of economic crisis was intensified by a far more important factor in terms of the overall British polity. The Anglo-Scottish dynastic union was in crisis by the early eighteenth century and required modification. In contrast to England, where the Act of Settlement of 1701 had recognised the Hanoverian Succession, the Scottish Parliament had adopted a position of aggressive constitutional nationalism in the sessions of

1703–1704, as evidenced in the Wine Act and the Acts of Security and Peace and War. The English response to this stance by her northern neighbour, the Alien Act of 1705, threatened to drain the lifeblood of the Scottish economy by banning the export of Scottish linen and black cattle to the dominant English market, unless the Scots agreed to appoint commissioners to negotiate for an incorporating union by Christmas 1705.[13] Political instability and the inability of the Court to control Scottish political life through various ministries had become all too obvious by 1706, most notably in the failure to secure the Hanoverian Succession in Scotland.

The Treaty of Union negotiated between the kingdoms of Scotland and England was primarily a political event. The representatives of the Scottish Parliament who negotiated the treaty with their English counterparts were distinctly unrepresentative of the Scottish political nation at large. Hence only one of the Scottish negotiators, the Jacobite George Lockhart of Carnwath, was opposed to the principle of an incorporating union. The Scottish negotiating delegation had been nominated by Queen Anne and as such was dominated by members who were in favour of an incorporating union. This was a direct result of the behaviour of James Douglas, 4th Duke of Hamilton, in the 1705 parliamentary session. Hamilton was one of the leading opponents of union, yet on 1 September 1705 he proposed in a poorly-attended session that negotiating commissioners should be chosen by the Queen. This was seized upon immediately by the Court to secure the motion, the parliamentary session was adjourned on 14 September, and negotiating commissioners were appointed by Queen Anne in February 1706. The motives behind Hamilton's actions have been the subject of some considerable debate ever since, but the end political result was to produce a Scottish negotiating delegation composed of pro-incorporationists.[14] As such, it can be argued that those commissioners sought to secure the best possible deal for Scotland but only in the full context of an incorporating union. Hence vulnerable sectors of the Scottish economy such as the coal and salt industries required protection, whilst Article 4 of the Treaty allowed for free Scottish entry into the English domestic and colonial markets.[15] Certainly the majority of Scottish elite political opinion sought a closer union with England, but the preferred option was a federal union which would have retained the Scottish Parliament as a political institution and would have involved further constitutional reform in Scotland limiting the powers of the Scottish monarchy.[16] For the English negotiating team, however, the only acceptable political solution was an incorporating union. A federal union was simply out of the question[17] and was also directly vetoed by Queen Anne herself; 'nothing can prove a solid and lasting settlement for the Peace and happiness of our Subjects of this Island but that of an entire Union'.[18]

The secure passage of the Treaty of Union through the Scottish Parliament in the session of 1706–1707 required substantial skills of political management on the part of the Court party, albeit this process was strengthened by the lack of unity among the Opposition in Parliament. Voting analysis clearly indicates that it was the votes of the Squadrone Volante which secured the acceptance of the Treaty by the Scottish Parliament. The two most important votes were on the first article on the principle of an incorporating union and the final vote which ratified the Treaty. The first article of the Treaty was voted on 4 November 1706 and was passed by a majority of 115 votes to 83 votes. The Squadrone Volante, which had 25 votes, played a central role in the balance of votes. The ratification of the Treaty was secured on 16 January 1707 by a majority of 110 to 67 votes with 46 absentions or absences. The increase in abstentions and absences from the first vote (25 in total) to 46 was particularly important. This has led one commentator to argue that the union was 'ratified by default rather than by absolute majority'.[19] Nevertheless, the Court vote remained relatively stable over both votes with 102 members voting for both the first article and ratification. Only 59 Members of Parliament, on the other hand, voted against the first article and ratification.[20] Members of the Court party also used their influence in their own localities and geographic spheres of influence to provide Members of Parliament in favour of an incorporating union. The Dalrymples of Stair, for example, provided four Members of Parliament in terms of shire and burgh representation in the last Scottish Parliament of 1703–1707; Sir Hugh Dalrymple of Stair, Lord President of the Session, (North Berwick), Sir David Dalrymple of Hailes (Culross), Solicitor-General to Queen Anne, George Dalrymple of Dalmahoy (Stranraer) for the burghs, and William Dalrymple of Glenmure and Drongan (Ayrshire) for the shires. Each of these individuals were Courtiers in terms of political alignment both Sir Hugh Dalrymple of Stair and Sir David Dalrymple of Hailes were two of the Scottish Commissioners who negotiated the Treaty of Union. Both had also served in the abortive union negotiations of 1702–1703. Dalrymple of Hailes proceeded to represent Haddington in the Parliament of Great Britain of 1708–1721. The peer Sir John Dalrymple, 1st Earl of Stair, was also a Courtier and voted in favour of the first article of the Treaty prior to his death in 1707 as the Treaty made its way through the Scottish Parliament.[21] Likewise, the influence of the House of Argyll also provided shire and burgh members, all of whom were Courtiers; John Campbell of Mamore represented Argyllshire and Charles Campbell represented Campeltown. Campbell of Mamore was a member of the first Parliament of Great Britain and represented the county of Dunbarton until 1722 and 1725–27.[22] The Campbell brothers, John Campbell, 2nd Duke of Argyll and Archibald Campbell, Earl of Islay, both played key roles in promoting an incorporating union. Both were firmly committed to a British political agenda, as was reflected in their virtual monopolistic control of Scottish politics through the Argyll interest in the first half of the eighteenth century. Both brothers served under Marlborough in Flanders and the second Duke had been created Earl of Greenwich in the English peerage in 1705. The overt political ambition of Argyll was noted by contemporaries; 'The Whig Lords say, half-a-crown will carry him'.[23]

From an English perspective, the securing of the Hanoverian Succession in Scotland and the securing of England's northern borders were of paramount concern. From 1707 onwards the accusation emerged that Scottish Members of Parliament had been bribed to vote away the national independence of the kingdom of Scotland and the dissolution of the Scottish Parliament. Thus, £20,000 sterling (£240,000 Scots) was sent north to Scotland by the English ministry to be strategically disposed of by the Scottish Treasurer, the Earl of Glasgow, to secure key votes in the Scottish Parliament for an incorporating union. In theory, this sum was designed to pay arrears and allowances from the civil list. In reality, the bulk of the money (£12,325 sterling) was placed at the disposal of the Queen's Commissioner, James Douglas, 2nd Duke of Queensberry, to strategically target votes and to pay Court informers. Financial inducement was also particularly important in the form of the Equivalent, estimated at £398,085 10s, which was to be used to liquidate the Scottish national debt and provide compensation for investors in the failed Company of Scotland, which had promoted the Darien Scheme. Of crucial importance here is the fact that members of the Squadrone Volante had invested heavily in this scheme. Acceptance of an incorporating union therefore had perceived direct financial benefit.[24] The perception that the Scots had been bribed was encapsulated in the verse of Scotland's bard, Robert Burns, with his assertion that Scotland had been 'bought and sold for English gold' by 'such a parcel of rogues in a nation'.[25] This view was also widespread in English political circles in the immediate aftermath of securing the Treaty and the Scottish nobility, in particular, were subjected to vilification. Johnston informed Baillie of Jerviswood of the view in London. Thus, the Whig Lords 'run you all down, particularly your nobility, who they declare, might have had better terms, if they had prest for them, and that they themselves were ashamed that they made themselves so cheap'.[26]

The securing of an incorporating union bewteen Scotland and England as a *British* political event must be fundamentally viewed in the context of English party politics and the partisan and factional rivalries between English Whigs and English Tories. In terms of English representative institutions, the House of Commons tended to be inclined towards Tory dominance, whilst the House of Lords was dominated by Whig power. Therefore, in every one of Queen Anne's Parliaments the majority of the House of Commons was Tory except for that of 1708. On the other hand, every one of the Whig junto in the reign of Queen Anne was a peer.[27] A major English political crisis had emerged in 1705 over the Occassional Conformity Bill and the Tory attempt to prevent English nonconformists from pragmatically receiving communion in the Anglican Church of England in order to qualify for civil or military office. This had been a major issue in the English Parliament where two Occassional Conformity Bills had been defeated in the sessions of 1702–1703 and 1703–1704 by virtue of Whig strength in the House of Lords. A third Occassional Conformity Bill (1704) had been 'tacked' to a Land Tax Bill and the voting of money for English involvement in the War of the Spanish Succession. Defeated by a Commons' alliance of Whigs and moderate Tories, the third Occassional Conformity Bill was once again rejected by the House of Lords.[28] The controversy over the Bill hindered the performance of the Tories in the English General Election of 1705 and the result of that election weakened the power base of the Tories in the Commons, by removing 54 Tory MPs, and the Court could only secure a viable majority by depending on the Whigs.[29] In turn, the promotion and securing of an incorporating union had a viable political objective for the Whigs in terms of the operation of *English* party politics. Thus, the addition of 45 Scottish MPs to an effectively enlarged English Parliament 'offered the one chance of changing a natural balance in the House of Commons that would always favour the Tories'.[30] Therefore incorporation solved an English poltical problem for the Whigs and 'Scotland was to be called into a British Parliament to redress the balance between London and the shires'.[31] This issue was all the more pertinent because the Tories traditionally had a higher number of safe seats and 30 of these 104 safe Tory seats were based in English county constituencies.[32]

Anti-unionism: petitioning

Petitioning constituted a formalised procedure whereby anti-incorporation resentment could be mobilised and public opinion from the localities formally articulated. J.R. Jones has noted that anti-union petitions constituted 'a more authentic and accurate indication of opinion in Scotland'[33] in gauging Scottish public opinion towards an incorporating union. Anti-union petitioning as a vehicle of public opinion appears to have drawn on an earlier Covenanting precedent for the expression of threats to Scottish national identity. Supplications and petitions had been mobilised by the embryonic Covenanting Movement in 1637–38 against the attempted imposition of the Scottish Book of Common Prayer by Charles I.[34] Petitioning in 1706–1707 was not restricted to any particular faction among the Opposition and cross-party support was secured with the common aim of preventing an incorporating union. In comparison, there was not one petition or address in favour of an incorporating union submitted to the Scottish Parliament.[35] Both the Jacobites and Presbyterian ministers were active in framing anti-incorporation addresses. Hence on 29 October 1706 Baillie of Jerviswood (Lanarkshire) noted not only that 'There is paines taken by the Tories to procure addresses from all places against the union' but also that 'Many of the Presbyterian ministers are against the Union, and acting such a pairt as they did in the late troubles; attempting to advise and interpose by the Commission of the Kirk in matters that not belong to them, and to raise objections against the Union from the Covenant'.[36] The thrust of Presbyterian petitions, emanating from presbyteries and parishes, was subsequently centralised and unified in an address from the Commission of the Kirk, the executive agency of the General Assembly of the Church of Scotland. Jerviswood noted on 5 November that 'the church is now upon framing one, for they alledge it is consistent with the Covenant to be united in one Parliament where bishops sit. They are not to be diverted from this, and it will influence a great many weak people'.[37] Furthermore, the infamous Jacobite George Lockhart of Carnwath, who was one of the representatives of the shire of Edinburgh in Parliament, observed that the ministers of the Church of Scotland 'roared against the wicked unions from their pulpits, made resolves and sent addresses against it from several presbyteries and the Commission of the Assembly'.[38] The impact of parliamentary legislation guaranteeing the security of the kirk was to ensure that 'most of their zeal was cooled, and many of them quite changed their notes and preached up what not long before they had declared anathemas against'.[39]

The Presbytery of Lanark petitioned Parliament on 14 November 1706 and pleaded *against* an incorporating union. A unitary kingdom, being represented by one Parliament, was perceived as being 'as destructive to the true interest of the nation as well as the church'.[40] The twenty-five articles of union had been inspected by the Presbytery and the 'fatal consequences thereof'[41] were dreaded. A closer union with England, focused on a Protestant successor, was certainly sought by the Presbytery but incorporation was out of the question: 'we are so far from being against all union with our neighbouring nation of England, that we very earnestly desire a good agreement, and such a firm union with them as may be honourable to the State, safe to the church, and beneficial to both'.[42] A Protestant successor was to be secured but only 'under such just and reasonable limitations as the circumstances of this kingdom do require'[43] and the Hanoverian Succession was *not* specified. In essence, the Presbytery of Lanark petitioned for a federal union which would retain the Scottish Parliament and involve a further programme of constitutional reform and limitations on the monarchy:

> Only as ministers, Scotsmen, and subjects of this free and independent kingdom, we cannot but wish and pray that our civill government may be rectified as to the execution of good laws Without being dissolved; our monarchy may be regulated and limited, without being suppressed; our Parliament may be secured from English influence, without being extinguished; and the just rights and liberties of the Nation, as to lawes, trade, and all other concerns, may be asserted, without being resigned in bulk, to the will and disposall of a British parliament, who are strangers to our constitution, and who may judge it for the interest of Britain to keep us low and intirely subject unto them, not only in those things that are unitable, but likewayes in all those that of their own nature are separat, and demand a solid security to keep them so.[44]

The Presbytery concluded that the 'guardianship of a Scots Parliament' was required to defend 'our known principles and covenants' and that an incorporating union was therefore 'destructive to the church and nation'.[45] The adjacent Presbytery of Hamilton was a hotbed of Cameronian activity and intrigue and the tenor and language of the Presbytery of Lanark's petition contain all the leitmotifs of Cameronian ideology. Robert Wodrow, Minister of Eastwood Parish in Renfrewshire, noted the natural enthusiasm of Hamilton Presbytery to defend the interests of the Kirk as far back as 1700.[46]

Grass-roots opposition to an incorporating union in Lanarkshire was partially reflected in the political allegiances and voting behaviour of Lanarkshire Members of Parliament in the last session of the Scottish Parliament in 1706–1707. The Act for Additional Representation in Parliament of the Greater Shires of the Kingdom of 1690 had accorded Lanarkshire four MPs in Parliament. In addition, the Royal Burgh of Lanark was represented in the burghal estate of Parliament by one Member of Parliament. In terms of the four shire representatives, three were members of the Opposition. Sir John Sinclair of Stevenson and William Baillie of Lamington both voted against the first article of the Treaty (on the principle of an incorporating union) and on the final vote of ratification. James Hamilton of Aitkenhead did not vote on the first article but voted against ratification and has been defined by Patrick Riley as a member of the Opposition. The remaining shire representative, George Baillie of Jerviswood, voted for an incorporating union in terms of both the first article and the final vote on ratification.[47] He was also one of the key figures in the Squadrone Volante, the group/faction whose votes secured an incorporating union in the Scottish Parliament, and his contemporary correspondence provides an excellent insight into the psyche and mentality of the Squadrone leadership as the Treaty progressed through the Scottish Parliament. In contrast to the dominant trend of the voting behaviour of the shire MP's, the burgh representative, William Carmichael of Skirling, was a member of the Court Party and voted for an incorporating union as per the first article and the final ratification vote.[48] Such voting behaviour was against the expressed mood of Carmichael's constituency as the Royal Burgh of Lanark petitioned against an incorporating union, as did the parishes of Blantyre, Bothwell, Cambuslang, Carnwath, Hamilton, Monklands Old and Monklands East. By way of comparison, Lanarkshire also petitioned against the union.[49] The parishes of Glasgow Barony and Glasgow Gorbals likewise petitioned against the union,[50] whilst the Member of Parliament for the Royal Burgh of Glasgow, Hugh Montgomerie of Busbie, voted against the union as per the first article and ratification. Montgomerie of Busbie has been defined as a Court 'cross-voter'.[51] Montgomerie of Busbie had no previous parliamentary experience yet in terms of political behaviour he had been involved in anti-Jacobite activity in 1689–90, he had subscribed £1000 to the Darien Scheme, and he had been one of the Scottish Commissioners to Treat for Union in 1702. Despite his opposition to the union, Montgomerie of Busbie was elected to the first Parliament of Great Britain.[52] Montgomerie's voting behaviour appears to be in line with that of his constituents as Glasgow formally petitioned against the union.[53]

Robert Wodrow, as a minister of the Church of Scotland, was fundamentally opposed to an incorporating union. In correspondence with George Ridpath, the anti-union pamphleteer, in April 1706, Wodrow noted that 'Ane incorporating union is quhat we deprecate, ane intire union, if by it we losse our Parliament, Privy Councill is quhat we cannot goe into, for we see litle security from preliminary stipulations'.[54] Wodrow had followed closely the fate of the Dissenters in England and much of his outlook on an incorporating union was governed by the crisis over the Occassional Conformity Bill and a belief that the Presbyterian structure of the Church of Scotland, only secured in 1690 after a period of intense persecution, would be under threat in a unitary kingdom where Presbyterianism would be in a minority and swamped by Anglicans and Episcopalians.[55] In January 1703 Wodrow noted that 'Things look very dark with respect to the Dissenters in England . . . The Toree party cary all'.[56] 'Our Jacobites are very high and conceive great hopes from England, and the clergy are the highest flyers of any'.[57]

Wodrow was particularly scathing of the attitude of his fellowcountrymen to the progress of the union negotiations in 1706: 'I am surprized to remarke the security, shall I say, or stupidity of all ranks in this poor country. Tho all might see we wer never at a more criticall juncture, yet noe concern, noe care'.[58] Wodrow lamented the strategic miscalculation of many who were opposed to an incorporating union: 'People feed themselves up in hopes that tho matters should get a wrong cast at the treaty all will be mended at our

Parliament'.[59] According to Wodrow, this constituted a strategic miscalculation on the part of opponents of incorporation. Rather, such a belief was folly and the Treaty itself would be bulldozed through Parliament; 'The secrecy (as some tell us, by oath) among the Commissioners looks odd, as if the Parliament members should knou nothing till they come to the House, and such fine important matter wer to be concluded or hudled over in ane afternoons sederunt'.[60] Rightly or wrongly, Wodrow believed that many of his fellow countrymen were being duped and that freedom of trade was being used as a stalking horse to secure an incorporating union through the Scottish Parliament:

> not a feu that are taken for men of sense and piety are like to goe in to ane incorporating union, and I forsee if Gods goodness prevent not, it may very easily take in Parliament. A great many are soe litle mindfull either of religion, liberty, or soveraingty that all are ciphers to a liberty of trade . . .[61]

Wodrow certainly had his own axe to grind and his comments do display the economic opinions and perceptions of a Presbyterian minister, but he was sceptical of how the Scottish economy could be improved in a larger entity without the protection of a Scottish Parliament; 'I see noe great things I can promise from a liberty in trade it self, without both a distinct kingdome and Parliament, and better limitations then we yet have, and regulations better suited to the temper of the inhabitants and situation of the country'.[62] For Wodrow incorporation would result in the relegation to provincial status for Scotland and the irrecoverable loss of religious and civil liberties in Scotland. Wodrow was well aware that this was a defining moment in Scotland's history. Previous crises, such as in 1572, 1638 and 1688, had been overcome. But this time was different: 'nou, once lost, ever lost'.[63] This fear of provincial relegation had been at the forefront of antagonism and then outright hostility to Charles I's administration of Scotland earlier in the seventeenth century.[64]

Whilst the Presbytery of Lanark petitioned against an incorporating union and Cameronian opposition was also located in Hamilton, the freeholders of Dunbartonshire drew up a petition on 28 October 1706 for submission to Parliament against the proposed incorporating union. The petition concluded that:

> Wee doe confidently expect that ye will not allow of any such incorporating union, But that ye will support 38; preserve entire the soveraignty and Independancy of the crown 38; Kingdom and the rights and priveledges of parliament, which has been so valliantly maintained by our heroike ancestours for the space of near two thousand years, that

> the samine may be transmitted to the succeeding generations as it hes been conveyed to us . . .[65]

A correlation can be made between the voting behaviour of the Members of Parliament for Dunbartonshire and anti-incorporation as articulated through the expressed wishes of the 'Barrons freeholders and others within the shire of Dumbartone'.[66] Dunbartonshire was represented by William Cochrane of Kilmaronock and Sir Humphrey Colquhoun of Luss in the Parliament of 1703–1707. Cochrane of Kilmaronock and Colquhoun of Luss both voted against the articles of the incorporating union in a consistent manner. Whereas Colquhoun of Luss had no previous parliamentary experience, Cochrane of Kilmaranock had represented the burgh of Renfrew in the 1689 Convention and the Parliamentary sessions of 1689–95.[67] Patrick Riley has identified both members as being part of the 'opposition (countrymen and cavaliers)'[68] and Cochrane of Kilmaronock was suspected of being a Jacobite in 1712, albeit he had subscribed the Act declaring the 1689 Convention to be a lawful meeting of estates and had signed the letter of congratulation to William of Orange.[69] Cochrane of Kilmaronock also appears to have been in close contact with Lockhart of Carnwath as part of a group of trusted advisors, including Fletcher of Saltoun, in the run-up to the opening of the treaty negotiations. Lockhart refers to this group as 'those of his party'.[70]

Whilst the shire commissioners for Dunbartonshire were clearly anti-incorporationist, the burgh representative, Sir James Smollett of Stainflett and Bonhill, was strongly pro-unionist. Not only was Smollett one of the Scottish commissioners who negotiated the Treaty, but his voting record was, unsurprisingly, consistently pro-incorporation and he was one of the key figures within the Court party for the burghal estate. Smollett had represented the burgh in Parliament consistently since 1689 (he was also present in the Parliament of 1685–6).[71] Smollett proceeded to be elected to the First Parliament of Great Britain and was later active in the politics of the electoral contest for the Glasgow District of Burghs (Glasgow, Dumbarton, Renfrew and Rutherglen), 1714–16. Ronald Sunter's case study of the mechanics of patronage and political management for the election of the Member of Parliament for the Glasgow District indicates that Smollett, 'the great man of Dumbarton', was allied to James Graham, fourth Marquis and first Duke of Montrose in his clash with John Campbell, second Duke of Argyll over who should hold the seat for the District. Hence the Montrose camp supported the sitting member, Thomas Smith, albeit it was outfoxed by the Argyll interest, which ultimately secured the election of Daniel Campbell of Shawfield.[72]

A similar picture of shire opposition and burgh support emerges with regard to the Stirling area. Lieutenant Colonel John Erskine represented the

Royal Burgh of Stirling and was pro-incorporation. Stirlingshire was represented by three commissioners; James Graham of Buchlyvie, John Graham of Killearn, and Robert Rollo of Powhouse.[73] According to Riley's classifications, all three were members of the 'opposition (countrymen and cavaliers)', although Graham of Buchlyvie and Graham of Killearn voted in half or fewer of the actual union divisions.[74] Lieutenant Colonel John Erskine, on the other hand, has been identified by Riley as a member of the Court party and voted in favour of an incorporating union. He was also elected to the First Parliament of Great Britain and represented Stirling District (Stirling, Queensferry, Inverkeithing, Dunfermline and Culross) there until 1710.[75] The shire representatives appear to have been more in line with their locality than their burgh counterpart. A series of anti-union addresses from the Stirling area was submitted to Parliament between 4 November and 26 December 1706, including an address submitted to Parliament on 23 November from the Provost, Baillies, Town Council and other inhabitants of the Burgh of Stirling.[76] Hence, Lieutenant John Erskine was clearly out of line with the expressed wishes of his own Town Council and Burgh.

Within a wider political context, the mechanics of patronage and management transcended the union of 1707. Hence the union was not a watershed in terms of patronage and management. Rather, such a system, as the eighteenth century progressed, operated in a larger British and imperial structure(s). Patronage could therefore be modified and redefined as circumstances demanded and/or times changed. Therefore the union did not represent a monolithic or static political event marking out a clear-cut watershed to Scottish politicians and parliamentarians active in Scottish and British public life. The cut and thrust of contemporary politics continued, but within a new structure which was evolving in its own right. Sir James Smollet (Dumbarton) and Lieutenant Colonel John Erskine (Stirling) therefore provide two examples of Scottish parliamentarians whose political careers and activities did not end in 1707 with the resolution of the 'union issue'. Both Smollett and Erskine were committed pro-incorporationists in 1707 and were aligned to the Court party, yet the same principle also applied to 'members' of other political factions as they existed in 1706–1707, especially the Squadrone Volante.

The geographic districts of Dunbartonshire, Stirlingshire and Perthshire were within a relatively close sphere or radius of influence, with particular regard to the Montrose interest. Perthshire was represented by four commissioners of shires in the Union Parliament, one of whom, Mungo Graeme of Gorthie, continued to play an important political function post-1707. In political terms, Graeme of Morphie has been identified as being a member of the Squadrone Volante, in common with one of the other Perthshire MPs John Haldane of Gleneagles, both of whom voted in favour of an incorporating union.[77] Morphie had been Chamberlain to the Duke of Montrose and was also elected to the first Parliament of Great Britain. Graeme of Morphie has been described as 'Montrose's principal agent in Scotland and a shrewd observer of the contemporary political scene'.[78] Morphie's career within the new British structure continued with appointment of Receiver-General of Customs in 1716 and that of Rector of Glasgow University in 1718–20. Appointment to both these positions would have been impossible without the patronage of Montrose.[79] Haldane of Gleneagles, Morphie's contemporary in the Squadrone Volante, had a parliamentary track record dating back to the 1689 Convention. Haldane of Gleneagles represented Perthshire between 1689 and 1693, before serving Dunbartonshire, 1700–1702. He represented Perthshire in the last Parliament of 1703–1707 and was also elected to the first British Parliament.[80]

Political and parliamentary careers in the post-1707 period were not restricted to members of the Court party and Squadrone Volante as constituted in 1707, but also applied to MPs who had voted against an incorporating union in 1707. Hence, William Cochrane of Kilmaronock who had voted against the union in 1707 as one of the commissioners of the shire for Dunbartonshire also represented Wigtown in the British Parliament of 1708–13. He was also appointed as Joint Deputy-Keeper of the Signet in 1711. Cochrane's continued employment could perhaps be explained by his close family links with the Montrose interest; his father-in-law had been the second Marquis of Montrose, for whom he had been a factor. His marriage to Grizel, the daughter of the second Marquis, had produced six children before Cochrane's death in 1717. Although differing political principles could affect voting behaviour and stances with regard to the union issue in 1707, patronage and close family ties could be reactivated in a new political context post-1707. This would appear to be clearly the case with regard to William Cochrane of Kilmaronock.[81]

Opposition to an incorporating union in the Stirling area was organised and mobilised from a variety of sources and in a variety of formats. Prior to the formal opposition of the Royal Burgh of Stirling and Stirling Town Council as evidenced by 23 November, an anti-union address had been submitted to Parliament on 4 November from the barons, freeholders and others within the shire of Stirling. The parishes of St Ninians and Clackmannan each petitioned against the union on 28 November and 26 December respectively. An address submitted on 11 December incorporated opposition from several sources within a single formal address. Such opposition came from the Presbytery of Dunblane, the heritors, ministers, elders and heads of families in the parish of Logie, and the parishes of Airth, Larbert, Dunnipace and Denny. Opposition from the parish of Logie clearly represented the voice of that local community and provides evidence of opposition down to the individual family level.[82] A similar pattern is apparent within a nearby geographical orbit with the parishes of Tulliallan, Saline, Carnock and Torie all petitioning against the union.[83] What is clear in overall terms is that whilst the formal opposition of the Church of Scotland leadership to the union waned after the Presbyterian supremacy in the Church of Scotland had been secured on 12 November 1706, Presbyterian opposition, emanating from the structures and institutions of the Kirk in the localities, continued to be voiced. The fears and apprehensions of provincial ministers and rank and file Presbyterians had still to be satisfied.

Anti-unionism: mob behaviour and rioting

Popular anti-unionism in Scotland was also expressed via direct action and mob rioting. Edinburgh and Glasgow both experienced substantial rioting and there was substantial mob activity in Dumfries and Stirling. The Scottish Parliament, as a national institution of Scotland's political elites, legislated against mob behaviour and unrest throughout October, November and December 1706. On 25 October Parliament commented on a 'rabble and tumult . . . by which several members of Parliament were threatened and insulted'.[84] The mob had 'offered to burst up the door' of the Parliament House and rampaged through the streets. The size of the mob was estimated at around 1000. Sir Patrick Johnston, a former Provost of Edinburgh (1700–2, 1704–6), was one of the Members of Parliament for the Burgh of Edinburgh, and was singled out for particular attention. The mob descended on his house and many of them appear to have been armed with 'forehammers'.[85] Sir Patrick Johnston may well have been singled out as a visible and familiar figure of the Edinburgh elites on which the mob could express its anger. However, Johnston had also been one of the Scottish commissioners who negotiated the Treaty and the hostility towards him may also have been connected to a combination of local familiarity and a grievance against Johnston's personal role in the union.[86] Johnston was also a Courtier in terms of political affiliation. Direct action against Sir Patrick Johnston may well have had an impact on his fear for his personal safety during the final stages of the passage of the Treaty of Union through Parliament. Whilst Johnston voted in favour of the first article (the principle of an incorporating union), he was absent from the vote on ratification of the Treaty as a whole.[87] The other Member of Parliament for the Burgh of Edinburgh, Robert Inglis, voted against the union both in terms of the first article (the principle of an incorporating union) and in terms of the ratification of the Treaty. Inglis has been identified as a Court 'cross-voter'.[88]

As a result of mob activity in the capital, troops were brought into Edinburgh who, along with the Town Guard, were instructed to secure the peace, albeit reservations were voiced that such forces could be used as a 'force on the Parliament'.[89] This failed to prevent attacks on Members of Parliament, however. Queensberry was attacked by a mob on 18 November and several of his servants were 'beat, wounded, and robb'd'.[90] On 29 November a Proclamation against Unlawful Convocations was issued in response to 'irregular and tumultuary meetings by people of the common and meanest degree'[91] in Glasgow, Kirkcudbright and several places in Lanarkshire. Lanarkshire was a particular cause for concern where a significant degree of organisation appeared to be underway for an armed march on Edinburgh. Letters had been issued inviting people to take up arms, provide ammunitions and provisions to march to Edinburgh 'to disturb the Parliament'.[92] This appeared to be focused on Shotts and Stonehouse as well as Lesmahagow and neighbouring Dumfriesshire. Letters issued in Shotts, Lesmahagow and Stonehouse required parishes to meet and be 'ready on a call with 10 dayes provision'.[93] The Proclamation against Unlawful Convocations stated that any individual found guilty of being 'Actors Abbettors or assistants in convocating or assembling in arms' were to be treated and pursued as traitors.[94] The civil and military forces of the Scottish state were empowered to 'disperse and subdue' any such convocations 'by open force and all manner of violence as enemies and open rebells to us and our Government'.[95] Indemnities and pardons were issued beforehand to any civil or military official who should happen to commit 'any slaughter blood bruises or mutilation'.[96] The following day, on 30 November, an Act against all Musters and Rendezvous was passed whereby all subjects of the kingdom of Scotland were prohibited from meeting or assembling together in arms without prior permission and licence. Failure to comply would be regarded as high treason.[97] This legislative process of reaction to potential insurrection was continued on 27 December. Petitions and addresses against an incorporating union had been presented to Parliament throughout the winter of 1706. Parliament had received information which indicated that letters were being distributed throughout the kingdom encouraging the subscribers of these petitions and addresses to convene in Edinburgh 'upon pretence of waiting the effect of the said Addresses and of knowing what Return the Parliament will give them'.[98] This latter justification was clearly a shrewd cover for exerting extra-parliamentary pressure on the Members of Parliament and it would also appear to bring back memories of the Whiggamore Raid of 1648 whereby an armed uprising and attack on Edinburgh had secured a change of political regime in Scotland. Following the approval of the first article of the Treaty, plans were made for an armed uprising based on the Cameronians and Highland clans who were ordered to convene near Hamilton with circa 7000–8000 men expected.[99] Fears of an armed uprising were countered in the Proclamation discharging Unwarrantable and Seditious Convocations and Meetings of 27 December. Furthermore, the motives and integrity of the Members of Parliament in terms of their consideration of the articles of union were stressed. Thus the subjects of the kingdom were assured that the Parliament 'have and will proceed in that matter with all due regaird and tenderness to the honour and interest of this our ancient Kingdom, both as to their civil and religious concerns'.[100] Nevertheless, a substantial opposition emerged in the House against the Proclamation against Unwarrantable and Seditious Convocations and Meetings. An overall majority of 48 votes was secured with 110 votes in favour of the Proclamation and 62 against. The opposition vote of 62 was composed of 17 noble votes, 29 votes of the commissioners of shires, and 16 votes from the commissioners of the burghs.

The Burgh of Glasgow responded to mob unrest in Glasgow by establishing rules for keeping the peace on 18 November 1706. Firstly, a town 'militia' based on merchants and tradesmen was to be established which was to serve on a daily basis. The Guard was to be mounted at 3 p.m. daily and was to continue on guard until 3 p.m. the following day. Social control of Glasgow's population was to be implemented by a nightly curfew. Secondly, all 'women, boys, young men, and servants' were banned from being on the streets after darkness. The head of each household was to be held personally responsible for any individual living in his house who was found to be part of mob unrest. All heads of families as well as 'private as of public houses' were to provide the Captain of the Guard with the names of any 'strangers they harbour in their houses' before 10 p.m. at night.[101] In addition, 200 dragoons were sent to Glasgow to maintain public order.[102] The Glasgow mob appears to have been composed largely of outsiders, primarily 'those from the country, demanding money and arms'.[103] The Articles of Union were also publicly burned in Dumfries and Kirkcudbright by anti-unionist mobs.[104]

English strategic security, the Treaty of Union and a military invasion of Scotland

The late seventeenth and early eighteenth centuries constituted a period of major European warfare. Within the context of Europe as a whole, there were 22 wars in the period 1648–1713 (from the Treaty of Westphalia in 1648, ending the Thirty Years' War, to the conclusion of the War of the Spanish Succession in 1713). France was directly involved in no less than 7 of these 22 conflicts and was the aggressor in 5 of these conflicts.[105] Military expenditure absorbed the vast bulk of the majority of the revenues of European states, especially those which sought to establish absolutist states with large standing armies as a central defining feature (France, Brandenburg-Prussia,

Sweden, Denmark, and Russia). The English state was no exception to this European trend. The creation of an elaborate English fiscal state went hand in hand with increased English military expenditure and the 'Schumpeter model' of the European state *vis-a-vis* state finances has identified the principal pressure for state financial reform emanating from the costs of warfare with the subsequent development of the 'tax state' and bureaucratic structures for revenue collection.[106] The size of English military commitments expanded rapidly to meet the demands of European warfare. Total staffing levels of the English military amounted to 116,666 men in the period 1689–97 (the Nine Years War) consisting of a navy of 40,262 men and an army of 76,404 troops. During the War of the Spanish Succession (1702–1713), the greatest war that England had ever been involved in,[107] the comparative total figure increased to 135,646 men consisting of a navy of 42,938 men and an army of 92,708 troops.[108] In terms of the number of ships, the Royal Navy expanded from 173 ships in 1688 to 247 ships in 1714. Military expenditure was only surpassed by that of France, which had a population of 19 million compared to the 'British' level of 5.2 million. In per capita terms, 'British' military expenditure was second only to the United Provinces of the Dutch Republic.[109] Whilst this unprecedented military commitment was intended primarily for a European theatre of war and zones of conflict, it also served as a powerful reminder of the military strength of the English state which could be unleashed in Scotland if required. Lord Belhaven, in a famous anti-incorporation speech delivered to the Scottish Parliament on 2 November 1706, pragmatically recognised English military strength when he correctly stated that 'the Royal Navy is the Terror of Europe'.[110] After the inconclusive Battle of Malaga in 1704 the Royal Navy faced no main enemy fleet and therefore 'could demonstrate the flexibility of superior naval power'.[111] The occupation of the Rock of Gibraltar in 1704 by Admirals Rooke and Byng, with the aid of a land force under Georg of Hesse, and Marlborough's famous victory at Blenheim one month later, had indicated the strength of the military might of the English state. The Battle of Blenheim 'registered Britain as a major European power' and the defeat of French forces under Marshal Tallard marked the first defeat of Louis XIV's armies in a direct encounter.[112]

By the later seventeenth and early eighteenth centuries, France had emerged as the dominant military power in continental Europe. French foreign policy and strategic aspirations had focused on the desire to create a French-centred European order and reconstruct the European balance of power which had been established at the Peace of Westphalia in 1648.[113] In short, French attempts at European hegemony had to be defeated, especially when the Spanish Sucession Crisis threatened the potential unification of France and Spain via the French and Spanish thrones through Philip V, the grandson of Louis XIV.[114] In addition, French military expansion accompanied this increased dynastic and hegemonistic threat. A detailed programme of military and naval expansion in France was put into place under the consecutive reforms of Jean-Baptiste Colbert, Controller General of Finances (1665) and Secretary of State for the Royal Household and Navy (1669), supplemented by the reforms of Louis XIV's War Minister, Sébastian François Michel Le Tellier, Marquis de Louvois, and Marshal Sebastien Le Prestre de Vauban, Royal Engineer and Commissioner General of Fortifications. Military reforms involved a more efficient reorganisation of regimental structures, drill and training procedures, the adoption of the cutting edge of technological innovation such as the flintlock and bayonet, and the construction of barracks and arsenals in all the major French cities.[115] A conscript militia was created in 1688 to augment peacetime forces and during the War of Spanish Succession the militia provided circa 350,000 men.[116] The growing size of the French armed forces reached circa 500,000 men during the reign of Louis XIV.[117] Under Colbert, the French naval budget increased from 300,000 *livres* per annum to 12 million *livres*. At the beginning of Louis XIV's reign, the French navy consisted of only 20 ships. By 1677 the French fleet numbered 144 ships of the line, 50 supporting vessels and 34 galleys.[118] By 1700 the French fleet consisted of 231 ships, albeit this had dropped to 192 ships by 1704.[119] A naval base was founded at Rochefort, the French northern ports of Brest, Le Havre, Calais and Dunkerque were all fortified, whilst naval dockyards and academies were also founded.[120] The defence of France's northern and eastern frontiers was enhanced by the construction of a chain of 160 fortresses along the French borders.[121] Marlborough's second famous military victory over the French at Ramillies in 1706 not only 'gave a final boost to the confidence and magnetism of England'[122] but it also destroyed the French threat to the Low Countries in the context of the War of the Spanish Succession. Linking these developments to the 'union crisis' in Scotland, the might of English military strength had now been clearly demonstrated at Blenheim and Ramillies against the most powerful military force and power in Europe. Acceptance of an incorporating union, on the best possible terms for Scotland, may well have been the preferred option to a military invasion and conquest of Scotland. After all, the Cromwellian conquest and occupation of Scotland (1651–1660) was not that far off in the past.

Given the context of French aspirations in terms of European dynastic rivalries, state structures and military expansion, the incorporating union of 1707 secured a number of political objectives on the part of the English ministry. Firstly, the 'Scottish problem' in terms of the ungovernability of Scottish parliamentary politics appeared to be solved via inclusion in an effectively enlarged English Parliament in which Scottish representatives could be controlled. More importantly, in terms of contemporary observations and polemics, were the securing of the Hanoverian Succession and the requirements of English foreign policy by the securing of England's northern border. Such considerations were discussed in detail in *Reasons For An Union Between the Kingdoms of England and Scotland*, a pro-union English pamphlet written in 1706. The author conducted an analysis of the European balance of power and concluded that France was 'yet a match for all other Powers'.[123] This raised fears for English strategic security given the sensitive nature of Anglo-Scottish relations. A potential Franco-Scottish military rapprochement was feared, harking back to the days of the Auld Alliance. Hence, it was argued that 'it was plain from all Experience, that all the Force of Scotland' was 'ever in the interest of France on our Disputes and War with that Kingdom'.[124] This was also recognised by James Johnston in correspondence with Baillie of Jerviswood in 1704 commenting on the English perception of the state of Anglo-Scottish relations; 'it was said, you and your independence are not so great but that you must depend either on France or England, and sure they will not suffer you to depend on France, if they can help it'.[125] The author of *Reasons For An Union Between the Kingdoms of England and Scotland* feared that the French would exploit the Anglo-Scottish crisis for their own ends by fomenting division. Accordingly, therefore, it was 'highly reasonable for all true English-Men, who have any Value for the Safety and Happiness of their Country, to wish and promote such a Union'.[126] Indeed, a union between England and Scotland was 'now absolutely necessary for the Safety of ourselves, and the defeating the Designs of our Enemy'.[127] Therefore a pragmatic yet realistic approach was adopted as to why the two kingdoms should unite, although it was confessed that the advantages of union 'would be much more so to Scotland'.[128] Two main benefits for the English kingdom were identified: 'What England would get by it, is only the Security of its Northern Borders, and having a Source of Men for our Common Wars'.[129] Scotland, on the other hand, would benefit by 'an Increase of Trade, and by Consequence an Increase of Money'.[130]

Issues of *British* strategic security were advanced on the Scottish side by William Seton of Pitmedden, a pro-incorporating union pamphleteer. Seton of Pitmedden represented Aberdeenshire in the last Scottish Parliament of 1703–1707 and was one of the Scottish commissioners who negotiated the Treaty of Union.[131] The Scottish negotiating team was packed by pro-incorporationists and in terms of 'party' alignment Seton of Pitmidden, unsurprisingly, was a member of the Court party. In terms of voting behaviour, he voted for the first article of the Treaty (based on the principle of an incorporating union) and voted in favour of ratification of the Treaty as a whole.[132] Whilst the author of *Reasons for An Union Between the Kingdoms of England and Scotland* emphasised the strategic interests of *England*, Seton of

Pitmedden emphasised the advantages of union for the strategic security of *Britain*: 'as an Union Secures our Religion, so it Procures the Safety, Prosperity and Peace of Britain'.[133] In common with the English pamphleteer, the mutual benefits of union were also assessed by Seton of Pitmedden and a common train of thought can be detected. Strategic security and foreign policy requirements would benefit the English side: 'England secures an old and dangerous Enemy to be their Friend, and thereby peace at Home, and in more safety to carry on designs abroad'.[134] In military terms England would also gain by 'a considerable addition of brave and courageous Men, to their Fleet, Armies and Plantations'.[135] Pitmedden assured his readership that Scotland should not be 'allarm'd by the Threatenings of a powerful and rich Neighbour' and Scotland would not be 'so easily put under the yoke of a foreign Enemy' because Scotland would be 'secured by their Protection, and inriched by their Labours'.[136] In economic and commercial terms, 'We send our Commodities and useful Manufactures to them, and have Money or other Necessaries remitted to us'.[137]

The short-term urgency of securing the Hanoverian Succession in Scotland was similarly emphasised by the author of *Reasons for An Union Between the Kingdoms of England and Scotland* as a pressing motive for union. The Scottish Act of Security opened up the possibility of Scotland and England having different monarchs. Therefore it was uncertain whether or not the Hanoverian Succession in Scotland would be carried and more importantly, it raised the issue of a possible Jacobite Restoration in Scotland. Hence fears were expressed that Scotland would become 'a distinct and separate Kingdom, as of old, and have Kings of their own, dwelling among them'. Therefore it was imperative that a union should be secured as quickly as possible:

> We see the fatal Time approaching, when, if this happy Union be not effected immediately, at least if not in her Majesty's Life, there can be no Prospect of accomplishing it afterwards. Her present most Gracious Majesty, is the last of the Race, that have an Hereditary Claim to the Crown of Scotland, and upon her Decease, it is reasonable to believe, that the Scots will either provide a Prince for themselves, or insist on Terms more difficult and hard, than now they are likely to do.[138]

Given the tense nature of Anglo-Scottish relations, an incorporating union would remove the worst possible scenario from the Scottish perspective, namely a military invasion of Scotland. This appears to have been recognised by Seton of Pitmedden when he stated that an 'honourable and advantageous union' would prevent 'the hazard and mischiefs of a Civil War, which may end in our utter Ruin and eternal Slavery'.[139] A military invasion of Scotland was one policy option considered if an incorporating union should fail to be secured, but it remains debatable whether or not this was a disguised threat designed to bully the Scots into a negotiating position or whether or not English military forces would have been sent into Scotland. James Johnston informed Baillie of Jerviswood in 1704 of the political mood in London; 'The spirit here runs upon conquest or union'.[140] A similar view was expressed in 1705; 'Its now noe more conquer or unite, but reduce or annexe'.[141] Threats of a direct military invasion were hinted at as early as 1705[142] whilst an English military force was situated near the Scottish border in December 1706, as the Treaty was proceeding through the Scottish Parliament, in preparation for movement if called upon by James Douglas, 2nd Duke of Queensberry, Her Majesty's Commissioner in Scotland.[143] James Johnston informed Baillie of Jerviswood of the prevailing mood in London in the winter of 1706:

> The discourse here is, that orders are sent down to the Ministry to despatch the business of the Union one way or other, and to assure them that there shall be troops at hand on the Borders and in Ireland, and from Flanders too, if they need them; and it's say'd ships of war too are order'd to your coasts.[144]

The option of military forces was not only considered as a means of enforcing an incorporating union but also for dealing with internal insurrection in Scotland and anti-union mob behaviour. Lord Treasurer Godolphin informed Marlborough in the winter of 1706 of the prospect of open revolt and insurrection in Scotland in response to the union:

> the mobb is uneasy at the Union in Scotland, and has been very unruly, the majority in the Parliament for it is so great, that they begin to find it cannot bee resisted but by tumult and open force. What effect this may have I doe not know, but I hope they won't prove the strongest.[145]

Johnston's information of troop movements in the winter of 1706 is also confirmed by correspondence between Lord Treasurer Godolphin and Marlborough. Thus, 'The Queen will have the precaution of making some regiments move towards the north of England and of Ireland, and if there were a reall occasion, I hope some of those at Ghendth would be as near'.[146] The main reason for the deployment of English military forces in Scotland, however, would be to suppress either an internal Jacobite uprising in Scotland either on its own or in tandem with an external French or pro-Jacobite invasion. This has an important long-term significance for the eighteenth century when viewed from the perspective of the period 1689–1746 as a whole.[147] Geoffrey Holmes and Daniel Szechi have noted that in the period 1689–1714, from the 'Glorious Revolution' to the Hanoverian Succession, when 'Britain' emerged as a 'Great Power', 'the establishment and defence of the Protestant Succession had become a keystone' of 'British' foreign policy.[148] Such an objective became of paramount importance following Louis XIV's recognition of Prince James Edward Stuart, the 'Old Pretender', as the rightful King of Scotland and England in 1701.[149] It was incorporated as one of the points in the Treaty of the Hague of 1702 in which French recognition of the Protestant Succession in the British Isles was demanded.[150] In conjunction with the constitutional nationalism of the Scottish Parliament in 1703–4, this led to a fear of a Jacobite invasion of Scotland. Godolphin was informed in July 1704 of the forces present in key strategic locations in Scotland. Edinburgh Castle was staffed by 120 men, Stirling Castle by 100 men, Dumbarton Castle by 40 men 'who are altogether insufficient'.[151] Godolphin was informed that 'if there were any stir here' then a small army of 3000 men in Scotland would be insufficient to deal with the problem. Three Highland regiments of 50 men each were included in these figures but it was asserted that these were 'of no use . . . if ther were any commotion'. This theme of certain Scottish regiments being unable to be trusted or relied on to put down domestic insurrection in Scotland resurfaced with a further Jacobite threat/scare in 1708 when the regiments of Alexander Grant of Grant and William Gordon, Lord Strathmore, were to be moved out of Scotland, partly for military commitments in the European theatre of war and partly because 'it seems to be agreed by all the Queen's servants in Scotland, that ther's no relying upon troops of that country in case of an invasion'.[152] In terms of English intelligence information, the Jacobite threat of 1704 was based on intelligence reports received by Marlborough from the Swedish envoy at The Hague, Johan Palmqvist, who had been contacted by the Swedish envoy in Paris. These reports suggested that a French invasion of Scotland, consisting of eight battalions of foot, was to be launched from the French Atlantic seaport of Rochefort.[153] In response to this information, Marlborough informed Lord Godolphin that he could ensure that six regiments could be despatched for Scotland within 24 hours.[154] Jacobite scares continued in 1708–10, whilst the move to repeal the incorporating union in the House of Lords in 1713 only narrowly avoided defeat. Despite French recognition of the Protestant Succession in the Treaty of Utrecht of 1713 which ended the War of the Spanish Succession,[155] Jacobitism continued to present problems on a variety of fronts. The Jacobite Rebellion of 1715 incorporated a wide diaspora of Scottish anti-union sentiment as well as Jacobite fundamentalists. The abolition of the Scottish Privy Council in 1708, the Treasons Act of 1709, the Brandon Case of 1709, the Greenshields Case of 1711, the Patronage Act of 1712 and the extension of the Malt Tax to Scotland in 1713 all contributed to widespread anti-unionism in Scotland.[156] The Rebellion of 1715 attracted between 12,000 and 20,000 rebels, which in terms of proportion to the Scottish population (circa one million), amounted to 5–

10% of the adult male population of Scotland.[157] Jacobitism remained a major thorn in the side of the British state until its ultimate demise on Culloden Moor in 1746. In terms of European power politics and diplomacy, by the Treaty of Aix-la-Chapelle of 1748 which ended the War of the Austrian Succession (1740–48), France finally recognised the House of Hanover in Britain and formally rejected the dynastic claims of the Young Pretender, Bonnie Prince Charlie.[158]

Conclusion

The Treaty of Union of 1707 has aroused intense historiographical controversy and debate as a defining moment in the nation's past. No single factor or historical approach satisfactorily explains the achievement of an incorporating union in 1707. Political instability and economic crisis provided the environment of uncertainty for contemporaries as to what the future would hold for the kingdom of Scotland. Nevertheless, the securing of an incorporating union at this particular time was a substantial short-term achievement which should not be underestimated in terms of the skills of the English ministry and the Scottish Court party. The type of Treaty secured in 1707 can be traced directly to the 1705 parliamentary session which opened the door for Queen Anne to nominate negotiating commissioners. The Treaty itself had to be carefully managed through the Scottish Parliament and the correspondence of George Baillie of Jerviswood, taken as a whole, clearly indicates that contemporaries were by no means certain that the Treaty could be secured in the Scottish Parliament in 1706–1707. Issues of Scotland's economic performance and future should not be underestimated when attempting to analyse the motives of Scottish Parliamentarians in accepting the Treaty of Union. However, the ultimate decision for an incorporating union between Scotland and England was based on unprecedented English military commitment in European warfare and the need to secure the Hanoverian Succession on a British basis. The decision for an incorporating union was primarily not a Scottish one and a variety of devices, sweeteners and threats were employed to secure this end. Nevertheless, the Treaty was distinctly unpopular in Scotland with a clear dichotomy between the elites and the people. The Treaty of Union, as a short-term political objective, was not ultimately secured until 1746 on Culloden Moor.

REFERENCES

1. *The Correspondence of George Baillie of Jerviswood* 1702–1708 (Bannatyne Club, 1842), p.190. Thomas Wharton, 1st Marquess of Wharton was one of the leading figures of the Whig Junto which secured the incorporating union of 1707. He was created Earl of Wharton in

1706 and raised to a Marquess in 1715. He was also Lord Lieutenant of Ireland 1708–1710. The Whartons were one of the most important Whig dynasties in England. Wharton was the uncle of George Lockhart of Carnwath, a Jacobite, and the only Scottish Commissioner who negotiated the Treaty of Union with representatives of the English Parliament who was not in favour of an incorporating union. Lockhart's inclusion appears to have been due to his uncle's influence; J.P. Kenyon, *Dictionary of British History* (Ware, 1994), p.359; D. Szechi (ed.), *Letters of George Lockhart of Carnwath 1698–1732*, Scottish History Society, Fifth Series, volume 2 (Edinburgh, 1989), pp.xvi-xvii.

2. Johnston was Secretary of State in Scotland, 1692–96, as well as Lord Clerk Register, 1704–5; H.L. Synder (ed.), *The Marlborough-Godolphin Correspondence* (Oxford, 1975), three volumes, volume two, p.647.
3. *Ibid*, p.737.
4. *Ibid*, p.765.
5. *The Marlborough-Godolphin Correspondence*, p.736.
6. *The Correspondence of George Baillie of Jerviswood*, p.27.
7. *Ibid*, p.177.
8. For a recent discussion and overview, see C.A. Whatley, *'Bought and Sold for English Gold'? Explaining the Union of 1707* (The Economic and Social History Society of Scotland, Dundee, 1994).
9. I.D. Whyte, *Scotland's Society and Economy in Transition, c.1500-c.1760* (London, 1997), p.151; T.M. Devine, 'The Union of 1707 and Scottish Development' in T.M. Devine, *Exploring the Scottish Past. Themes in the History of Scottish Society* (East Linton, 1995), p.39.
10. Whyte, *Scotland's Society and Economy in Transition*, pp.154, 158.
11. For a discussion of the economic issues, see C.A. Whatley, 'Economic Causes and Consequences of the Union of 1707: A Survey', *The Scottish Historical Review*, volume LXVIII, 2, No. 186: (1989), pp.150–181.
12. Devine, 'The Union of 1707 and Scottish Development', pp.41, 45–46, 50
13. The English Alien Act was repealed in November 1705 but the distinct possibility remained that it could be introduced as an economic and political inducement for incorporation in the future (Whyte, *Scotland's Society and Economy in Transition*, p.156).
14. W. Ferguson, *Scotland 1689 to the Present* (Edinburgh, 1968), pp.46–47.
15. Whyte, *Scotland's Society and Economy in Transition*, 158; Devine, 'The Union of 1707 and Scottish Development, p.37.
16. Ferguson, *Scotland 1689 to the Present*, p.43.
17. *Letters of George Lockhart of Carnwath 1698–1732*, p.30.
18. B.C. Brown, *The Letters and Diplomatic Instructions of Queen Anne* (London, 1935), pp.190–191. Queensberry was instructed by the Queen that 'If in opposition to an entire and complete Union as is now treated by the Commissioners, a Federal Union, the settling the succession with Limitations or any other measure shall be proposed, You are to let all Our servants know that We expect their joint and hearty concurrence with you for the throwing out thereof' (*ibid*).
19. P.G.B. McNeill & H.L. MacQueen (eds.), *Atlas of Scottish History to 1707* (Edinburgh: The Scottish Medievalists and Department of Geography, University of Edinburgh, 1996), pp.151–153.
20. *Ibid*.
21. M. Young (ed.), *The Parliaments of Scotland. Burgh and Shire Commissioners*, two volumes, (Edinburgh, 1992–1993), volume one, pp.173–175; S. Lee (ed.), *Dictionary of National Biography. Index and Epitome* (London, 1903), p.314; P. Riley, *The Union of England and Scotland* (Manchester, 1978), pp.330–331.
22. Young (ed.), *The Parliaments of Scotland. Burgh and Shire Commissioners*, volume one, pp.100, 102; Riley, *The Union of England and Scotland*, p.331.
23. *The Correspondence of George Baillie of Jerviswood*, p.162.
24. McNeill & MacQueen (eds.), *Atlas of Scottish History to 1707*, pp.151–153; Ferguson, *Scotland 1689 to the Present*, pp.48–49.

25. See C.A. Whatley, 'Burns and the Union of 1707', in K. Simpson (ed), *Love and Liberty. Robert Burns: A Bicentenary Celebration* (East Linton, 1997), pp.183–197.
26. *The Correspondence of George Baillie of Jerviswood*, p.190.
27. J. Carswell, *From Revolution to Revolution: England* 1688–1776 (London, 1973), p.55.
28. G. Holmes, *The Making of A Great Power. Late Stuart and Georgian Britain* 1660–1722 (London, 1993), pp.202–203, 324, 339, 340, 344, 362–363. Occassional Conformity was successfully legislated for in 1711 but in general was evaded and was ultimately repealed in 1719.
29. G. Holmes, *Religion and Party in late Stuart England* (Historical Association Pamphlet, London, 1705). Holmes states that the Whigs gained some 60 seats in the General Election of 1705 (p.17). See also for the wider issue and mechanics of Occassional Conformity.
30. Carswell, *From Revolution to Revolution*, p.60.
31. *Ibid.*
32. *Ibid*, pp.55–56. In contrast to the Tories, the Whigs only had 74 safe seats and only four counties were regularly Whig seats.
33. J.R. Jones, *Country and Court. England* 1658–1714 (London, 1993 edition), p.332.
34. McNeill & MacQueen (eds.), *Atlas of Scottish History to* 1707, p.392; A.I. Macinnes, *Charles I and the Making of the Covenanting Movement* 1625–1641 (Edinburgh, 1991), pp.161–166.
35. McNeill & MacQueen (eds.), *Atlas of Scottish History to* 1707, p.391.
36. *The Correspondence of George Baillie of Jerviswood*, p.167.
37. *Ibid*, p.168.
38. D. Szechi (ed.), *'Scotland's Ruine'. Lockhart of Carnwath's Memoirs of the Union* (Aberdeen, 1995), p.135.
39. *Ibid*, p.135.
40. J. Robertson (ed.), *Ecclesiatical Records of the Presbytery of Lanark* 1623–1709 (Abbotsford Club, Edinburgh, 1889), pp.140–141. I am very grateful to Mrs Linda Fryer, research assistant for Professor Allan Macinnes of Aberdeen University, for passing on a transcribed copy of the address from the Presbytery of Lanark located in the USA; John Carter Brown Library, Providence, Rhode Island, 'Unto his Grace Her Majesty's High Commissioner and the Right Honourable Estates of Parliament. The Address of the Presbyterie of Lanerk'. This version contains the signatures of 14 members of the Presbytery, three of whom were elders.
41. *Ecclesiastical Records of the Presbytery of Lanark*, pp.140–141.
42. *Ibid.*
43. *Ibid.*
44. *Ibid.*
45. *Ibid.*
46. L.W. Sharp (ed.), *Early Letters of Robert Wodrow* 1698–1709, Scottish History Society, Third Series, 24 (Edinburgh, 1937), pp.xxxiv-xxv, 135. Sharp somewhat confusingly describes the Cameronians and Hamilton Presbytery as 'extremists'(p.xxxiv).
47. Young (ed.), *The Parliaments of Scotland. Burgh and Shire Commissioners*, volume one, pp.30, 32, 314, volume two, 644; Riley, *The Union of England and Scotland*, pp.332–334. Hamilton of Aikenhead voted in half or fewer of the union divisions.
48. Young (ed.), *The Parliaments of Scotland. Burgh and Shire Commissioners*, volume one, p. 107; Riley, *The Union of England and Scotland*, p.331.
49. Scottish Records Office, PA. 7/28, Addresses against the Union; PA.7/28/10–12 (Lanarkshire), PA.7/28/39 (Lanark), PA 7/28/52 (Blantyre), PA. 7/28/53 (Bothwell), PA. 7/28/56 (Cambuslang), PA. 7/28/60 (Carnwath), PA. 7/28/71 (Hamilton), PA.7/28/77 (Monkland East), PA. 7/28/78 (Monkland West), PA. 7/28/81 (Shotts).
50. SRO PA.7/28/35–36 (Glasgow Barony and Glasgow Gorbals).
51. Riley, *The Union of England and Scotland*, p.332.
52. Young (ed.), *The Parliaments of Scotland. Burgh and Shire Commissioners*, volume two,

p.505.

53. SRO PA. 7/28/34.
54. *Early Letters of Robert Wodrow*, p.287.
55. *Ibid*, pp. xxxiv-xxv, 280 .
56. *Ibid*, p.248.
57. *Ibid*, p.250.
58. *Ibid*, p.290.
59. *Ibid*.
60. *Ibid*.
61. *Ibid*.
62. *Ibid*, p.291.
63. *Ibid*.
64. See A.I. Macinnes, *Charles I and the Making of the Covenanting Movement 1625–1641* (Edinburgh, 1991).
65. Glasgow City Archives, Mitchell Library, Glasgow, Hamilton of Barns Papers TD 589/1030. This is a manuscript copy of a petition subscribed by the 'Gentlemen, Heretours, and others at Kilpatricke'. The copy was made by John Lang, a schoolmaster in Kilpatrick and is a contemporary copy.
66. *Ibid*.
67. Young (ed.), *The Parliaments of Scotland. Burgh and Shire Commissioners*, volume one, pp.127, 138.
68. Riley, *The Union of England and Scotland*, p.333.
69. Young, (ed.), *The Parliaments of Scotland. Burgh and Shire Commissioners*, volume one, p.127.
70. Lockhart of Carnwath, *'Scotland's Ruine'*, pp.119–120.
71. *Ibid*, p.118; Young (ed.), *The Parliaments of Scotland. Burgh and Shire Commissioners*, volume two, p.650; Riley, *The Union of England and Scotland*, p.332; K.F. McAlister, 'The Making of the Treaty of Union of 1707: A Case Study of the Localities with particular reference to the Members of Parliament for the Royal Burgh of Stirling and the Shires of Stirling and Clackmannan', (University of Strathclyde, BA Honours Dissertation, 1997), Appendix 5: comparative analysis of Members of Parliament for Dunbartonshire and the Royal Burgh of Dumbarton.
72. R. Sunter, *Patronage and Politics in Scotland, 1707–1832* (Edinburgh, 1986), pp.199–210.
73. Shire representation had been increased by the Act for Additional Representation in Parliament of the Greater Shires of the Kingdom in 1690. Eleven shires were accorded two additional members to give a total of four shire representatives each (Aberdeen, Lanark, Perth, Midlothian, Berwick, Roxburgh, Dumfries, Haddington, Ayr, Fife, and Forfar). The Stewartry of Kirkcudbright and three further shires (Stirling, Argyll, and Renfrew) were each accorded one additional member to give three representatives each, Young (ed.), *The Parliaments of Scotland. Burgh and Shire Commissioners*, volume one, pp. xviii, xix; R.S. Rait, *The Parliaments of Scotland*, (Glasgow, 1924), pp.235–236; C.S. Terry, *The Scottish Parliament: Its Constitution and Procedure* (Glasgow, 1905), pp.36–37.
74. Riley, *The Union of England and Scotland*, pp.328, 333.
75. *Ibid*, p.331; Young (ed.), *The Parliaments of Scotland*, volume one, p.232.
76. McAlister, 'The Making of the Treaty of Union of 1707', Appendix 6: Petitions and Addresses against the Union by the Shires of Clackmannan and Stirling and the Royal Burgh of Stirling. See also McNeill and MacQueen (eds.), *Atlas of Scottish History to 1707*, pp.152–153.
77. Riley, *The Union of England and Scotland*, p.334; Young (ed.), *The Parliaments of Scotland*, volume one, pp.292–293.
78. Sunter, *Patronage and Politics in Scotland*, p.200.
79. Young (ed.), *The Parliaments of Scotland*. Burgh and Shire commissioners, volume one, pp.292–293.
80. *Ibid*, p.306.

81. *Ibid*, p.127.
82. McAlister, 'The Making of the Treaty of Union of 1707', Appendix 6.
83. The parish of Tulliallan petitioned in a single address, whereas the address of Saline, Carnock and Torie was based on a cluster format (McNeill and McQueen (eds.), *Atlas of Scottish History to 1707*, p.153).
84. *The Acts of the Parliaments of Scotland* [*APS*], T. Thomson 38; C. Innes (eds.), twelve volumes, (Edinburgh, 1814–75), volume XI, p.309.
85. *A Diary of the Proceedings in the Parliament and Privy Council of Scotland, May 21 1700-March 7 1707*. By Sir David Hume of Crossrigg, One of the Senators of the College of Justice (Bannatyne Club, Edinburgh, 1828), pp.176–177.
86. Young (ed.), *The Parliaments of Scotland. Burgh and Shire Commissioners*, volume one, p.384.
87. Riley, *The Union of England and Scotland*, p.331.
88. *Ibid*, p.332; Young (ed.), *The Parliaments of Scotland. Burgh and Shire Commissioners*, volume one, p.367.
89. *The Correspondence of George Baillie of Jerviswood*, p.166.
90. *A Diary of Proceedings in the Parliament and Privy Council of Scotland*, pp.184–185.
91. *APS*, XI, p.341.
92. *Ibid*.
93. *A Diary of Proceedings in the Parliament and Privy Council of Scotland*, pp.187–188.
94. *APS*, XI, p.343.
95. *Ibid*.
96. *Ibid*.
97. *Ibid*, p.344.
98. *Ibid*, p.369.
99. McNeill 38; MacQueen (eds.), *Atlas of Scottish History to 1707*, pp.152–153.
100. *APS*, XI, p.372.
101. R. Renwick (ed.), *Extracts from the Records of the Burgh of Glasgow A.D. 1691–1717* (Scottish Burgh Records Society, Glasgow, 1908), pp.399–401.
102. Ferguson, *Scotland*. 1689 to the Present, p.50.
103. *A Diary of the Proceedings in the Parliament and the Privy Council of Scotland*, pp.187–188.
104. *Ibid*; Sir H. Maxwell, *A History of Dumfries and Galloway* (Edinburgh, 1896), 306; Glasgow University Library Special Collections Unit, Mu 29-e. 20/41, *An Account of the burning of the Articles of the Union at Dumfries* (1706).
105. K.J. Holsti, *Peace and War: Armed Conflicts and International Order 1648–1989* (Cambridge, 1991), pp.47, 68. See also D. McKay 38; H.M. Scott, *The Rise of the Great Powers 1648–1815* (London, 1983), pp.1–66; P. Kennedy, *The Rise and Fall of the Great Powers. Economic Change and Military Conflict from* 1500 to 2000 (London, 1988), pp.100–108.
106. M.J. Braddick, *The Nerves of State. Taxation and the Financing of the English State*, 1558–1714 (Manchester, 1996), pp.12–13.
107. Holmes, *The Making of A Great Power*, p.232.
108. Braddick, *The Nerves of State*, p.33.
109. *Ibid*, p.191. These levels of military expansion created a problem of escalating debt. By 1697 English debt levels amounted to £16.7 million and had increased to £36.2 million by the end of the War of the Spanish Succession in 1713 (*ibid*, p.33).
110. Glasgow University Library Special Collections Unit, James Dean Ogilvie Collection, Ogilvie 955, *Lord Belhaven's Speech in Parliament, The Second Day of November 1706*. On the Subject-Matter of an Union betwixt the Two Kingdoms of Scotland and England (London, 1706) (7).
111. Kennedy, *The Rise and Fall of the Great Powers*, p.104.
112. J. Carswell, *From Revolution to Revolution: England 1688–1776* (London, 1973), pp.53–54.
113. Holsti, *Peace and War*, pp.44, 60.
114. *Ibid*, pp.56, 61.
115. N. Davies, *Europe. A History* (Oxford, 1996), p.619; J.B. Collins, *The State in Early Modern*

France (Cambridge, 1995), pp.90–91. Colbert enjoyed a wide ministerial portfolio in the administration of Louis XIV. He died in 1683 and it has been noted that 'more than any other minister, Colbert was responsible for providing the resources which enabled Louis XIV to establish absolutism in France, and France to become the chief power in Europe'; E.N. Williams, *The Penguin Dictionary of English and European History 1485–1789* (Harmondsworth, 1980), p.100. Louvois died in 1691.

116. D. Parker, *The Making of French Absolutism* (London, 1983), pp.124–125.
117. R. Price, *A Concise History of France* (Cambridge, 1993), p. 61.
118. Parker, *The Making of French Absolutism*, p.125.
119. Braddick, *The Nerves of State*, p.191
120. Davies, *Europe. A History*, p.619.
121. *Ibid.*
122. Carswell, *From Revolution to Revolution*, p.60.
123. Glasgow University Library Special Collections Unit, James Dean Ogilvie Collection, Ogilvie Q34, *Reasons For An Union Between the Kingdoms of England and Scotland* (London, 1706), (33).
124. *Ibid*, (32).
125. *The Correspondence of George Baillie of Jerviswood*, p.22.
126. *Reasons For An Union Between the Kingdoms of England and Scotland*, (34).
127. *Ibid.*
128. *Ibid*, 36.
129. *Ibid.*
130. *Ibid.* The author proceeds to state that 'The other Advantages which would arise particularly to Scotland can't be so well describ'd, unless we knew in what manner this Union was to be, whether an entire Union of Laws, Liberties and Religion, or only a partial Union, which does not take in the whole State of each Nation'. It was therefore unclear at the point when this pamphlet was written whether or not an incorporating or a federal union was to be achieved, but the basic intellectual and strategic case forwarded by the author remains the same.
131. Young (ed.), *The Parliaments of Scotland. Burgh and Shire Commissioners*, volume two, p.629.
132. Riley, *The Union of England and Scotland*, p.331.
133. Glasgow University Library Special Collections Unit, James Dean Ogilvie Collection, Ogilvie 954, William Seton of Pitmedden, *Scotland's Great Advantages By An Union with England: Showen in a Letter From the Country, To a Member of Parliament* (1706), (5).
134. *Ibid*, (7).
135. *Ibid.*
136. *Ibid.*
137. *Ibid.*
138. *Reasons For An Union Between the Kingdoms of England and Scotland*, (39).
139. *Scotland's Great Advantages By An Union with England: Showen in a Letter From the Country, To a Member of Parliament*, (8). Seton of Pitmedden's analysis was fundamentally related to the mutual benefits of union and he only made a passing reference to a 'civil war'. Thus, Seton asserted, 'I think the matter may be reduced to this Alternative, either Union with Peace and Plenty, or Dis-union with Slavery and Poverty'.
140. *The Correspondence of Baillie of Jerviswood*, p.22.
141. *Ibid*, p.85.
142. *HMC, Mar and Kellie*, volume I (1904), p.233.
143. Ferguson, *Scotland.* 1689 to the Present, pp.50–51.
144. *The Correspondence of George Baillie of Jerviswood*, p.170.
145. H.L. Synder (ed.), *The Marlborough-Godolphin Correspondence*, three volumes (Oxford, 1975), volume two, p.727.
146. *Ibid.*
147. Three main periods of Jacobitism have been identified by H.T. Dickinson; 1688–96,

1714–24 and 1745–50. See H.T. Dickinson, 'The Jacobite Challenge', in M. Lynch (ed.), *Jacobitism and the 45*, The Historical Association (London, 1995), pp.7–22.

148. G. Holmes and D. Szechi, *The Age of Oligarchy. Pre-industrial Britain 1722–1783* (London, 1993), p.71.
149. G. Holmes, *The Making of A Great Power. Late Stuart and early Georgian Britain 1660–1722* (London, 1993), pp. 253–254.
150. *Ibid*, pp.253–254, 436.
151. British Library, London, Add. MSS. 28, 055. Sidney 1st Earl of Godolphin. Official Correspondence Home 1701–1710 (Correspondence of Lord Godolphin, chiefly in reference to Scotch affairs, 1701–1710), folio 98.
152. *The Marlborough-Godolphin Correspondence*, volume 2, p.1123.
153. *Ibid*, volume 1, p.265. Reports of a French invasion of Scotland are confirmed in *The Correspondence of George Baillie of Jerviswood*, pp.33–34.
154. *The Marlborough-Godolphin Correspondence*, volume 1, p.359.
155. Holmes, *The Making of A Great Power*, p.437.
156. *Ibid*, pp.317–318.
157. Holmes and Szechi, *The Age of Oligarchy*, p.98.
158. *Ibid*, p.372.

Four

A Commercial Empire: Scotland and British Expansion in the Eighteenth Century

MICHAEL FRY

ADAM SMITH PERCEIVED, and described in terms moving for one of such sober temper, his compatriots' urge to burst the bonds imposed on them by nature: 'It is a sort of instinctive feeling to us, that the destiny of our name and nation is not here, in this narrow island which we occupy'.[1] The instinctive feeling he identifies is surely at odds with the image of Scots imparted by the traditional Whig historiography.[2] In deterministic fashion, this has taught that the Union changed almost everything about Scotland as it raised her from primitive darkness into the light of modernity. Imperialism is without doubt an aspect of modernity. Yet Scottish imperial activity, if encouraged by the Union of 1707, also formed a continuous line of its own cutting across that crux, along which certain experiences of the separate nation moved to shape its future within the United Kingdom. The position and outlook of Scots in the Empire for the rest of the eighteenth century owed something to both the old Scotland and the new Britain.

Of several independent Scottish colonial endeavours the Darien Scheme, just at the turn of the century, formed the climax. Though it is somewhat ill-served by the existing literature, recent work has extended our understanding of it.[3] It no longer looks so much like the madcap venture of a minnow in the contemporary international system, born of economic despair, doomed to failure and fit for showing only that the Union was desirable, if not inevitable. Of course the scheme did fail, but most early colonial schemes of all nations failed, so it cannot be dismissed on that account. Of course it was projected by a small, weak country, but small, weak countries such as Portugal and the Netherlands proved perfectly capable of mounting colonial enterprises, more capable than some much bigger and stronger countries. By 1700, after all, the vast Spanish territories in the New World were impoverishing rather than enriching the mother country, while another European power, the Holy Roman Empire of the

German Nation, had despite its best endeavours and inducements from its rulers never got off the ground in expanding overseas.

Instead of lamenting the failure of Darien, it is more instructive to look at what it actually tried to do. This is not simple to define. The Scottish state under the Union of the Crowns suffered many handicaps, but remained able to follow a reasonably independent economic policy. Through most of the seventeenth century the policy took on, with fits and starts, an increasingly mercantilist character. The trend culminated in 1681 under the viceregal rule of the Duke of Albany, later James VII. He dragooned the merchant class into accepting a regime which encouraged domestic manufactures while severely restricting foreign competition. Another face of it was the foundation of colonies, which would ship their exotic produce back for processing in the mother country. Colonies were actually founded in New Jersey and South Carolina, if without ever fulfilling their purpose. The policy anyway soon ran into trouble through retaliation from Scotland's trading partners. Even so, it was not wholly abandoned. The eventual establishment in 1695 of a chartered Company of Scotland, which would go on to set up at Darien, was in a way the continuation of it.[4]

But it was also different, because meanwhile a deep change in the political and economic environment, indeed in the whole course of Scottish history, had taken place. The 1680s saw the final phase of royal absolutism, a last chance to show that in the special form of absentee monarchy it was not intolerable. The House of Stewart failed the test, tried beyond its limits the Scots' allegiance to the legitimate descent of Robert Bruce and dissipated much of their loyalty for good. The Revolution of 1688–9 brought something of a national liberation, a way out from previous false turns. It assumed many forms, but here we must confine ourselves to the economic ones, those which bore on Scotland's position in foreign trade, especially on the intercontinental trade opened up by the age of discoveries and European expansion.

Since the Reformation, Calvinist thought had broken new ground beyond the narrow bounds of the absolutist suspicion, owed to the Roman Catholic Church, of commerce, profit, credit and interest. It took some while for a fresh orthodoxy, in other words for the intellectual foundations of capitalism, to be laid down. Not even the elementary ideas were immediately accepted in Scotland. But, in order to kindle intellectual ferment, it was enough for them to become known. At once known to Scots, for example, was the liberalism of Hugo Grotius in the Netherlands, centred on *mare liberum*, the freedom of the seas basic to intercontinental trade. William Wellwood, professor of civil law at the university of St Andrews, wrote as early as 1613 a rebuttal of the Dutch scholar-statesman's theory, the only one which the latter thought worthy of a reply by himself. But already, under the Union of

Crowns, Scots were enjoying economic advantages from more open exchange with England, first as a result of Calvin's case (1608) and establishment of the right to acquire property in all the dominions of James VI and his successors. Gradual elaboration of reciprocal economic rights resulted in complete free trade between the two countries under the Cromwellian Union. The Restoration and the extension to Scotland of the English Navigation Acts then reversed the trend, yet not fully. Among other things, they encouraged illegal free trade, that is to say, Scottish smuggling, a major industry up to 1707 and beyond. Internally, too, this fresh mercantilist diversion brought contrary reactions, as in efforts to curtail the exclusive trading rights of the royal burghs. If the accompanying debates were inconclusive, they still counted. By the end of the seventeenth century, Scots such as William Paterson and Andrew Fletcher of Saltoun had become, to judge from the contents of their libraries, well aware of the early development of political economy in Europe.[5]

With the end of royal absolutism in 1688, Scots had a chance to begin testing for themselves the respective merits of mercantilism and free trade. In general, mercantilism got the worse of it. Out of royal privilege and monopoly emerged a system of corporate law capable of sustaining robust commercial structures, which continued to serve till replaced by the modern law in the mid-nineteenth century. Instead of a sterile obsession with accumulation of specie came also, in the shape of the Bank of Scotland in 1696, the foundation of the old Scottish banking system, that is, of banking without gold. As economic theory and practice interacted before the Scots' eyes they found that, poor as they were, they could still aim realistically at economic growth, above all through trade. They did not quickly succeed, but that is no surprise, because the theory remained immature and the practice a matter of trial and error. Scotland did, however, suddenly become a party to the economic debates which had been going on for a century, in similarly inconclusive fashion, among the three great commercial nations of northern Europe, England, France and Holland. Scots began to speak the European language of political economy in a dialect of their own. They could not yet produce a classic text worthy of universal recognition, but only a flurry of pamphlets concerned with the national interest.[6] Yet it was enough to prompt them to a fundamental reappraisal of their needs, and a realisation that these were now bound up with those of a global commercial system.

In this context, the history of the Company of Scotland appears in a different light from that in received accounts. Its initial mercantilist purpose came to nothing. The hostility to it in England, the political intervention against it there and the consequent failure of the underwriting in the City of London showed Scots that their country was too small and weak to erect mercantilism on the same scale as the great European powers. The alternative strategy came in 1696 from Paterson, who had been involved in the company from the outset and was, by the standard of the times, a free trader. He proposed the scheme for a commercial emporium on the Isthmus of Panama:

> Trade will increase trade, and money will beget money, and the trading world shall need no more to want work for their hands, but will rather want hands for their work. Thus, this door of the seas and the key of the universe, with anything of a sort of reasonable management, will of course enable the proprietors to give laws to both oceans and to become arbitrators of the commercial world without being liable to the fatigues, expenses and dangers, or contracting the guilt and blood of Alexander and Caesar.[7]

However we might rationalise this advertising puff, it is not a mercantilist statement: it does not advocate control by the state, or some surrogate, over the factors of production with a view to excluding their exploitation by others and so supposedly contributing to the security of the state. When the Company of Scotland committed itself to Darien, its first, rather confused, mercantile purpose was resolving itself under the inherent difficulties of the project into, relatively speaking, a free-trading one. Mercantilism was in any event not working for Scotland, and a small country's circumstances commended a more liberal course. The new aim was to set up an apolitical entrepôt, where anybody could exchange goods without bothering about control over the factors of production.

Amid a sharpening of European imperial rivalries, the aim was certainly original. Yet if we mark the Scots' general position in international commerce in 1700, they did perhaps identify a window of opportunity. To a nation of few resources, the entrepôt might offer a fast track to mercantile wealth, as it often does to this day. In particular, the Scots stood poised between the English and Dutch systems of navigation, having entered into a closer but unstable relationship with the first since 1603, yet not cut loose from the second, to which by tradition they rather belonged. The English system had not been fully shut off, and probably never could be, as no system of navigation ever could. In that case, some traffic between England's colonies and England's competitors seemed likely to continue. Scots were only marginally in the running as competitors, and might be able to take over the function of entrepôt for that traffic. Lucrative it would doubtless prove, but it would also threaten to expose the system of navigation as hollow, a matter unlikely to be overlooked by England, or rather by those English interests with a stake in it. One thing it could do was unite the Scots. For example, it allied Paterson and Fletcher, who shared no other views, but who now convinced themselves that the scheme would launch a take-off in economic growth and solve the political problem that Scotland was unable to exercise sovereignty overseas. Unhappily these two and others had, beyond the bright idea, little conception how it might all actually work, and no better means than before to compete with larger, richer nations. Still, the concept of Darien was not itself a bad one. The basic faults in 1700 were that its time had not yet come, and that the means to realise it were lacking. But this, so far as Scotland is concerned, is an old story.[8]

Despite failure, Darien did leave a legacy. We can trace it in Smith's argument in *The Wealth of Nations* that the English system of navigation was useless anyway, setting off the process which brought about its disintegration by the middle of the nineteenth century. But that was only one conclusion of the wider arguments that gave political economy its prime role in the Scottish Enlightenment. A precocious technical debate continued through John Law to Sir James Steuart on the mercantilist side, and on the liberal side through Francis Hutcheson to Adam Smith and far beyond. It only ran out of steam with John Ramsay MacCulloch and the full transition to an English kind of utilitarianism in Victorian times. It remained intense and fruitful because closely linked to the central question of moral sentiment, whether there is some sympathy, some non-rational impulse, enabling us to work, as by an unseen hand, with people far removed from us in time or space and intent on nothing more than their own self-interest. The inquiry is ultimately connected to the rival claims of freedom and authority which take us back to the Reformation, and forward again to the insistence of Scots in 1707 on cultural autonomy, on saving all their other institutions even if the Parliament had to go. In considering those rival claims under the head of political economy, they just enlarged the debate. To be sure, this aspect of it was argued out, to a greater extent than others, in a new context, in a faster evolution of Scottish experience and its assimilation to a larger system. But that did not negate the native cast of the general principles applied to the particular issues arising. It was another example of how Scots maintained a national culture after the Union of 1707, in what George Davie has defined as 'unification in politics, separation in ethics'.[9]

In the end Scotland decided to tackle her economic problems through the Union. This is not the place to argue its merits and demerits, except to say that it was not the only possible or plausible answer, nor in itself a simple one. But in the matter of trade, and of intercontinental trade especially, the Scots clearly knew what they were doing. They insisted on free trade - something denied to Ireland, which till this point had had much the closer relationship to England. And since they got what they wanted, it meant they were in a sense entering the Union on their own terms. To be more precise, they were entering a mercantilist system on free-trading grounds. This was a piece of intellectual ingenuity, perhaps presbyterian hypocrisy, typical of many they would devise in their complex relations with their larger neighbour for the next 300 years.[10]

What happened after 1707, then, when people with a Scottish mentality could go out without let or hindrance into what had been till then an English Empire? It was as strange to Scots as they were strange to it. It had not been formed for their needs and, being mercantilist in its principles, did not follow the lessons of their experience or the more progressive economic conceptions they were starting to form. No doubt, in most ports of the English Empire, Scots were to be found, though that was true of the Dutch, French or Danish empires as well. But little permanent emigration or colonisation from Scotland had taken place, and was not to take place till the last third of the eighteenth century. While a large Scottish settlement lay in Ulster, its status as a colonial society was ambiguous, and will not be further discussed here. Scots colonies in the New World remained small. Colonies of settlement were unScottish, just as they were unDutch or unDanish, in other words difficult for any small nation with few people to spare. Far into the future it was trade rather than colonisation that lured Scots overseas. Empire meant to them first and foremost a commercial Empire.

The potential for imperial development of the Scottish mentality soon showed itself in these new fields. India offered the contemporary model for a trading rather than colonising Empire. Empire was indeed almost a misnomer for the European entrepôts through which alien peoples exchanged resources remaining in their own possession and normally exploited by traditional methods. A few Scots had already, in the service of the English or of the Dutch East India Companies, made their way to the sub-continent. But these individuals could not, any more than individuals of other nations, leave much of an impression on the societies they encountered. The evidence suggests, on the contrary, that Scots made themselves at home, often setting up house with local women and adopting local customs: one notable, if slightly later, example was that of David Ochterlony, British resident at Delhi, who lived like an oriental potentate in manners and dress, keeping 13 wives and parading them round the city, each on her own elephant.

The Scots usually shut their eyes to abuses they found, not being in a position to control the conduct of other Europeans. But the knowledge they transmitted home was lapped up by philosophical countrymen. These felt alarmed at the situation in India. Their disdain for the sordid gain available there was barbed by the sight of what it could buy at home. David Hume went so far as to wish for 'the expulsion of the English from the East Indies'. Adam Smith coolly applied his usual arguments against mercantilism: whatever the monopoly's original justification it had now gone, and the East India Company's commercial interests were incompatible with the sovereign power over conquered territories which it won notably with the *diwani* of Bengal in 1765. Allan Ramsay warned of corruption spreading into the sanctum of British liberty, for the nabobs grew rich enough to come back and buy seats in Parliament. George Dempster thought Indian acquisitions would ruin the mother country much as an Asian *imperium* had ruined the Roman republic.

This last thought shows how the literati started to fit empirical observation of India into their general intellectual inquiry. Enjoying a recognised status in their own hierarchical society, in others they were inclined to seek and admire a caste like themselves. Such they supposed Indian brahmans to be, men of enlarged minds and sympathies benevolently guiding humanity, drawing on the resources of classical language and philosophy embodied in Sanskrit learning. These represented the vista of an immemorial civilisation, with attainments quite as high as Europe's yet different in quality. With the analogy established, India could begin to take her place in conjectural history. Finding one for her was a challenge the Scots gladly took up.[11]

William Robertson, no less, did so in his *Historical Disquisition concerning the Knowledge which the Ancients had of India* (1791). The title pointed western readers aware of their own culture's origins towards its links with the Orient, which were just as old. They might know what classical texts had to say of Egypt or Persia, and need only be shown that India also formed part of this one great story. Comparison of ancient with modern knowledge would demonstrate besides that her culture enjoyed a continuity proper to itself. Neither Europe nor India represented anything unique: the civilisations were equivalent, and admirable in themselves. Yet readers could scarcely overlook the contrast between progress in the West and decline in the East. They were entitled to note it, for if Indians resembled westerners, westerners could live among them, develop and judge them by western standards. They still ran the moral hazard of feeling superior. So Robertson counselled against conscious westernisation, or even christian proselytising. He did, however, urge the free circulation of knowledge, as good for all societies, and useful in this case to fulfil the specific, benevolent mission of the British. It was to bring India up to the higher level of commercial society and draw her into the emergent global economy, crowning another chapter of the great story with a happy ending.[12]

Robertson's project thus had not only an intellectual but also a moral purpose, to explain why exploitation of Indians should end, and to compel respect for their natural rights, which included cherishing their culture and preserving their heritage. This would let them advance in harmony with their own laws, traditions and historic achievements. In accepting such obligations, Britain would vindicate her imperial role more surely than by subjection or domination. She would do it, too, on Scottish criteria, in conservative awareness of the prerequisites for India's healthy development towards universalist goals, in other words, towards assimilation of her experience into the narrative of human development.[13]

Though an academic work, the *Disquisition* therefore had practical value, as a basis for rational and benevolent Indian policy. It showed strong parallels with what was done by Henry Dundas, political boss of Scotland in the last quarter of the century and also President of the Board of Control for India from 1793. At this distance in time we cannot be sure who was influencing whom, but the parallels strengthen the case for seeing in Dundas one who, consciously or unconsciously, realised enlightened principles. He understood sooner than most British statesmen the importance of intercontinental trade. Partly through his Scottish background, and partly through daily contact with the practical problems, he was among the first British politicians to shake himself free from a still widely prevalent mercantilism. Having accepted instead the principles of free trade (if in a limited sense compared with what was taken for granted a century later) he began to discern the outlines of Britain's future as the centre of an imperial system, with commodities from the outposts feeding consumption and industry in the mother country. Equally striking were the political implications. In Dundas's view, India should never become a colony of settlement. He effectively prohibited permanent residence by British subjects, who were allowed out only under licence, had their conduct closely monitored while they stayed and were pressed to come home once they had done their business. Native rulers were not to be deposed unless incapable, though their domains might be reduced to tributary states. Social and especially religious institutions were to be preserved or if possible restored: no Christian missionary ever got permission to set foot in Dundas's India. In all, he brought about a decisive change from the previous regime of the English East India Company, the servants of which often acted on a casual assumption that Indian culture was worthless and Europeans at liberty to rape it. Here Scottish moral philosophy and commercial empire enriched and reinforced each other.[14]

That also held true for very different climes. During the Seven Years' War, in 1759, Simon Fraser's Lovat Highlanders helped to storm Quebec and bring the history of New France to an end. By the Treaty of Paris in 1763, King George III became the sovereign of Canada. The first military, then civil governor of the territory, James Murray of Elibank, won the admiration and respect of the conquered French by clemency and by guarantees for their religion and laws, similar to those for Scotland under the Treaty of Union. Some Scots soldiers were rewarded for their service by grants of land, their numbers being slowly swelled by emigrants, notably from the Highlands, and later, after 1776, by many loyalists from the 13 colonies. Dundas took an interest in Canada too, applying the same general principles as in India but always bearing specifically in mind the genesis of the United States. The intensive peopling of colonies would irresistibly, he believed, create demands for autonomy, then independence, with disruption or loss of British commerce. Of a Canada still largely empty he wrote in 1792 that 'an ingrafted population' would bring 'a want of that regularity and stability which all, but particularly colonial, governments require' – this was a logical counterpart of his domestic policy of discouraging Highland emigration. Where settlers had already established a presence, he retarded political development. He supported the division of Canada into Upper and Lower provinces, to keep the British and French communities separate and incapable of forming common interests.[15]

In this case, too, Dundas's views seem to have squared with those of many countrymen who actually went out into the Empire. For them, Canada long remained first a field for trade. Unlike India, where statutory monopoly required all traffic to be channelled through London, Canada was fully open to Scots from the conquest. Their experience of acting outside systems of navigation stood them in good stead here, though it had its price. Contrabandism frequently worked through cliques and clans, and this tradition Scots carried to Canada. They mainly traded with their home ports, often showing great generosity to one another but an utter lack of scruple towards outsiders. At their most successful, which could mean their most ruthless, they might reveal in their methods the same tendency to monopoly as they were wont – again hypocritically, it must be said – to deplore in Englishmen. But otherwise, Canada was by her size and resources ideal for the practice of liberal and flexible commercial principles. In her early history the wealth of the usually temporary Scots residents, such as the merchant community of Montreal, made them more important than the peasants who had found a permanent abode on the land: it was a country that lived rather off the appropriation and shipping of its natural resources than off the domestic production of its inhabitants.

One reason why Canada only filled up slowly was that Scots wanted to keep her empty, and their commercial pre-eminence gave them means to do so. Their trade in furs through the North West Company and later the Hudson's Bay Company could indeed only continue so long as the country remained empty, since tilled land yielded no furs. The merchants therefore aimed, by whatever means were necessary, to bar colonists from the vast stretches to the north and west of the narrow strip already populated along the St Lawrence River and the shores of the lower Great Lakes. This policy was fully maintained for the first half-century of British sovereignty, coming under serious threat only in 1817 when Lord Selkirk sent settlers far into the interior, to the Red River in the Manitoba of today. The factors of the North West Company arranged a convenient massacre of them by savage half-castes living roundabout. As a result, settlement in the West remained unattractive till after the Confederation of 1867.[16]

We can see from two major examples in India and Canada how an inherent bias against colonies of settlement in the imperial thinking of a small country could evolve towards a principle of preserving the original character of peoples and lands touched by European expansion. Better still, with a helping hand from sympathetic Scots, these peoples and lands might be induced to develop on their own terms by the transformatory power of commerce, and so proceed along the stages of civilisation revealed by conjectural history. It was a sophisticated enlightened position, marrying commercial advantage and moral principle. But, even in this best of all possible Scottish worlds, it still did not cover every case.

The Scots' intellectual apparatus stood baffled where Europeans had already brought about changes entirely severing certain regions from whatever history they had had. The West Indies developed a profitable economy of plantations exploited through slavery. By the late eighteenth century three different Scottish attitudes towards this form of economic organisation can be discerned. There was dislike of slavery among those in direct contact with it, men like James Ramsay, minister of St Kitts, or Zachary Macaulay, who went out aged 16 from the manse of Inveraray to Jamaica as a trainee overseer, both destined to become leaders of the abolitionist movement. There was more open intellectual censure at home, by enlightened figures such as Adam Smith and John Millar. There were growing scruples among Scots at large, evidenced by Dundas's successive efforts to find a political solution, starting with his plan for staged abolition of the slave trade in 1792. Yet while hope remained of amelioration, to use the contemporary parlance, in the slave trade or in the treatment of negroes, Scots seemed wary of denouncing slavery for itself. At any rate they let no doubts of its morality affect their conduct of business in the colonies dependent on production of tobacco, sugar and cotton. Ever ready to debate the theory of slavery, they saw little need to do anything about it. Perhaps this was another case of presbyterian hypocrisy, but there may be a better explanation.[17]

If overawed by the scale of British imperial enterprise, Scots hardly yet felt it was their Empire, to be ordered on their principles. Scotland was still the centre of their world. When they went out to economies of plantation they again went as transients, a phenomenon which has been analysed for both West Indies and Chesapeake Bay by Alan Karras.[18] They were often men of academic education or professional training: doctors, lawyers, factors, merchants and tradesmen, the range of occupations being more varied in the West Indies where there were few free settlers to perform skilled jobs. The aim of going out with a profession was to make money, save up and buy an estate, from the proceeds of which a man could then live, preferably as an absentee. Most did not even marry till they got home again, but cohabited with black women. 'We all come here to improve and not spend fortunes, and of consequence, devote our whole thought and attention to the former', wrote one migrant, James Gillespie.

Prospects in these places beckoned because their more fluid society offered greater upward mobility than Scotland could. This was, in an exotic setting, the normal Scottish quest for self-advancement. With the dearth of domestic opportunities, a national tradition had grown up of seeking them out abroad and coming back the richer for having exploited them. In previous ages that had been done in Europe; now it could be done overseas. For most, the real purpose in wandering was to move up the social ladder once they returned. Henry Brougham noted that the West Indians went out 'not to subsist in the colonies, but to prepare for shining in the mother country'. So these Scots seldom severed their connections with home, or with each other: in the Americas, too, they won notoriety for their cliques and mutual self-help. They were not losing or forswearing their Scottishness, but trying to keep and affirm it. Even far away, they remained preoccupied with the families, communities and nation they had left behind.[19]

The contact with other cultures did of course enrich theirs, prompting them to question it, explain changes in it, reckon what price was paid for them. But in then applying the lessons, Scots showed a becoming diffidence. When they analysed alien societies, they looked for more lessons to learn rather than for chances to teach their own. When they analysed less advanced ones, such as Africa, they did so in order to draw inferences about excessive liberty, here held to manifest itself in savagery. The critique of slavery was thus not meant to solve the problem of slavery. It was instead just one extreme aspect of a completely different problem, of the balance between authority and freedom, between tradition and enlightenment, the general problem with which Scots saw themselves confronted at every turn. In their philosophical speculation about it, they weighed with care the conflicting claims. This could not be done by simple standards of white and black, good and bad, innocent and guilty. There lay the difference between the way enlightened Scots thought about slavery, and the way their children came to think about it once abolition turned into a great moral cause. This happened with the rise of evangelical religion, and of the deeper social and spiritual forces beneath it.

A yet more salient example of failed Scottish analysis lies in the 13 Colonies, the originally English settlements of North America. On the whole, Scots did not understand them or their evolution. A couple of eminent exceptions only proved the rule. David Hume supported the independence of Americans as early as 1768, before most of them did. He continued to even when war polarised British opinion: 'I am American in my principles, and wish we would let them alone to govern or misgovern themselves as they think proper'. He believed England to be succumbing to that imperial corruption of which antiquity gave awful warning, under ruling cliques in London propagating a warlike nationalism destructive of culture and liberty. In October 1775, the year before his death, Hume wanted royal forces withdrawn from the other side of the Atlantic Ocean: 'Let us, therefore, lay aside all anger; shake hands and part friends. Or if we retain anger, let it be against ourselves for our past folly'. Adam Smith was never so outspoken, even in private. But he verged on the same conclusions through his critique of mercantilism. While recommending its gradual relaxation, he doubted if the quarrels could end there. The colonies would still cause war and expense they did not pay for. There were two possible solutions, independence or imperial union. He perhaps preferred the latter, which would have granted the colonies economic equality and parliamentary representation, another scheme surely suggested by the Anglo-Scottish Treaty of 1707; with their continuing advance, the seat of the Empire might in time shift to America. But he thought few in Britain would concur.[20]

In Scotland hardly anyone did. Hume and Smith remained quite unrepresentative of Scottish opinion. From the enlightened literati down to the strapping youngsters who joined up to fight the Americans, Scots on both sides of the Atlantic were overwhelmingly hostile to them. In philosophical terms, this might be explained by a shift from the originally radical position in Scottish political thought, positing a right of resistance to tyranny. Instead a consensus evolved which, still liberal in its way, counselled moderation and reform to correct abuse, but gave the benefit of the doubt to legitimate authority. This was the position taken, for example, by Robertson in his unfinished history of British America. He thought the cure for the crisis lay in rendering the exercise of authority more rational, so as to strike a balance between the excess of it in a Virginia burdened with vain economic constraints and the deficiency of it in a New England prey to religious fanaticism.

What I propose to add here is an argument derived not from Scottish philosophy but from Scottish history, the history of a small country with a natural bias towards an Empire of commerce rather than of settlement, and a consequent distaste for the autonomy of colonised lands. Scots did not act like Englishmen even when they went to live in America. A good example is the community round the Chesapeake, largely recruited from the West of Scotland for the trade in tobacco. These Scots were therefore, like others elsewhere, transients with no desire to become Americans. The New World was not to them a home, but a place to make money for a better life on return to the mother country. They did business with neighbours, some intermarried, some represented their county or town in colonial institutions. Yet they were alienated from Virginians by nagging economic friction, by their own dependence on imperial trade, by their clannishness and by Scottish notions of authority. When they had to choose, they stayed loyal. Or else, as early as 1774, they began to leave, for the spreading unrest made them ready targets to radicals. With the outbreak of fighting in the northern colonies, latent prejudice and hostility towards them boiled up here in violent incidents. This confirmed to them, as to other non-English colonial minorities, that for their safety they could only trust the Crown, rather than the Anglo-American majority round them.[21]

This was true even of ostensibly non-transient communities, such as the Highlanders who in the wave of emigration after 1763 went to the back-country of Virginia and the Carolinas. They too remained conspicuously loyal, and suffered still more for it. Among those mustering forces in the name of George III was Allan MacDonald of Kingsburgh, husband of Flora, the Jacobite heroine, a tacksman from Skye who had taken his people to the banks of the Cape Fear River in North Carolina, to a settlement now known as Fayetteville. In February 1776 he sent round the fiery cross. He assembled about 3500 men under the royal standard in the square of the town, where they were given their envoi in sonorous Gaelic by Flora herself, mounted on a white horse. They set off to march to the port of Wilmington, seized by revolutionaries after the governor sought safety on a ship offshore. But the pipes skirled in vain. Rebels ambushed and routed the force at Moore's Creek Bridge, an early sign that restoration of British authority was going to be at best difficult. Even then, revolution made no appeal to these Scots. Some did win release on parole, and went back up the Cape Fear River to live out their days quietly farming their land. But others, including Kingsburgh himself, preferred to return to Scotland.[22]

Such evidence must heavily qualify the view taken of Scottish colonisation in America by Ned Landsman, generalising from a study of New Jersey. He claims that the Scots here, descendants of settlers in the reign of James VII, nurtured an ethnic cohesion. Many of their forefathers had been Quakers or Episcopalians, but in later generations they tended to simplify their Scottishness, or perhaps become more Scottish, by conforming to Presbyterianism. Landsman finds this Presbyterianism fully compatible with the principles of the American Revolution. The link is John Witherspoon, the evangelical minister from Paisley who became in 1768 the principal of the College of New Jersey (now University of Princeton), later a revolutionary leader who in his writings offered a Calvinist justification for the new republic. Thus a presbyterian element of Americanism is traced far back towards the origins of Americans. But if there was a coherent body of Scots supporting the Revolution, it seems odd that nobody else noticed it. On the contrary, the Scots' true-blue loyalty waxed so strong that not just the Americans remarked on it, and resented it, but even the English did. Scots had their ethnic ways, when they came to America as traditionalists or transients. But Scots truly intent on making a new life in the New World had to discard their ethnicity, because it was inconsistent with American radicalism, an outgrowth of progress from settlement to autonomy which represented a break with the cultures of the Old World. Only such permanent colonists from Scotland as by design or desuetude had cast off her values might be receptive to its ideals. After 1776 they could simply become Americans, if by the change in their situation and outlook they were not so already. Those wanting to remain Scots could not stay in America. And they appear to have formed the majority. They were losers from the war, many long grudging it. But at least their demonstrative loyalty made their countrymen permanently welcome in the rest of the British Empire, assuring them a place in the colonial development that stretched two centuries into the future.[23]

Our best way of assessing the Scots' place in British expansion may not lie in comparison with certain durable traits of English imperialism, and their evolution in an Empire of conquest, occupation and settlement. Scotland, a small nation, could never emulate that. The context ought perhaps to be wider. It may not be idle to choose the very widest context, the opening of the European mind which started with the age of discoveries and, propelled by Renaissance and Reformation, brought vast changes in consciousness and a tremendous cultural flowering. The evolution was as rich in small nations as in large ones, sometimes richer in small nations. What proved true of the Portugal of Camoêns, proved true of the Holland of Rembrandt, the Sweden of Queen Christina, the Denmark of Holberg. Nor was the achievement confined to high culture. It also spread among ordinary folk, in the diffusion of a popular literature of travels and wonders, in the invention of ancient and modern myths about themselves. A general explanation is hard to find on the basis of political conditions, different in each country. We have to look rather to the new cultural universals replacing the religious unity now lost in the West. Some experiences remained common – Reformation or Counter-Reformation, political revolution, the age of discoveries, the rise of science – though in every instance they took a specific form and evoked an individual response. That response often turned out crucially formative of small nations. It answered a psychological need for self-assertion in a world where they were not held to be of much account, and drew on a national pride coexistent with a nagging sense of national inferiority.

All this illumines the case of Scotland, even if she in these times lost her independence. It suggests that she owed her own cultural flowering and share in the expansion, not to speak of her economic transformation, to influences more numerous and general than the Union of 1707. In other words, that arrangement was permissive, and the real reasons for much of the subsequent headlong progress lay elsewhere. At the turn of the century, Scotland seemed an unlikely candidate for it. But its engines had already been stoked by internal improvements. Scots began to exploit their resources better, stimulated by easy access to oceanic routes, though also by privation, to name but two of many forces at work. Altogether, though, trade became vital to them. They opened their country to products, techniques and ideas from abroad, essential elements in their agricultural, then their commercial, then their industrial revolutions. Though often hampered by discord, famine and war, they reached the point of being able to aim realistically to develop their economy. In so aiming, not least in seeking as far as circumstance allowed a share in the expansion of Europe, they were quite typical of the continent's small nations, with which a comparison has much to tell us. They also made one individual response of unique importance. They became aware of the diversity of manners among mankind, and awakened in themselves the ethical scepticism which formed a foundation of their Enlightenment.

When they sought what Adam Smith called the destiny of their name and nation, they were also fulfilling something profound in themselves. It seems unlikely that this could have been divorced by the Union from their previous national experience. True, the political structure of the Empire, its institutions being everywhere English, never replicated the diversity even of the narrow island. And no crude contrast can be drawn between the imperial conduct of liberal, progressive Scots and reactionary, oppressive Englishmen; on the contrary, Scots could be the most violent, destructive and extortionate of all. But they did preserve much of what had been their own before 1707 and develop it further afterwards. When they did, it let them meet and trade with distant peoples on equal terms, and prompted them to the study of alien cultures to do so the better. There they found their conception of a commercial Empire both practically and morally vindicated.

REFERENCES

1. A Smith, *The Wealth of Nations* (Oxford, 1976; first published, 1776) II, p. 473.
2. Briefly surveyed by me in 'The Whig Interpretation of Scottish History', in I. Donnachie & C. Whatley (eds.), *The Manufacture of Scottish History* (Edinburgh, 1992), pp.72–89.
3. See especially D. Armitage, 'The Scottish vision of empire: intellectual origins of the Darien venture', in J. Robertson (ed.), *A Union for Empire, political thought and the Union of 1707* (Cambridge, 1995).
4. Gordon Marshall, *Presbyteries and Profits, Calvinism and the development of capitalism in Scotland 1560–1707* (Edinburgh, 1980), pp.198–207.
5. For Paterson's library, see the appendix to vol.3 of S. Bannister (ed.), *The Writings of William Paterson* (New York, 1968; first published, 1859); for Fletcher's library, see NLS MS 17864.
6. See notably Bannister, *Paterson*; J. Law, *Proposals and Reasons for Constituting a Council of Trade in Scotland* (Glasgow, 1751; first published, 1700); *Money and Trade Considered*

(Edinburgh, 1705); *Oeuvres Complètes* (Paris, 1934); Anon., *A Full and Exact Collection of all the Public Papers relating to the Company of Scotland Trading to Africa and the Indies* (n.p., 1700a); J. Spreul, *An Accompt Current Betwixt Scotland and England Balanced* (Edinburgh, 1705), and the rest of the economic pamphlet literature at the time of the Union, for which a useful bibliography can be found in C.A. Whatley, *"Bought and Sold for English Gold"?* (Dundee, 1994).

7. Paterson to Sir Robert Chiesly, July 9, 1695, NLS MS Adv. 83.7.4, f.4, the same sentiment recycled in his letter to the Company of Scotland, Jan. 17, 1700, NLS MS Adv.83.7.5, f.56.
8. For the development of these points with particular reference to Glasgow, see G. Jackson, 'Glasgow in Transition' in T.M. Devine & G. Jackson, *Glasgow, vol.*1, Beginnings to 1830 (Manchester, 1995), p.77.
9. G. Davie, *The Democratic Intellect* (Edinburgh, 1961), p.xv.
10. The standard literature on the economics of the Union, now showing its age, consists of W.R. Scott, 'The Fiscal Policy of Scotland before the Union'', *Scottish Historical Review*, i, 1904; T. Keith, 'Scottish Trade with the Plantations before 1707', *Scottish Historical Review*, vi, 1909; T.C. Smout, *Scottish Trade on the Eve of the Union* (Edinburgh, 1963); all soon to be supplemented by the work of D. Armitage, as in 'Colonial Theory in a Provincial Society, Scotland before 1707', unpublished paper, 1996.
11. For Scottish criticism of the old British regime, see A. Ramsay, *An Enquiry into the Rights of the East India Company* (London, 1772), especially the introduction; Sir J. Steuart, *The Principle of Money applied to the Present State of the Coin of Bengal* (n.p., 1772), especially pp.56–7; Smith, *Wealth of Nations* II, pp.637–41; G.R. Gleig, *The Life of Major-general Sir Thomas Munro* (London, 1830), especially II, p.260. For modern comments see V.A. Narain, *Jonathan Duncan and Varanasi* (Calcutta, 1959); J. Dwyer, *Virtuous Discourse, sensibility and community in late eighteenth-century Scotland* (Edinburgh, 1987), especially p.44; B. Lenman, 'The Transition to European Military Ascendancy in India 1600–1800' in J.A. Lynn (ed.), *Tools of War* (Urbana, Ill., 1990), especially p.183.
12. In Robertson, see especially pp.262, 335–6. For modern comments, see G.D. Bearce, *British Attitudes to India* 1784–1858 (Oxford, 1961), especially p.24; J. Rendall, 'Scottish Orientalism from Robertson to James Mill', *Historical Journal*, xxv, 1980, pp.43–59. I am indebted to Jeffrey Smitten of Utah State University for allowing me to read and make use of his unpublished paper, 'Power and Authority in William Robertson's *Historical Disquisition concerning India* (1791)', 1992.
13. Such criteria lie, of course, at the heart of what has become known today, following the work of Edward Said (1978), as orientalism. The modern critique of it is that it attributes to western culture knowledge about other cultures that they do not possess themselves, so contains no sense of them which might test, rather than confirm, western values. Still, it did bring an advance on the belief that Indian culture was worthless, and Europeans at liberty to rape it.
14. Michael Fry, *The Dundas Despotism* (Edinburgh, 1992), pp.111–29.
15. For early Scottish views on Canada, see R. Lamond, *Narrative of the Rise and Progress of Emigration from the Counties of Lanark and Renfrew to the New Settlements in Upper Canada* (Glasgow, 1821), pp.1–7, 25; J. Galt, 'Bandana on Colonial Undertakings' and 'Bandana on Emigration', *Blackwood's Edinburgh Magazine*, cxv, 1826, pp.306 et seqq, pp.471 et seqq; R. & K. Lizars, *In the Days of the Canada Company* (Toronto, 1896), especially I, 379. For modern comments, see J.M. Cameron, 'A Study of the Factors that Assisted and Directed Scottish Emigration to Upper Canada 1815–1855' (unpublished Ph.D. thesis, University of Glasgow, 1970); Fry, *Dundas*, p.199; M.E. Vance, 'The Politics of Emigration, Scotland and assisted emigration to Upper Canada 1815–1826' in T.M. Devine (ed.), *Scottish Emigration and Scottish Society* (Edinburgh, 1992).
16. In the extensive literature on these subjects, works which which deal especially with Scottish involvement are: M.W. Campbell, *The North West Company* (Toronto, 1957); G.C. Davidson, *The North West Company* (New York, 1918); H.A. Innis, *The Fur Trade in Canada* (Toronto, 1956); C. Martin, *Lord Selkirk's Work in Canada* (Oxford, 1916); E.A. Mitchell,

'The Scot in the Fur Trade', in W.S. Reid, *The Scottish Tradition in Canada* (Toronto, 1976); E.E. Rich (ed.), *Hudson's Bay Company* 1670–1870 (New York, 1960); W.S. Wallace (ed.), *Documents relating to the North-west Company* (Toronto, 1934).

17. For some contemporary Scottish literature, see J. Ramsay, *Enquiry on the Treatment and Conversion of African Slaves in the British Sugar Colonies* (London, 1784); *Objections to the Abolition of the Slave Trade, with answers* (London, 1784); *A Reply to the Personal Invectives and Objections contained in two Answers . . . to an Essay on the Treatment and Conversion of African Slaves* (London, 1785); J. Marjoribanks, *Slavery* (Edinburgh, 1792); H. Brougham, *An Inquiry into the Colonial Policy of the European Powers* (Edinburgh, 1803), especially p.68; *A Concise Statement of the Question regarding the Abolition of the Slave Trade* (London, 1807); R. Wedderburn, *The Horrors of Slavery* (London, 1824). See also C. Booth, *Zachary Macaulay* (London, 1934) and Anon., 'An Early Glasgow-West Indian Miscellany', *Three Banks Review*, liv, 1962, pp.37 et seqq. For modern comments, see C.D. Rice, 'Abolitionists and Abolitionism in Aberdeen', *Northern Scotland*, i, 1972; *The Rise and Fall of Black Slavery* (London, 1975); 'Archibald Dalzel, the Scottish Intelligentsia and the Problem of Slavery', *Scottish Historical Review*, lxii, 1983, pp.121–36; J.D. Hargreaves, *Aberdeenshire to Africa, North-east Scots and British overseas expansion* (Aberdeen, 1981), p.5; B. Fontana, *Rethinking the Politics of Commercial Society, the Edinburgh Review* 1802–1832 (Cambridge, 1985), p.63; P.D. Morgan, 'British Encounters with Africans and African-Americans, circa 1600–1780', in B. Bailyn, & P.D. Morgan (eds.), *Strangers within the Realm, cultural margins of the first British Empire* (Williamsburg, 1991), p.193.
18. *Sojourners in the Sun, Scottish migrants in Jamaica and the Chesapeake* 1740–1800 (Ithaca & London, 1992).
19. Karras, *Sojourners*, pp.20–1, 46–7, 54; E. Long, *The History of Jamaica* (London, 1774), II, p.286; C. Campbell, *Memoirs* (Glasgow, 1828), p.18; T.M. Devine, 'An Eighteenth-century Business Elite, Glasgow-West India merchants 1750–1815', *Scottish Historical Review*, lvii, 1978, pp.40–67.
20. (ed.), J.Y.T. Greig, *Letters of David Hume* (Oxford, 1932), II, pp.300–3; Smith, *Wealth of Nations*, II, pp.946–7.
21. A. Hast, *Loyalism in Revolutionary Virginia* (Ann Arbor, 1979), pp.9 et seqq.
22. D. Meyer, *The Highland Scots of North Carolina* 1732–1776 (Chapel Hill, 1957), pp.157 et seqq; H.F. Rankin, *The Moore's Creek Bridge Campaign* (Conhoshocken, Pa., 1986).
23. W.H. Nelson, *The American Tory* (Oxford, 1961), pp.90, 110; W. Brown, *The Good Americans, the loyalists in the American Revolution* (New York, 1969), pp.46–50; N.C. Landsman, *Scotland and its First American Colony* 1683–1775 (Princeton, 1985), especially pp.165, 256–8; 'Witherspoon and the Problem of Provincial Identity in Scottish Evangelical Culture', in R. Sher & J. Smitten (1990), pp.29–45.

Five

Scottish Jacobitism: in Search of a Movement

ALLAN I. MACINNES

LONG REPUDIATED AS a peripheral theme in European diplomacy, yet a persistent irritant to successive British governments, support for the exiled House of Stuart was the mainstay of political polarisation in Scotland for almost six decades after the deposition of James VII in 1689. Nonetheless, the question remains whether Jacobitism was a developed political movement or an episodic interruption in the body politic. Scottish Jacobites were involved in a series of major risings in 1689–91, 1715–6, 1745–6; of minor risings in 1708 and 1719; and of plots to assassinate William of Orange in 1695–6 and to effect changes of government in 1702–3, 1706, 1717, 1723 and again in 1753. Despite the persistence of such commitment, Jacobitism in Scotland cannot unequivocally be said to have demonstrated structured organisation, strategic coherence or even ideological conformity.

Historiographically, the case for a movement has tended to focus on the Courts of the exiled House of Stuart in Paris, Lorraine, Avignon, Madrid and Rome not on sustained political collaboration on their behalf either within Scotland or the British Isles.[1] Furthermore, by focusing on the Courts in exile, primacy is given to diplomatic and campaigning issues which facilitated the risings and plots in favour of first James VII and then his heir, James 'VIII' whose dynastic legitimacy has been disparaged by the Whig sobriquet of the 'Old Pretender'. While international recognition gave credibility to Jacobitism, this support was expendable, unreliable and manipulative. British governments could depend on the haemorrhaging of information about Jacobite activities not only through espionage and double-agents, but through factional infighting among European powers temporarily promising assistance to the exiled House of Stuart. At the same time, rivalries within and between Jacobite Courts, notably those in Paris and Rome, have derailed considerations about the effectiveness of liaison between the constituent kingdoms of the British Isles.[2]

A British revisionist perspective, while rehabilitating the political, intellectual and commercial viability of Jacobitism from Whig polemical disparagement, effectively makes the case for a unifying cause being pursued concurrently but not concertedly in the three kingdoms.[3] As well as the manifest lack of co-ordination between Scotland, England and Ireland in all the risings, plotting was debilitated by espionage and susceptible to agents provocateurs. Co-ordinated endeavours within as well as among the three kingdoms were notable for their rarity. Moreover, political labelling of Scottish, English and Irish Jacobites was only superficially uniform. Jacobitism differed according to the Revolutionary Settlement in each kingdom.

In Scotland, James VII was unequivocally deposed by a Convention of Estates in which few Tories remained after a walkout of militant Jacobites. The Whigs were thus given free reign to complement their parliamentary dominance in the State by their establishment of a Presbyterian ascendancy in the Kirk. From 1689, therefore, Jacobites were effectively Tories prepared to resort to direct action to restore the Stuarts. However, some career minded Tories were prepared to forswear Jacobitism in order to secure political office, while others were prepared to accept an accommodation, first with William of Orange, then Queen Anne and the Hanoverians, in order to secure religious toleration for Episcopalians. Nonetheless, Jacobites in Scotland continued to draw support primarily from the Episcopalian majority not inclined towards oaths of allegiance that abjured the Stuarts. This support was supplemented by the Catholic interest which, notwithstanding the Roman affiliations of James VII, his son and his grandsons, remained a minority pursuit in Scotland. Jacobitism in the run up to Union also attracted vestigial support from Presbyterian dissenters opposed to the erastian nature of the Revolution Settlement. But few Presbyterians, apart from a handful of Highlanders committed as much by clannish as by religious commitments, actually campaigned for Jacobitism in the 'Fifteen and the 'Forty-Five.[4]

The association of Jacobitism with Tories prepared to resort to direct action also prevailed in Ireland during the first major rising of 1689–91. Following rigorous suppression and wholescale forfeitures among the political elite, support for Jacobitism subsequently continued as a largely passive expression of confessional nationalism in the eighteenth century. Irish Jacobitism, though ostensibly thirled to failure, was sustained through the dream imagery of eventual national liberation. This appeal remained enduringly popular among the Catholic majority rigorously excluded from power with the unfettered establishment of the Anglican supremacy by 1693. However, the supplementary application of civil and religious penal laws to Presbyterians and other Protestant dissenters did not lead to a Jacobite common front for political protest. The appeal of Jacobitism to Protestants was marginal. Nonetheless, exiled Irish brigades in the service of Spain and France remained a professional reserve of striking potential if harnessed to militant Jacobitism elsewhere in the British Isles.[5]

Although the Revolution Settlement in England confirmed the Anglican supremacy in the national Church, constitutional issues of State reflected the compromising of Whig ideology to retain Tory support for William of Orange. Accordingly, James II was not deposed. He was deemed to have abdicated the throne. As in Ireland, Presbyterians and other Protestant dissenters, though subject to civil and religious discrimination, made no tangible common front with Jacobitism. Albeit Jacobite traditions and sentiments were never sublimated among Tories who sought neither office nor favour at Court under William of Orange and then Anne, few were provoked to direct action by the Hanoverian Succession. During the 'Fifteen there was desultory participation on the Borders and in the north of England, primarily by the Catholic minority. Jacobitism was also adopted as a label of convenience for localised, community protest as for alternative theatre. In terms of the political discourse, the tendentious association of Jacobites and Tories in England was not expressed through direct action but, more usually, through drinking, discreteely in Oxford colleges and excessively in the social clubs of disaffected members of the ruling elite.[6]

Indeed, most Tories were reconciled to political acquiescence after the 'Fifteen. It can be tempting to associate Tories in the early eighteenth century with a Country interest in England, similar to the opponents of the Court who sought a return to the political equilibrium of 'the ancient English constitution' in the early seventeenth century. However, Tories featured as the Court influence in the reign of Anne and, in the wake of their removal from power at the accession of George I, featured only as one in a series of misplaced political interests during the Whig hegemony subsequently established by Sir Robert Walpole. The most distinctive sound emanating from Tory circles in England during the 'Forty-Five was silence.[7]

Unlike Ireland or England, a constructive case based primarily on recruitment patterns, prisoner lists and protest songs can also be made for Scottish Jacobitism as a sustained national endeavour; a case that certainly serves as a corrective to the over-identification in Whig polemics of Jacobitism with clanship.[8] While Jacobitism was notably vital in Scotland north of the Tay, not just in the Highlands, the clans remained the military bedrock of Scottish support for the House of Stuart bearing the brunt of the fighting and dying in the front lines during the major risings. Yet, the mobilisation of Scottish support depended primarily on the tradition of passing around the fiery cross among the clans, supplemented by personal connection and patriarchal power to call out the host elsewhere. A cohesive organisation to effect nationwide recruitment appears to have been lacking. At the same time, the clans like other Scottish families and communities were divided by the civil wars occasioned by the major risings, albeit support for Jacobitism remained consistently higher than that for the Whigs. Even within the clans espousing Jacobitism, support fluctuated, switched and declined in all three major risings.[9]

In assessing whether Jacobitism was more a movement than a cause there are two cognate models – albeit from the opposite side of the political spectrum – on which to draw comparisons. The first is the early Covenanting Movement, which instigated the Scottish Revolution against Charles I in 1638 and triggered the Wars for the Three Kingdoms during the 1640s. The success of this Movement was based essentially on its power to mobilise forces of persuasion and coercion. Unprecedented nationwide demands for ideological conformity, financial supply and military recruitment were grounded on the direct importation of the Swedish version of the military revolution. A conscripted army with a professional backbone, trained in the latest continental techniques of warfare, was sustained by a centralised State. The export of revolution and armed intervention in England and Ireland was sanctioned by the rigorous management of constitutional assemblies and broadcast through the pulpits of the Presbyterian Kirk. Not only did the early Covenanters repeatedly raise national armies in excess of 20,000 men, their forces were continuously replenished from the localities through shire committees of war between 1639 and 1651.[10] Accordingly, numbers recruited – from a similar demographic base – vastly outstripped Jacobite performances in the major risings, albeit the numbers engaged on particular campaigns were ostensibly comparable.[11] A more significant indicator in terms of support for the House of Stuart was the undoubted capacity of the Jacobites to raise more forces in their regional heartlands of the Highlands and the north-east than those mobilised through clan hosts and personal levies for the Royalist cause in the 1640s.[12]

A second and, perhaps more germane, organisational model is provided by the later Covenanters as a Movement of protest following their exclusion from power with the Restoration of Charles II. As well as developing an atomised ideology of protest in seeking to justify resistance through recourse to godly communities rather than national endeavours, the later Covenanting Movement depended on atomised rather than nationwide organisation. The Movement was sustained not by constitutional assemblies but by covert praying societies and, more overtly, by field conventicles. The three decades between the Restoration and Revolution Settlements were marked by episodic uprisings as well as regular armed conventicles involving the mobilisation of numbers between 4,000 and 14,000. These figures were similar to the range mobilised for the three major Jacobite risings, albeit later Covenanting endeavours were largely confined to Scotland south of the Tay.[13]

The willingness of the Jacobites to sustain an armed struggle in pursuit of power was part of a Scottish tradition of partisanship now turned against the

Whigs as the political heirs of the Covenanting Movement. Their repeated recourse to armed struggle meant that Scottish Jacobites could not be so readily accommodated within a political structure of party and patronage that operated in England and which has confuted the debate about the extent to which Jacobites and Tories were compatible as unplaced political interests.[14] At the same time, the Jacobites, whether operating covertly as plotters and insurrectionists, or overtly as Tories were an identifiable element in Scottish political life. After the Revolution, the Jacobites were permanently associated with the Country interest opposed to the Court's dominance of Scottish affairs and played a significant role in the Confederated Opposition which resisted the making of the Treaty of Union. Because of continuous and incremental Court interference in Scottish affairs between 1689 and 1707, the Jacobites could claim to represent an alternative national interest, a stance which drew support from disaffected constitutional reformers in the assassination plot of 1695–6 as from Presbyterian dissenters formerly associated with the later Covenanting Movement in the abortive plans for a coup d'état in 1706. Conversely, the Jacobite alternative made the Court particularly suspicious of most leading Scottish politicians during the putative 'Scotch Plot' of 1702–3. Purported association with Jacobitism became a particularly potent smear among political rivals.[15]

After 1707, the Jacobite alternative became the restoration of the nation state; a threat to the incorporating union that resulted in the British government apprehending suspect Jacobites among the landed classes prior to the first elections to the parliament of the United Kingdom in 1708. While this pre-emptive tactic certainly contributed to the termination of the intended diversionary raid on Scotland – that was not so much a minor rising as a Jacobite hiccup – the removal of over 20 nobles, clan chiefs and other landed gentry to London was viewed among the foremost grievances North Britain was obliged to endure in the wake of Union. The crass insensitivity of the British government was further highlighted by the precipitate measure to encourage loyalty in 1715, which cited around 50 leading landowners to disown their suspect Jacobitism on pain of forfeiture. This measure, subsequently given the misnomer 'the Clan Act', aided and abetted recruitment for the 'Fifteen.[16]

Notwithstanding dynastic, denominational and constitutional differences with the Whigs, the association of Jacobitism with alternative national politics was strengthened by shared ideological beliefs in associating property with progress and prosperity with commercial opportunities, colonial ventures and co-partneries. Whereas Irish Jacobitism after the first major rising and, more selectively, English Jacobitism after the 'Fifteen were subject to rigorous repression, Scottish Jacobitism was sufficiently well connected to the Whig political elite that no such repression was feasible until after the failure of the 'Forty-Five. Indeed, the Whig establishment within Scotland was enraged by the process of forfeiture and other punitive measures along Irish lines that the British government proposed to implement after the 'Fifteen. Although estates were forfeited in both Lowlands and Highlands, there was an ongoing determination that landed families and their commercial associates should not be utterly ruined by laws based on the presumption rather than proof of participation in or association with rebellion. At the same time, although Non-Juring and Catholic Jacobites faced penal laws, until the aftermath of the 'Forty-Five they were spared the summary justice meted out to the later Covenanters. While the righteousness of their cause was thus not validated by the systematic oppression of a suffering remnant, there were particular features which made Jacobite commitment distinctive in Scotland.[17]

The dynastic appeal of the House of Stuart was not only based on indefeasible hereditary right, divine right to suspend and dispense laws and non-resistance to lawful authority, the essential British facets of Jacobite support for an organic rather than a contractual theory of government. Nor was Scottish Jacobitism content with a patriarchal spin in favour of their ancient and native kings. Support for the Stuarts was grounded in direct Scottish experience of James governing, first as Duke of York and then as King of Scots. Whig historiography has focused on the continuous harassment of Covenanters, the suppression of conventicling and the infliction of summary justice, known as 'the killing times' throughout the 1680s. Yet, his government of Scotland awaits rehabilitation. His reversal, albeit temporary, of the Restoration policy of fiscal repression in favour of judicial conciliation was particularly appealing to the clans. He was also sensitive to Scottish commercial aspirations in a mercantilist age in seeking economic development through colonialism rather than unionism. The flirtatious pursuit of political and commercial union with England by the previous Restoration regime during the 1670s was abandoned in favour of substantive Scottish colonial ventures in South Carolina and East New Jersey.[18] While his suspension of the penal laws against Catholics led to rioting in Edinburgh, his comprehensive toleration afforded Presbyterians relief from the fiscal sanctions associated with conventicling as well as time to organise and associate publicly. Nonetheless, as James II, he was so obsessed with English problems that he fatally underestimated the potential strength of his support in Scotland at the Revolution. Despite his subsequent failure to provide timely reinforcements from Ireland where he concentrated his campaigning endeavours during the first rising, the clans in the forefront of the Jacobite campaign remained in arms for two years. Although they failed to break out of the Highlands, the Whig government was obliged to sue for peace and rescind its policy of punitive forfeitures.[19]

Although the House of Stuart consistently promised to uphold a Protestant establishment maintained with parliamentary approval in both Scotland and England, the use of his prerogative by James VII and II to set aside the penal laws against Catholics was instrumental in his removal from the British thrones. Subsequently his son, James VIII and III refused overtures from his half-sister, Queen Anne, after the death of her own children, to declare himself a Protestant in order to pave the way for his restoration instead of the planned Hanoverian succession. By 1741, the Old Pretender was dropping hints to leading British politicians that he was prepared to disclaim absolutely all pretensions that the royal prerogative conveyed a power to suspend and dispense with parliamentary law. His son, Charles Edward Stuart, 'the Young Pretender', declared pragmatically in favour of Protestantism – but not until the 'Forty-Five was lost. Such persistent if not always pious adherence to Catholicism, while reinforcing the confessional nationalism of Jacobites opposed to the Anglican Ascendancy in Ireland, served as a considerable political handicap for Tories sympathetic to Jacobitism but fearful for the Anglican Ascendancy in England.[20]

In Scotland, the promise of religious toleration, coupled to the refusal of the exiled House of Stuart to sacrifice its faith for the thrones, stiffened the resolve of both Catholics and Non-Jurors not to be reconciled to the Presbyterian Ascendancy which had been specifically guaranteed by the Treaty of Union. While the confessional nationalism associated with Scottish Jacobitism can be associated more with the Non-Juring majority rather than the Catholic minority, the main appropriators of this concept were the upholders of the Presbyterian Supremacy in a British context. Presbyterians disenchanted with the Union, but dreading the restoration of a Popish king, were usually no more than passive sympathisers with Jacobitism. However, the majority, content with having secured national establishment as the price of national independence, vigorously promoted a British identity as the only guarantee of Protestantism, property and progress. In return for the occasional licence to prosecute Non-Jurors as well as Catholics, notably in the aftermath of Union and prior to the 'Fifteen, the Kirk of Scotland served not only as the Whig interest at prayer, but also as an eager monitor of purported Jacobite activities, especially in the Highlands and the north-east.[21]

Confessional nationalism notwithstanding, the provincial standing of Ireland affirmed by the Revolution Settlement was confirmed by the rejection of parliamentary union with England in 1703. Conversely, the implementation of parliamentary union accorded the added ingredient of political nationalism to Scottish Jacobitism. Appeals to end the incorporating union, not an issue of known significance among their English counterparts, became a major plank of Scottish Jacobitism that justified the issuing not only of interim declarations pledging the restoration of a Scottish parliament but of separate national manifestos in the 'Fifteen and the 'Forty-Five. Their respective plans to revoke the Union and settle civil and ecclesiastical affairs for an independent Scotland were rendered inoperative by the inept timing of James VIII's participation in the former rising and the inconsistent campaigning of Prince Charles in the latter.[22]

Nationalism and antipathy to the Union were given popular currency through folk-songs as well as polemical pamphlets. As there appears to be no convincing evidence of concerted or commissioned publications to sustain Jacobitism, such propaganda testifies to spontaneous combustion in the popular imagination.[23] Moreover, the cultural appeal of Jacobitism was reinforced by the oral tradition of the Gael as well as in Scots literature. Gaelic polemics built not only upon bardic traditions of eulogy and elegy but, more pertinently, upon vernacular traditions of political and social criticism which gave a cutting edge to Jacobitism that was absent in Irish Gaelic dream poetry. Nonetheless the optimistic equation that the triumph of Jacobitism would end Scottish political subjugation gave way to an unredeemed fatalism with the failure of the 'Fifteen and the 'Forty-Five.[24]

Terminating the Union, however, had a more material objective than the reassertion of Scottish nationalism. The passage of Union had constricted the places of profit and patronage at the disposal of the Court in Scotland: the ending of Union would reinvigorate the politics of influence which, by 1725 was firmly under the acquisitive control of the House of Argyll. In the interim, differing constitutional traditions, the clash between the English doctrine of parliamentary sovereignty and the Scottish appeal to fundamental law was manifested by a series of adjustments to the letter and spirit of the Treaty which were propagated as breaches of the Union in relation to religion, law, administration and economics. Indeed, as the Union had been partially conceived to foster free and equal trade between two unequal nations, Scotland, as the weaker partner suffered a recession that lasted until mid-century and was little ameliorated by fiscal rebates from Westminster. Arguably, development funds, channelled from 1727 through the Board of Trustees for Fisheries and Manufactures in association with the Royal Bank of Scotland, were primarily forthcoming because of the fear of Jacobitism. At the same time, the exclusion of the sheep farming districts in the north-east from access to woollen bounties was a further grievance fuelling Jacobitism. More meaningfully for Scottish economic development, the provision of drawbacks for linen exports in the early 1740s, promoted the formation of co-partneries as British endeavours.[25]

The Shawfield Riots in Glasgow and strikes among brewers in most towns in west-central Scotland against the malt tax in 1725 were compounded by the Porteous Riots against the execution of smugglers in Edinburgh in 1736. Jacobitism was also particularly advantaged by persistent mis-management of

Scottish affairs that resulted from the scrapping of the Privy Council to curtail patronage during the first elections to the parliament of Great Britain in 1708. At a stroke, executive government was deprived of its central intelligence agency in Scotland, an agency never satisfactorily replaced or compensated for by the occasional placement of Secretaries of State and other leading Scottish politicians in the emergent cabinet council in London. Nonetheless, Jacobitism was not the only means of protesting against the Union as is evident from the persistence of religious schism and the clandestine development of smuggling as the national sport. While government particularly feared the association of Jacobitism with the latter, political capital for the exiled House of Stuart rarely if ever accumulated outwith the Highlands and the north-east.[26]

Notwithstanding its distinctive identity as well as a ready awareness of pertinent organisational models for armed struggle, the extent to which Scottish Jacobitism can be deemed a movement remains problematic on both military and political grounds. The major, if not the minor risings, did demonstrate a degree of military cohesion. Although the Jacobites were unable to capitalise on their victory at Killiecrankie in July 1689 and break out of the Highlands, the predominantly clan campaigners did remain in arms five months after the Whig government offered peace at Achallader in July 1691. In the 'Fifteen, the Jacobites were not defeated in Scotland. But, the drawn engagement at Sheriffmuir in November effectively terminated the restoration of James VIII. During the 'Forty-Five, the Jacobites actually gained control of Scotland and remained a viable military force until crushed at Culloden in April 1746. Moreover, in the latter two risings, the Jacobites had an effective game plan for retaking the three kingdoms from Scotland that was devised by Colonel Nathaniel Hooke in the wake of Union. Building upon the successful invasion of England by the Covenanting Movement in 1640 and the possibilities opened up by the establishment of the Bank of England to service the national debt in 1694, Hooke advocated the seizure of Newcastle to cut off the coal supplies to London once revolt in Scotland had been sufficiently consolidated. The resultant financial crisis would have made the escalating national debt unserviceable. An effective trading stop on the Bank of England would deprive the British government of their power to finance their allies and muster sufficient reinforcements to counter a Jacobite rising backed by their continental opponents. Unfortunately for the Jacobites, this game plan was disastrously set aside by their respective commanders in the 'Fifteen and the 'Forty-Five – John Erskine, 6th Earl of Mar and 'Bonnie Prince Charlie'.

Despite their campaigning inconsistencies, both Mar and Prince Charles were in a position to establish their forces as the army of a provisional government. Although Mar fatally delayed in Perth rather than pressing on to Edinburgh, Jacobites did assert control over local government and taxation north of the Tay – notably in the town and shire of Aberdeen. Prince Charles did establish a provisional government in Edinburgh. Aberdeen again gave the lead to localities declaring for a Jacobite polity and there was a general expectation even in Whig districts that taxes would be exacted in the name of the provisional government. However, the determination of Charles to march on London by way of north-west England, allowed the government forces to regroup on a British basis, permitted civil war to flourish in Scotland and prevented the establishment of a secure bridgehead to await or encourage foreign intervention.[27]

Although there was an overt Jacobite parliamentary presence after the Revolution, their performance as a political party was noted more for their shifting alliances than their pursuit of principled opposition; a feature particularly evident in the parliamentary session which enacted the Union in 1706–7. Nominally led by John Murray, 1st Duke of Atholl, they formed part of the Confederated Opposition ineptly headed by James Douglas-Hamilton, 4th Duke of Hamilton. The 19 identifiable Jacobites among the 83 members of the Scottish Estates who voted against the principle of Union actually abstained when the Treaty was eventually ratified. Their abstention was done in protest at Hamilton's failure to countenance extra-parliamentary resistance, mass lobbying by constituents, and the wholescale boycott of a parliament by the Confederated Opposition prior to the vote on ratification. This later tactic to force a general election had been used successfully to scupper proposals for Union in 1702. Indeed, throughout the last parliamentary session, the Jacobites exhibited a high indulgence in cross-party voting and limited enthusiasm for parliamentary as distinct from extra-parliamentary protest co-ordinated by George Lockhart of Carnwath.[28]

In the wake of Union, operations became covert as Jacobitism was proscribed and abjured within the civil, military and ecclesiastical establishments. Nonetheless, despite the petering out of the Fifteen, the failure of the minor risings in 1708 and 1719, and the aborting of a planned rising in 1723, Lockhart of Carnwath did preserve a measure of coherent organisation between 1707 and his flight to the continent on being exposed as a leading Jacobite in 1727. During the remainder of Anne's reign, he enjoyed moderate success both in securing the return of Scottish Tories and in his guerrilla campaigning with parliamentary procedures. His parliamentary career eclipsed by the Hanoverian Succession, he gave a measure of coherence to Jacobite conspiracies. After the failure of the Swedish plot of 1717 to get off the ground and the abortive Spanish-backed rising that was terminated in Glenshiel in 1719, the laird of Carnwath played a prominent role in convincing James VIII in 1720 to establish a Commission of Trustees in Scotland to promote the affairs of the exiled House of Stuart. As Secretary to this rather shadowy Commission of Jacobite Trustees, Lockhart was primarily involved in reporting on internal politics rather than preparing for risings, plotting the removal of the government or capitalising on continuing unrest with Union. The Commission became embroiled in the factions surrounding the rise and fall of the Secretaries of State attending James VIII. More damagingly, as a disillusioned Lockhart diagnosed, was the failure of James VIII to assert his authority over factions in civil and ecclesiastical affairs and to provide sufficiently strong leadership to sustain the political organisation required by a movement.[29]

The resultant fissiparous character of Scottish Jacobitism was a more fundamental flaw than the lack of consistent support from magnate families which has been deemed an inherent, if not fatal, weakness.[30] The Whig cause would certainly appear to have derived more credibility from the relatively consistent support of the ducal House of Argyll than Jacobitism did from the equivocation of the ducal Houses of Hamilton, Gordon and Atholl. Yet, not only prominent noble families from the Whig heartlands south of the Tay, but even the House of Argyll was prepared to flirt with Jacobitism. John, the 2nd Duke, the Whig hero of the 'Fifteen, was stripped of his military posts in 1740 for persistent opposition to the foreign policy of the Whig ministry over the previous 18 years and especially following the outbreak of the War of the Austrian Succession. Sources close to the House of Argyll appear to have elicited an overture from James VIII on 25 May 1741, which sought to woo the Whig grandee with the assurance, 'I am fully resolved to make the Law the rule of my Government and absolutely disclaim any pretensions to a dispensing power'.[31]

Moreover, analysts of Scottish politics should be wary of the neo-Whig prism that focuses on the often turbulent relationship of the Crown and magnates since the later middle ages, a prism that becomes more difficult to sustain given the political rise of the gentry in the course of the seventeenth century. Albeit their political clout was episodic and uneven, the gentry were integral to the constitutional opposition to the House of Stuart as manifested by the Covenanting Movements and the Revolution Settlement. Subsequently, gentry were to be key players in providing the organisational framework for Jacobitism as a political as well as a military force. Notwithstanding the unreliable presence of political opportunists, there is considerable evidence of continuity among the associates of Lockhart of Carnwath and the Commission of Jacobite Trustees in the 1720s with the Scottish Jacobite Association formed in 1739, in response to the diplomatic opportunities opened up by the Austrian War. Although this Association eventually prepared the ground for the 'Forty-Five, as the testimony of its secretary, John Murray of Broughton, subsequently bears out, liaison with the Court in exile through unreliable agents strained political credibility and severely hampered preparations for a major rising.[32]

A further drawback was the capacity of careerist politicians to jump on and derail the Jacobite bandwagon. Thus, the Earl of Mar, who had actively campaigned for Union but was removed from his office as Secretary of State for Scotland at the Hanoverian Succession, was able to play on the Scottish Jacobites' need for a prominent leader in unilaterally launching the 'Fifteen. His reputation as 'Bobbing John' was reaffirmed by his subsequent role in political factions at the Jacobite Courts in exile and his willingness to turn informer for the British government. No less flagrantly, Simon Fraser, 11th Lord Lovat, having been convicted of treason for rape and abduction in securing his ennoblement, escaped to the Jacobite Court in France. But, he turned informer by disclosing the plot of 1702–3 in order to pave the way for his political rehabilitation at the British Court. He went out on the side of the Whig forces during the 'Fifteen, yet re-engaged fleetingly with the Jacobites in 1723 and more determinedly from 1737. Having had limited success in electoral politics for Westminster, he hoped not only to regain the position of lieutenant-general over the Highlands offered to him by James VII in the 1690s, but also to acquire a British peerage at the rank of duke. During the Forty-Five, he forced his estranged son, Simon, Master of Lovat, to lead out his clansmen to join the Jacobite forces. Despite voluminous disclaimers about his political influence, he was duly convicted and executed for treason in 1747.[33]

Notwithstanding its fissiparous character, its campaigning inconsistencies and its vulnerability to political opportunism, Jacobitism was deemed to be so deeply ingrained, particularly in the Highlands, that the government after the 'Forty-Five indulged in state-sponsored terrorism to ensure the eradication of clanship. At the same time, the crushing of Scottish Jacobitism – through show-trials, deportations and executions in tandem with the forfeiture and annexation of estates – was viewed as a necessity for advancing the British State. The trial and execution of James Stewart of the Glens in 1752, as accessory to the assassination of Colin Campbell of Glenure, an agent for the forfeited estates, was framed judicially to remind the clans in the Jacobite heartlands of Appin and Lochaber of the government's punitive powers. In the following year, the exemplary execution of Dr Archibald Cameron, a continental agent from the Lochiel family, for his involvement in the ill-fated Elibank Plot confirmed that Jacobite activity in Scotland was largely an emigré endeavour. Most potently, the British government decided to recruit erstwhile clansmen, regardless of past political allegiances, for service in North America a year after the outbreak of the Seven Years' War in 1756. Thus, the Highland Regiments, in marked contrast to the Irish Brigades in France and Spain, became bulwarks of the British Empire.[34]

Like the Southern Confederacy of nineteenth-century America, Scottish Jacobitism has carried an emotional resonance for a stateless nation; a situation that requires a new research agenda to establish its credentials as a movement. The current generation of researchers had been given a powerful steer to look for fresh perspectives on the movement through the extensive networks of the Scots Colleges in Paris and Rome.[35] Despite tempting glimpses of political activity in correspondence between the Colleges and the Jacobite Courts in exile, the papers of the Sacred College of Propaganda, as the co-ordinating body for the Scots Colleges, offer limited scope for fresh insights on Scottish Jacobitism.

In a rare display of unity, the Catholic bishops resident in Scotland, supported by the resolve of politically prominent Catholic laity, by clergy and trainee priests in both Scots Colleges and by their associates in the Jacobite Court, then in Paris, successfully persuaded the Sacred College that no clerical union with England was desirable in the wake of the Treaty of Union. In turn, the Sacred College, boosted by favourable reports of conversions on the Scottish Mission, created a separate Highland district in 1731. However, faction was more prominent than unity as was confirmed by the patronage and intrigue applied to ecclesiastical appointments. Moreover, during the 1730s, an acrimonious split between the clergy in the Highland and Lowland districts of the Scottish Mission spread to the Scots Colleges as to the Jacobite Courts at Paris and Rome. Ostensibly, the issue at stake was the Jansenist heresy, purportedly rife in the Lowland district as at the Scots College at Paris. However, no less pressing from the point of view of the clerical instigators of dissent from the Highland district was the discriminatory division of limited funding for the Scottish Mission which was loaded in favour of the Lowland district, where the priests tended to serve in the households of landed society rather than travel among communities dispersed in the isles, glens and straths. The acrimony engendered by this dispute all but emasculated the Scottish Mission and its capacity to provide reliable intelligence for Jacobite aspirations in the run up to the Forty-Five. Indeed, the primary value of these papers is perhaps to demonstrate the prospects of movement from Non-Juring Episcopacy to Roman Catholicism, particularly in selected areas of the Highlands. Jacobitism as well as a pastoral commitment was thus a significant factor in defining denominational allegiance in resistance to the Presbyterian establishment in the Kirk.[36]

Undoubtedly, there is ample scope for renewed searches for Jacobite material in continental archives, especially in Spain, Sweden, Prussia, Austria, Russia and the Netherlands to complement exploratory ventures in France and Italy. Ultimately, however, the continental archives may no more than supplement the pronounced bias in favour of the Jacobite Courts in exile manifest in the Stuart Papers at Windsor, which effectively treats of the cause not the movement in Scotland.[37] Despite extensive publication of sources for Jacobite activity at home and abroad since the nineteenth century, archival searches for new Scottish sources remains an imperative. These searches will require to be conducted not only in Scottish public and private archives, but in other national and local repositories in England and Ireland as in the state and institutional libraries in North America.[38] Nonetheless, the establishment of Scottish Jacobitism's credentials as a movement still requires the thorough exploration of the dynastic, commercial and ideological networks which provided the essential fabric of political life in the eighteenth century.

Too much importance can be given to marriage alliances, but not necessarily to the accompanying legal contracts as snapshots for commercial exchange rather than lasting political affiliations. Marriage contracts offered the facility to move around money between Jacobite families that would otherwise be liable to tighter surveillance by the British government.[39] Commercial co-partneries were usually even more short-lived than marriages and subject to greater fiscal scrutiny. At the same time, illicit links through smuggling were only detectable if unsuccessful. Co-partneries were by no means restricted to political affiliates and, given a shared commercial ideology between Whigs and Jacobites, no barrier to cross-party co-operation. In addition to the extensive marketing portfolio of the Campbells of Ardchattan and their landed associates among the Whigs of Argyllshire, Caithness and Perthshire, their commercial networking straddled the political divide prior to the 'Forty-Five. Their trading partners included the Camerons of Lochiel and their Jacobite affiliates in Lochaber whose enterprises ranged from smuggling from France to legitimate trading with the West Indies and the American colonies. This co-partnery was also to the fore in financing Jacobite endeavours during the last major rising. Laundering of money through commercial networks gives added weight to investigating foreign activities of Scottish Jacobites, notably fund-raising through the Swedish East India Company of those exiles based in Gothenburg.[40]

The development of clubs cut across as well as liberalised political barriers in the first half of the eighteenth century. In some cases, in both Scotland and England, purported Jacobite clubs served mainly as safety valves to confound rather than conspire against the British government. In other cases, clubs became a means of channelling Jacobite endeavours towards an Enlightened rather than a rebellious Scotland. Yet, speculative freemasonry had more than a social or intellectual function. Masonic lodges had strong links with the supporters of James VII even before the Revolution and these links were maintained with the Court in exile beyond the 'Forty-Five. Unlike England where the ritual of freemasonry was purged of its Jacobite associations in the Whig reconstitution of that country's Grand Lodge in 1723, freemasonry in Scotland continued to cut across political and denominational barriers. Indeed, among the prominent members of landed society involved in the separate reconstitution of the Grand Lodge of Scotland in 1723, were leading families like the Montgomery Earls of Eglinton who were flirting with Jacobitism. Even in the fallow years between the apparent demise of the Commission of Jacobite Trustees in 1727 and the formation of the Scottish Jacobite Association in 1739, agents from the Court in exile could move freely around sympathetic Masonic lodges in Scotland.[41]

A challenge can therefore be offered to the upcoming generation of historical scholars to embark upon the thorough research of these networks. While continuing to bear in mind the polemical impact of Jacobitism on the national consciousness, research should focus on the elites who may have helped shape a movement rather than on the rank and file who drank and died for the cause. The elites are more likely to be bound by legal and commercial contracts, especially such judicial proceedings involving bankruptcy which trace the associates and commercial contacts of known Jacobites like Sir James Campbell of Auchinbreck over several decades. A prime mover among entrepreneurial Argyllshire landowners establishing colonies in Jamaica and North Carolina in the 1730s, his commitment to Jacobitism from the 1720s overstretched his resources and bankrupted his family – albeit legal action in the Court of Session was not fully underway until 1760.[42]

The primary task in this research agenda must be the identification of a body of Jacobites from the risings, from the conspiracies, from parliamentary activity against the Union and from membership of the Commission of Jacobite Trustees and the Scottish Jacobite Association.[43] Thereafter, there are three important methodological operations. Firstly, archival searches should seek to establish the involvement of identifiable Jacobites in dynastic, commercial and ideological networks and the extent to which these networks serve as a basis for political management and association. This task is undoubtedly painstaking and almost inevitably fruitless if reliance is placed on traditional methods of searching voluminous materials, as in the Registers of Deeds, for legal and commercial contacts. Searches will require to be targeted towards selective sampling rather than general serendipity. Secondly, recourse must be had to data processing, preferably following on from the scanning of apposite archival material. The extraction of material in machine readable format allows the work of political association to be expedited, scrutinised and challenged through effective modelling of interrelational data sets. Given well founded caveats against the reinvention of the wheel by pioneering practitioners of historical computing, it is not necessary to devise original programmes, merely to tweak perfectly serviceable commercial programmes such as ACCESS, which offer both textual and alphanumeric facilities. Linking to a mapping package such as GIS can demonstrate the extent to which Jacobitism was a national or predominantly a regional endeavour in Scotland. Thirdly, research must be driven by disciplinary standards of intellectual rigour, structured analysis and systematic presentation that carries academic conviction throughout a chronological framework of six decades of Jacobitism. Such work will inevitably require international collaboration and major funding as befitting a research agenda of transnational significance.

The challenge to the upcoming generation of historical scholars to face up to this agenda concludes with a warning. The danger of not doing so will confine popular perceptions of Scottish Jacobitism to the shortbread tin. Jacobitism should not be submerged in antiquarian studies of memorabilia, in hypothesis about freemasonry based more on architectural drawings than actual buildings or in reconstructed literary criticisms unable to differentiate, nationally or regionally, between movements of power and movements of protest. Jacobitism, whether a movement or a cause, must be saved from the disconnected depths of post-modernist cultural studies which are currently masquerading as interdisciplinary approaches to history.[44]

REFERENCES

1. Sir C. Petrie, *The Jacobite Movement: The First Phase, 1688–1716* (London, 1950) & *The Jacobite Movement: The Last Phase, 1716–1807* (London, 1950).
2. D. Szechi, *The Jacobites: Britain and Europe, 1688–1788* (Manchester, 1994); F.J. McLynn, *The Jacobites* (London, 1985); G.P. Insh, *The Scottish Jacobite Movement: A Study in Economic and Social Forces* (Edinburgh, 1952).
3. B.P. Lenman, *The Jacobite Risings in Britain, 1689–1746* (London, 1980) & *The Jacobite Cause* (Glasgow, 1986).
4. W. Ferguson, *Scotland: 1689 to the Present* (Edinburgh, 1968), pp.1–101; K.M. Brown, *Kingdom or Province: Scotland and the Regal Union, 1603–1715* (London, 1992), pp.70–96.
5. B. O'Buachalla, *Aislig Ghear: Na Stiobhartaigh Agus An tAos Leinn, 1603–1788* (Dublin, 1996), pp.231–448; J.G. Simms, *Jacobite Ireland, 1685–91* (London, 1969); M. Hennessy, *The wild geese: the Irish soldier in exile* (London, 1973).
6. E. Cruikshanks, *Political Untouchables: The Tories and the '45* (London, 1979); E. Cruikshanks 38; J. Black (eds.), *The Jacobite Challenge* (Edinburgh, 1988); J.C.D. Clark, *English Society, 1688–1832* (Cambridge, 1985); E. Gregg, *Jacobitism* (The Historical Association, London, 1988); P.K. Monod, *Jacobitism and the English People, 1688–1788* (Cambridge, 1989).
7. J.A. Cannon, 'Historians and the '45: Listening to the Silence' in M. Lynch (ed.), *Jacobitism and the '45* (The Historical Association, London, 1995), pp.23–31; I.R. Christie, 'The Tory Party, Jacobitism and the Forty-Five: a note', *Historical Journal*, XXX, (1987), pp.921–31; L. Colley, *In Defiance of Oligarchy: The Tory Party, 1714–60* (Cambridge, 1982); P.S. Fritz, *The English Ministers and Jacobitism between the Rebellions of 1715* and *1745* (Toronto, 1975); L. Gooch, *The desperate faction?: the Jacobites of the north-east England, 1688–1745* (Hull, 1995).
8. M. Pittock, *The Myth of the Highland Clans* (Edinburgh, 1995).
9. A.I. Macinnes, *Clanship, Commerce and the House of Stuart, 1603–1788* (East Linton, 1996), pp.159–209.
10. E.M. Furgol, *A Regimental History of the Covenanting Armies, 1639–1651* (Edinburgh, 1990); J.R. Young, *The Scottish Parliament, 1639–1661*: A Political and Constitutional Analysis (Edinburgh, 1996).
11. M. Pittock, 'Who were the Jacobites? The pattern of Jacobite Support in 1745' in *Jacobitism and the '45*, pp.58–70.

12. Macinnes, *Clanship, Commerce and the House of Stuart*, pp.98–104, 182, 242–9.
13. I.B. Cowan, *The Scottish Covenanters*, 1660–88 (London, 1976); C. Kidd, 'Religious realignment between the Restoration and Union' in J. Robertson (ed.), *A Union for Empire: Political Thought and the British Union of 1707* (Cambridge, 1995), pp.145–68.
14. For a helpful summation of this debate see H.T. Dickinson, 'The Jacobite Challenge' in *Jacobitism and the '45*, pp.7–22. For a contemporary polemical flavour see Anonymous, *The anatomy of a Jacobite-Tory: in a dialogue between Whig and Tory, occasioned by the act for recognising King William and Queen Mary* (London, 1690); R. Ames, *The Jacobite conventicle, a poem* (London, 1692); D. Defoe, *A Dialogue betwixt Whig and Tory* (London, 1693) & *Whigs turn'd Tories, and Hanoverian Tories, from their avow'd principles, prov'd Whigs* (London, 1713); Anon., *The new revolution; or, the Whigs turn'd Jacobite* (London, 1710); C. Leslie, *The good old cause further discussed* (London, 1710); C. Lambe 38; B. Lintot, *The possibility of leaving the Tories, and speaking the truth afterwards: in a short answer to an impudent stupid pamphlet, publish'd by the Jacobite faction, entitled, Two wolves in lambskins, or, Old Eli's sorrowful lamentation over his two sons* (London, 1716); Anon., *The Faction: a poem on the new Jacobite and Swedish conspiracy* (London, 1717).
15. Ferguson, *Scotland's Relations with England*, pp.180–253; P.W.J. Riley, *King William and the Scottish Politicians* (Edinburgh, 1979) & *The Union of England and Scotland: A Study of Anglo-Scottish politics of the eighteenth century* (London, 1978); W.A. Speck, *The Birth of Britain: A New Nation, 1700–1710* (Oxford, 1994), pp.98–158; British Museum [BM], Scotch Plot, 1702–04: Papers of Simon Fraser, Lord Lovat, Add. MSS 31,250; Anon., *The Great danger of Scotland . . . from these who are commonly known by the name of Jacobites* (Edinburgh, 1704).
16. Inveraray Castle Archives [ICA], bundles 73/1, 109/30; Dumfries House [DH], Loudoun Papers, bundle 17/1, /11, A235/1–10, A237/5, A239/3, A261/2, A1320/2, A2173/2, A2201/6: material extracted from both these archives has been sponsored by major research grants from the British Academy; J.S. Gibson, *Playing the Scottish card: the Franco-Jacobite invasion of 1708* (Edinburgh, 1988); C. Sinclair-Stevenson, *Inglorious rebellion: the Jacobite risings of 1708, 1715 and 1719* (Edinburgh, 1971).
17. S. Lambert ed. *House of Commons Sessional Papers of the Eighteenth Century: Reports & Papers, 1717–25* (Scotland) (Wilmington, Delaware, 1975), pp.262–3, 320–8, 405–23, 439–49; Huntington Library [HL], Loudoun Scottish Collection, box 1, LO 7745–6, LO 7746; box 5, LO 11080; box 7, LO 8093, LO 8104, LO 8109, LO 8113, LO 8134; box 10, LO 11171–2; box 11, LO 11859, LO 11861; box 14, LO 10928–9; box 18, LO 8325; box 20, LO 7603, LO 7651, LO 7670, LO 7676; box 22, LO 11409; box 25, LO 11514; box 27, LO 8931, LO 11604, LO 11653–4; box 28, LO 11669; box 32, LO 10552.
18. D. Douglas (ed.), *History of the Union of Scotland and England by Sir John Clerk of Penicuik* (Scottish History Society, Edinburgh, 1993), pp.78–83; K.M. Brown, 'The vanishing emperor: British kingship in decline' in *Scots and Britons: Scottish political thought and the union of 1603* (Cambridge, 1994), pp.58–87; L.G. Fryer, 'Robert Barclay of Ury and East New Jersey', *Northern Scotland*, 15 (1995), pp.1–17.
19. P. Hopkins, *Glencoe and the End of the Highland War* (Edinburgh, 1986) provides an erudite and exhaustive account of the first Jacobite rising in Scotland.
20. E. Gregg, 'Was Queen Anne a Jacobite?', *History*, 57 (1972), pp.358–75; Aberdeen University Library [AUL], MacBean Collection, C5, 'Copy letter from King James Pretender to the Duke of Argyll, 1741'; E. Bohun, *The doctrine of non-resistance or passive obedience no way concerned in the controversies now depending between the Williamites and the Jacobites* (London, 1689); Sir R. Steele & J. Addison, *The Quaker's sermon, or, A holding-forth concerning Barabbas* (London, 1711); Anon., *Hereditary right not indefeasible* (London, 1747).
21. Scottish Record Office SRO, Church Papers CH 1/2/5/2–3; HL, Loudoun Scottish Collection, box 3, LO 7362, LO 10850; box 5, LO 11073; box 6, LO 9958–9, LO 9987; box 15, LO 10927; box 16, LO 7017; box 18, LO 8327, LO 8333, LO 8351; box 27 LO 8647, LO 11604, LO 11636, LO 11655; box 30, LO 10534–5; DH, Loudoun Papers, bundle 1726/3–4; bundle 1728/1; A 30/1–3; ICA, bundle 81/1–2; H. Clark, *A converse betwixt two Presbyterians of the Established Church an elder and a preacher: wherein the Presbyterian Dissenters from the*

Establish'd Church are vindicated from the charge of Jacobitism, (n.p., 1714); W. Wright, *The Jacobite curse, or, Excommunication of King George and his subjects* (Glasgow, 1714); Mr Adam Ferguson, Chaplain to the Regiment, *A Sermon preached in the Ersh Language to his Majesty's First Highland Regiment of Foot commanded by Lord John Murray at the Containment at Camberwell on* 18 December 1745 (London, 1746); Anon., *A comparison of the spirit of the Whigs and Jacobites: Being the substance of a discourse delivered to an audience of gentlemen in Edinburgh,* 24 December 1745 (Edinburgh, 1746).

22. *Historical Papers relating to the Jacobite Period,* 1699–1750, 2 vols, J. Allardyce ed. (New Spalding Club, Aberdeen, 1895), I, pp.177–92; B.P. Lenman & J.S. Gibson (eds.), *The Jacobite Threat: A Source Book* (Edinburgh, 1990), pp.122–6; Windsor Castle Royal Archives [WCRA], Stuart Papers, microfilm volumes 153/134, 161/3, /7, 162/52–3, 254/93, 296/39, box 3/41.
23. W. Donaldson, *The Jacobite Song: political myth and national identity* (Aberdeen, 1988); M. Pittock, *Poetry and Jacobite Politics in Eighteenth Century Britain and Ireland* (Cambridge, 1994).
24. Macinnes, *Clanship, Commerce and the House of Stuart*, pp.188–9, 193; J.L. Campbell (ed.), *Highland Songs of the 'Forty-Five* (Scottish Gaelic Texts Society, Edinburgh, 1984).
25. R. Mitchison, 'The Government and the Highlands, 1707–1745' in N.T. Phillipson & R. Mitchison (eds.), *Scotland in the Age of Improvement* (Edinburgh, 1970), pp.24–46; D. Warrand (ed.), *More Culloden Papers*, 5 vols. (Inverness, 1923–30) provides probably the most comprehensive coverage of published papers relating to the tergiversions of government policy throughout Scotland during the Jacobite period.
26. A.I. Macinnes, 'Jacobitism' in J. Wormald (ed.), *Scotland Revisited* (London, 1992), pp.29–41; *Historical Papers relating to the Jacobite Period*, I, pp.1–27, 131–65; Anon., *Jacobitism triumphant: or, The Whigs weigh'd in the ballance and found light* (London, 1752).
27. BM, Negotiations of Col. Hooke in Scotland, 1705–07, Add. MSS 20,858 fos 143–4; *Correspondence of Colonel N. Hooke, agent from the Court of France to the Scottish Jacobites in the years* 1703–1707, 2 vols, W.D. Macray (ed.) (Roxburghe Club, Edinburgh, 1870–1); *Historical Papers relating to the Jacobite Period*, I, pp.39–54, 195–205; *The Jacobite cess roll for the county of Aberdeen in* 1715: from the MS. of John Forbes of Upper Boyndlie, A.N. 38; H. Tayler eds. (Third Spalding Club, Aberdeen, 1932).
28. A.I. Macinnes, 'Studying the Scottish Estates and the Treaty of Union', *History Microcomputer Review*, 6 (Kansas, 1990), pp.11–25; , D. Szechi ed., *Scotland's Ruine: Lockhart of Carnwath's Memoirs of the Union* (Aberdeen, 1995).
29. A. Aufrere ed. *The Lockhart Papers: Memoirs and Correspondence upon the Affairs of Scotland from 1702 to 1715*, by George Lockhart Esq. of Carnwath, 2 vols. (London, 1817); D. Szechi ed., *The Letters of Lockhart of Carnwath, 1698–1732* (Scottish History Society, Edinburgh, 1989).
30. Lenman, *The Jacobite Risings in Britain*, pp.126–54; Brown, *Kingdom or Province*, pp.92–6.
31. AUL, MacBean Collection, C5, 'Copy letter from King James Pretender to the Duke of Argyll, 1741'; Macinnes, *Clanship, Commerce and the House of Stuart*, pp.198–9.
32. WCRA, microfilm volumes 48/92, 68/30–9, 100/8–9, box 1/22–3; HL, Loudoun Scottish Collection, box 14, LO 7973; box 29, LO 8973; Edinburgh, Brodrick Haldane Collection, H 1725/1, H 1744/1; W.B. Blaikie ed. *Origins of the 'Forty-Five* (Scottish History Society, Edinburgh, 1916), pp.3–68; R.F. Bell (ed.), *Memoirs of John Murray of Broughton, Sometime Secretary to Prince Charles Edward, 1740–1747* (Scottish History Society, Edinburgh, 1898), pp.7–147.
33. Macinnes, *Clanship, Commerce and the House of Stuart*, pp.166–8, 193, 214; G. Sewell, *The Earl of Mar marr'd: with the humours of Jockey, the Highlander: a tragi-comical farce* (London, 1715).
34. A.I. Macinnes, 'Scottish Gaeldom and the Aftermath of the '45: the Creation of Silence?' in *Jacobitism and the '45*, pp.71–81; B.P. Lenman, *The Jacobite Clans of the Great Glen, 1650–1784* (Edinburgh, 1986), pp.177–212; DH, Loudoun Papers, A58/3, A65/1, A966/1, A972/1, /9, /13, /16–7, /25, /27, A998/1, A1002/1; Edinburgh, Brodrick Haldane Collection, H 1757/1.

35. B. Neveu, 'A Contribution to an Inventory of Jacobite Sources' in E. Cruikshanks ed. *Ideology and Conspiracy: aspects of Jacobitism, 1689–1759* (Edinburgh, 1982), pp.38–58.
36. Macinnes, *Clanship, Commerce and the House of Stuart*, pp.175–6, 186; J. MacMillan, 'Jansenists and Anti-Jansenists in Eighteenth Century Scotland: the Unigenitus Quarrels on the Scottish Mission, 1732–1746', *Innes Review*, XXXIX (1988), pp.12–45.
37. Stuart Papers from the original manuscripts in the Royal Archives, Windsor Castle are microfilmed in 281 reels with indexes in another five reels (Wakefield, 1969). Extracts from these papers have been published in various formats including the extensive appendices to J. Browne, *A History of the Highlands and of the Highland Clans*, 4 vols (Glasgow, 1835); F. Atterbury, *The Stuart Papers printed from the originals in the possession of Her Majesty the Queen*, J.H. Glover ed. (London, 1847); A.N. & H. Tayler (eds.), *The Stuart Papers at Windsor: being selections from hitherto unprinted royal archives* (London, 1939). Other useful collections include the 3 reels of microfilm from the Stuart Papers from the *Denys Eyre Bower Collection, Chiddingstone Castle, Kent* (Wakefield, 1969); *Stuart papers relating chiefly to Queen Mary of Modena and the exiled court of King James II* (Roxburghe Club, Edinburgh, 1889); F.J.A. Skeet (ed.), *Stuart papers, pictures, relics, medals and books in the collection of Miss Maria Widdrington* (Leeds, 1930). The Scottish History Society has also published a plethora of Jacobite material. In addition to those already cited in the text, the following are worth consulting, A.D. Murdoch (ed.) *The Graemeid, an heroic poem on the Campaign of 1689* by James Philip of Almerieclose (Edinburgh, 1888); W.K. Dickson (ed.), *The Jacobite Attempt of 1719* (Edinburgh, 1895); H. Paton (ed.), *The Lyon in Mourning*, 3 vols. (Edinburgh, 1895–6); A.H. Millar ed. *A Selection of Forfeited Estate Papers, 1715, 1745* (Edinburgh, 1909); Sir B.G. Seton 38; J.G. Arnot (eds.), *The Prisoners of the '45*, 3 vols. (Edinburgh, 1928–9); H. Taylor (ed.), 'Jacobite Papers at Avignon', in *Scottish History Society Miscellany* V (Edinburgh, 1933); H. Tayler (ed.), *The Jacobite Court at Rome in 1719* (Edinburgh, 1938).
38. The Scottish Record Office has produced an extremely helpful *A Jacobite Source List* (Edinburgh, 1995), while the Manuscripts Division of the National Library of Scotland has recently published a *Collections and Named Manuscripts Index* (Edinburgh, 1995), which can be used to target Jacobite families. Rivalling the extensive resources of the British Museum and Library on the topic of Jacobites are the materials described in M.D. Allardyce (ed.), *Aberdeen University Library MacBean Collection: a catalogue of books, pamphlets, broadsides, portraits, etc. in the Stuart and Jacobite Collections gathered together by W.M. MacBean* (Aberdeen, 1949). The 39 boxed volumes in the Loudoun Papers at the Huntington Library in San Marino, California have proved an undoubted treasure trove with regard to the shaping of British public policy towards Scottish Jacobitism.
39. Useful starting points are J.B. Paul (ed.), *The Scots Peerage*, 9 vols. (Edinburgh, 1904–14); *Henry de Massue, Marquis of Ruvigny & Raineval, Jacobite Peerage, Baronetage, Knightage and Grants of Honour* (Edinburgh, 1904); Jacobite extracts of births, marriages and deaths: E.C. Lart (ed.), *The parochial registers of Saint-Germain-en-Laye, 1689–1720*, 2vols. (London, 1910–12).
40. Macinnes, Clanship, *Commerce and the House of Stuart*, pp.224–6; G. Behre, 'Sweden and the Rising of 1745', *Scottish Historical Review*, LI, (1972), pp.148–71; J. Mackay ed. *The Letter Book of Bailie James Steuart of Inverness, 1715–52* (Scottish History Society, Edinburgh, 1915).
41. D. Defoe, *The history of the Jacobite Clubs: with the grounds of their hopes from the P—T m—Y: as also a caveat against the Pretender* (London, 1912); W.J. Hughan, *The Jacobite Lodge at Rome* (Torquay, 1910); D. Stevenson, *The Origins of Freemasonry: Scotland's century, 1590–1710* (Cambridge, 1988) & *The First Freemasons: Scotland's early lodges and their members* (Aberdeen, 1988); N. Paton, *The Jacobites: their roots, rebellions and links with Freemasonry* (Fareham, 1994); B. Graham, 'Lowland reaction to the '45 Rebellion with particular relation to the estates of Lord Kilmarnock' (unpublished M.Litt. thesis, University of Glasgow, 1979).
42. SRO, Court of Session Productions, CS 96/1626.
43. Additional useful texts to those already cited on Jacobitism include edited works by C.S.

Terry, *The Chevalier de St. George and the Jacobite movements in his favour, 1701–1720* (London, 1901); *The Albemarle Papers: Correspondence of William Anne, Second Earl of Albemarle, Commander-in-Chief in Scotland, 1746–47*, 2 vols. (New Spalding Club, Aberdeen, 1902); *The Jacobites and the Union* (Cambridge, 1922) & *The Forty-Five* (Cambridge, 1922): likewise the following, *Faithful Register of the late rebellion: or, an impartial account of the impeachments, trials, attainders, executions, speeches, papers etc. of all who have suffered for the cause of the Pretender in Great Britain* (London, 1718); R.C. Jarvis, *Collected Papers of the Jacobite Risings*, 2 vols. (Manchester, 1972); *Muster Rolls of Prince Charles Edward Stuart's Army, 1745–46*, A. Livingstone, C.W.H. Aikman & B.S. Hart eds. (Aberdeen, 1984); *Jacobite correspondence of the Atholl family during the Rebellion, 1745–1746*, J.H. Burton & D. Laing (eds.), (Abbotsford Club, Edinburgh, 1840); T.L.K. Oliphant, *The Jacobite lairds of Gask* (Grampian Club, London, 1840); *Patrick Lindesay the Jacobite: founded on his letters in the possession of the Earl of Lindesay*, A.F. Steuart (ed.) (Edinburgh, 1927); *Jacobite letters to Lord Pitsligo 1745–46*, preserved at Fettercairn House, A.N. & H. Tayler (eds.) (Aberdeen, 1930); A.N. & H. Tayler, *Jacobites of Aberdeenshire and Banffshire in the rising of 1715* (Edinburgh, 1934); Sir J. Fergusson, *Argyll in the 'Forty-Five* (London, 1951).

44. In the summer of 1995, as part of the quincentenary celebrations of the University of Aberdeen, the Thomas Reid Institute, in conjunction with Eighteenth Century Scottish Studies Society and the Association for Scottish Literary Studies, ran an interdisciplinary conference on the theme Jacobitism and Enlightenment. Short on erudite scholarship and long on self-indulgent rhetoric, the treatment of Jacobitism would largely appear to confirm the predilection of practitioners of cultural history towards intellectual masturbation.

Six

Mission Accomplished? The Catholic Underground

JAMES F MCMILLAN

Introduction

In 1779, against a background of proposals in parliament to introduce a relief bill to remove the long-standing penal legislation against Catholics, a Protestant mob rioted in the streets of Edinburgh and burned down the home of Bishop Hay in Chalmers' Close. Hay gave his own description of what happened in a report he sent to Rome a few days after the event:

> 'No sooner did this (ie the proposal to extend Catholic emancipation to Scotland) become publicly known than the fanatic party among the preachers commenced to excite the alarm of the people . . . No Catholic could appear abroad without being pointed at, and saluted with these or similar cries: See the papist, the black Papist! Shoot him! Kill him!

The Bishop was not actually in the house at the time of the attack but two of his priests were. His report states: 'So thickly rained the stones from all quarters that they (the priests) could make no resistance, and only escaped with the greatest difficulty'. By 5pm the mob had battered its way into the house, which they then set on fire. Returning to Edinburgh at the height of the blaze and seeing the crowds gathered outside, Hay enquired of a woman bystander what was going on. 'Oh sir', she replied, 'we are burning the Papists' chapel and we only wish we had the bishop to throw into the fire'. The house was completely destroyed and other houses known to belong to Catholics in the city were also attacked and looted.[1]

The Edinburgh rioting had been preceded by similar disturbances in Glasgow. As soon as word of a Catholic relief bill got about, a 'no popery' crusade was launched by various Protestant divines, such as the Glasgow minister Dr Gillies. In October 1778, the Synod of Glasgow and Ayr declared a general fast day on account of 'awful signs of divine displeasure which are visibly displayed at this time, particularly the encouragement given to and growth of Popery'. The following Sunday a mob gathered outside of a house where it was known that mass was celebrated. As the small group of worshippers emerged, they were subjected to catcalls and physical abuse and the house itself broken into and wrecked. When the Catholics found another house at which to worship, it too was attacked and vandalised (on 9 February 1779) by a mob calling itself the 'Friends of Protestantism', who likewise torched warehouses belonging to its owner, Mr Bagnall, an English manufacturer.[2]

This chapter is not about the perpetrators of this violence – though the pathology of anti-Catholicism in Scotland remains a subject which could do with further illumination – but about its victims, the members of the tiny Scottish Catholic community. It looks at a group of Scots men and women who have largely been absent from mainstream Scottish histories of the period, though it is good to see trenchant and perceptive pages devoted to them in recent works by Michael Lynch and Allan Macinnes.[3] Apart from the fact that, as we have just seen, the story of the minority Scottish Catholic community has not been unaffected by the master narratives of the Protestant majority, minorities need to be studied as well as majorities, to ensure that history is genuinely inclusive and not merely the propaganda of the victors. My starting point is that the Scottish Catholic community has a history of its own which requires to be related in its own right and on its own terms, in the manner of the superb study of the English Catholic community carried out by John Bossy.[4]

But how is one to write the history of the Scottish Catholic community? On the one hand, it is necessary to avoid viewing it exclusively through hostile eyes as the remnants of a defeated and discredited, but still potentially subversive, popery, since Scottish Catholics, in their own eyes, were both Catholics, that is members of a universal Church centred on Rome, and Scots, every bit as conscious of their membership of a historic nation as was the Presbyterian majority. On the other hand, we need to avoid the pitfalls of Catholic recusant history – antiquarianism, partisanship and a lack of any critical perspective – which only serve to justify the marginalisation of the subject on the part of academic historians.

Bossy's agenda was to recover 'the religious and social experience of the average Catholic', which he succeeded magnificently in doing in a volume of some 446 pages. That larger agenda, however, will have to keep for another occasion. Here the purpose is twofold: first, to perform an act of reclamation which will restore a Catholic voice to the history of the eighteenth century (and no apologies are required for employing the extensive quotations which permit that voice to be heard): and, secondly, and more ambitiously, as well as more controversially, to attempt an overview of the achievements and shortcomings of the mission from the time of the appointment of the first vicar-apostolic Thomas Nicolson in 1694 to the 1770s, a period when the

Catholic Church in Scotland was still essentially an underground Church, operating in conditions of clandestinity.

A crucial point to appreciate in this exercise is that in Scotland, as in England, by the mid-seventeenth century at the latest the Catholic community was not the rump of a medieval Scottish Christianity which had somehow survived the Reformation unscathed but an altogether new, small and expanding body shaped by the ideals of the Counter-Reformation. The history of that body is certainly the history of lay people, but as Bossy has pointed out, in the context of Counter-Reformation Christianity, the dynamics of the community depended on the clergy. What is true of England is also true of Scotland: to cite Bossy again, 'The mission did not by itself suffice to create the community, but without the mission no community could have been created'.[5]

We should ask, therefore, what exactly the mission accomplished. How effectively was it run? How far did it meet its targets? Was it adequately funded? These and other questions are all the more relevant since in the correspondence of the missionary priests, preserved in the Catholic archives in Edinburgh and in the archives of Propaganda Fide in Rome, the Church was described as a 'company' and its business, religion, was referred to as 'trade'. Priests featured as 'merchants' or, more commonly, as 'labourers': ecclesiastical students were 'prentices'. Head of the company was Mr Cant (the Pope) who presided at trading headquarters in Hamburg (Rome), the location also of the Change (Propaganda). The company, operating out of Prussia (Scotland) had other business connections with Amsterdam (Paris), notably regarding its 'shops' (colleges). A balance sheet of the mission is therefore in order, based partly on primary research in Rome and Edinburgh but also on some of the excellent pioneering work done by others and published over the years in the indispensable *Innes Review*, the journal of the Scottish Catholic Historical Association.

Background: the creation of a missionary Church

But before we take a closer look at the performance indicators, it might be useful to give some relevant background information which will help to clarify the missionary enterprise and how this missionary church came into being. Following the Reformation of 1560 the collapse of the old Church in Scotland was comprehensive. The last Catholic bishop of the pre-Reformation period, James Beaton, died in exile in 1603 and for almost another century Scottish Catholics remained without episcopal leadership. Penal laws were enacted to discourage adherence to the old religion. After 1560, Mass attendance was to be punished by the confiscation of goods and corporal chastisement for a first offence; banishment was the penalty for a second offence; and death for a third. Subsequent parliaments renewed and extended these measures, which were enforced in the reign of Charles I in the 1620s as a sop to the Kirk for the King's other ecclesiastical innovations. Further penal legislation followed in the wake of the Whig Revolution of 1688. In May 1700, a new Act of Parliament offered a reward of 500 merks for the capture of priests and prescribed instant banishment for Catholic clergymen on pain of death should they return to Scotland. The same statute declared Catholics incapable of inheriting property or educating their children.[6]

It took the papacy some time to adjust to the situation in which it had to organise missionary activity not only in the non-Christian world of the Orient and the Americas but also in Protestant countries like Scotland. Its solution, eventually, was the establishment under Gregory XV in 1622 of the Congregation for the propagation of the faith, Propaganda Fide, which under the direction of its first secretary Francesco Ingoli (1622–49) elaborated a mission strategy in which the key role in missionary activity was assigned to the individual missionary priest, trained in Tridentine theology and working directly under the control of the papacy by reporting to Propaganda. These missionary priests were to be secular clergy rather than regulars, whose independence and political intrigues were viewed with deep suspicion at Propaganda, which laid down as its top priority the creation of a native clergy able to effect and sustain personal conversions among a missionary population rather than to bring about conversion by means of political or commercial pressure.[7] This was a 'bottom-up' rather than a 'top-down' missionary strategy and it meant that a Rome-inspired drive to recatholicise Scotland was never a serious possibility. Nor was it attempted by the Scots Catholic clergy. Their preoccupation was first and foremost with ministering to their existing flock rather than seeking to convert Protestants. To make an assessment about the success or otherwise of the Scottish Catholic mission, we should first be clear about its objectives.

That there was still a flock for the secular clergy to tend in the eighteenth century was due largely to the work of various religious orders such as the Jesuits and the Benedictines in the late sixteenth and seventeenth centuries, though a trickle of secular priests arrived on the mission after being educated at one of the Scots colleges on the continent. Most crucial to the maintenance of a Catholic presence in the Highlands and Islands in the first half of the seventeenth century were the endeavours of Irish Franciscans, who operated out of Antrim, and received funding from Propapaganda after 1622.[8] After 1646, they were succeeded by Irish Vincentians, likewise supported by Propaganda, and by a number of Irish Dominicans.[9] It was 1653 before Rome formally established a secular Scottish Mission which in the first instance was placed under the leadership of a Prefect-Apostolic rather than a

Vicar-Apostolic, or bishop *in partibus infidelium.*[10] Only with the consecration of Thomas Nicolson as bishop of Peristachium in 1694 did Scotland finally have its own Vicar-Apostolic, by which time the contours of the counter-Reformation Catholic population were clearly discernable.[11]

The majority (ie about two-thirds) were to be found in the Highlands, especially places such as Knoydart, Moidart, Arisaig, Morar and Lochaber in the west, along with the islands of Barra, Eriskay, South Uist, Benbecula, Canna, Rum and Eigg. Strathglass, Strathfarrer and the Aird were Catholic strongholds in the central and northern Highlands, as were Glengairn in upper Deeside, Braemar, Inveravon, Strathavon, Strathdon and Glenlivet in the eastern Highlands. Lowland Catholicism was also concentrated in the north-east, especially in the Enzie of Banff in the territories of the Duke of Gordon. Bishop Nicolson established his headquarters at Presholme in the Enzie and mission stations were set up at Aberdeen, Angus, the Mearns, Strathbogie and Strathisla, though there was also a Catholic presence in Edinburgh and in the vicinity of aristocratic houses such as Stobhall and Drummond Castle in Perthshire, Traquair and Terregles.[12] Glasgow, which in the nineteenth century would become a huge centre of Irish Catholic immigration, never had more than a handful of Catholics until the end of the eighteenth century, and was served from Edinburgh. In the 1780s Bishop Geddes looked after a little flock of about five.[13] The rioting in Glasgow and Edinburgh in 1779 with which we began can hardly be attributed to the threat of a Catholic takeover.

Organising the mission: the role of the vicars-apostolic

The appointment of Thomas Nicolson as vicar-apostolic finally allowed the Scottish Mission to develop in conformity with Propaganda's grand design and Nicolson wasted no time in drawing up a set of Ordinances or *Statuta* for the Mission which mirrored those laid down by the Congregation. Agreed upon at a meeting of the clergy in April 1700, these were approved by Rome in 1706 and regulated the Scottish mission until 1780, when Bishop Hay incorporated them into a new code. A number of *monita*, or admonitions, preceded the *statuta*, and stressed the importance of the need for priests to set standards for their flocks by themselves living blameless Christian lives and avoiding all internal dissensions. The missionaries were to have fixed places of residence which could not be changed without due authority. The *statuta* further stipulated that all clergy, including regulars, were to be subject to the authority of the bishop for the administration of the sacraments and in 1701 the Jesuit missionaries in Scotland made a complete submission to the vicar-apostolic. By this date, it is clear that their lives as missionary priests did not differ substantially from those of the seculars.[14]

To put the organisation of the mission on a more secure basis, Propaganda agreed to the appointment of a coadjutor bishop for Bishop Nicolson and decided on James Gordon, a secular priest from Glastirum in the Enzie, a cousin both of the Duke of Gordon and of the Roman Agent for the Scots Clergy, William Leslie, and a relative of some of the leading Jacobite families in Scotland, who was consecrated Bishop of Nicopolis in April 1705 in a secret ceremony conducted by Cardinal Barbarigo at Montefiascone, north of Rome.[15] Following the death of Bishop Nicolson, Bishop Gordon in his turn petitioned Propaganda for a coadjutor and was successful in obtaining the appointment of John Wallace in 1720. A native of Arbroath, Wallace was a son of the town's provost and had converted to Catholicism after serving as an Episcopalian minister. He was consecrated Bishop of Cyrrha in Edinburgh by Bishop Gordon, assisted by two of his priests, on 8 April 1720.

Increasingly, however, it became apparent that, given the massive problems involved in ministering to two communities, Highland and Lowland, whose pastoral needs were very different, what was required was a coadjutor bishop who would be permanently stationed in the Highlands. In 1726 Bishop Gordon and Bishop Wallace proposed to Propaganda that Scotland be divided into two vicariates, the Highland and the Lowland districts and that the first vicar-apostolic of the Highland District be Mr Alexander Grant, who had proved himself a successful missioner on his seven years on the mission after his return from the Scots College Rome, where he had also earned plaudits for making a public defence of the controversial bull *Unigenitus*. Propaganda approved, as did Pope Benedict XIII in 1727 and a reluctant Grant was dispatched from the braes of Glenlivet to set out for Rome. He never made it: having run out of money and suffered a nervous breakdown at Genoa, he simply vanished from view. Another four years were to elapse befor the post of Vicar-Apostolic for the Highland District was filled by Hugh Macdonald, son of the Laird of Morar and a Clanranald, who was consecrated in Edinburgh as Bishop of Diana on 18 October 1731 by Bishop Gordon, with the assistance of Bishop Wallace.[16]

The mission remained organised on the basis of these two vicariates until 1827, when the influx of Irish Catholic immigrants in the west of Scotland necessitated the creation of a third vicariate, and the mission was organised into eastern, western and northern districts. For the record, the other vicars-apostolic of the eighteenth century were Alexander Smith, who was preferred to Colin Campbell as coadjutor in the Lowlands after the death of Bishop Wallace in 1733 and consecrated Bishop of Missinopolis in Edinburgh in 1735. He became Vicar-apostolic of the Lowlands when Bishop Gordon died in 1746 and only obtained a coadjutor in the person of James Grant in 1755. Bishop Hugh Macdonald had to wait until 1761 for his coadjutor, who was his nephew John Macdonald. George Hay, an Episcopalian convert who had received a training in medicine, was appointed coadjutor to Bishop Grant in 1768 and succeeded him as Vicar-Apostolic of the Lowlands when he died in 1778. John Geddes became coadjutor of the Lowland District in 1780, while yet another Macdonald, Alexander Macdonald, succeeded Bishop John Macdonald the same year.

The pastoral zeal of the Scottish vicars-apostolic was always exemplary and sometimes, as in the case of Bishop Gordon, nothing short of heroic. Throughout his forty years as a bishop he carried out visitations to his flock, touring the entire country some thirty times. His first visit to the Highlands, undertaken in 1707 and repeated many times, typified his pastoral methods and is worth recounting in detail from the narrative compiled by the eighteenth-century priest-chronicler John Thomson.[17] Setting off from the Enzie on 5 June along with a deacon who could speak Gaelic, Gordon reached Glengarry on 10 June, having survived on a diet of milk and cheese and slept in leaky huts on beds of straw and heather. Having met up with two fellow missionary priests, he left to avoid the soldiery stationed in Glengarry and headed for the remotest corners of the Highlands and Islands on foot, dispensing with horses 'with a view to conceal himself the better, and that his fellow-travellers might have the less reason to complain of the fatigues of the journey, bad roads, and bad food, since he had to bear all these circumstances in common with them'. At Glenquoich, which they reached on 16 June, 'they began to experience how bad, perilous and fatiguing the roads were; for they were either so steep that they had to crawl with hands and feet along high and rugged mountains, with danger of falling down precipices every moment, or so wet and boggy that they were often in danger of sinking, and never had a dry foot. The Bishop, however, bore these fatigues with cheerfulness, and encouraged his fellow-travellers by his example'.

After resting with the brother of Glengarry for two nights, they set off again for the safe house belonging to the laird of Knoydart, where on 20 June the Bishop began his missionary activity by administering the sacrament of Confirmation. Then it was on to Loch Morar, Arisaig, and the Isles. Landing on Eigg on 25 June he taught the catechism while the two priests heard confessions in preparation for more Confirmations. At Mass, one of the priests preached in Gaelic and afterwards the Bishop himself delivered a short homily which was translated into Gaelic. This became a standard procedure adopted elsewhere – on Uist, where they lodged with Clanranald, on Barra and Watersay, followed by Uist again, and then Canna and back to Eigg, before returning to the mainland on 16 July. Working his way back through Strathglass, the Bishop continued to administer the sacraments despite falling ill to fever and dystentery, to which he finally succumbed at Badenoch in mid-August. He finally obtained the rest he needed back in Balnacraig on Deeside at his brother's house on 21 August. In the course of his arduous tour, the good Bishop succeeded in confirming some 2242 people.

Blessed with such leadership, the mission made modest, if unspectacular progress. Numbers increased. The exact size of the Scottish Catholic community remains a matter of some dispute, but the best estimate would appear to posit a rise from a mere 6.000 in the 1690s to perhaps 16.500 in 1763.[18] According to the demographer Alexander Webster, Catholics therefore still accounted for less than 2% of the Scottish population in the mid-eighteenth century. The number of priests on the mission also expanded. Whereas there was a mere handful of five seculars in 1653, by the 1730s and 1740s the total number of missionary priests operating on the mission at any one time was around 40, seculars and regulars combined. In 1734 for example it was reported to Propaganda that there were 24 missionaries labouring in the Lowlands (14 seculars and 10 regulars) and in the Highlands 13 missionaries (8 seculars and 5 regulars). Presbyterian clergymen who expressed alarm about the 'encrease of popery' in the first half of the eighteenth century exaggerated a great deal, no doubt because they wanted to continue to receive government subsidies for the ongoing fight against Jacobitism, but it gave the vicars-apostolic and the misssioners a sense of achievement to think that their work was rewarded with conversions.[19]

Another source of immense satisfaction for Bishop Gordon and the other vicars-apostolic was the foundation of a native seminary where boys could be trained for the priesthood without having to be sent abroad to one of the Scots colleges. In 1714, or possibly even before, he opened a seminary on the island of Eilean Ban in Loch Morar, in the heart of Clanranald territory, where one of the first pupils was Hugh Macdonald, the future vicar-apostolic. After the failure of the 'Fifteen, when the West Highlands were no longer so safe, the seminary was transferred to Scalan in the remote braes of Glenlivet in the country of the Duke of Gordon where it opened for business again in 1716. This time the seminary had found a home which would be a nursery of Catholic priests for the next eighty years, despite repeated attempts on the part of Presbyterian ministers to have it closed down and the destruction of the original house after the 'Forty-Five. In its time, Scalan produced more than 100 priests who served on the Scottish mission, five of whom became bishops. In the *Rules* which he personally drew up for Scalan in 1722, Bishop Gordon ensured that the Scottish seminary was modelled on continental Tridentine ideals on the education and training of aspirants to the priesthood.[20] A Presbyterian source, a memorial presented to the General Assembly in 1720, gives perhaps the best succinct summary of the key role it played in the spread of Counter-Reformation Christianity to Scotland:

> . . . there is a famous Popish school in the foresaid Scalla in Duke Gordon's countrey under the inspection of one Father Innes, who still

> resides there, and keeps a correspondence with fforeign Popish colleges; to this nursery are sent children from the Isles and many other places, and such as Father Innes judges promiseing are educated and maintained here, and after [some time of] study at this school sent abroad, and when they have been a competent time at Popish universities are returned in orders to Scotland, and by those means the nation is furnished with Priests suited to the Genious and Language of every Countrey, and with such as have friends and Blood relations to Countenance and Shelter them.[21]

Scalan, quite simply, may be regarded as the *lieu de mémoire* par excellence of the Scottish Catholic mission.[22] In 1798, when a move to a new college at Aquorties had been decided for the following year, a former pupil who went on to be Rector of the Scots College at Douai, wrote:

> Old Scalan's approaching dissolution affects me much for the sake of old long syne; next summer I intend – God willing – to shed a few tears over it.[23]

It was also a priority of Bishop Hugh Macdonald to establish a Highland seminary where Highland boys could be educated for the priesthood in the language of the Gael but his efforts did not meet with the same success as Bishop Gordon experienced at Scalan. Too often, Bishop Hugh told Propaganda, young Highland boys fell by the wayside when they got to the continent of Europe, even to the point of forgetting their own native tongue.[24] Straightaway in 1732 at the beginning of his episcopate he re-established a seminary in Loch Morar, which in 1738 was transferred to Arisaig. Crippled by a lack of funds, however, the seminary had to be abandoned altogether after Culloden and for the next 24 years the Highlands remained without a seminary, though the Bishop seems to have tried to have some of his youths educated at Fochabers. A subsidy from Propaganda allowed a Highland seminary to reopen again at Glenfinnan, but it too soon folded for want of further funding. Throughout the eighteenth century all attempts to establish a Highland seminary on a sure financial footing came to naught, but the seriousness with which the Highland Vicars-Apostolic addressed the problem does at least testify to their commitment to the creation of a native, Gaelic-speaking, Highland clergy, which was the key to any future progress on the Highland mission.[25]

Assessing the missionary achievement

Any verdict on the Catholic mission needs to take account of the exceedingly harsh conditions under which it was obliged to operate, partly on account of nature, climate and the poverty of the people, and partly on account of the penal conditions which drove the mission underground. Reports of Jesuit missioners of the early eighteenth century testify to the difficulties and dangers encountered by the missionary priest. Father John Innes wrote:

> For nearly fifteen years I have been wandering over different parts of this, my native country, with what difficulty, hardship and peril He only knows, Who knows all things. I have had to accommodate myself to the manners and customs of the rudest and most uncouth country people, to be hid in caverns or in forests, and to travel at night, and in winter nights, over mountains, rocks, and through woods, over the most difficult roads, often without guide or companion, not without peril to my life. And not unfrequently when tired out by these journeys, whether by night or day, I have had to lie down without food or drink in barns or stables among the brute animals, upon a little straw, or sometimes on the hard, bare earth. It cost me immense toil and much time to speak the extremely difficult language of this country, but by God's favour I am master of it now, and can get through all the duties of my office by means of it. My business in these parts has given me, and is giving me still, the greatest possible anxiety, has caused and causes me many vigils and much toil. What disguises have I not worn, what arts have I not professed! Now master, now servant, now musician, now painter, now brass-worker, now clock-maker, now physician, I have endeavoured to be all to all, that I might save all. I found that such skill as I had acquired in the medical art was most useful for the purpose I had in view, and I have cultivated and used it most generally. But while it readily obtained me access to the sick, of whatever condition, age, or sex they might be, at the same time it involved me in much anxiety and no little peril. For I often had to get up in the middle of the night, even when I was ill myself, and make my way over hill and forest, and rapid streams and torrents, with evident danger of my life.[26]

Fellow Jesuit Father Hugh Strachan, a convert to Catholicism while a student at the University of Aberdeen, testified in like manner concerning the conditions of the Jesuit mission on Upper Deeside, which he served from Braemar between 1701 and 1737: 'The region I dwell in is steep and sterile, mountainous and rugged, and much hardship and inconvenience has to be put up with. The people are so poor that they keep their cattle in their own dwellings. We live as we can on butter, cheese and milk, rarely get flesh, fish hardly ever. We usually drink water, sometimes beer, wine we never taste but at the altar. We lie on the ground, or on a little straw or heather'.[27] Strachan's colleague, Fr Macrae S.J., who had charge of the mission at Strathglass in the valley of the river Beauly, beyond Glengarry, confirmed these observations in another report, noting how in the summer months his people took off to the hills with their sheep and cattle: 'I cannot track them in the mountains and forests without the greatest difficulty; and if I find them, I find with them very little of the comforts of life. The huts they live in are so low and narrow that they will barely hold their families, and I am very often obliged to sleep in the open air, even in very cold weather'.

Notwithstanding these conditions, Fr Macrae spoke highly of the piety and commitment of those in his charge, rejoicing in 'the ardour of mind and soul with which they worship God. They are often glad to walk eight or nine miles on a Sunday to hear Mass and a Sermon; nor will even persecution hinder them from joining in this public worship. Scarcely a Sunday passes without some of them coming to the holy table. They never pass me without going down on their knees and asking my blessing, unless they suspect some of the heterodox are in sight, whose testimony might bring themselves and me into danger. When anyone is taken ill, the first care is to send for the spiritual physician, whatever the distance may be. I have never once seen anyone die without feeling the strongest consolation when I witnessed their perfect submission to the will of God, their patience, even in extreme suffering, their piety in receiving the sacraments of the Church, the ardour with which they asked for prayers of all present, and I always feel this is a sufficient reward for all the labour I have undergone'.[28]

Among secular priests, some mission stations had the reputation of being more difficult to work in than others. Lochaber, for instance, was often described as lawless. The first priest to be stationed there on a permanent basis after the Reformation was Mr John Macdonald, a native son and a Clanranald on his father's side, who returned to the mission in 1721 after studying in Rome and discovered that only three families in the district still observed Catholic religious practices, not because the others had converted to Protestantism but because they had allowed their observance to lapse. Mr Macdonald laboured there for some forty years until his death in 1761, obviously to good effect, since it was reported to Rome in 1763 that Lochaber had 3.000 communicants.[29] Another demanding station was Shenval, in the Cabrach, the district in the dividing line between Banffshire and Aberdeenshire, which was reckoned to be a Scottish Siberia, bitingly cold and stormy as well as isolated.[30]

Clandestinity remained the normal condition of the Catholic Church in Scotland for most of the eighteenth century on account of the penal laws, despite the fact that the governing classes of the British state increasingly showed themselves sympathetic to the idea of religious pluralism after the Revolution of 1688, extending religious toleration to all Protestants in England by law in 1689 and in Scotland in 1712, and in practice often turning a blind eye to the discreet practice of Catholicism. What preoccupied the authorities about Catholics was less their religion than their politics, and it is usually argued that penal legislation was maintained more as a deterrent against Jacobitism than as a means of extirpating the Catholic religion. Except in times of crisis, such as 1689–92 and 1745–46, local lairds evinced little desire to meddle in the religious affairs of their neighbours and it was in similar circumstances that the military set out to apprehend members of the clergy. True, sometimes priests were arrested because of their misfortune in encountering a particularly zealous magistrate, and there were also some soldiers who were attracted to bounty-hunting by the reward of 500 merks (£333–6/8 Scots) offered for the capture of a priest after 1700. The primary duties of the army, however, remained the catching of cattle thieves and the suppression of Jacobites. In any case only after the 'Forty-Five was there a military presence in the Highlands in sufficient numbers to carry out any systematic persecution of Catholics.[31] Thus there were many periods which passed without the arrest of a single secular priest (eg between 1705 and 1726 and 1727–1745), though the odd regular, such as the Jesuit Father Hudson, chaplain to the Jacobite Earl of Nithsdale, was seized in 1715.

As Daniel Szechi has argued in a recent article, however, it is probably a mistake to underestimate the impact of persecution on the development of the Scottish Catholic mission. When the state did decide to crack down on Catholic recusancy, it cracked down hard. Among the 24 secular clergy on the Scottish mission in 1689, 6 were arrested and 5 imprisoned for a year or more; 7 Jesuits were captured as part of the same round-up, and nearly all the missionaries were constrained either to go into hiding or take the path of exile. In the aftermath of the 'Forty-Five it was again the Jesuits who bore the brunt of the repression. Five were captured (four of them from Highland mission stations) and two died in prison. Only 4 out of 29 secular priests were arrested, though to these must be added one who fell at Culloden and two others who were forced to flee the country. Even if arrests were made on a random rather than a systematic basis, the total number detained in the period 1653 to 1755 has been shown by Szechi to be high, amounting to 23 out of 105 secular priests (21.9%). None suffered the death penalty as prescribed by the penal statutes but all were banished from Scotland and threatened with execution if they returned. It might be thought that, since most did return and some were captured and exiled yet again, the state once more can be represented as exercising a degree of leniency, but it was certainly the case that, after a year spent languishing in jail, missioners often needed a long period of recuperation on the continent, and some, like the Jesuit John Farquarson after his imprisonment in the wake of the 'Forty-Five, showed a marked reluctance to return to the Highlands. While no priest was executed in Scotland between 1653 and 1755 at least 5 (2 seculars, 2 Jesuits and 1 Dominican) died as a direct consequence of incarceration and others, broken in body, died soon after their release.[32]

Merely to have survived in such adverse conditions, let alone to have undergone a modest expansion, might be thought to have been no mean achievement on the part of the mission. That is certainly the view of a recusant historian like Mgr Sandy McWilliam, whose pathbreaking researches on the activities of both secular and regular missionary priests were fuelled by the belief that 'They were giants in those days'.[33] That was also the contemporary view which Bishop Gordon was keen to convey to his paymasters in Rome, doubtless because his generosity of spirit made him always think well of his priests, but also because he hoped to convince Propaganda that the excellent work already being done could be improved if only the Congregation would fund the mission a little more generously.[34]

Without in any way wishing to belittle the heroism and commitment of the missionary priests, it may be suggested that it is necessary to view eighteenth-century underground Scottish Catholicism with a more critical eye than some of its earlier historians have done. If Counter-Reformation Catholicism never succeeded in implanting itself on Scottish soil on any significant scale, this was not entirely because it had to operate in a hostile environment. This short survey of the Scottish Catholic Mission will therefore conclude with a brief examination of certain factors which suggest that it may well have underperformed as a result of internal weaknesses.

An undoubted handicap was systematic underfunding from Rome, allied to the unequal division of mission funds between Lowland and Highland districts. The Scottish Catholic Mission was financed by money from three sources: Rome, Paris and Scotland. The Roman funds were the most important, being those donated by Propaganda when it set up the Mission in 1653 and bequeathed Prefect Ballantyne an annual sum of 500 crowns (£120). At this time, there were only 10 secular priests to be supported, so each received 50 crowns or £12 a year for maintenance. Despite the vote of periodic extraordinary subsidies and the donation of another 50 crowns or £12 a year for the care of sick and superannuated clergy, Propaganda resolutely set its face against any increase in the amount of the basic annual subsidy, even when the number of missionary priests increased. By the 1720s this was causing a considerable degree of resentment among the missioners, particularly those working on the Highland mission, as the turbulent Benedictine monk Gregor McGregor informed Thomas Innes: 'Our trading was never in a lower condition than it is at present, not but that we have work enough only the encouragement is so little that we cannot live by it, viz seven pounds sterling yearly . . . I have been these seven years bypast in Glengary in the ruggedest and most painfull Station in Scotland. The inhabitants are not wont nor doe they contribut in the least to my temporall assistance, neither shall I ever introduce that custome in my own favoure unless it were allready established, or to be removed thence.'[35]

Underfunding, as we have already seen, was the crucial reason for the relative lack of success on the Highland mission, notably in regard to the creation of a native clergy. Here Rome was not solely to blame because the administrators of the Lowland District resolutely refused to help out with the training of Highland priests and fought off attempts to amalgamate the Highland and Lowland seminaries. Bishop Grant feared overcrowding at Scalan but as he told Bishop Hay in 1775 that was not his only fear. At bottom his objections were as much cultural as financial since 'a very great difference there visibly is between the natural disposition of our country boys and that of the Highlanders, which often occasions disagreements and quarrels and jars, to the great detriment of regular discipline'.[36]

A second debilitating factor was internal divisions over so-called 'Jansenism', to which the same lethal combination of underfunding coupled with cultural antagonisms was not unrelated, since as the present author has shown elsewhere, they underlay the quarrels which proved so divisive in the 1730s and early 1740s. Disputes which ostensibly concerned the spread of so-called Jansenist heresy on the mission had less to do with doctine than with a clash of cultures between Highlanders and Lowlanders and which made much of the fact that, though the bulk of Scottish Catholics lived in the Highlands, the majority of the priests – and the greater part of the mission's funds – were located in the Lowlands. Scottish anti-Jansenism and the financial grievances of the Highland missioners were largely one and the same thing.[37] The consequences of these troubles were considerable: pastoral activity on the mission was disrupted; the Scots College Paris incurred suspicion which never really lifted; individual missioners such as Bishop Smith likewise became the object of suspicion at Propaganda: episcopal authority was subverted; and badly needed funds were withheld from the mission by Rome, as in 1741.

A third factor which contributed significantly to the mission's failure to achieve its full potential was politics, and more particularly the ultimately disastrous attachment of Catholics to the cause of the house of Stuart. Despite the fact that the mission statutes expressly forbade involvement in politics, missionaries were Jacobites to a man. Priests such as James Carnegie acted as Jacobite secret agents.[38] Bishop Gordon encouraged the Old Pretender to rise in 1715.[39] Bishop Macdonald blessed the cause of Bonnie Prince Charlie in 1745 and appointed chaplains to his forces, who wore Highland dress, complete with sword and pistol, and were given the rank of captain. Colin Campbell fell on the field of Culloden. As has been seen, the Jacobite connection was the main justification for the maintenance of the penal legislation against Catholics, and to that extent the missionary priests were authors of their own woes.

The final defeat of the Jacobites brought disaster on the Highland mission.

Bishop Hugh Macdonald was forced to flee to France, where he became a political refugee at the Scots College and a pensioner of the French government. Many priests were arrested and imprisoned. The little seminary at Scalan was burned down and known Catholic chapels and houses suffered the same fate. Bishop Smith was obliged to go into English exile between 1747 and 1751. What made these sufferings all the more useless and galling was the cynicism in regard to religion displayed by Charles Edward Stuart, who converted to Anglicanism in 1750 and lived a wastrel, dissolute life. The failure of the 'Forty-Five probably held back the progress of the Catholic Mission in Scotland for more than a generation.

Finally, it has to be recognised that clerical shortcomings played their part in limiting the success of the missionary enterprise. The key figure on the mission was the missionary priest, but not all the missioners could be described as spiritual giants. This is a point which recusant historians rarely mention, but it has been rightly raised by Szechi in his recent article as another factor which did the mission no good. By his calculations there was a significant rate of priestly apostasies in the period 1653–1753, amounting to some 16 priests in total, of whom 11 were seculars, who accounted for 10.5% of the strength of the secular mission. It is true that 2 apostates subsequently returned to the fold but Szechi still puts the figure at 9 priests, or 8.6% of the total. Two (one of whom was the pilgrim Colin Campbell) suffered from some kind of nervous breakdown. Two others became Presbyterian ministers. Others, like John Gordon of Glencat, succumbed to the temptations of the flesh. Moreover, some of those who remained, particularly on the Highland mission, were far from exemplary models of priestly virtue, but given over to alcohol abuse.[40] To a significant degree, the story of Scottish Catholicism in the eighteenth century can be written as a story of missed opportunities, particularly in the Highlands.

REFERENCES

1. A. Bellesheim, *History of the Catholic Church of Scotland*, trans. D.O. Hunter Blair, 4 vols. (Edinburgh 1887–90), vol 4, pp. 236–7.
2. *Ibid*, p.235.
3. M. Lynch, *Scotland: A New History* (London, 1991): A Macinnes, *Clanship, Commerce and the House of Stuart* (East Linton, 1996).
4. J. Bossy, *The English Catholic Community* 1570–1850 (London 1975).
5. *Ibid*, p.194.
6. A.I. Macinnes, 'Catholic Recusancy and the Penal Laws, 1603–1707', *Records of the Scottish Church History Society*, 23 (1987), pp.27–63.
7. L. von Pastor, *History of the Popes* (London, 1938), pp.129ff.
8. C. Giblin OFM, *The Irish Franciscan Mission to Scotland 1619–1648* (Dublin, 1964).
9. P.F. Anson, *Underground Catholicism in Scotland 1622–1878* (Montrose, 1970), pp.57–9.
10. *Ibid*, p.54.

11. W. Doran, 'Bishop Thomas Nicolson: First Vicar-Apostolic 1695–1718', *Innes Review*, 39 (1988).
12. On the cultural divisions between Highland and Lowland Catholicism, see A. Roberts, 'Aspects of Highland Catholicism on Deeside', *Northern Scotland*, 10, 1990, pp.9–30.
13. C. Johnson, *Developments in the Roman Catholic Church in Scotland* 1789–1829 (Edinburgh, 1983), p.22.
14. The *Statuta* are discussed by Bellesheim, *History* vol.4, pp.168–174.
15. On Gordon, see Canon W. Clapperton, *Memoirs of Scotch Missionary Priests*, unpublished ms in the Scottish Catholic Archives (SCA) and J.F.S. Gordon, *The Catholic Church in Scotland from the Suppression of the Hierarchy to the Present Time* (Aberdeen, 1874), pp.3–6.
16. George M. Dorrian, *Hugh MacDonald (1699–173): First Vicar Apostolic of the Highland District in His Religious and Social Context* (M.Phil, University of Strathclyde, 1990).
17. John Thomson, *A History of the Scottish Mission* (unpublished manuscript, SCA).
18. The figures are discussed by D. Szechi, 'Defending the True Faith: Kirk, State, and Catholic Missioners in Scotland, 1653–1755', *The Catholic Historical Review*, 82 (1996), p.399.
19. N. MacDonald Wilby, 'The "Encrease of Popery" in the Highlands 1714–1747', *Innes Review*, 17 (1966).
20. Bishop Geddes, 'A Brief Historical Account of the Seminary of Scalan', *Innes Review*, 1963.
21. Quoted by Johnson, *Developments*, p.66.
22. The 'site of memory' concept is developed in P. Nora, ed., *Les lieux de mémoire*, 7 vols (Paris, 1984–93).
23. Blairs Letters (BL), SCA, Mr Farquarson to abbé Macpherson, 19 October 1798, quoted by Johnson, *Developments*, p.69.
24. Report of Bishop Hugh MacDonald to Propaganda Fide, 18 March 1732, quoted and translated in Bellesheim, vol 4, pp.390–1.
25. C. Johnson, *Developments*, pp.71–78.
26. W. Forbes-Leith, SJ, *Memoirs of Scottish Catholics during the xviith and the xviiith centuries* (1909), vol. 2, pp.195–6.
27. *Ibid*, p.204.
28. *Ibid*, p.194–5. See also A. MacWilliam, 'The Jesuit Mission in Upper Deeside, 1671–1737', *Innes Review*, 23 (1972).
29. Dom Odo Blundell, *The Catholic Highlands of Scotland*, 2 vols (1909, 1917), vol. 1, pp.178ff.
30. *Ibid*, p.15.
31. MacInnes, *Clanship*, p.210ff.
32. Szechi, 'Defending the True Faith', pp.397–411.
33. MacWilliam, 'The Jesuit Mission in Upper Deeside', p.36.
34. SCA, Blair's Letters, Bishop Gordon to Propaganda Fide, 17 June, 1735, stressing the fidelity of Scots Catholics to the Holy See. On the finances of the mission, see Bishop Hay, *A Full State of All Company's Funds, with a Historical Account of the Same as They Stand in the Present Year*, 1772, reproduced in J. Carman, *History of the Scottish Clerical Quota Fund* (privately printed, Girvan, 1883).
35. Quoted by A. Roberts, 'Gregor McGregor (1681–1740) and the Highland Problem in the Scottish Catholic Mission', *Innes Review*, 39 (1988), p.97.
36. Quoted by Johnson, *Developments*, p.74.
37. On Jansenism, see J.F. McMillan, 'Scottish Catholics and the Jansenist Controversy: the Case Re-opened', *Innes Review*, 32 (1981): id., 'Jansenism and Anti-Jansenism in Eighteenth-Century Scotland: The *Unigenitus* Quarrels on the Scottish Catholic Mission, 1732–1746', *Innes Review*, 39 (1988): id., 'The Root of All Evil? Money and the Scottish Catholic Mission in the Eighteenth Century', *Studies in Church History*, 24 (1987), p.267–82.
38. On Carnegie, see SCA, Clapperton, *Memoirs*.
39. SCA Bl, 13/24 August 1714, James Gordon to Thomas Innes.
40. D. Szechi, 'Defending the True Faith' *passim*.

Seven

Scotland and the Idea of Britain in the Eighteenth Century

ALEXANDER MURDOCH

RECENTLY THERE HAS BEEN an increase of interest in 'the idea of Britain' amongst professional historians, and the success of Linda Colley's study *Britons: Forging the Nation 1707–1837* (1992) has epitomized this development, the idea, and reactions to it, particularly in relation to the eighteenth century. In one sense it might be argued that Colley's argument reiterates traditional views of empire and patriotism, but this would be unjust. She has developed the abstract but brilliant insights of John Pocock, first published in a famous article, 'British History, a Plea for a New Subject', and related those ideas to 'real' social and political history.[1] Her book demonstrates that 'Britishness' was not an elite concept, but an idea which affected the lives of thousands of ordinary people in England, Wales and Scotland over the course of the eighteenth century, and that the number of people whose lives it did affect increased over the course of the eighteenth century. Britishness was an expanding idea that originated in the intense Protestant sectarianism of the 'second' protestant reformation, about which many specialists in eighteenth century British and Scottish History have less than complete knowledge. In a Scottish context, although not mentioned by Colley, the work of John Pocock's former students Arthur Williamson and Roger Mason demonstrates the intellectual pedigree of the idea, as well as the tension it created in the Scottish literary and political community over a division of loyalty towards an ancient Scottish history which acted as a kind of origin myth for the nation and the emerging sectarian British conception of protestantism as a religion and a cause.[2]

Essentially what happened in the eighteenth century was that Britishness in a Scottish, English and Welsh context ceased to be sectarian and became imperialistic; it also, to an extent which historians have been reluctant to discuss, became racist. As C.A. Bayly has pointed out, in 1750 the population of the British dominions including the American colonies had been 12.5 million at most; in 1820 population of territory under British authority was in the order of 200 million, representing something like 26 per cent of the population of the world at that date. It is interesting that the primary source for Bayly's statement is work published by Patrick Colquhoun in 1815. Colquhoun was a former provost of Glasgow who had been appointed a magistrate of London through the influence of the Scottish politician Henry Dundas in 1792. His book was an attempt to publicize the possibilities of empire after the end of the wars with France, drawing on his experiences of American and West Indian trade acquired during his years as a merchant in Glasgow. It was no mistake that it was a Scot who took this task upon himself of instructing an English speaking audience of the possibilities of British empire.[3]

The purpose of this chapter is to support Colley's and Bayly's arguments about both the popular element in the British idea as it developed over the eighteenth century, and the evangelical edge combining religious mission with imperial power which would give it such resonance not just in the emerging empire, but in Scotland itself, not least in that city created by the wealth of empire, Patrick Colquhoun's own Glasgow. In seeking to do this it does not only add support to relatively recent work that attempts to relate Scottish history to a wider British and imperial context, but to develop earlier research which has contributed to their recent work and to incorporate new work from a related project.[4] A good starting point for this purpose is the most adept of the critical reviews which have appeared of Colley's *Britons*, Edward Thompson's long piece published under the title 'Which Britons?', which argued that in one sense Colley's book incorporated nothing more than an account of the integration of elite groups in the English provinces, Wales and Scotland into the emerging British imperial state. Where Thompson encountered difficulty was that Colley produced impressive evidence supporting the proposition that by the end of the eighteenth century 'Britishness' was not just a phenomenon restricted to the emerging identity of a self-serving elite, but had become an expression of a popular movement born out of war-time patriotism which commanded the loyalty and contributed to the identity of most of the population on the island of Great Britain. Significantly, Colley never attempted to include Ireland in her argument. Although Thompson was able to produce evidence of individual dissent from patriotic wartime values on the part of, for example, men enlisted in Volunteer regiments who were later indicted for political sedition, he had to concede that by the first decade of the nineteenth century, 'the Colley thesis is probably right'.[5]

Let us consider an example Colley gives us in her book of popular British patriotism which also gives some idea of how this ideology affected Scotland at the end of the eighteenth century. Peter Laurie was the son of an East Lothian farmer who started work as a printer's apprentice in Edinburgh during the 1790's. He became embroiled in radical politics in Edinburgh as an apprentice, and as a result was packed off to London by his family and put into a less ideological calling as a saddler. Once in London Laurie transformed himself from radical into patriotic Volunteer soldier, and in the process improved his business by selling saddles and uniform belts to his fellow soldiers at discount prices. Later he used his military contacts to acquire profitable orders from the East India Company's regiments in India for similar products. 'I much disliked soldiering', he wrote in his memoirs, 'but I never failed to avail myself of any thing that should increase my business and reputation'.[6] If not quite the complete eighteenth-century precursor of Samuel Smiles, his fellow native of East Lothian, and the gospel of self-help, Laurie still ended his days as a Director of the East India Company and Lord Mayor of London, a human monument to self-help and the power of the modern Briton for endless re-invention of himself and his politics.

Another Scottish immigrant to England, Thomas Hardy, is seldom identified as a Scot by those who became fascinated by his career as Secretary of the London Corresponding Society and eminent member of the British political reform movement of the 1790s. Hardy was born in Larbert, Stirlingshire, in 1752, and brought up as a shoemaker by his maternal grandfather, Thomas Walker. His emigration to London in 1774 signified his Britishness, but did not necessarily make him less of a Scot. It is remarkable to this writer, that it was Hardy in London who pressed for English delegates to be sent to a 'National' (meaning British) Convention of the Friends of the People held in Edinburgh in November 1793. Indeed Hardy was instrumental in organising the demonstration attended by thousands of people at Hackney in London in October 1793.[7] In a similar manner in Scotland, Thomas Palmer the English Unitarian minister in Dundee represented the English and British input into Scottish radicalism as an active member of the Scottish Association of the Friends of the People, and victim of the authoritarian Scottish legal system. A British dimension which received additional emphasis when Maurice Margarot and Joseph Gerrald as delegates from England played such a key role in the so-called National Convention and the political trials in Scotland which followed its breakup by the Scottish legal authorities.[8]

Like Hardy, Thomas Spence of Newcastle and London is often seen as a quintessential English radical of the later eighteenth century, valued for his spirited response to the diatribes of Burke (he responded to Burke's dismissal of the 'swinish multitude' by calling his journal for working men *Pig's Meat*) as well as his early ideas about land nationalisation, although these were more related to traditional ideas of localised, communal landholding than any early advocacy of collectivisation. In at least one publication, Spence is presented as the personification of a distinctive radical tradition associated with the Northeast of England, but how English really were Spence's radical ideas?[9] Can they really be accommodated in an 'English' national framework? Spence was, after all, the child of Scots from Orkney and Aberdeen who had emigrated down the coast to Newcastle. In addition, while still in Newcastle, Spence had become a member of the congregation of James Murray, graduate of Edinburgh University, presbyterian dissenting minister at Morpeth and Newcastle, and a vigorous pro-American in the Newcastle-upon-Tyne area until his death in 1782. Murray has been described as descended from 'an old Covenanter family', and he embodied an anti-Erastian religious tradition with a radical analysis of the American conflict from 1765–1782 in which British colonial policy was seen as the creation of 'Tories', 'Jacobites' and 'Papists', while the American war was being fought, in his view, not by rebels but by those who were resisting the imposition of an 'era of slavery to both them and us'.[10] James Thomson's lyrics for his song *Rule Britannia* proclaimed that Britons never would be slaves. James Murray's analysis of the American war linked the Americans with the seventeenth century traditions of the Covenant and English Parliamentarianism in a deliberately inclusive, rather than nationally exclusive, appeal to the protestant British tradition of the Solemn League and Covenant of 1643.

Murray's work can be linked with that of the Scottish minister John Erskine in Edinburgh, member of the so-called Popular Party of the Church of Scotland during the eighteenth century as one of the ministers of Greyfriars' Kirk, Edinburgh. Thus Erskine's pamphlet, *Why Should I Go to War with my American Brethren?*, perhaps the best known Scottish publication in the Pro-American cause in Scotland, coincides with Erskine's own support for the agitation against the extension of Roman Catholic Relief to Scotland in 1778.[11] Just as the Americans were right to suspect the anti-libertarian and slavish motives for extending toleration to Roman Catholics under the Quebec Act, went this point of view, so Scots were fighting the same fight in opposing toleration for Roman Catholic worship in Scotland, just at a time when the British government was significantly increasing the number of Roman Catholics in the army as part of its efforts to maintain the American War. The failed attempt to extend Roman Catholic Relief to Scotland, which Robert Kent Donovan has shown was based on a deal between Henry Dundas and the Scottish Roman Catholic hierarchy to secure at least one regiment for the war effort from the Roman Catholic population in the Highlands, coincided not just with extension of relief to Roman Catholics in England, but also Ireland, where the measure was explicitly linked to the needs of military recruitment.[12]

This resistance in America, Ireland and Scotland to Roman Catholic Relief looked back to the sectarian issues of the seventeenth century and sought to perpetuate them, but also resisted the move to an imperial centralised constitution which marked British political development from 1775. This British sectarian aspect linked the Scottish Catholic Relief riots of 1779 very closely with the Gordon Riots in London during 1780, as Donovan has shown.[13] Lord George Gordon himself personified the link between the elite British imperial identity and a popular (and overtly sectarian) British popular patriotism which historians of British radicalism have been reluctant to concede existed, linking as it does 'liberty' with sectarian bigotry.[14] Negative aspects of this 'British' side of the riots were the attacks on both opposition and ministerial figures at the time, including Burke and Rockingham from the opposition and Lord North and the Scottish born Lord Chief Justice of England, Lord Mansfield. Mansfield's library was destroyed by the mob both because he was a warm advocate of Catholic Relief, which was true, and because the rumour spread through the crowd during the riots that 'he had advised the dragoons to ride over the Protestants, that he was a Roman Catholic and that he had made the King one'.[15] Murray's family in Scotland was not untainted with Jacobitism, but it has always been part of the Scottish Episcopalian tradition. Nevertheless Jacobitism in general could not but be associated with Roman Catholicism in the demonology of British politics in the third quarter of the eighteenth century.[16]

Recent studies of the public demonstrations which occurred in Scotland during the annual celebration of the King's Birthday emphasize their Hanoverian and British ethos, even when they involved the expression of plebeian resentment at patrician privilege through ritualised violence fuelled by copious amounts of alcohol.[17] The burning of effigies of John Wilkes during the Edinburgh King's Birthday celebrations were reported well into the nineteenth century, not as an expression of rejection of radical politics, but as a ritual demonstration of a rejection of Wilkite insistance on excluding Scots from inclusion in the benefits of what had become after 1707 a British constitution.[18] The Wilkite use of the numeral '45' in such elaborate and insistent ways had not been coincidence, but an emphatic rejection of the Scottish Whig tradition and its advocacy of a British rather than English political identity.[19] The intensity of Scottish reaction to the Wilkite movement therefore represented far more than reaction to political radicalism in England. It was a reaction to English chauvinism in the British political arena. Indeed when political radicalism can be associated with the mobbing prevalent in the Scottish King's Birthday riots, as in the case of Edinburgh in 1792, the violence was directed against the leaders of the native Scottish political class, Henry and Robert Dundas, rather than against the monarchy. The ideology expressed by such radicalism was that Scottish subjects of a just king were being denied their rights as Britons by the machinations of a selfish Scottish landowning elite intent on preserving their own feudal privileges in Scottish society. Hence the demonology associated with Henry Dundas, political saviour of the Scottish landowning elite, amongst Scottish Whig reformers and radicals whose agenda was frustrated for generations by his career and its legacy.[20]

There was an irony involved in this division between traditional resistance to an Erastian state, and sceptical Enlightenment rejection of the intellectual authority of both church and state in favour of legal institutions. In Scotland the landowning elite was associated with feudalism and an atavistic constitution, yet the very Enlightenment ideas so powerful in motivating American and French republicanism had in Scotland been largely the preserve of the middle class clerical and legal servants of that same landed elite. It was an ideological development which circumvented both Scottish historical traditions of feudal law and reformation religion and left them lacking in relevancy to the revolutionary developments of what was then the modern world.[21]

This division within the Socttish reform movement can be illustrated by reference to a speech given by Alexander Aitchison of Edinburgh to the second Scottish Convention of the Association of the Friends of the People in May 1793. Aitchison's speech, reported at length in the Edinburgh press, appealed to two rules of conduct beyond which, he submitted, the reform movement could not go. These he identified as the Magna Carta of England and the Claim of Right of the Scottish Convention which offered the throne of Scotland to William and Mary in 1689. These two documents, Aitchison argued, 'comprehended our rights as Britons'; but, he continued, the expression, 'our rights as men', took in a much wider range of political ideas . . . comprehending the essence of the French Constitution and Tom Paine's *Rights of Man*. While Aitchison supported universal manhood suffrage, he continued, he would not do so at the expense of encouraging anarchy. Therefore, he concluded, 'let us stick to our rights as Britons, but delete the words, "rights of man,"[22] It is interesting that Aitchison's concept of British rights included both English Magna Carta and Scottish Claim of Right, but equally interesting that the Magna Carta was taken as a guarantee of individual liberty of the subject while the Claim of Right of 1689 essentially asserted Scottish national identity on a Sectarian basis against arbitrary Stewart kings who were, unfortunately for Scottish Whigs, representatives of the ancient national dynasty, and by implication constitution, of Scotland.[23]

There are connections between Aitchison's ideology and that expressed by politicians in the burgh of Dumfries in 1760, when they confronted the political influence of the third Duke of Queensberry. There the appeal was also to the Claim of Right, as an opposition including lawyers, merchants and craftsmen appealed to constitutional rights safeguarded by the Scottish Convention of 1689.[24] While at the same time others of their supporters asserted their rights by seizing the council house on election day and singing hymns to keep their spirits up as they continued their occupation. Later, the outgoing burgh magistrates were physically attacked when they attempted to attend church in their official capacity as the burgh council of Dumfries. Yet in Dumfries the Scottish context of the Claim of Right does not explain everything about the political opposition that appealed to it, which included 'British' appeals to traditional rights of liberty and property. On the day of the disputed council election, it was later testified, Francis Maxwell of the incorporation of hammermen had displayed a length of 'sky blue ribbon' in his bonnet, and when asked, 'Frank, what call you that is about your bonnet', replied, 'I call it property and liberty, and be damned to you'.[25] What was so British about Frank Maxwell's appeal to the blue ribbon and liberty and property in Dumfries during 1760? There are interesting parallels with another example of popular protest at the time, not in Scotland but in Birmingham in 1772, when resistance by gun finishers to lower wages led to a demonstration in front of the merchant who had attempted this, where in addition to breaking his windows and singing a specially commissioned song denouncing him, seventy men staged a formal parade to dramatise their protest in which each wore a blue cockade, the colour and badge of traditional rights. The blue ribbon and the blue cockade suggested loyalty to tradition, to mutual obligation in a hierarchical society and resistance to attempts to change it.[26]

This emphasis on traditional rights across national boundaries evidenced in Aitchison's speech to the Scottish Convention of the Association of the Friends of the People in 1793, the example of political opposition to aristocratic influence in Dumfries in 1760 and the Birmingham gun finishers strike of 1772 raises the problem of how to relate the idea of Britain not just to Scottish national and historical identity, but to ideas of continuity and tradition versus change over time in Scottish society. Edward Thompson had no doubt how to relate Scotland to historical change and the idea of British History. His analysis was organized along something like the following lines. Once there was a golden age of English tradition embodied by the sturdy, independent and free English peasantry. Then came union with Scotland, of little consequence except that it provided the means for the ideas of Adam Smith to influence British government by the end of the eighteenth century, with the result that ever since the English working class and the socialist and labour movement which arose out of it has been in retreat, driven on the right by the disciples of Smith and their advocacy of market efficiency, and on the left, although this aspect of his thought is never fully developed in his writings, by Irish, and Scots and Welsh radicals whose uncompromising behaviour demonstrated that they were not capable of understanding the nuances of English exceptionalism in History, illustrated by Thompson's dismissal of the views of Tom Nairn on the British Labour Movement at one point in his political writings as those of 'a Marxist kirk elder.[!]'[27] Thompson's work embodies a rejection of the ideas of modern social and economic development associated with the Scottish Enlightenment in favour of a defence of the traditional rights identified in this essay in Aitchison's speech, the opposition at Dumfries in 1760, and the Birmingham labour unrest of 1772. Thompson's history enshrines the heroic defence of traditional rights by working people wherever evidence of their struggle has been preserved, but perhaps what makes his work so English, and hence relatively inaccessible to Welsh and Scottish social historians, is his identification of 'Old Corruption' with English ideology.[28] Yet his desire to see the British landed class as 'a sophisticated system of brigandage' prevented him from accurately identifying 'Old Corruption' as liberal reinvention of traditional institutions rather than feudalism, drawing on the ideas of the Scottish Enlightenment on the one hand and on the other, *pace* his famous attack on Methodism, the evangelical and international protestantism of late eighteenth century northern Europe and its colonial peoples; both systems of belief utterly foreign to a secular Marxist like Thompson. On both counts it would be wrong to see these developments as confirmation that British ideology and patriotism was merely a vehicle for the colonisation of English and Scottish working class culture as well as overseas empire.[29]

Support for this view has been demonstrated recently in work by the Israeli historian of British History, Dror Wahrman, who rather than take the so-called 'four nations' route to understanding British History posits a different distinction between an emerging 'national society' at the end of the eighteenth century, in contrast to a traditional 'communal culture' which was essentially local.[30] Thus Wahrman's view of the historiography abandons the perception of a metropolitan English state using its control of British ideology to colonise other nations in Britain in favour of a confrontation between national and local culture transcending the 'proto-national' and feudal identities of England, Wales and Scotland. The British national culture of Adam Smith, James Watt, the Foulis Academy of Glasgow and Sir John Sinclair's *Statistical Account of Scotland* extended outwards into traditional communities, following urban lines of communication whether it be in Northampton, Newcastle or Glasgow. It was a culture which after mid-century came to include more and more people, partly because it began to become more influential at a time when population in Britain began to grow, and as a result the population as a whole grew younger and more open to change. It included a very significant Scottish element which reinforced rather than questioned its British perspective. Nevertheless, it was a culture which excluded those who rejected its commercial ethos or did not have access to it. In Scotland this included many Gaelic speakers, certainly all those who could not speak English as well as Gaelic.[31] It also, however, excluded those like Archibald Bruce who still looked back to the seventeenth century Scottish Church of the Covenant, and emphasised doctrine and the authority of scripture rather than the new evangelical religious movement towards spirituality and self development independent of the authority of a ministry of the gospel as well as Erastian political influence.[32] Conversely those who were included in British national culture were not only the members of the Scottish elite, no matter how that term is defined. Working people were included as well as soldiers, weavers, and urban dwellers of all descriptions, a growing number of whom participated in the ever expanding culture of print by reading themselves or having access to those who read to them.[33] An important part of this new national British society was as much influenced by evangelical ideas of Christianity which were international as it was by the commercial ethos of Adam Smith.[34]

No more vivid example of this evangelical protestant Christian, rather than sectarian, British culture can be given than that of Philip Doddridge's published biography of Colonel James Gardiner of East Lothian, killed at the battle of Prestonpans in 1745 when he declined to follow his own regiment in precipitate flight before the onslaught of the Jacobite army. Philip Doddridge was a well known English dissenting minister whose academy at Northampton attracted students from English Anglican families as well as many English dissenters and Scots. It offered a 'modern' curriculum in English rather than Latin which emphasised science and philosophy rather than the Classics. Amongst the Scots who attended were David Fordyce, son of an Aberdeen merchant who became Professor of Moral Philosophy at King's College Aberdeen, and George Gillespie, who returned to Scotland to become a minister and eventually was expelled from the Church of Scotland, later to help found the so-called 'Relief' secession presbytery in Scotland in 1761. Students from the Scottish gentry included Sir Harry Munro of Foulis in Easter Ross and John Fergusson, son of the Scottish Court of Session judge Sir James Fergusson of Kilkerran.[35]

Doddridge's biography of Gardiner was written in the aftermath of news of Gardiner's death reaching England, occasioned by Doddridge's friendship with him, formed while Gardiner's dragoons were stationed in Northampton. Its appearance in 1747 might be thought to elicit little comment in this essay; Gardiner came from minor Lothian gentry stock, Doddridge was a dissenting minister in a provincial English Midlands market town. Their friendship might be thought part of the elitist rather than the more problematic popular aspect of British identity during the eighteenth century. Clearly Doddridge's little book was intended for an English audience and its message was that the '45 rebellion was not a Scottish but a Jacobite rebellion in which many Scots who were loyal Hanoverians like Gardiner lost their lives, which was why an account of his former student Munro of Foulis' family was included as an appendix to his life of Gardiner as an example of Hanoverian loyalty in the Highlands. There is even what Doddridge terms 'a pardonable aside' in the book on the origins of the 1745 rebellion, which was explained to an English readership as the result of the 'ignorance and idleness' of the Scottish Highlanders, a condition which prevented their access to the very real benefits of being a Briton, and had led them instead into Jacobite rebellion.[36]

The information related above about Doddridge's book on Gardiner could be dismissed as no more than an indication of some degree of the integration of elites on a British level, but this would not take into account evidence available regarding the probable readership of this work. The National Library of Scotland holds more than 45 editions of Doddridge's *Life of Gardiner*, from the first edition in octavo of 1747, to a London edition of 1864. Most editions were published in 12mo, 16mo or even 24mo (London, 1831), cheap editions intended for a mass market. In addition to the many editions published in Edinburgh and London, Doddridge's book was published at Wigan in 1782, at Aberdeen in 1786, Philadelphia in 1795, at Bungay in Suffolk in 1808 and 1817, at Gainsborough in 1813 and 1814, at Knaresborough in 1817 and at Halifax in West Yorkshire at the height of the years of Chartist agitation in 1841, 1844, 1850 and 1855. Clearly, noting editions of books only takes us so far in placing them in relation to their readership, but equally clearly, Doddridge's *Life of Gardiner* had become part of a protestant Christian literature which was both evangelical and *British*, illustrating the life of a Christian soldier who died defending king and country in a way which looks forward to the Britishness of David Livingstone rather than backwards to the mission of the Scottish Covenant of the seventeenth century. It originated in a British provincial culture which included Scotland, but it also included the protestant dissenting academies and congregations of Ireland, most obviously through the links represented by Francis Hutcheson and the other Irishmen who studied at Glasgow.[37]

This was a culture which established itself in Scotland during the eighteenth century not in opposition to Enlightenment culture but as a religious manifestation of it.[38] It looked outwards towards Ireland and America as well as England, although of course awareness of the legacy of Scottish presbyterianism of the seventeenth century continued to be current in Scotland. Yet many of the losses in membership of the Church of Scotland during the eighteenth century occurred not to the traditional presbyterianism of the original secession, but to congregations influenced by the evangelical Christianity of the eighteenth century which rejected the Church of Scotland as much for its Calvinism as its Moderatism, although until we have more social studies of religion in a meaningful local context it will be difficult to achieve a more precise idea of the popular manifestation of this emerging religious culture.[39] Popular religion influenced the politics and patriotism of many Scots in a way which meant that at the end of the century its landed class, retaining its authority and identity, attracted more support for its leadership in pushing for a British imperial agenda than opposition to the continuation of its dominance of the Scottish political system. After 1815 that would change, a development not unexpected by the leaders of the political elite. Much of Professor Colley's argument for the existence of a popular patriotism rested on evidence from the muster lists of Volunteer regiments indicating the extent that former radical sympathisers like Peter Laurie had become involved in the war effort. In a Scottish context as early as 1797 Henry Dundas had written to his colleague and supporter in the defence of the interests of the Scottish landed class, the third duke of Buccleuch, stating that of course the regiments of yeomanry raised for defence against possible French invasion would remain in existence at the conclusion of the war, as they would be needed to maintain order amongst the population of the expanding cities, no longer directly under the authority of a landowner.[40]

The ultimate beneficiaries during the eighteenth century of Scotland's participation in the construction of a British state were its landowning class, but they could not have succeeded in circumnavigating the difficulties they faced as a class in the second half of the eighteenth century unless they had been able to draw upon considerable popular and patriotic support in a society that witnessed rapid urbanisation and consequent industrial activity in some areas at the end of the eighteenth century, but not to such an extent that a sustainable challenge to the existing regime could have any opportunity of emerging.[41] To argue otherwise is to anticipate the politics of Victorian Scotland in the very different historical context of the eighteenth century. Nevertheless, the legacy of eighteenth century Scotland's increasing integration with the British state was the evolution of a system of concurrent identities which John Pocock identified in 1974 and which T.C. Smout discussed in a Strathclyde seminar of 1988.[42] That concurrent relationship between Scottish and British identities was created in the second half of the eighteenth century in Scotland, and subsequently exported to England and the rest of the second British Empire. Through it Scots who adopted British national culture as part of their identity were able to retain not just a distinctive identity as Scots and Britons, but a sense of superiority as a poor but virtuous people, morally superior both to the luxury-ridden degeneration of metropolitan England and the primitive underdevelopment of traditional Scottish rural society, Gaelic or Scots speaking, which continued to exist in much of the country.[43] This was not a development imposed from without but one invented from within, and its impact on the history of Scotland in the eighteenth century and after has yet to be fully explored.

The author would like to acknowledge receipt of a British Academy Research Leave Award held while an employee of Nene College of Higher

Education Corporation, Northampton, England, from January to June 1995 and to record his appreciation of the efforts made by those at the college who attempted to ensure that he benefited from this award, particularly its Director, Dr. S. Martin Gaskell.

REFERENCES

1. John Pocock, 'British History: A Plea for a New Subject', *Journal of Modern History*, 47 (1975); several times updated, most recently in 'Conclusion: Contingency, Identity, Sovereignty' in Alexander Grant and Keith J. Stringer (eds.), *Uniting the Kingdom?: The Making of British History* (London, 1995).
2. Arthur H. Williamson, *Scottish National Consciousness in the Age of James VI* (Edinburgh, 1979); A.H. Williamson, 'Scotland, Antichrist and the Invention of Great Britain' in J. Dwyer, R.A. Mason and A. Murdoch (eds.), *New Perspectives on the Politics and Culture of Early Modern Scotland* (Edinburgh, 1982); [R.A. Mason] 'Introduction', in J. Dwyer et al (eds.), *New Perspectives*; Roger A. Mason (ed.), *Scots and Britons: Scottish Political Thought and the Union of* 1603 (Cambridge, 1994).
3. Christopher A. Bayly, *Imperial Meridian: The British Empire and the World,* 1780–1830 (London, 1989), p.3, for perceptive comments on race and the British Empire see pp.7, 136–147; on Colquhoun see the *DNB* and T.M. Devine and G. Jackson (eds.), *Glasgow Volume I: Beginnings to* 1830 (Manchester, 1995), pp.250, 293 38; 312.
4. Linda Colley, 'The People Above in Eighteenth-Century Britain', *The Historical Journal*, 24 (1981), pp.971–979; L. Colley, *Britons*, pp.106, 118, 141; Alexander Murdoch, *The People Above: Politics and Administration in Mid-Eighteenth-Century Scotland* (Edinburgh, 1980), p.133; John Dwyer and A. Murdoch, 'Paradigms and Politics: Manners, Morals and the Rise of Henry Dundas, 1770–1784', in J. Dwyer et al (eds.), *New Perspectives*, pp.210–211, 215–216, 238–243; J. Dwyer and A. Murdoch, 'Henry Dundas Revisited but Not Revised', *Studies on Voltaire and the Eighteenth Century*, 256 (1988), pp.325–33; A. Murdoch, 'Lord Bute, James Stuart Mackenzie and the Government of Scotland' in Karl Schweizer (ed.), *Lord Bute: Essays in Re-interpretation* (Leicester, 1988), p.140.
5. Edward P. Thompson, 'Which Britons?', *Dissent*, (Summer 1993), reprinted in E. Thompson, *Persons and Polemics* (London, 1994); also see Thompson's reaction to Geoffrey Best's, 'The making of the English Working Class', *Historical Journal*, 8 (1965) in the 'Postscript' first published with his *The Making of the English Working Class* when it appeared in paperback (Harmondsworth, 1968).
6. Colley, *Britons*, pp.301–2.
7. *DNB*; Thompson, *Making of the English Working Class* (paperback edn 1968), pp.19–22, 31, 132–4, 145–50; particularly p.31: 'Thomas Hardy gained some of his first experiences of organization in the factional struggles of the Presbyterian congregation in Crown Court, off Russell Street.'
8. William Ferguson, *Scotland: 1689 to the present* (Edinburgh and London, 1968), pp.258–9, 261; Elaine W. McFarland, *Ireland and Scotland in the Age of Revolution* (Edinburgh, 1994), p.105, quoting Palmer's hope, expressed in a letter written to a colleague in Dublin, that he hoped in time to return to 'my country', by which he meant 'Britain'; also see p.160 on continuing links between the London Corresponding Society with Scotland.
9. Harry T. Dickinson (ed.), *The Political Works of Thomas Spence* (Newcastle, 1982), p.vii; Dickinson, *The Politics of the People in Eighteenth-Century Britain* (Basingstoke, 1995), pp.184–5, 188–9, 231, 241, 247, 249.
10. Dickinson (ed.), *Works of Spence*, p.viii; J.C.D. Clark, *The Language of Liberty* 1660–1832 (Cambridge, 1994), pp.329–31.
11. Robert Kent Donovan, *No Popery and Radicalism: Opposition to Roman Catholic Relief in Scotland,* 1778–1782 (New York, 1987), pp.82–83, 92, 176, 178, 272; Robert Kent Donovan,

'The Popular Party of the Church of Scotland and the American Revolution' in R.B. Sher and J.R. Smitten (eds.), *Scotland and America in the Age of Enlightenment* (Edinburgh, 1990), pp.84–85, 89–90, 97.

12. R.K. Donovan, 'The Military Origins of the Roman Catholic Relief Programme of 1778', *The Historical Journal*, 28 (1985), pp.90–92, 95–96; R.B. McDowell, *Ireland in the Age of Imperialism and Revolution* 1760–1801 (Oxford, 1979, reissued 1991), pp.184, 189.
13. Donovan, 'Military Origins', pp.100–101.
14. Donovan, *No Popery*, pp.xi, 6–7, 313; Donovan, 'Popular Party', p.94.
15. George Rudé, 'The Gordon Riots', originally published in *The Transactions of the Royal Historical Society*, 5th series, VI (1956), reprinted in Rudé, *Paris and London in the Eighteenth Century: Studies in Popular Protest* (paperback edn London, 1974), pp.272–73.
16. Colley, *Britons*, pp.110–11; Daniel Szechi, *The Jacobites* (Manchester, 1994), p.133; Allan I. Macinnes, *Clanship, Commerce and the House of Stuart*, 1603–1788 (East Linton, 1996), pp.180–81.
17. Christopher A. Whatley, 'Royal Day, People's Day: The Monarch's Birthday in Scotland, c1660–1860' in Roger Mason and Norman Macdougall (eds.), *People and Power in Scotland* (Edinburgh, 1992), pp.170, 174, 178, 180, 183.
18. *Ibid*, p. 83; A. Murdoch, 'Lord Bute' in Schweizer (ed.), *Lord Bute*, pp.138–40.
19. John Brewer, 'The Number '45: A Wilkite Political Symbol' in Stephen Baxter (ed.), *England's Rise to Greatness* 1660–1763 (Berkeley, 1983), pp.351, 356, 367.
20. Whatley, 'Royal Day', p.183; Kenneth J. Logue, *Popular Disturbances in Scotland* 1780–1815 (Edinburgh, 1979), pp.8–9, 133–43; Michael Fry, *The Dundas Despotism* (Edinburgh, 1992), pp.167–68; David J. Brown, 'Henry Dundas and the Government of Scotland' (University of Edinburgh Ph.D. thesis, 1989), pp.167–68.
21. This issue has not yet been explicitly addressed by historians but it is implicit in Colin Kidd's brilliant book, *Subverting Scotland's Past: Scottish Whig Historians and the Creation of an Anglo-British Identity*, 1689-c.1830 (Cambridge, 1993), especially chapters 8 and 9; Colin Kidd, 'North Britishness and the Nature of Eighteenth-Century British Patriotisms', *The Historical Journal*, 39 (1996), pp.361–82. From another perspective work by John Brims illustrates the same point, 'The Scottish "Jacobins", Scottish Nationalism and the British Union' in Roger A. Mason (ed.), *Scotland and England* 1286–1815 (Edinburgh, 1987); and John Brims, 'The Covenanting Tradition and Scottish Radicalism in the 1790's' in Terry Brotherstone (ed.), *Covenant, Charter, and Party: Traditions of Revolt and Protest in Modern Scottish History* (Aberdeen, 1989). For comparative purposes a historians of Scotland would find much of interest in John Murrin, 'A Roof Without Walls: The Dilemma of American National Identity' in Richard Beeman et al (eds.), *Beyond Confederation: Origins of the Constitution and American National Identity* (Chapel Hill, 1987), pp.333–48; and Edmund S. Morgan, *Inventing the People: The Rise of Popular Sovereignty in England and America* (New York, 1988).
22. quoted in John D. Brims, 'The Scottish Democratic Movement in the Age of the French Revolution' (University of Edinburgh Ph.D., 1983), p.414.
23. The text of the Claim of Right is available in W. Croft Dickinson and Gordon Donaldson (eds.), *A Source Book of Scottish History* (Edinburgh, 1954), Vol. 3, pp.200–7. It has of course been appealed to many times in Scottish History, for example at the time of the Disruption of the Church of Scotland in 1843: see Stewart J. Brown, *Thomas Chalmers and the Godly Commonwealth* (Oxford, 1982), pp.328–32.
24. A. Murdoch, 'Politics and the People in the Burgh of Dumfries, 1758–1760', *The Scottish Historical Review*, 70 (1991), p.158.
25. *Ibid*, p.159.
26. Clive Behagg, 'Custom, Wealth and the Continuity of Small Scale Production', a paper given at a conference held at the University of Liverpool 27–28 March 1995: 'Conflict and Change in English Communities and Regions', citing Galton Papers, 550, 552; also see A.J. Randall, 'The Industrial Moral Economy of the Gloucestershire Weavers in the Eighteenth Century' in J. Rule (ed.), *British Trade Unionism*, 1750–1850 (London, 1988), and A.J. Randall, *Before the Luddites* (Cambridge, 1991).

27. Edward Thompson, 'The Peculiarities of the English', an essay which first appeared in 1965 in *The Socialist Register*, edited by Ralph Milibrand and John Saville, consulted here in E.P. Thompson, *The Poverty of Theory and Other Essays* (London, 1978), p.65. Also see pp.58–59, 62–3, 74, 77, 78, 80 38; 82 of the same essay, which varies considerably in its use of the terms 'English' and 'British'.
28. See E.P. Thompson, *Customs in Common* (London, 1991), pp.29–30, 43–44, 86–87, 90, 92, all of which refer exclusively to England, and compare them with Thompson's brief and unacknowledged, in the assumption that it was universally known, quotation from Burns on p.96. Also see Thompson, 'Peculiarities of the English', pp.49–50, 52, 56.
29. Thompson, 'Peculiarities of the English', p.48; *Customs in Common*, pp.29–30, 162, 201, 202–4, 207–8, 261, 268–71, 273–84, 287, 288, 296, 303; *Making of the English Working Class*, chapters 2 38; 11, and the 'Postscript' first published in the paperback edition of 1968, pp.917–23; 'Which Britons?' in *Persons and Polemics*, pp. 328–31; David Eastwood, 'E.P. Thompson, Britain, and the French Revolution', *History Workshop Journal*, 39 (1995), pp.78–88.
30. Dror Wahrman, 'National Society, Communal Culture: An Argument about the Recent Historiography of Eighteenth-Century Britain', *Social History*, 17 (1992), especially pp.52–53, 70–71, which can be followed up in chapters 1 and 2 of Dror Wahrman, *Imagining the Middle Class: The Political Representation of Class in Britain, c.*1780–1840 (Cambridge, 1995).
31. Charles W.J. Withers, 'Kirk, Club and Culture Change: Gaelic Chapels, Highland Societies and the Urban Gaelic Subculture in Eighteenth-Century Scotland', *Social History*, 10 (1985); Charles W.J. Withers, *Highland Communities in Dundee and Perth,* 1787–1891: A Study in the Social History of Migrant Highlanders (Dundee, 1986).
32. Ned C. Landsman, 'Evangelists and Their Hearers: Popular Interpretation of Revivalist Preaching in Eighteenth-Century Scotland', *Journal of British Studies*, 28 (1989).
33. Alexander Murdoch and Richard Sher, 'Literary and Learned Culture' in T.M. Devine and R. Mitchison (eds.), *People and Society in Scotland, Volume I,* 1760–1830 (Edinburgh, 1988), pp.127–30, 133–38.
34. Ned C. Landsman, 'Presbyterians and Provincial Society: The Evangelical Enlightenment in the West of Scotland, 1740–1775' in J. Dwyer and R.B. Sher (eds.), *Sociability and Society in Eighteenth-Century Scotland* (Edinburgh, 1993).
35. Peter Jones, 'The Polite Academy and the Presbyterians, 1720–1770' in J. Dwyer et al (eds.), *New Perspectives*, pp.159–171; James Fergusson, *John Fergusson* 1727–1750 (London, 1948), pp.26–35, 52–55, 91–2, 182, 200, 205; Ian R.M. Mowat, *Easter Ross* 1750–1850: *The Double Frontier* (Edinburgh, 1981), p.133.
36. Philip Doddridge, *Some Remarkable Passages in the Life of Col. James Gardiner, who was slain at the Battle of Prestonpans, September* 21, 1745. With an appendix relating to the antient family of the Munros of Fowlis (London, 1747), pp.239–41.
37. Ian McBride, 'The School of Virtue: Francis Hutcheson, Irish Presbyterians and the Scottish Enlightenment' in D. George Boyce, Robert Eccleshall and Vincent Geoghegan (eds.), *Political Thought in Ireland Since the Seventeenth Century* (London, 1993), pp.73–99,
38. Landsman, 'Presbyterians and Provincial Society', pp.195–96; Ned C. Landsman, 'Witherspoon and the Problem of Provincial Identity in Scottish Evangelical Culture', in Sher and Smitten (eds.), *Scotland and America*, pp.29–45.
39. Callum Brown, *The Social History of Religion in Scotland Since 1730* (London, 1987, reissued 1996), pp.109, 112, 136–37, 140; Brown, 'Religion and Social Change' Devine and Mitchison (eds.), *People and Society*, pp.150–1, 155; Brown, 'Protest in the Pews' in T.M. Devine (ed.), *Conflict and Stability in Scottish Society* 1700–1850 (Edinburgh, 1990), especially p.87; R.H. Campbell, 'The Influence of Religion on Economic Growth in Scotland in the Eighteenth Century' in T.M. Devine and David Dickson (eds.), *Ireland and Scotland* 1600–1850 (Edinburgh, 1983), pp.223–24, 227, 231–32.
40. David J. Brown, 'Henry Dundas and the Government of Scotland', pp.201–2. I am very grateful to Dr. Brown, now of the Scottish Record Office, for discussing this point with me.

41. T.M. Devine, 'The Failure of Radical Reform in Scotland in the Late Eighteenth Century: the Social and Economic Context' in Devine (ed.), *Conflict and Stability*, especially pp.54–57; N.T. Phillipson, *The Scottish Whigs and the Reform of the Court of Session* 1785–1830 (Edinburgh, The Stair Society, 1990), pp.1–41, 165, 183; N.T. Phillipson, 'Nationalism and Ideology' in J.N. Wolfe, ed., *Government and Nationalism in Scotland* (Edinburgh, 1969), pp.167–88; Fry, *Dundas Despotism*, pp.99–241.
42. Pocock, 'British History', pp.614–617; T.C. Smout, 'Problems of Nationalism, Identity and Improvement in later Eighteenth-Century Scotland' in T.M. Devine (ed.), *Improvement and Enlightenment* (Edinburgh, 1989), pp.1–21; Linda Colley, 'Britishness and Otherness: An Argument', *Journal of British Studies*, 31 (1992), pp.314–16; Smout has developed Pocock's ideas with a focus on modern Scotland in T.C. Smout, 'Perspectives on the Scottish Identity', *Scottish Affairs*, No. 6 (Winter 1994), pp.101–13.
43. J. Dwyer and A. Murdoch, 'Paradigms and Politics', pp.214–20, 230–37; Dwyer and Murdoch, 'Henry Dundas Revisited', pp.325–33; R.B. Sher, *Church and University in the Scottish Enlightenment* (Edinburgh, 1985), pp. 213–61; Colin Kidd, *Subverting Scotland's Past*, pp. 205–15; N.T. Phillipson, *Hume* (1989), pp.53–75, 140–41.

Eight

Keeping the Covenant: Scottish National Identity

RICHARD J. FINLAY

THE PERIOD FROM 1707 to 1832 was one of profound economic, social, cultural and, ultimately, political change. There are few eras in Scottish history which have witnessed such a complete transformation as the nation metamorphosed from a rural, subsistence society to one which was commercial, urban and, increasingly, industrial.[1] Even the iron grip of the Scottish governing classes began to falter as the forces of the 'new' middle-classes prepared an assault on the bastions of aristocratic privilege, which were breached with the passing of the Great Reform Act in 1832.[2] Whereas, the Scots, on their own admission, 'had contributed little to the progress of civilization' in the period before the Union, the latter half of the eighteenth century witnessed a prolific outpouring of Scottish genius.[3] That Scotland in 1830 was a very different place from what it had been in 1707, few would dispute. Nor would many historians challenge the reasons and the dynamic which produced this transformation. After much ground-breaking work, there is a reasonable degree of consensus on most of these issues.[4] There is, however, less agreement regarding the vexed question of Scottish identity. Its ephemeral nature and the concept's intangible qualities has meant that the authority of empirical testing, which has characterized so much of the scholarship on eighteenth century Scotland, cannot be called upon for a Solomon like judgment. Instead, the reader is faced with a variety of historical explanations; some more convincing than others.

The debate is dominated by an attempt to resolve the relationship of Scottish identity to the emergence of the newly created British state and the evolution of its particular national identity. Marxists have the simplest and easiest explanation, though probably the least convincing. It is argued that national identity is a bourgeois construct which does not figure until the time of the French revolution. So for most of the eighteenth century, the Scots do not have a national identity until one is invented for them in the period of the turn of the nineteenth century. Apart from displaying an appalling ignorance of Scottish history and the popular character and mass participation of the Anglo Scottish Wars of the fourteenth century, the Reformation, the

Covenanting Wars and the evidence of medieval and early modern popular culture, the analysis is crude and rudimentary and does not command, nor deserve, serious attention from most historians.[5] For many, the answer lies in concentric loyalties, i.e. the Scots could be loyal to both their Scottish and British identities without any sense of contradiction. Indeed, this sophisticated model allows the Scots to compartmentalize their national identities into appropriate categories. For example, the Scot could regard himself or herself as Scottish when it came to an identification with a particular locality and culture, yet could think of himself or herself as British when it came to issues concerning the empire, foreign policy or the Crown.[6] In many ways, this is a more convincing explanation of the duality of eighteenth century Scottish identity than the notion of cultural schizophrenia, which tends to be judgmental in its attitude by expecting Scots to be *either* Scottish *or* British and implicitly suggests that the ability to combine both was evidence of a flawed society.[7]

Whereas, the Union of 1707 deserves little more than a footnote in the grand sweep of English history, the same cannot be said of Scotland. England retained its sense of historical continuity, but few could argue that the Union was not a dramatic turning point in the history of Scotland.[8] It is only in recent times that historians have become aware of the British dimension in English history and Linda Colley's acclaimed study of the 'forging' of British identity in the eighteenth century was an attempt to address this neglect. For Colley, British identity was built on the common strands of Protestantism, shared economic priorities, the monarchy and a fear of the Catholic, continental 'other'.[9] While offering an attractive and simple explanation, a number of significant problems remain with this thesis. Firstly, as with others who have studied this question, there is a tendency to focus on the intellectuals and elites of society.[10] While this is valuable in itself, it cannot be taken for granted that this represented the values and ideas of the people. A critical aspect of national identity must be the fact that it has to have a vision of the nation with which most of the nation can identify. This problem is further compounded in the Scottish case by the fact that popular nationalism has a significant historical pedigree before the eighteenth century. An elitist examination of national identity runs the danger that it ignores important lines of historical continuity. A second related problem is that the British nation had only a minimal impact on most Scots throughout the eighteenth century.[11] If the economic benefits of Union were slow in appearing, it can be argued that the appearance of British identity was even slower. Indeed, the Scottish intellegensia only actively work towards the creation of a north British identity in the second half of the century. The fact that it had to be constructed by intellectuals reveals that it was not a natural evolution. Furthermore, and this is most significant, the idea of North Britain was a failure. By the early nineteenth century the idea had gone out of fashion and it is questionable whether it had any significant popular following. A third and final problem with the issue of British identity in eighteenth century Scotland, is that it either ignores or relegates the fact that there were different competing versions of Scottish identity and that these visions of Scottishness were arguably more important than the abstract notion of Britain which was the concern of a narrow elite.

It is the purpose of this essay to argue that religion was central to Scottish national identity in the eighteenth century. Although much research on this issue has yet to be done, there is enough evidence to suggest that the case of Scottish identity in the eighteenth century needs to be reopened and that modern day historians' obsessions with the emergence of the British state and the role of intellectuals in eighteenth century Scottish society have obscured the importance of an issue which used to be considered important but has, in recent times, gone out of fashion. There are two principal reasons why religion should be put at the heart of the debate on eighteenth century Scottish identity. Firstly, even in spite of evidence to show that church attendance in pre-industrial society was not as high as was once thought, religious beliefs had a much greater impact on the lives of most Scots than abstract political concepts. The Kirk remained a powerful force in local government, education and culture. In short, it pervaded Scottish society in the eighteenth century in a way that was unmatched by any other institution. Secondly, religion was conceived as a 'national' project. The settlement of 1690 left the Presbyterians as the established 'national' church with full territorial rights to extend its influence throughout the land. The displacement of Episcopalianism as the national church remained a grievance in the North East and the Jacobite project was closely allied with plans to extend and restore the Episcopalians to their rightful position. Although it is tempting to project Scotland in the eighteenth century as a nation divided between Episcopalianism and Presbyterianism, there were in fact three competing claims on national identity, each of which was bound up with a particular religious vision of the nation. There was the Episcopalian Jacobite vision, the Moderate Presbyterian vision and the radical Covenanting Presbyterian vision. While many studies have focused on the issue of religious divisions in Scotland in the eighteenth century, the relationship of this to national identity has largely been ignored.

In many ways, the Jacobites are the most easy to deal with. Firstly, while much attention has focused on nationalist iconography in Jacobite studies, the fact remains that the movement failed in its programme of national mobilization and was unable to break out of its Highland/North East ghetto.[12] Overt resistance in the West and largely passive resistance in the East Lowlands demonstrated that Jacobitism was handicapped by the fact that it was a minority movement which was located in the periphery of Scotland. While Jacobitism could call upon its own vision of the Scottish past and its own ideas of Scottish nationhood, it could not break the alternative visions of national identity in the lowlands which were supplied by the Covenanting legacy of the seventeenth century and the triumph of Presbyterianism in 1690. Indeed, these had been forged in opposition to Stewart 'Catholic despotism' and the defence of Presbyterian liberties. After the 1715 rebellion, the city of Glasgow increasingly identified itself with the cult of William of Orange as the liberator from 'popery and slavery' and the victor of the Presbyterian triumph.[13] Furthermore, as the social and economic transformation of Scotland in the eighteenth century gathered pace, the traditional heartland of Jacobite support was subject to increasing marginalization as the central belt became more dominant. As Jacobitism had ceased to be an effective military and political force after 1746, the real conflict over Scotland's religious and national identity was between the Covenanting and Moderate vision of Presbyterianism and it is this conflict which is the main focus of this essay.

In many ways, the Covenanting tradition had a head start.[14] The movement had mobilized a national effort in the seventeenth century and while focused on religion, the Covenanting language was replete with images of nationhood. Scotland as a nation, was covenanted with God.[15] In terms of conceptionalization, and almost in practice, the Covenanters had created a 'national' church.[16] Central to this vision was the idea of the 'Godly Commonwealth' which arguably received legitimization in 1690. Whatever the leaders of Scottish and English society may have thought of it, especially in terms of its theocratic and radical tendencies, it was powerful enough to ensure its accommodation to allow the passage of the Union in 1707.[17]

Thanks largely to Jacobite propagandists, the dangerous qualities of the Covenanting tradition were well known to the ruling elite. Attention focused on the activities of the Cameronians, an extremist faction of the Covenanting movement which had dangerous republican tendencies. Furthermore, it was claimed that the unconstitutional and violent nature of the Covenanting movement had been absorbed by the Church of Scotland.[18] To accommodate the Church to the changed political circumstances of the Union and the changing intellectual environment engendered with the Enlightenment, attempts were made to 'modify' the Presbyterian tradition. Wodrow, in his *History of the Sufferings of the Church of Scotland*, played down the influence of seventeenth century radicals and passed them off as extremists who were not representative of the movement as a whole. It was an endeavour to portray the Covenanting tradition as one of 'civic constitutionalism' as Presbyterians had taken to arms only after patient suffering in an act of self defence to preserve civil values. Yet, as critics pointed out, Covenanting was not repudiated, nor was the radicalism of Samuel Rutherford disowned.[19] Wodrow's *History* demonstrated a clear effort to reinvent the Scottish religious tradition into one more suited to the changed political and intellectual environment of the early eighteenth century.

At the same time as the Covenanting tradition was facing an intellectual assault from both within and without the Kirk, patronage was introduced in 1712 which enabled the governing classes to monitor and select the type of minister for churches. Efforts were made to promote those of a more gentile and 'moderate' leaning against those who were branded as 'wild' and fanatical. Evidence of the influence of the power of the Covenanting tradition can been seen in the early secessionist church which avowed that patronage went against the Covenanting tradition. According to Ebenezer Erskine, the leader of the Seceders, he was upholding true Presbyterian principles and was leaving because of 'the prevailing party in this established church . . . who are carrying on a course of defection from our reformed and covenanted principles'.[20] Erskine was able to tap into covenanting memories and utilized the services of the evangelical preacher, George Whitefield, to good effect. Firm endeavours were made to impress upon their evangelical guest the Covenanting principles and the purity of the seceders cause, although Whitfield was reluctant to support their claims. This led to a fall out with Erskine denouncing Whitefield as a 'wild enthusiast, who was engaged in doing the work of Satan'.[21] Yet, the visit did set a template which brought evangelicalism and the Covenanting tradition together. The revival at Cambuslang in 1742 was a great success which attracted about 30,000 people. Yet, much of this success can be explained by the fact that it was an area with a strong Covenanting tradition and a record of patronage disputes. Indeed, Sir John Clerk of Penicuik described the whole affair as a 'gadding after conventicles'.[22] As the eighteenth century wore on, patronage disputes became more frequent and increasingly bitter.[23] While patronage was used to reassert ideological control and promote Moderatism in the Church, the intellectual endeavours continued to reinvent the Scottish Presbyterian and Reformation tradition along lines which were more conducive to the cultural and political climate of the Enlightenment.[24] The leader of the Moderates, William Robertson, discredited Presbyterian radicalism in his history of Scotland and referred to Covenanting as having its origins in banditry. Furthermore, for good measure, he claimed that 1638 and 1643 advanced violent and unconstitutional methods.[25] His message was plain, the Covenanters of the seventeenth century were not an appropriate model for the Enlightenment constitutionalism of the eighteenth century.

While many historians have focused on the dramatic changes associated with religious outlook in the era of Enlightenment, less attention has been paid to the remarkable degree of continuity. It is easy to describe the rise of

Moderatism as a rationalist reaction to the bigoted fanaticism of the seventeenth century.[26] Yet, the Moderates were quite circumspect in holding on to certain traditions and, as will be argued, endeavoured to present their claims as the legitimate outcome of the Presbyterian inheritance. Rather than a break with the past, the Moderate vision was a reinvention of the Scottish reformation tradition. As David Allan has pointed out, Moderatism has its roots in the Scottish Calvinist/Humanist tradition and the tensions which these two apparently contradictory philosophies generated.[27] While there has been much talk about the decline of Calvinism, it is more accurate to talk about the modification of Calvinism in eighteenth century Scotland. The relationship between rational observation and Calvinism has been well charted and the emphasis on order and structure was another feature which entered into the mainstream of eighteenth century Scottish intellectual thought.[28] Hugh Blair was a great advocate of stoicism, which had echoes of a Calvinist tradition in Scotland. His campaign for a Militia was rooted in the belief that it would act against the growth of effeminacy, vice, corruption and laziness.[29] Echoes of Calvinist predestination are to be found in the writings of Adam Smith and the 'invisible' hand of historical change.[30] Furthermore, Moderates related political developments to the will of God and, drawing on natural theology to show the perfection and ordered structure of the universe, applied this to the hierarchical society to provide an intellectual vindication of the status quo. The American Revolution, for example, was cited as evidence of God's wrath against a society which had become corrupt and vicious.[31] This and other similar messages were delivered within the traditional framework of Presbyterian oratory which was regarded as an essential tool of any minister's trade.[32] While much attention has been focused on the rise of rational thought in the Enlightenment, less attention has been devoted to the fundamental religious underpinning which dominated it. The Moderate objective was still to maintain a Godly society and the best way to achieve this was through order and structure. The action of the Covenanters had brought Scottish society to a state of chaos in the endeavour to create the Godly Commonwealth.[33] The Moderates never eschewed the idea of the Godly society, they rejected the Covenanting tradition as a means to achieve it.

Although the Moderates were able to exert great influence over Scottish society, they were unable to eradicate the Covenanting tradition. There is ample evidence to the popularity of works by Rutherford, Shields and Boston in the lower echelons of society.[34] Popular texts such as *Scots Worthies*, recited Scotland's Reformation tradition in an accessible form and did not omit any of the most zealous Covenanters.[35] Glasgow, as the nation's fastest growing city was stronghold of the Covenanting tradition and contemporaries talked about the 'gloomy, enthusiastical cast' which inflicted the common people.[36] Further evidence can be cited from the survival of oral testament and folk memory, which was utilized to great effect by Robert Burns and Sir Walter Scott.[37] As has been shown, there is strong evidence to show that the memories and the traditions of the Covenanters were a principle source of motivation for the secessionist churches of the early eighteenth century. Patronage, which was to remain the running sore in Scottish ecclesiastical establishment, was frequently denounced as a betrayal of the Covenanting tradition. If memories of the Covenanters were important in fueling anti-patronage sentiment, then it must be acknowledged that this group constituted almost a third of Presbyterian adherents by 1820.[38] Whatever the claims of the Moderates, the Scottish religious success story of the eighteenth century were the seceders. Furthermore, this figure becomes more impressive when we take into account the fact that the Evangelicals in the Established Church of Scotland constituted a majority by 1833. Again this is clear evidence of how the Covenanting tradition was allied to contemporary concerns regarding patronage as a betrayal of Scotland's religious inheritance. Free Church propaganda made great play of the fact that it represented the true Reformation and Covenanting tradition which was reinforced by liberal use of pictures of martyrs being burned at the stake and the signing of the National Covenant. [39]

Central to the debate of religion in Scottish society in the eighteenth century has been the 'decline of Calvinism'.[40] This has been noted both in the rise of Moderatism and in the rise of Evangelicalism. Yet, little attention has focused on the theological implications of this and less attention has been paid to important lines of continuity. Firstly, Calvinism has been used as a shorthand term to describe religious fanaticism. Secondly it has been obsessed with notions of the elect. In many ways it is easy to see not so much the demise of Calvinism in eighteenth century Scotland, but rather its modification and transformation. We have already noticed that the Moderates utilized the rationalist components of Calvinism to great effect. What is more contentious is the idea that Evangelicalism was driven by a desire to convert all and that redemption was universal. In many ways there is no sense of contradiction here. Firstly, conversion could be tied to notions of restoring the Godly Commonwealth. As members of the elect, it was a duty to bring all in the Covenanted nation of Scotland to Christ and to ensure that society as a whole obeyed His commandments. This 'national' aspect of the programme is often overlooked in the description of Scottish Calvinism as being the preoccupation of individuals who are obsessed in trying to find out if they are saved. Secondly, the conversion of others could furnish evidence that an individual was an instrument of God and thus one of the elect. While it is no doubt the case that Arminianism did exert a greater influence among the evangelicals, it is by no mean obvious that older precepts and ideas such as upholding the Godly Commonwealth and proving one's elect status as an instrument of God were abandoned. This is an area which is crying out for further research.

While it has been fashionable to look for socio-economic factors in the disputes over patronage, the fact remains that the stalwart opponents of patronage were the winners in the changing socio-economic circumstances of eighteenth century Scotland. Dissent was most strongly supported by the growing commercial middle-class who could tap into anti-aristocratic sentiment of which the Covenanting tradition was replete.[41] In Glasgow, the presence of many self-made men in the ranks of the Seceders is striking. While much attention has focused on the Moderates, less has focused on the Evangelicals and there has been a tendency to record little more that the accusations which were often leveled against them. Known as the 'wild' party, Evangelicals were denounced for their intolerance and fanaticism.[42] Witherspoon, for example, would often use the language of liberty in both his denunciations of Moderatism and his support for the American revolution.[43] Arguably, it was the rise of the commercial middle-class which did most to further the image of the Covenanting tradition. This aspect of class conflict between the new aspiring bourgeoisie and the aristocracy has been well noted by historians of ecclesiastical disputes in the eighteenth century. What has been less studied is the relationship between ideas of the Covenanting tradition and the middle-class assault on the citadels of aristocratic patronage. The middle class appealed to the values of hard work and the covenant of Adam. The radical and anti-aristocratic strain in the Covenanting Tradition could be utilized for contemporary assaults on aristocratic privilege and patronage. Notions such as the equality of souls and the theocratic elements of Covenanting had a direct appeal to middle class aspirations. Evidence of this can be seen from the fact that it was the middle class who formed the vanguard of the Evangelical movement.

The anti-Catholic riots of 1779 provide some of the clearest evidence of the survival of the Covenanting tradition. Why the Scottish population should have risen up in protests at the attempt by Henry Dundas to repeal penal legislation against the Catholics in Scotland is not clear. Firstly, the Catholic population was extremely small and could not be conceived in any way to pose a threat to the population. Secondly, although Episcopalian demagogues may have tried to draw fire away from their own precarious position by targeting Catholics, and in this endeavour they were supported by Presbyterian fundamentalists, this does not entirely explain the extent and ferocity of the riots, nor does it explain why the Moderate leadership should have been targeted by the mob.[44] Anti-Catholic pamphlets may have initiated the spark, but it does not explain the intensity of the heat which was generated. One possible explanation is to borrow E.P. Thompson's idea of the 'moral' economy of the crowd and adapt it to notions of religion and tradition.[45] Popular disturbances in Scotland had a tradition of being motivated by a sense of injustice and betrayal which contravened the accepted moral limitations of the crowd.[46] Upholding tradition was also an important feature of popular celebrations and riots.[47] If a grain merchant was hoarding grain to raise the price, it was seen as immoral and thus a target for direct action. The same type of argument could be applied to the anti-Catholic riots. Anti-Catholicism was deeply embedded in the traditions and psyche of the lowland mob. The attempt to introduce toleration would be seen as a betrayal of this tradition which was beyond the limitations of acceptable conduct. Given that anti-Catholicism had a historical and official legitimacy, the attempt to introduce toleration would be seen a violation of accepted conventions and would justify the direct action which was taken. According to Howie's historical account: 'Charles II being dead and the Duke of York a professed Papist being proclaimed . . . Renwick could not let this opportunity of witnessing against the usurpation of a Papist government of the nation and his design to overturn the Covenanted work of the Reformation and introducing Popery'.[48] Catholic toleration could also be seen to violate traditional concepts of liberty, in that the official restoration of Catholicism would be seen as a return to the days of the Covenanters and Stuart despotism. Pamphlets printed at the time are replete with Covenanting images and the mob were well aware of their religious traditions. The death threats to Robertson were couched in echoes of the assassination of Archbishop Sharp in 1679 which 'is still no murder in the opinion of 20,000 people inhabitants of this city of (Edinburgh)'.[49] Furthermore, Howie's description of the assassination made no concessions to genteel Enlightenment taste: 'The Commander (of the assassins) struck, which was redoubled by the rest, until he was killed. And so he received the just demerit of his sorceries, villanies, murders, perfidy, perjury and apostasy.'[50] Also, it has to be remembered that the anti-Catholic riots were the one striking success of popular agitation in eighteenth century Scotland. Not only was repeal removed from the legislative agenda, Robertson's career was effectively brought to an end and the reputation of the Moderate party never recovered.[51] Whatever the reasons for the riots, they were a striking demonstration of the power of popular religious tradition.

Catholic toleration was just another incident in a catalogue of failure which evangelicals used to claim that the Moderates were failing in their endeavours to maintain the Godly society. The beginnings of urbanization and the lapse of many from the church together with associated social evils were used to denounce Moderate laxity. According to John Howie, Scotland had lapsed from its previous Godliness and had degenerated into moral laxity:

> Ah Scotland, Scotland. How is the Gold become Dim. How is the most fine Gold changed. Ah! Where is the God of Elijah and where is his Glory! Where is that Scottish zeal which one flamed in the breasts of thy nobility, barons, ministers and commoners of all sorts. Ah where is that true courage and heroic resolution for religion and the liberties of the nation, that once did animate all ranks in the land. Alas, Alas! True Scots blood now runs cool in our veins.[52]

Although benefiting from the process of commercialization and industrialization, the middle class were quick to draw attention to moral decline. According to one contemporary account, Glasgow's once celebrated fame for piety has 'long been sinking, and is now on the very brink of perishing'.[53] Moderate other worldliness, its aloofness and rationality, together with its lack of passion were cited as reasons for the moral decay of the nation. The Moderates were condemned for their dependency on 'old' corruption and their failure to maintain the ideals of the Godly Commonwealth.[54]

Finally, evidence of the power of Covenanting tradition can be seen in the turmoil surrounding the demand for radical reform in the 1790s.[55] The Scottish Convention of the Friends of the People made numerous references to the Covenanting past. And, as John Brims has demonstrated, the Covenanters were an important icon of democratic aspirations and the history of the movement was a source of inspiration for many radicals. Yet, at the end of the day, it was the extreme radicalism of the Covenanting movement, and its potentially devastating power, which meant that the moderate leadership of the Friends of the People decided that it would not serve as a useful model for the democratic movement.[56] At the close of the century, the Covenanting tradition still had the power to mobilize and inspire many Scots, in spite of the best endeavours of the Scottish ancien regime to eradicate its memory. The re-emergence of the cult of the Covenanters in the nineteenth century demonstrated a remarkable degree of historical continuity. If anything, this essay would suggest that too little attention has focused on the competing claims within Scotland regarding Scottish national identity and that the emergence of the British state and the rise of rationalism in the eighteenth century has distracted historians from the more obvious factors which were much closer to home and more widely spread throughout society than lofty ideals or political ideology.

REFERENCES

1. T.M. Devine & R. Mitchison, *People and Society*, 1750-1830, vol. I (Edinburgh, 1988); T.M. Devine (ed.), *Conflict and Stability in Scottish* Society (Edinburgh, 1990); T.M. Devine, *The Transformation of Rural Scotland: Social Change and the Agrarian Economy*, 1660-1815 (Edinburgh, 1994); R.H. Campbell, *Scotland Since 1707: the Rise of an Industrial Society*

(London, 1965); T.M. Devine & Gordon Jackson (eds.), *Glasgow: Volume I, Beginnings to 1830* (Manchester, 1995).

2. H.W. Meikle, *Scotland and the French Revolution* (Glasgow, 1912); John Brims, 'From Reformers to 'Jacobins': The Scottish Association of the Friends of the People', in Devine (ed.), *Conflict and Stability*, pp.31–50, William Ferguson, *Scotland: 1689 to the Present* (Edinburgh, 1975 edn.), pp.266–91.
3. R. Mitchison & N. Phillipson (eds.), *Scotland in the Age of Improvement* (Edinburgh, 1970); A. Chitnis, *The Scottish Enlightenment: A Social History* (London, 1976); A. Broadie, *The Scottish Enlightenment: An Anthology* (Edinburgh, 1998); D. Daiches, P. Jones & J. Jones (eds.), *A Hotbed of Genius: The Scottish Enlightenment, 1730–90* (Edinburgh, 1986); John. Dwyer & Richard B. Sher (eds.), *Sociability and Society in Eighteenth Century Scotland* (Edinburgh, 1993); David Allan, *Virtue, Learning and the Scottish Enlightenment: Ideas of Scholarship in Early Modern Scotland* (Edinburgh, 1993); Colin Kidd, *Subverting Scotland's Past: Scottish Whig Historians and the Creation of an Anglo-British Identity,* 1689-c. 1830 (Cambridge, 1993).
4. In particular see Devine, *The Transformation of Rural Scotland;* Devine & Mitchison (eds.), *People and Society;* T.M. Devine, *The Tobacco Lords: A Study of the Tobacco Merchants of Glasgow and their Trading Activities c.* 1740–90 (Edinburgh, 1990 edn), T.M. Devine, 'The Union of 1707 and Scottish Development', *Scottish Social and Economic History*, 5 (1985) and L.M. Cullen & T.C. Smout (eds), *Comparative Aspects of Scottish and Irish Economic and Social History* 1600–1900 (Edinburgh, n.d.) for a comparative perspective.
5. In particular see T. Dickson (ed.), *Scottish Capitalism: Class, State and the Nation from before the Union to the Present* (London, 1980) for a crude Marxist perspective. Tom Nairn, *The Break-up of Britain* (London, 1987 edn), is a more sophisticated treatment. E.J. Hobsbawm & T. Ranger (eds.), *The Invention of Tradition* (Cambridge, 1987) takes a wider perspective on national identity. A good summary on the latest thinking regarding Scottish national identity before the Union of 1707 is to be found in D.Broun, R.J. Finlay & Michael Lynch (eds.), *Image and Identity: The Making and Remaking of Scotland Through the Ages* (Edinburgh, 1998).
6. T.C. Smout, 'Problems of Nationalism, Identity and Improvement in Late Eighteenth Century Scotland', in T.M. Devine (ed.), *Improvement and Enlightenment,* (Edinburgh, 1989), pp.1–22. For a literary perspective see K. Simpson, *The Protean Scot: The Crisis of Identity in Eighteenth Century Scottish Literature* (Aberdeen, 1988).
7. See D. Diaches, *The Paradox of Scottish Culture: The Eighteenth Century Experience* (Oxford, 1964).
8. See Kidd, *Subverting Scotland's Past*, pp.33–51.
9. Linda Colley, *Britons: Forging the Nation,* 1707–1837 (Yale, 1992).
10. Kidd, *Subverting Scotland's Past;* Allan, *Virtue, Learning and the Scottish Enlightenment;* J. Robertson, *The Scottish Enlightenment and the Militia Issue* (Edinburgh, 1985); J. Dwyer, *Virtuous Discourse: Sensibility and Community in Eighteenth Century Scotland* (Edinburgh, 1987); R.Sher, *Church and University in the Scottish Enlightenment: The Moderate Literati of Edinburgh* (Edinburgh, 1993), N.T. Phillipson, 'Politics, Politeness and the Anglicization of Early Eighteenth Century Scottish Culture', in R.Mason (ed.), *Scotland and England:* 1286–1815 (Edinburgh, 1987), pp.226–46.
11. See Devine, 'The Union of 1707' for the economic aspects and J. Shaw, *The Management of Scottish Society,* 1707–64 (Edinburgh, 1983) and A. Murdoch, *The People Above: Politics and Administration in Mid-Eighteenth Century Scotland* (Edinburgh, 1980) for the political dimension. A wider theoretical perspective is provided by Lindsay Paterson, *The Autonomy of Scotland* (Edinburgh, 1995).
12. On the Jacobites see, B.Lenman, *The Jacobite Risings in Britain,* 1688–1746 (London, 1980); B. Lenman, *The Jacobite Clans of the Great Glen* (Edinburgh, 1995 edn); A.I. Macinnes, *Clanship, Commerce and the House of Stuart,* 1607–1788 (East Linton, 1996); M.G.H. Pittock, *The Myth of the Jacobite Clans* (Edinburgh, 1995). For Jacobite iconography see M.G.H. Pittock, *The Invention of Scotland: The Stuart Myth and the Scottish Identity,* 1638 *to the present.*

13. Quoted in I. Maver, 'The guardianship of the community: civic authority before 1833', in Devine and Jackson (eds.), *Glasgow,* p.259.
14. On the Covenanters see E.J. Cowan, *Montrose: For Covenant and King* (London, 1977); A.I. Macinness, *Charles I and the Making of the Covenanting Movement,* 1625–41 (Edinburgh, 1991); J.R.Young, *The Scottish Parliament* 1639–1661: A Political and Constitutional Analysis (Edinburgh, 1995); I.B. Cowan, *the Scottish Covenanters,* 1660–1688 (London, 1976).
15. Macinnes, *Charles I,* pp.56–72.
16. Young, *Scottish Parliament,* pp.54–83.
17. See J.R. Young's article in this volume.
18. Kidd, *Subverting Scotland's Past, pp*.54–55.
19. *Ibid*., pp.68–9.
20. A.L. Drummond and J. Bulloch, *The Scottish Church,* 1688–1843 (Edinburgh, 1973), p.41.
21. *ibid*., p.53.
22. *ibid*., p.55.
23. R.B. Sher, 'Moderates, Managers and Popular Politics in Mid-Eighteenth Century Edinburgh: The Drysdale 'Bustle' of the 1760s', in J. Dwyer, R.A. Mason & A. Murdoch (eds.), *New Perspectives on the Politics and Culture of Early Modern Scotland* (Edinburgh, 1982), pp.179–210; Drummond & Bulloch, *Scottish Church, pp*.21–3, 57–9, 223–39; C. Brown, 'Protest in the Pews. Interpreting Presbyterianism and Society in Fracture During the Scottish Economic Revolution', in Devine (ed.), *Conflict and Stability,* pp.83–106.
24. Kidd, *Subverting Scotland's Past,* pp.185–204.
25. *ibid*., p.194.
26. The classic espousal of this is H.T. Buckle, *A History of Civilization in England* (London, 1873).
27. Allan, *Virtue, Learning and the Scottish Enlightenment.*
28. See R.H. Campbell, 'The Enlightenment and the Economy', in R.H. Campbell and A.S. Skinner (eds.), *The Origins and Nature of the Scottish Enlightenment* (Edinburgh, 1982), pp.8–26; Allan, *Virtue, Learning and the Scottish Enlightenment,* pp.209–18.
29. Robertson, *The Scottish Enlightenment and the Militia Issue*; Sher, *Church and University,* pp.213–42.
30. Allan, *Virtue Learning and the Scottish Enlightenment,* p.211.
31. Sher, *Church and University,* pp.262–77.
32. ibid., pp.187–212; Allan, *Virtue, Learning and the Scottish Enlightenment,* pp.186–91.
33. Sher, *Church and University,* pp.324–8.
34. J. Brims, 'The Covenanting Tradition and Scottish Radicalism the 1790s' in T. Brotherstone (ed.), *Covenant, Charter and Party: Traditions of Revolt and Protest in Modern Scottish History* (Aberdeen, 1989), pp.50–63; Drummond and Bulloch, *Scottish Church,* pp.50–3.
35. John Howie, Scots Worthies: Containing a brief historical account of the most eminent *Nobles, Gentlemen, Ministers and others who testified for the cause of Reformation in Scotland , from the beginning of the sixteenth century to the year* 1688 (1775), edited by William McGavin (Glasgow, 1846).
36. R.Sher, 'Commerce, religion and the enlightenment in eighteenth century Glasgow', in Devine and Jackson (eds.), *Glasgow,* p.317.
37. See L. McIlvanney, 'Sacred Freedom: Presbyterian Radicalism and the Politics of Robert Burns', in K. Simpson (ed.), *Love and Liberty: Robert Burns, A Bicentenary Celebration* (East Linton, 1995), pp.168–83; Rev. George Gilfillan, *The Martyrs, Heroes and Bards of the Scottish Covenant* (Edinburgh, 1852); John Howie, *Sermons Delivered in Times of Persecution in Scotland* (Edinburgh, various edns); Sir Walter Scott, *Old Mortality* (various edns).
38. Brown, ' Protest in the Pews', pp.29–31.
39. T. Brown, Annals of the Disruption (Edinburgh, various edns).
40. See Brown, 'Protest in the Pews', for example.
41. Howie, *Scots Worthies.*
42. Drummond and Bulloch, *Scottish Church,* p.108.
43. Sher, *Church and University,* pp.263–8; 127–9.

44. *Ibid.*, pp.277–97, R.K. Donovan, 'Voices of Distrust: The Expression of Anti-Catholic Feeling in Scotland, 1778–1781', *Innes Review*, 30 (1979), pp.62–76.
45. E.P. Thomson, 'The Moral Economy of the English Crowd in the Eighteenth Century', *Past and Present*, 50 (1971) pp.76–136.
46. See K. Logue, *Popular Disturbances in Scotland*, 1780–1815 (Edinburgh, 1979).
47. See Chris Whatley, 'Royal Day, People's Day: The Monarch's Birthday in Scotland. 1660–c.1860', in R.Mason & N. Macdougall (eds.), *People and Power in Scotland: Essays in Honour of T.C. Smout* (Edinburgh, 1993).
48. Howie, *Scots Worthies*, p.523.
49. Sher, *Church and University*, p.290.
50. J. Howie, God's Justice exemplified in his Judgment upon persecutors in a brief *Historical account of the wicked lives and miserable Deaths of some of the most remarkable Apostates and bloody persecutors in Scotland*. (Glasgow, 1775) reprinted in McGavin (ed.), 1846 edn., p.584.
51. *ibid.* pp.295–97.
52. Howie, *Scots Worthies*, p.xxxv.
53. Sher, 'Commerce, religion and the enlightenment', in Devine and Jackson (eds.), *Glasgow*, p.317.
54. See Sher, *Church and University*, pp.296–7.
55. John Brims, 'The Covenanting Tradition'.
56. *ibid.*, pp.58–9.

Nine

Clio, Mars and Minerva: The Scottish Enlightenment and the Writing of Women's History

JANE RENDALL

> It is, indeed, the conquerors and disturbers of the earth, to whose actions the attention of succeeding ages has been chiefly devoted; 'for' as it has been well observed by a venerable historian, 'it has unfortunately happened, the Muse of History hath been so much in love with Mars, that she hath conversed but little with Minerva.' [Henry's *Hist. of Britain*, vol. iv, p. 91][1]

IN JANE AUSTEN'S *Northanger Abbey*, first drafted in the 1790s, the heroine Catherine Morland laments the absence of women from the historical record:

> . . . history, real solemn history, I cannot be interested in . . . I read it a little as a duty, but it tells me nothing that does not either vex or weary me. The quarrels of popes and kings, with wars or pestilences in every page; the men all so good for nothing, and hardly any women at all – it is very tiresome.[2]

She does so in the context of a conversation with Henry Tilney and his sister Eleanor, who were both 'fond of history', conventionally instructed by the reading of the works of David Hume and William Robertson. It is a rich conversation, full of irony and ambiguities, which signals much to us about the relationship between Catherine, Henry, and Eleanor, just as it indicates the imaginative possibilities of even the masculine historical canon, from which Eleanor Tilney admires the nation's heroes of the most distant past, including Caractacus and Alfred.

I suggest that this was a period, not as Catherine Morland suggested, of the absence of women but of contest over their appearance in the historical record. As Gianna Pomata – to whom I owe the reference to *Northanger Abbey* – has argued so powerfully, both the presence and the absence of women in the major national narratives of European history need still to be established.[3] There is, however, evidence of such contested territory in the narratives of the male historians of the Scottish Enlightenment. Women writers, both Scottish and English, still found the formal boundaries of the masculine genre of historical writing hard to cross, although a few, like Elizabeth Hamilton, were to engage with it through different routes.[4]

Within late eighteenth-century Scottish historiography, as elsewhere in enlightened Europe, different but historicized approaches to the situation of women and to gender differences were apparent, recognised and contested. Such approaches served a variety of purposes. In these works women were understood to be central to the history as to the fabric of civil society, even though they were not full political citizens.[5] Their condition could serve to illustrate the desired degrees of difference between the present and the past, or between the cultural varieties of the present. Different national histories of women, or of gender relations, might also symbolise the superiority of an earlier stage of society, distinguishing the competing genealogies of ancient Britons, Celts, and Anglo-Saxons. Such histories might also convey powerfully gendered and moralizing strategies for the civil society of the future.

The historiography addressed here has been the subject of much recent re-interpretation, though little attention has been paid to these debates.[6] However, Karen O'Brien and, more directly, Mark Phillips, have both alluded to the growing significance of the appeal to sentiment and sympathy in historical writing, and their implications for a female readership.[7] It is true that the issues discussed here may appear peripheral in the major historical narratives, although they were central to some of the works of John Millar, Lord Kames, Gilbert Stuart and William Alexander. Yet even incidental references, sometimes more extended, in the works of Adam Ferguson, Adam Smith, William Robertson, Robert Henry, James Macpherson, James Beattie, John Gregory and James Dunbar could be given significance by writers who focused, prescriptively or historically, on the condition of women.

One work frequently cited as initiating historical writing about women in Britain is William Alexander's *History of Women* (1779).[8] Alexander practised medicine in Edinburgh in the 1760s, and took his MD there in 1769. His work deserves to take its place among Enlightenment histories of civil society, in spite of its length and rambling inconsistency. The reader does sometimes understand why one contemporary, William Hayley, felt impelled to the crude but direct satire of his *Philosophical, Historical and Moral Essay on Old Maids* (1785).

Writing about women historically was certainly not simply a product of the eighteenth century. In his Introduction, Alexander referred to the lengthy traditions in European literature both of misogyny, and of that celebration of famous women which emerged to counter such hostility. He intended, he said, to argue neither for or against women, in the spirit of the 'querelle des femmes', but to offer a historical picture of 'the character and manners of women from the destruction of the Roman Empire to the present time', a character to be contrasted also with the unchanging histories of women in eastern and savage societies.[9] In spite of his disclaimer, Alexander made considerable use of past literature, as of classical authors, the Bible and theological writings, travel literature and contemporary French writers including Montesquieu, Buffon and Raynal.

His method of proceeding was thematic rather than chronological, and themes included 'The Employments and Amusements of Women', 'The Treatment, Condition, Advantages and Disadvantages of Women, in Savage and Civil life', and 'The Chastity of Women'. Each was discussed through repetitive retelling of broadly identical narratives. The central narrative began with a chapter which unconvincingly paid lip service to the Biblical account of womanhood, in 'a short history of antediluvian women' (rendered by William Hayley as 'Conjectures concerning the Existence of Old Maids before the Deluge'). Discussion of each theme, in grouped chapters, began with the harsh conditions experienced by women in savage life. In savage states, where hunting, fishing and war were the only occupations, women, lacking strength and courage, were largely oppressed. But:

> pasturage, agriculture, and every thing that brings mankind into society, is generally in favour of women.[10]

He commented on the harshness of women's seclusion in ancient Greece, in contrast with the glory of its masculine classical learning. Though he praised the heroic qualities of the women of republican Rome, he lamented the degeneration and corruption of the later Empire. He contrasted the classical worlds with the spirit of the 'northern nations' of Europe, who universally held their women in a greater degree of respect, even though they fell some way short of the refinement of civil society.[11] He identified the potential of the coming of Christianity to improve women's condition, though he perceived the Christian institutions of medieval Europe, its monastic institutions, convents, and celibate priesthood, as hostile to progress for women.[12]

He gave detailed attention to the condition of women in eastern societies, suggesting in commonplace 'orientalist' terms that for so-called eastern women 'no alteration for the better has ever taken place', and that Asiatic ideas on women were 'coarse and indelicate'. This absence of change in the east was contrasted directly with the impact on medieval Europe of the coming of chivalry, with its origins in early Germanic practices, which brought a refinement of manners and reverence for women, a refinement to be lost as later chivalry was corrupted into gallantry, especially in France.[13]

Alexander concluded with a short survey of the condition of women in contemporary England, in which he attempted to weigh in the balance what he regarded as their privileges and their disadvantages. He had little to say specifically of Scotland.

Alexander's view of what constituted 'progress' for women needs to be examined. He constantly compared the potential of women's lives in a 'civilized' society favourably with those in a less developed condition both in past worlds and contemporary societies. He argued against the view that monogamy and masculine superiority were providentially intended, and asserted the civil rather than divine origins of marriage, indicating that the 'boasted pre-eminence of the men is at least as much the work of art as it is of nature'.[14] But his work still carried a didactic charge, a prescriptive message for his own day, since he also stressed the complementary nature of the qualities of men and of women. In savage states, he wrote, the difference between men and women was far less evident than it was in civilized societies. He was inclined to attribute the differences to women's lack of education and style of life, differences which could be remedied, although he was critical of the pedantry of 'learned ladies' as of the education in accomplishments that girls received in his own day. The right kind of education could bring out the complementary qualities of women and of men:

> to each sex [the Author of our being] has given its different qualifications; and . . . these, upon the whole, when properly cultivated and exerted, put men and women nearly on an equal footing with each other, and share the advantages and disadvantages of life impartially between them.[15]

Alexander strongly endorsed the belief that human societies had progressed in their treatment of women, expressing doubts, though citing some evidence, on the existence of any 'golden age' for women in the historic past. In modern Europe alone were women neither 'abject slaves' nor 'perpetual prisoners', but 'intelligent beings'.[16] Progress, nevertheless, could be accidental, variable, and unpredictable. This brief account of his work is intended to suggest that Alexander's *History of Women* drew not only upon older traditions and upon travel literatures, but upon the methodologies and contested narratives of gender to be found in eighteenth-century Scottish 'philosophical' history. Alexander shared with John Millar and with William Robertson the assumption that

> the rank . . . and condition, in which we find women in any country, mark out to us with the greatest precision, the exact point in the scale of civil society, to which the people of such country have arrived.[17]

But he also followed Lord Kames, James Macpherson and Gilbert Stuart in his interest in the distinctive history, even a 'golden age,' of the women of the 'ancient northern nations'. And like James Fordyce and John Gregory he stressed the significance of the relationship between historical understanding and educational intervention, in the need to shape and direct that form of moral sensibility and propriety most appropriate to a modern civil society.

The most significant features of eighteenth-century Scottish 'philosophical' history have frequently been traced.[18] They include the adoption of a stadial theory of development, through three or four stages, mainly understood as stages defined by material development, from what were regarded as savage states to contemporary western European civilisation. The 'conjectural' use of comparative material to fill in the gaps was also common, though not especially original. These Scottish historians shared with European counterparts like Montesquieu a sense of the totality of the manners, culture, and political institutions of any society. In spite of the progressive nature of their history, they retained a sense of the significance of the accidental and unpredictable variety of human history. And finally they shared a common politics which was broadly whiggish if socially conservative, though within that definition there remained ample room for disagreement.

Within this broad framework, I consider here three particular contexts which may help to explain the distinctive interest in histories of women and gender relations in Scotland between 1760 and 1790. The first lay in the systematic and historically comparative study of law, especially by Adam Smith and John Millar in the University of Glasgow. The second lay in the complex rewriting within late eighteenth-century Scotland of myths of origins, of histories of the 'northern nations', most notably here by James Macpherson for ancient Scotland, and Gilbert Stuart for an ancient Germanism. Thirdly, it is suggested that there was a relationship between such historical themes, and the strength of prescriptive and educational writing in the 'virtuous discourse' of late eighteenth-century Scotland.[19]

The significance of a historical and comparative approach to the study of law is most apparent in the lectures on jurisprudence given by Adam Smith, and those on civil law by John Millar. Smith lectured on jurisprudence in Glasgow as a part of his teaching as Professor first of Logic then of Moral Philosophy from 1751 to 1763. These lectures drew upon, though amended, the framework of his predecessors Francis Hutcheson and Gershom Carmichael, deeply grounded in natural jurisprudence.[20] Millar, the protégé of Lord Kames and friend and disciple of Smith, lectured as Professor of Civil Law at Glasgow from 1761 to 1801. The development of the teaching of Roman law, and indeed of organised university instruction in national law, in Scottish universities, is relevant to the development of a sociologically-oriented history. [21]

Both Smith and Millar, but especially Millar, used in their lectures on law principles of organisation ultimately derived from the *Institutes* of the Emperor Justinian, first issued in AD 533. In the classic Justinian structure, which was also that of early modern natural jurisprudence, these principles were based on the rights of persons, things and actions. The rights of *persons* were subdivided into those of the individual, the member of a family and the member of a community. The rights of members of families were subdivided into the relationships of husbands and wives, parents and children, masters and servants. Smith and Millar in their lectures used these principles of organisation, not only for descriptive accounts of Roman, Scottish, and English law. They constructed comparative and sociological accounts of changing practices and sentiments, in relation to the family and household as for the political community.

Smith, as a moral philosopher as well as a political economist, indicated the outlines of a historical account which offered not only a descriptive account of the marriage contract, but one which located it within the moral sentiments of societies, sentiments which would vary from time to time and place to place. Student notes on Smith's lectures show him addressing the history of marriage and divorce, polygamy and consanguinity, a history which was rooted in the response of the male spectator to the injury afforded by infidelity. The self-interest of this is not concealed:

> The laws of most countries being made by men generally are very severe on the women who can have no remedy for this oppression.[22]

He traced the history of Roman and European marriage compared to that of savage and polygamous societies, indicating, though briefly, the implications for the status of women, for whom the indissolubility of marriage in modern societies, and the greater refinement of manners since the coming of chivalry, had secured a more respected position.

In 1771 John Millar published his pioneering essay, 'Of the rank and condition of women in different ages' in his *Observations concerning the Distinction of Ranks in Society* (1771).[23] It is clear from the unpublished lecture-notes left by Millar's students that the second part of his course in civil law, though nominally on Roman law, was a course in general jurisprudence which drew extensively on Smith's model but also went beyond it. In total, nine sets of student notes survive for this course, from 1778 to 1794, and although there are no sets which precede the first edition of the *Observations*, it is very clear that its material emerged from these lectures.[24] While lecturing, Millar referred his law students to his published work on the condition of women as to other sections of the book, and responded to his critics.

The *Observations* was broadly a history of progress, conceived not only in material terms but also in terms of manners, assuming 'a natural progress from ignorance to knowledge, and from rude, to civilized manners'. Such progress was however most frequently traced through four stages of material development, leading ultimately towards commercial western civilisation. For the situation of women, Millar suggested focusing on:

> the cultivation of the arts of life . . . the advancement of opulence; and . . . the gradual refinement of taste and manners. From a view of the progress of society, in these respects, we may in a great measure, account for the diversity that occurs among different nations, in relation to the rank of the sexes, their dispositions and sentiments towards each other, and the regulations which they have established in the several branches of their domestic economy.[25]

In writing of the situation of women in 'savage' and 'barbarous' societies, he used what was by the second half of the eighteenth century a very familiar trope of European commentary : the 'savage' woman as drudge, labourer, slave and servant.[26] That representation was relevant not only to contemporary peoples elsewhere in the world, such as the American Indian populations, but also to the European past. Millar argued that in early Germanic nations, as in all other such societies, women were treated as slaves, servants, labourers, purchased in marriage by payment of a bride-price, sometimes polygamously and excluded from the succession of property.[27] Millar's work borrowed heavily from previous writers, such as the Abbé Lafitau and Pierre de Charlevoix, as in his chapter on 'The influence acquired by the mother of a family, before marriage is completely established'. Though this is described by Ronald Meek as 'a path-breaking section dealing with group marriage and matriarchy in primitive society', what was significant for Millar about the public power of older women, and established patterns of female and agnatic inheritance and succession, was that they were indicative not of progress but of a very early stage of civilisation.[28]

To Millar, it was only the later stages of material development, and particularly the acquisition of settled property which brought, with inequality of property and rank, a higher status for women. It brought a degree of leisure and tranquillity, and also notions of honour, jealousy between families, and constraints upon women of higher rank, which allowed romantic and imaginative attachments to develop, even though they might be frustrated by familial concern for the protection of legitimate succession. Like William Robertson in his 'View of the Progress of Society in Europe' (1769), Millar wrote of the coming of chivalry as one of the many signs of a new dawn in late medieval European society, signalling a profound shift in gender relations. Millar is clear that the 'politeness, delicacy and attention' derived from an age of chivalry was unknown to the classical and antique worlds and was 'a valuable improvement'.[29] Yet not until the emergence of commercial society, its divisions of labour, its surplus productivity, and its sociability, were women's talents, both the useful and the agreeable, properly valued. Only then according to Millar did 'women become, neither the slaves, nor the idols of the other sex, but the friends and companions'. And as friends and companions their situation was perceived as particularly qualified for rearing and maintaining children, for employments requiring skill and dexterity, and for the exercise of particular delicacy and sensibility. Yet wealth and luxury brought with it also the danger of the corruption of sexual relations and the importance of guarding against that corruption, for Millar's version of material progress did not exclude the maintenance of virtuous manners.[30]

Much of this analysis was followed by contemporaries like Lord Kames and William Robertson. Lord Kames in his *Sketches of Man* wrote that:

> After traversing a great part of the globe with painful industry, would not one be apt to conclude, that originally females were everywhere despised, as they are at present among the savages of America; that wives, like slaves, were procured by barter; that polygamy was universal; and that divorce depended on the will of the husband?[31]

Robertson's brief but influential portrait of the American Indian woman similarly allowed no doubt:

> To despise and degrade the female sex, is the characteristic of the savage state in every part of the globe.[32]

Yet it has also to be stressed that this view of a progress rooted in material developments was in no sense simple, uniform or irreversible. Millar and his contemporaries saw historical development as diverse and unpredictable. And both Millar and Kames noted one outstanding exception to the historical pattern I have sketched above, in the manners of ancient Caledonia. In the poems of Ossian Millar found:

> a degree of tenderness and delicacy of sentiment which can hardly be equalled in the most refined productions of a civilized age.[33]

His confusion was echoed by Kames:

> Had the Caledonians made slaves of their women, and thought as meanly of them as savages commonly do, Ossian could never have thought, even in a dream, of bestowing on them those numberless graces that exalt the female sex, and render many of them objects of pure and elevated affection.[34]

Certain themes in the writing of Millar, Robertson, and Kames were to become controversial in late eighteenth-century Scotland: the status of savage or barbarian women, the existence of polygamy in such societies, the implications of the public power of women, the origins of chivalry. Those who wrote of the shaping of a modern civil society were challenged by historians for whom the myth of a 'golden age' for women in a distant past could serve different national purposes and political needs.

In much European scholarship on the origins of peoples from the early seventeenth to the mid-eighteenth centuries, the common roots of Germanic and Celtic peoples were assumed, confusing much historical writing from the early seventeenth to the late eighteenth century. It was in this context that in 1755, the Genevan Paul-Henri Mallet published in Copenhagen his *Introduction à l'histoire de Dannemarc*, to retell the history of the manners of the loosely defined 'northern nations' of Scandinavians, Teutons, Celts and Germans, all here given a common Gothic inheritance. Mallet identified within that inheritance the origins of a system of chivalry in these northern nations, to be carried from there to the other nations of Europe, ultimately contributing to the shaping of a modern sensibility.[35]

In the early 1760s, a small group of Edinburgh literati, inspired by national sentiment and the hope of a Scottish epic, encouraged James Macpherson to publish his version of the works of the ancient Celtic bard, Ossian. If read together with Hugh Blair's *Critical Dissertation on the Poems of Ossian* (1763), and Macpherson's own *Introduction to the History of Great Britain and Ireland* (1771), the poetry of Ossian and its reception is relevant to the theme of this paper.[36] In his *Introduction* Macpherson was to argue, against Mallet and others, that the Celtae were the dominant peoples of western Europe, and those of northern Germany, including Angles and Saxons, simply a hybrid of east and west. The Scandinavian sagas simply illustrated the barbarism of those who were the ancestors of the Anglo-Saxons, as in their treatment of women, excluded from Valhalla in the after-life.[37]

However, like Mallet, Macpherson had for the most part recreated his heroic past in the language of the eighteenth century. Contemporaries immediately noted the refinement of the manners and the extraordinary delicacy of sentiment that appeared in the relationships between the women and men of ancient Scotland. Hugh Blair stressed that the poetry of Ossian clearly established both 'the superior excellence of the Celtic bard' and the direct contrast between Celtic and Scandinavian (or Gothic) manners:

> when we open the works of Ossian, a very different scene presents itself. There we find the fire and the enthusiasm of the most early times combined with an amazing degree of regularity and art. We find tenderness, and even delicacy of sentiment, greatly predominant over

> fierceness and barbarity. Our hearts are melted with the softest feelings, and at the same time elevated with the highest ideas of magnanimity, generosity and true heroism. When we turn from the poetry of Lodbrog to that of Ossian, it is like passing from a savage desart, into a fertile and cultivated country.

Blair firmly distinguished the politeness of the sentiments and manners of the ancient Scots from those of the Gothic and Teutonic peoples, among whom 'even their women are bloody and fierce'.[38] In arguing that ancient Scotland was still in the first stage of society, he suggested that Ossianic heroes showed 'refinement of sentiment . . . but none of manners'; but elsewhere he wrote of the 'imaginary refinement of heroic manners' as recalling the age of chivalry.[39] Contemporary doubts of the genuineness of Ossianic poetry limited the force of this case. But the notion of the unique delicacy of ancient Scottish manners in an early stage of society was to have a much longer appeal, and to contribute more generally to discussion of the condition of women in the early stages of society.

The appeal to a 'golden age' for women did not depend simply on Macpherson's representations of the Celtic past. Other Scottish historians also wrote of the situation of women among the early peoples of the northern nations, including ancient Britons, Scots and Germans. In 1771–4 Robert Henry, an Edinburgh minister, wrote the first volumes of his *History of Great Britain*, covering the period up to 1066, as a history of manners as well as of politics, and paid particular attention to the condition of women throughout ancient Britain. In Henry's references Ossian is prominent yet jostles indiscriminately Mallet, Giraldus Cambrensis, Tacitus and many other classical writers, as well as Martin Martin's *Description of the Western Isles of Scotland* (1716). Henry wrote of the remarkable devotion shown to women:

> among the ancient Britons and all the other Celtic nations of Europe, even when they were in the lowest stages of civilization and but little removed from savages in some other respects. These brave, rough, unpolished nations treated their women with much attention and respect, as the objects of their highest esteem and most sincere affection.[40]

The historian who did most, however, to recover a golden age for the women of the northern nations, and particularly the women of early Germany, for his own age was the Edinburgh historian, and journalist, Gilbert Stuart.[41] A major theme of his *View of Society in Europe* (1778) was that the earliest stages of society were most favourable to women, including the women of ancient Germany featured in the *Germania* of Tacitus. His arguments were directed quite specifically and indeed vitriolically, for personal as well as political reasons, against Millar, Kames and Robertson. I 'scruple not to contradict positions which have the sanction of distinguished names', he wrote in an eleven-page endnote on the history of bride-price and dowry.[42] Stuart stressed, first, that marriage among the Germans meant that a wife enjoyed 'her equality with her husband', as 'the partner and the companion of his toils and his cares', a partnership marked by her fidelity and chastity, as by her contribution in war. Secondly, he wrote of German women acquiring rights to property, and denied the existence of a bride-price denoting marital slavery.[43] Thirdly, he stressed the attention paid by women to business and affairs, to the public councils of the community:

> what evinces their consideration beyond the possibility of a doubt, is the attention they bestowed on business and affairs. They felt, as well as the noble and the warrior, the cares of the community . . . They went to the public councils or assemblies of their nations, heard the debates of the statesmen, and were called upon to deliver their sentiments.[44]

Finally, he identified the origins of chivalry itself in the early Germanic tribes. His description was not only of an age of equality and power for women, but the decline of that happy condition, in the later growth of an increasingly venal, money-oriented and debauched society, a process which he regarded as underway by the thirteenth century.

Conflicting definitions of national identity here found their focus in alternative representations of womanhood. Millar's responses to Stuart can be identified within his lectures. His young law students heard him defend his interpretation of the existence of the bride-price and polygamy among the early Germans. He reiterated that a matriarchal pattern of inheritance, and a public role for women, were indicative of the earliest stages of civilisation.[45] The debate lay between those who looked to the 'golden ages' of the past, whether Celtic or Germanic, in the spirit of a humanist and republican vision of a commonwealth, and those who looked towards the modern civil society of the future. To the latter, the brutalised condition of 'savage' women was a significant index of the distance that had to be travelled in the achievement of a desirable civil society. It was to be the modernizing version of the nation's history which dominated by the end of the eighteenth century, yet a version which would nevertheless incorporate elements of a 'golden age' for women located in the distant past, though that which survived was to be not the Celtic but the Anglo-Saxon.[46]

Yet there is also a third context in which approaches to the history of women in late eighteenth-century Scotland need to be placed. That is the relationship between historical writing, and the ethical strategies of late eighteenth-century Scottish writers. John Dwyer has traced the concern of writers and preachers like Hugh Blair, James Fordyce, and John Gregory to develop the kind of social and moral sensibility appropriate to a modern commercial society. Mark Phillips has pointed to the fluidity of the boundary between genres, between the moral sentiments of history and the sentiment of the novel.[47] The prescriptive writings addressed to women in late eighteenth-century Scotland drew in different ways upon that relationship between history, virtue and sensibility, a relationship which carried with it ambivalent messages for the woman reader.

The Scottish authors of some of the most influential prescriptive works of the period, including James Fordyce's *Sermons to Young Women* (1766), Dr John Gregory's *A Father's Legacy to His Daughters* (1774) and Lord Kames' *Loose Hints upon Education* (1781), were, directly or indirectly, engaged in a conversation with Jean-Jacques Rousseau's portrait of the education of Sophie in *Emile* (1762).[48] Each wrote of the different destiny and abilities of women. Fordyce wrote of their faculties as shaped by a 'Nature', which had excluded them from 'war, commerce, politics, exercises of strength and dexterity, abstract philosophy, and all the abstruser sciences'. Gregory, in attempting to write of 'the peculiar propriety of female manners' stressed: 'I want to know what Nature has made you, and to perfect you on her plan'. For Lord Kames too women had the 'peculiar province' of the 'culture of the heart'.[49]

Nevertheless, such texts may still be placed within the historical understanding traced above. Fordyce distinguished the treatment of women in savage and 'eastern' societies from their position in periods and societies of distinction:

> Look into the history of the world at large: do not you find, that the female sex have, in a variety of ways, contributed largely to many of its most important events? Look into the great machine of society, as it moves before you: do not you perceive, that they are still among its principal springs? Do not their characters and manners deeply affect the passions of men, the interests of education, and those domestic scenes, where so much of life is past, and with which its happiness or misery is so intimately blended.[50]

Gregory referred in the preface to *A Father's Legacy* to 'a little Treatise of mine just published' in which he had considered women 'not as domestic drudges or the slaves of our pleasures, but as our companions and equals; as designed to soften our hearts and polish our manners'. His *Comparative View* (1763) drew extensively though not uncritically upon Rousseau, in its admiration for an early, though not the earliest, state of society as showing mankind to its best advantage. The preface to the edition of 1788, published after his death, reflected on the alternative lessons of Ossianic poetry, and on an ancient Scottish society in which:

> as they required no slaves to do the laborious and servile offices of life, they were still less disposed to degrade their women to so mean and so wretched a situation . . . The women described by Ossian have a character as singular as that of his heroes. They possess the high spirit and dignity of Roman matrons, united to all the softness and delicacy ever painted in modern romance.[51]

The loss of the virtues of that early stage, succeeded by the pursuit of wealth and commerce, was inevitable. Yet for Gregory, it was such a contemplation of humanity in what he called 'the progressive stage of society' that led him to advocate what he describes the uniting of 'the peculiar advantages of these several stages'. For 'civil and natural history' could not only amuse but it could serve the purposes of the improvement of the species. And, for women, that meant a recognition of the importance of their domestic and educative role; 'we should either improve the women or abridge their power'.[52] Similarly Lord Kames looked to parents and above all to mothers to replace the censors of the early republics, by taking up 'the parental censorian office', the responsibility for stemming the 'tide of corruption' in the complexity and opulence of a modern society.[53]

Dwyer's studies of the 'virtuous discourse' of late eighteenth-century Scotland help us understand the way in which the term 'women' was positioned within both the prescriptive and the historical writing discussed here. The message of Henry Mackenzie's Mirror Club was directed 'at all above the lower ranks, of all who claim the station or the feeling of the gentleman', to the professional and middling classes as well as to the landed. The modern white western 'women' of whom John Millar wrote were clearly not the labouring women of industrialising Scotland.[54] Like James Fordyce in his *Sermons to Young Women*, John Millar placed at the heart of his commercial society that 'virtuous woman' drawn by Solomon, in Proverbs xxxi.10–13, as 'highly expressive of those ideas and sentiments, which are commonly entertained by a people advanced in commerce and in the arts of life'.[55] Historical writing, like prescriptive writing, was didactically directed towards the inculcation of a social sensibility in the middle and upper ranks, within a moralised domestic framework entailing both a sharper differentiation between the sexes, and Gregory's imperative, 'improve the women or abridge their power'.

But the study of history was not exclusively masculine. Fordyce called for it to occupy a considerable proportion of women's leisure:

> Those pictures which it exhibits, of the passions operating in real life and genuine characters; of virtues to be imitated, and of vices to be shunned; of the effects of both on society and individuals; of the mutability of human affairs; of the conduct of divine providence; of

> the great consequences that often arise from little events; of the weakness of power, and the wanderings of prudence, in mortal men; with the sudden, unexpected, and frequently unaccountable revolutions, that dash triumphant wickedness, or disappoint presumptuous hope; the pictures, I say, which History exhibits of all these, have been ever reckoned by the best judges among the richest sources of instruction and entertainment.

That call was echoed by Lord Kames and others, though not all the histories discussed above could be recommended to the female reader without reservation.[56] William Alexander had excused his lack of references by indicating that his work was intended 'solely for the fair sex'. But his frank and even voyeuristic discussion of the cultural variety of sexual practice was strongly attacked by his reviewers, and there is little evidence of a female readership.[57] The middle- and upper-class women who were the prospective readers of such works may well have been deterred from acquiring the broader anthropological and ethnographic knowledge they promised.

In *Northanger Abbey*, Jane Austen had recognised both didactic and imaginative impulses in Eleanor Tilney's reading of David Hume and William Robertson. In 1810, the Unitarian Lucy Aikin, in her *Epistles on Women*, appealed to 'the impartial voice of History' to 'testify for us', in opposition to the 'politic legacy' of Dr John Gregory. Her aim was to trace the 'progress of human society', and the 'accompanying and proportional elevation or depression of woman in the scale of existence'.[58] The aims of Aikin were not dissimilar from those of her Scottish friend, Elizabeth Hamilton, who like Catherine Morland, had noted the invisibility of women in the historical narratives of men, 'the conquerors and disturbers of the earth'; though in Robert Henry she had also found women as historical subjects. The social history of this network of women writers, uniting English rational dissent and Scottish Whiggism, across Edinburgh, Glasgow, and northern England, as well as London and Bath, remains to be written. But their common recognition of the ambivalent possibilities of historical writing about and for women is apparent. Gary Kelly, in his study of women's writing in the period after the French revolution has discussed different approaches to the feminizing of history, through poetry, the national tale, the novel of antiquity or even the chivalric romance.[59] To writers such as Lucy Aikin and Elizabeth Hamilton, and to their readers, such genres were to offer alternative modes of intervention within a modern civil society, as within the circle of the national or the regional community, as writers and educators as well as wives and mothers.

REFERENCES

1. Elizabeth Hamilton, *Memoirs of the Life of Agrippina, the wife of Germanicus*, 3 vols. (Bath, 1804), p.xxvi.
2. Jane Austen, *Northanger Abbey* (New York, 1965), Ch.14, pp.91–2.
3. Gianna Pomata, 'History, Particular and Universal: on reading some recent women's history textbooks', *Feminist Studies*, xix (Spring 1993), p.11.
4. Natalie Zemon Davis, 'Gender and Genre: Women as Historical Writers, 1400–1820', in Patricia H. Labalme (ed.), *Beyond Their Sex. Learned Women of the European Past* (New York and London, 1984); Bonnie Smith, 'The Contribution of Women to Modern Historiography in Great Britain, France and the United States, *American Historical Review*, 89 (1984); Jane Rendall, 'Writing History for British Women: Elizabeth Hamilton and the *Memoirs of Agrippina*', in Clarissa Campbell-Orr (ed.), *Wollstonecraft's Daughters. Womanhood in England and France 1780–1920* (Manchester, 1996).
5. On the concept of civil society, see John Keane, 'Despotism and democracy: the origins and development of the distinction between civil society and the state', in John Keane. ed., *Civil Society and the State. New European Perspectives* (London, 1988); David McCrone, *Understanding Scotland. The Sociology of a Stateless Nation* (London and New York, 1992), pp.20–6.
6. Colin Kidd, *Subverting Scotland's Past. Scottish whig historians and the creation of an Anglo-British identity, 1689-c.1830* (Cambridge,1993); David Allan, *Virtue, Learning, and the Scottish Enlightenment* (Edinburgh, 1993).
7. Karen O'Brien, *Narratives of Enlightenment. Cosmopolitan history from Voltaire to Gibbon* (Cambridge, 1997), pp.60–2, and 'Robertson and eighteenth-century narrative history', in Stewart J. Brown (ed.), *William Robertson and the Expansion of Empire* (Cambridge, 1997), pp.83–5; Mark Phillips, '"If Mrs Mure be not sorry for poor King Charles": History, the Novel, and the Sentimental Reader', *History Workshop Journal* 43 (Spring 1997).
8. On Alexander, see Jane Rendall, 'Introduction' to William Alexander, *History of Women, from the Earliest Antiquity to the Present Time, giving some account of almost every interesting particular concerning that sex, among all nations, ancient and modern . . .* 2 vols (1779; 1782 ed. reprinted Bath, 1994), pp.v-xxvi. References are to the latter edition unless otherwise indicated.
9. *Ibid.*, I, p.xiv. On the 'querelle des femmes', see Joan Kelly, 'Early Feminist Theory and the Querelle des Femmes', in *Women, History and Theory* (Chicago, 1984).
10. *Ibid.*, I, pp.256–60, 283.
11. *Ibid*, I, pp.53, 218, 360–89.
12. *Ibid.*, II, pp.318–21, 415–432.
13. *Ibid*, I, pp.xv–xxii.
14. Alexander, *History of Women* (1779), II, p.185; *History of Women*, II, pp.48, 385–7.
15. *Ibid*, I, pp.65–6, 502, II, pp.56–8; *History of Women* (1779), I, p.48.
16. *History of Women*, I, p.300.
17. *Ibid*, I, p.151.
18. Kidd, *Subverting Scotland's Past*, pp.107–122; Allan, *Virtue, Learning and the Scottish Enlightenment*, Part II; Ronald Meek, *Social Science and the Ignoble Savage* (Cambridge, 1976), *passim*; and see the bibliography of Richard Sher, *Church and University in the Scottish Enlightenment. The Moderate Scottish Literati* (Princeton, 1985), pp.366–368.
19. John Dwyer, *Virtuous Discourse. Sensibility and Community in late Eighteenth-Century Scotland* (Edinburgh, 1987).
20. The natural jurisprudence referred to here was that school of early modern writers, including Hugo Grotius and Samuel von Pufendorf, who grounded a theory of natural rights in a natural law to be distinguished from divine law, ordained by God yet knowable through 'right reason'. See: Knud Haakonssen, *The Science of a Legislator. The Natural Jurisprudence of David Hume and Adam Smith* (Cambridge, 1981); Ian Simpson Ross, *The Life of Adam Smith* (Oxford, 1995), pp.107, 121–7; Jane Rendall, 'Virtue and commerce:

women in the making of Adam Smith's political economy', in Ellen Kennedy and Susan Mendus (ed.), *Women in Western Political Philosophy* (Brighton, 1987).

21. See Donald R. Kelley, 'Gaius Noster: Substructures of Western Social Thought', *American Historical Review*, 84 (1979), p.648; Dario Castiglione and Lesley Sharpe (eds.), 'Preface', *Shifting the Boundaries. Transformation of the Languages of Public and Private in the Eighteenth Century* (Exeter, 1995), p.x. In the paragraph which follows, I have relied upon: Knud Haakonssen, 'John Millar and the Science of a Legislator', *Juridical Review* (1985); John W. Cairns, 'John Millar's Lectures on Scots Criminal Law', *Oxford Journal of Legal Studies* 8 (1988); *idem*, 'Rhetoric, Language and Roman Law: Legal Education and Improvement in Eighteenth-century Scotland', *Law and History Review*, 9 (1991).
22. Adam Smith, *Lectures on Jurisprudence* R.L. Meek, D.D. Raphael, and P.G. Stein eds. (Indianopolis, 1982), p.146. More generally, on the implications of Smith's moral philosophy and political economy, see also: Henry C. Clark, 'Women and Humanity in Scottish Social Thought: the Case of Adam Smith', *Historical Reflections/Reflexions Historique* 19 (1993); Kathryn Sutherland, 'Adam Smith's master narrative: women and the *Wealth of Nations*', in Adam Smith's *Wealth of Nations. New interdisciplinary essays* ed. Stephen Copley and Kathryn Sutherland (Manchester, 1995).
23. *Observations concerning the Distinction of Ranks in Society* (London, 1771) reprinted as *Origin of the Distinction of Ranks . . .* 3rd ed. (London, 1779).
24. The relevant lectures are those which form the second part of the course on Roman law. Both parts of the course are contained in the following MSS: National Library of Scotland (NLS) MS 3930 and Adv. MS 28.6.8; Glasgow University Library (GUL) MSS Murray 76–82 and 96–8, and MSS Gen. 812–4. The second part only can be found in NLS Adv. MSS 20.4.7; GUL MS Murray 332, and Hamilton 117; Edinburgh University Library (EUL) Dc. 2. 45–6. I have relied primarily on GUL Murray 96–8 and on EUL Dc. 2. 45–46. See Cairns' 'John Millar's Lectures'.
25. Millar, *Origin of the Distinction of Ranks*, reprinted in W. C. Lehmann, *John Millar of Glasgow* (Cambridge, 1960), pp.176, 203. On Millar's account, see P. Bowles, 'John Millar, the four stages theory, and women's position in society', *History of Political Economy* (Winter, 1984); *idem*, 'Millar and Engels on the history of women and the family', *History of European Ideas*, 12 (1990); Michael Ignatieff, 'John Millar and Individualism', in Istvan Hont and Michael Ignatieff (eds.), *Wealth and Virtue* (Cambridge, 1983).
26. See, for instance, Adam Ferguson, *Essay on the History of Civil Society* (1767; reprinted Edinburgh, 1966), p.83.
27. Millar, *Origin*, in Lehmann, *John Millar of Glasgow*, pp.190, 195–7.
28. Meek, *Social Science and the Ignoble Savage*, p.167; Joseph Francis Lafitau, *Moeurs des sauvages amériquains comparées aux moeurs des premiers temps* (1724); Pierre Charlevoix, *Histoire et description générale de la Nouvelle France; avec le journal historique d'un voyage fait par ordre du roi dans l'Amerique septentrionale*, 6 tom. (Paris, 1744). On the many precedents for such historical writing, see: Margaret Hodgen, *Early Anthropology in the Sixteenth and Seventeenth Centuries* (Philadelphia, 1964); Roger L. Emerson, 'American Indians, Frenchmen, and Scots Philosophers', in Roseann Runte, ed., *Studies in Eighteenth Century Culture* (Madison, Wisconsin, 1979), and 'Conjectural History and the Scottish Enlightenment', Canadian Historical Association, *Historical Papers* (1985).
29. Millar, *Origin*, in Lehmann, *John Millar of Glasgow*, p.218; William Robertson, *History of the Reign of the Emperor Charles V, with a View of the Progress of Society in Europe*, 3 vols., (1769), in *The Works of William Robertson D.D.*, 12 vols, (London, 1818), IV, pp.25–98.
30. Millar, *Origin of Ranks*, in Lehmann, *John Millar*, pp.219–28.
31. Henry Home, Lord Kames *Sketches of the History of Man*, 4 vols. (1774, 2nd ed. Edinburgh, 1778), II, p.69. On Kames, see Ian Simpson Ross, *Lord Kames and the Scotland of his Day* (Oxford, 1972); William C. Lehmann, *Lord Kames and the Scottish Enlightenment* (The Hague, 1971).
32. Robertson, *History of America* (1777) in *Works*, IX, 103; O'Brien, *Narratives of Enlightenment*, pp.156–61.

33. Millar, *Origin of Ranks*, in Lehmann, *John Millar of Glasgow*, pp.206–7.
34. Kames, *Sketches*, I, pp.421–2, 450.
35. *Ibid.*, Paul-Henri Mallet, *Introduction à l'histoire de Dannemarc, où l'on traite de la religion, des lois, des moeurs, & des usages des anciens Danois* (Copenhagen, 1755), pp.199–201. More generally on this debate, see Jane Rendall, 'Tacitus Engendered: Gothic Feminism and British Histories 1750–1800', in Geoffrey Cubitt (ed.), *Imagining Nations* (Manchester, 1998).
36. There is here no space to address the complexity of modern reinterpretation of Ossianic poetry; I am indebted to the important recent discussion of Ossian in terms of the enlightened representation of sensibility and feeling by John Dwyer, 'The Melancholy Savage: Text and Context in the Poems of Ossian', in Howard Gaskill (ed.), *Ossian Revisited* (Edinburgh, 1991).
37. Kidd, *Subverting Scotland's Past*, pp.219–39; James Macpherson, *Introduction to the History of Great Britain and Ireland . . .* (1771; 2nd ed. London, 1772), pp.268–77, 307.
38. Yoshiaki Sudo, 'An Unpublished Lecture of Hugh Blair on the Poems of Ossian', *The Hiyoshi Review of English Studies*, 25 (March 1995), p.168; Hugh Blair, *A Critical Dissertation on the Poems of Ossian* (1765 ed.), in James Macpherson, *The Poems of Ossian and Related Works* ed. Howard Gaskill (Edinburgh, 1996), pp.349–52, 378. Ragnar Lodbrog was the ninth-century Danish king whose funeral ode was partially translated in 1756 by Mallet, *Monumens de la Mythologie et de la poesie des Celtes et particulièrement des anciens Scandinaves . . .* (Copenhagen, 1756), pp.155–6.
39. Blair, *Critical Dissertation*, pp.354, 375–6.
40. Robert Henry, *The History of Great Britain, from the first invasion of it by the Romans, under Julius Caesar. Written on a New Plan* (1771–93; 2nd ed., London, 1788–95), 12 vols.,I, p.321.
41. On Stuart, see William Zachs, *Without Regard to Good Manners. A Biography of Gilbert Stuart 1743–1786* (Edinburgh, 1992), p.24; Kidd, *Subverting Scotland's Past*, pp.239–246.
42. Gilbert Stuart, *A View of Society in Europe, in its Progress from Rudeness to Refinement* (1778; 1792 edition reprinted Bath, 1995), pp.223–234.
43. *Ibid.*, pp.17–18, 28–34.
44. *Ibid.*, 15; see also pp.169–70, 244–5.
45. John Millar, MS lectures on civil law, Edinburgh University Library Dc. 2. 45–6, ff. pp.32–8.
46. See Rendall, 'Tacitus Engendered'.
47. John Dwyer, *Virtuous Discourse*, Ch. 5; *idem*, 'Clio and Ethics: Practical Morality in Enlightened Scotland', *The Eighteenth Century* 30 (1989); Phillips, '"If Mrs Mure be not sorry for poor King Charles"'.
48. John Gregory, *A Comparative View of the State and Faculties of Man with those of the Animal World* (1764; Edinburgh, 1788), pp.41, 51, 66, 185; 'An account of the life and writings of Dr John Gregory' prefixed to John Gregory, *A Father's Legacy to His daughters* (Edinburgh, 1788), pp.73–4; Lord Kames, *Loose Hints upon Education, chiefly concerning the Culture of the Heart* (1781; 2nd ed., enlarged, Edinburgh, 1788), pp.15, 27, 36–8, 52–7, 64, 68, 81, 120, 143, 238–45, 258, 277; Paul Wood, 'The science of man', in N. Jardine, J. A. Secord and E.C. Spary (eds.), *Cultures of Natural History* (Cambridge, 1996).
49. James Fordyce, *Sermons to Young Women* (1764; Dublin, 1766), I, pp.257–8; Gregory, *A Father's Legacy to his Daughters* (1774; here in *The Young Lady's Pocket Library, or Parental Monitor*, 1790, reprinted with an introduction by Vivien Jones, Bath, 1995), pp.3–4, 22; Kames, *Loose Hints*, p.8.
50. James Fordyce, *The Character and Conduct of the Female Sex, and the advantages to be derived by young men from the society of virtuous women . . .* (London, 1776), pp.6–8, 4–7.
51. Gregory, *Father's Legacy* (1995), p.3; *idem*, *Comparative View* (1788), p.xi.
52. *Ibid*, xvi-xviii, pp.18–19, 121–22.
53. Kames, *Loose Hints*.
54. *The Lounger*, p.102, quoted in Dwyer, *Virtuous Discourse*, p.113.
55. Fordyce, *Sermons*, I, pp.7, 195, 198–211; Millar, *Origin*, in Lehmann, *John Millar of Glasgow*, pp.220–1.

56. Fordyce, *Sermons,* I, pp.260–1; Kames, *Loose Hints*, 277; compare the comments of Kames' biographer, who struggled to account for the indelicacy of those sections of the *Sketches* which dealt with the progress of the female sex. Alexander Fraser Tytler, *Memoirs of the Life and Writings of the Honourable Henry Home of Kames . . .* (Edinburgh, 1807), pp.160–1.
57. Rendall, 'Introduction', Alexander, *History of Women*, pp.xxiii-iv.
58. Lucy Aikin, *Epistles on Women, exemplifying their Character and Condition in Various Ages and Nations with Miscellaneous Poems* (London, 1810), Introduction. For a discussion of the ambivalent relationship of Mary Wollstonecraft to the Scottish historiographical tradition, see Jane Rendall, '"The grand causes which combine to carry mankind forward"': Wollstonecraft, history and revolution', *Women's Writing: the Early Modern Period*, 4 1997.
59. Gary Kelly, *Women, Writing and Revolution,* 1790–1827 (Oxford, 1993), pp.187–91.

Ten

William Robertson and America

BERNARD ASPINWALL

'I CAN SCARCE CONCEIVE a Scotchman, capable of liberality, but utterly incapable of impartiality.' wrote a friend to Rev Richard Price, the Unitarian philosopher, dissenter and American sympathiser, 'That nation is compos'd of such a sad set of innate cold hearted, impudent rogues, that I sometimes think it a comfort when you and I shall walk together in the next world, which I hope we shall see as well as this, we cannot possibly then have any of them sticking to our skirts. It is a melancholy thing that there is no finding other people that will take pains, or be amenable even to the best purposes.'[1] Earlier, an American correspondent had bitterly assailed the Scottish character: it was 'impossible to wean them from the principles of perfidy, slavery and ingratitude which are native to them; and which mark them as a people *hostis humani generis*'. Whatever John Witherspoon did at Princeton or in signing the Declaration of Independence, the image of Scotland in America then remained essentially negative during the War of Independence. By the early nineteenth century, the image was positive, warm and vital. How had this change come about?

William Robertson was part of the explanation. Americans knew him and his historical work: both were greatly respected. His history had a social and political agenda. He showed a quiet confidence in humane and providential progress. In the eighteenth century, he provided providential roots and rational purpose: in the nineteenth national purpose. He reflected the confident Edinburgh of the Enlightenment, the growing assertiveness of the Scottish aristocracy and the subtle absorption of the nation into the English provinces. Robertson was Whiggish, respectable and comfortable in his elitism. Accepted and secure in the larger British society, he retained a strong sense of Scottish identity. The particular, the province and the locality might contribute to the larger humane, British imperial mission. In his reasonable restatement of older Calvinist notions, the 'right' people would make the correct decisions. At home and abroad, reasonable Protestantism, educated leadership and commerce made for progress. It was antiseptic, orderly, peaceful and advantageous. Hardly a utopian, Robertson envisaged social uplift. He did not contemplate the reordering of society or the redistribution of wealth. Self-confident Scots would remodel the world in the image of reason.

Robertson served two distinct purposes. In his lifetime his writings reassured the Scottish elite in its self-confidence and conceit. The Scottish Enlightenment proved their superiority. Robertson's *History* integrated Scotland and the colonies into the British transatlantic world. In his work he justified himself as a preacher, teacher and university principal. Religious, political and cultural leadership demanded virtue, discipline and intelligence. In 'modernising' Protestantism, Edinburgh and Scotland, Robertson restated old truths in new guises. In a developing society, effective leadership needed education, the work ethic, stewardship and responsibility. Enlightened Protestantism and education, property and thriving commerce were irresistible forms of providential purpose. In short Robertson endorsed 'the redemptive role of the technically trained professional middle class'.[2] Scotland was fit to lead.

In the colonies and the early American republic to the Civil War, Robertson served another purpose. Without tradition, America needed moral purpose. The colonies and Scotland shared a common outlook: they had a similar set of cultural assumptions. To these interests Robertson naturally appealed. The later popularity of his writings demonstrated the conservatism of the American revolution. It was a moral revolt of high-minded civil libertarians against irresponsible power. It was not allegedly a revolt of the untutored masses: the American constitution ensured they were contained. Careful checks and balances held ruler and ruled in equilibrium. The disinterested men of virtue, property and education allegedly had prevailed. In reality an elite group, comfortable in its assumptions of superiority, virtue and wealth dominated. Inevitable progress, better education and efficiency followed. Compassion, understanding, democracy and equality were less in evidence.

In Robertson's work a civilised property–owning citizenry, educated and pursuing peaceful commerce, respected responsible rulers. Men were mobile but not restless. Society was stable but not static. Religion was flexible rather than routine. That was Robertson's message, one of orderly progress. The guarantee of providential favour therefore lay in increasingly educated masses, sensitive to their moral duties and in the creation of a purposeful national identity. Individualism was not licence. It demanded even high moral stewardship. Education, moral awareness and calm judgement of the individual were essential in democratic society. How else could norms be established?

Robertson himself sympathised with colonial constitutional aspirations and privately seemed resigned, reluctantly, to American independence at some point: 'I do not apprehend revolution or independence sooner than these must and should come'.[3] At the same time he was a close friend of William Smith (1728–93), historian and chief justice of New York. He vainly sought to conciliate the colonies and government before abandoning his Whiggish views for Tory exile.[4] Another of Robertson's friends, Edmund Burke, followed a similar pattern. His sympathies shifted to Toryism.[5] Like Robertson they shared a distaste for the masses. As the only volunteer to provide himself with a horse during the Jacobite scare, Robertson clearly preferred union with England to a potentially irresponsible populace and to weak liberal nations struggling in an autocratic Catholic world.[6]

Robertson also knew Benjamin Franklin: they had shared some five days' convivial companionship with Lord Kames at Blair Drummond. Franklin had become a firm friend. Although differing philosophically, he greatly admired Franklin and accepted his several recommendations for Edinburgh degrees.[7] Thomas Jefferson read him and made sure his family did too.[8] John Adams read him throughout his long life.[9] He even wrote a considerable article on Robertson, Chalmers and Hutcheson for the *North American Review* in 1831. Alexander Hamilton similarly read his work. Benjamin Rush, although less than impressed by Robertson's personality, remained a fair admirer of his work.[10] In the early nineteenth century the American newspaper editor and former professor at Dartmouth, Nathaniel A. Carter, made a pilgrimage to Robertson's manse.[11] Even though more than a decade before some American critics had derided Robertson as outdated, an article in the *North American Review*, in 1826, claimed he remained the most widely read historian in America. In the same journal shortly afterwards, John Adams was to write a major analysis of his work.[12]

That renewed interest demonstrated the considerable popularity, abiding influence and contemporary usefulness of his work. His histories had sold well before the War of Independence. An immense American boom followed in the first decades of the nineteenth century: editions appeared in Philadelphia, 1799, 1811–12, and 1821; Walpole, New Hampshire, 1801; Albany, New York, 1822. Not all Americans were uncritical admirers. Ralph Waldo Emerson discerned 'superiority and spiritual pride' in Robertson's departure from the 'popular faith'.[13] Washington Irving, the novelist and historian of Spain, found the work read 'like a romance'.[14] That was hardly surprising. Robertson was a close friend of Sir Walter Scott: both were tapping similar reading markets.[15] Later, William Hinkling Prescott produced a version of *Charles V*, extended by his own work in 1855: a gentleman scholar with clear racial, social and religious prejudices, he found the work coincided with his own vision of an ideal America. A relaxed Calvinism, a practical industrious self-reliant spirit gave shape and direction to the civilising forces of man.[16] The Bible and religion permeated both Scottish and American consciousness: God, history and national purpose were interchangeable. Prescott preferred British rationality to the excesses of the continent.[17]

The most interesting feature for our consideration is the use of Robertson's *The History of America* as a school textbook. Every year from 1831 to 1859, Harper's published John Frost's version with additional examination questions. Frost (1800–59) was a school teacher from Kennebunk, Maine, educated at Bowdoin and Harvard. He taught in Cambridgeport, Boston and Philadelphia until 1845. In his spare time he produced a short-lived improving magazine for children and wrote textbooks. His educational influence then continued unchallenged until the Civil War. Frost was building the moral purpose of the nation. He not only produced a version of Robertson and of Kames's *Elements of Criticism* (1839), but he also wrote some four hundred other inspirational, nationalist works. They included studies of Webster, Clay, Zachary Taylor, Penn, Washington and philanthropic American merchants' deeds for youngsters; eulogies of American heroes in the army, navy and the West, American heroines, popular histories of America and California. He also published studies of Kossuth and the Hungarian rising. On receiving an honorary degree from Marischal College, he gave an address. It was entitled *The Duty of the American Scholar to the Life of his Country* (1841). Robertson, then, was a rare foreign contributor to Frost's notions of American identity.[18]

That was hardly surprising considering the dominance of Scottish thinkers, writers and religious outlook in the colonies and the emerging nation. Readers found great solace in their works.[19] Although some American historians still overlook that influence, substantial studies make an irresistible case.[20]

John Witherspoon at Princeton and a host of Scottish educators shaped the nation: civil and religious liberties were indivisible.[21] Moderate evangelicals and evangelical moderates were not always so clearly distinguishable in their zeal to 'liberate' man. Evangelicals, restrained and otherwise, found like-minded souls in Scotland and America. Scottish weavers and ironmoulders introduced new technologies to infant industries. Scottish entrepreneurs supplied the material needs. Scottish educated doctors treated the American ills. Even the expression 'Americanism' was a Scotticism invented by Dr. John Witherspoon.[22] He also gave it campus common usage. Robertson allegedly invented 'interference'.[23] The Atlantic was little more than a Scottish loch.

Scottish Common Sense philosophy was a dominant element. That form of modified Enlightened-Evangelicalism or Evangelical-Enlightenment provided cohesion in a fragmented evolving society. It established virtue by consensus. It provided the framework within which to develop an American national identity. Robertson and his history gave 'reasonable' religious, political and social roots. Reason and faith in providential evolutionary progress proved a revolution had not taken place. The elite, pious and reasonable, right thinking and dominant, still set the agenda. Duty and obligation were paramount in the community: at best freedom and rights were secondary. It helped to solidify an evolving British identity in the aftermath of Jacobitism, dislocated old order and increasing commercialism. While quietly maintaining the superiority of Protestantism, especially Presbyterianism, other traditions were not excluded: 'A progressive group is always united because the beliefs of its members come from their acts and impulses; a stationary group falls apart through the tendency of each faction to emphasise a past in which other groups do not share.'[24] Men of Common Sense had to unite in particular against Scottish-American free thought.[25] As an Edinburgh divine told the American Alexander Dallas Bache, if popular education in Scotland 'has not produced distinguished men, it has infused into the industrious classes a considerable number of sober citizens'.[26] Like Professor John Nichol later, Robertson was perhaps apprehensive lest excessive criticism led to nothingness.[27] It was a philosophy of creative containment in a common transatlantic culture.

My purpose, then, is to suggest that Robertson was part of a transatlantic network. He manufactured tradition for export. He baptised the Enlightenment and made it safe for Christianity: a reasonable Christian morality would inform the new Enlightened order. Robertson, Chalmers and Bryce, a Scot by tradition and adoption, were its main exponents: they found echoes in numerous American commentators and disciples. Part of an educated and informed elite, Robertson, Chalmers and Bryce and their kind were Liberal Unionists or Liberal Tories. They accepted change within an orderly, rational British environment: but the onus was on the critics. They provided mobile servants of the enterprise culture of the English-speaking imperial states. They were vital components in the mental structure or furniture of that world; educated for a dynamic leading role and above all technicians of Progress. 'Wha's like us? Damn few and they're a' deid.' The world was going and should go their way. The demands of humanity, ideals of social service, were enough. No lesser breeds, faiths, ideals or races need apply.

While not actively persecuting less able, less fortunate or less 'Protestant' elements, these writers were sure of their own mental, moral and economic superiority. Sir George Campbell similarly recognised the better qualities of America owed much to the diffusion of Scottish blood, endeavour and intelligence through the society. They could easily mistake one of their own for an American. A Paisley Member of Parliament visited Chicago. Eager to meet a typical American, he 'found at last a man who exactly came up to his ideas and entering into conversation with him, he said 'Have you been here long ? 'Na,' was the answer, 'I'm just a month frae Glasgow'.[28] The popularity of David Macrae's numerous entertaining travel books on both sides of the Atlantic was further proof.[29] In so far as the group or individual approximated to the perceived Scottish qualities, they were acceptable. Scotland was a mirror for Americans, and America, a mirror for Scots.

Shared values and shared assumptions made for a democracy of the like-minded: pluralism was a long way off. That dominance continued, slowly eroding after the Civil War as industrialism developed and new migrant groups arrived in America. Sabine Gould's hymn 'Onward Christian Soldiers' in 1865 was a symptom of the change. Commonsense Christian faith was giving way to a more intense, emotional and less 'reasonable' expression of faith. However liberal Bryce may appear, he still reflected the assumptions and values of the older American elite. As Simon N. Patten, the American economist, said: 'No nation which had been through Calvinism can ever be truly democratic'.[30]

The change to a more thoroughly democratic, more diverse mentality followed from the 1920s. The growing dominance of the cities, industry and the new ethnics coincided with the emergence of the later Sir Denis W. Brogan. The Glasgow-born and Jesuit-educated son of an Irish Catholic migrant tailor and founder of the Glasgow Gaelic Association, he won a Snell scholarship from Glasgow to Balliol and became a remarkable scholarly commentator on American life. His many books like *The American Character* (1944) show a more democratic, more relaxed, less moralising view. He reflected a social revolution in the Atlantic world. Diversity of race, gender and ethnicity challenged the old order. In more recent times a more thoroughly pluralist yet equally 'real' American character has developed.[31] Yet the link between *local*, ethnic, gender and racial loyalties and *universal* loyalty to liberty remains well established. Robertson and his tradition had served their purpose.

Education was the key ingredient in the transatlantic tradition to which William Robertson contributed. Scottish Common Sense philosophy dominated through the first half of the nineteenth century. Even after 1868 James McCosh of Princeton still maintained its importance. In a sense it provided a featherbed for fading Calvinists. Against the background of evangelical zealots and wild Jacksonian democrats, it inculcated restraint. That in turn was effected through a largely Scottish-inspired educational programme. Scotland and New England had, according to Orville Dewey, 'a people in both instances, industrious, virtuous, religious almost beyond example-carrying popular education to the point of improvement almost unexampled in the world'.[32] It was practical as a Scottish observer believed 'he carried no burden of learning he could not use'.[33] The American Unitarian William Ellery Channing extolled the social role of teachers: 'that skill to form the young to energy, truth and virtue is worth more than the knowledge of all other arts and sciences'.[34] At a philosophical academic level, Francis Wayland's *Elements of Moral Science* (1835), the popular American vehicle for

Scottish philosophy, exercised widespread influence. His visit to Scotland sealed that association. At a more popular level the work of William Russell, a Glasgow graduate, and Robert Cunningham, an Edinburgh graduate, established the professional character of school teaching, introduced new teaching techniques and formed the necessary American values among pupils. In their hands Robertson became a vital element in building American national tradition.

What, then, was this tradition to which Robertson contributed? First it sustained a good self-conceit. It was primarily defensive. Fear as much as benevolence directed education. It was a form of social insurance. It protected society against extremists of religious zealotry or radical free thinkers like the Scottish Fanny Wright and her friends. For migrants lose 'that vital force which is the organic and conserving order of society. All the old roots of local love and historic feeling – the joints and bands which minister nourishment – are left behind'.[35] Robertson and his kind injected a useful, practical version of Christian tradition into a new democratising society. If it was imposed on the populace, they believed such notions were naturally inherent in humanity. Certain personal and social values were 'natural'. The legal imposition of such ideas was unnecessary and in a vast, mobile America impossible. A self-disciplined virtuous individual functioned more efficiently than one regulated by external legal compulsion. Robertson and the rest were gerrymandering a moral majority for traditional Protestant values and for the absent God. It was democratic and restraining. People, as de Tocqueville saw, were free, free to conform to the norms sustained by local public opinion.

If Robertson endorsed the status quo, he accepted intelligent political evolution. For Robertson and his American supporters, moral philosophy was vital in higher education: it was part of the university mission to inculcate a love of religion and virtue and 'to teach our sons when boys what we desire they may retain and profit by when they are men'.[36]

Education, then, was the battleground: the soul of the republic was at stake.[37] Scottish religious concern aroused American observers.[38] Hard work was a better guide and more fruitful than brain work in America: it also crushed vice, luxury and pretension.[39] As another Princeton exporter of this tradition, John Witherspoon saw intuition was the first principle of morality: the right environment would create the 'right' disposition.[40] Another Scot at Princeton, James McCosh, saw 'the formation of good habits was more than half of education'.[41] Character was, so this tradition would suggest, 'aroused by vivid ideas and long sought ends. It is never built out of new material or improved by hardship and restraint'.[42] Robertson's *History*, like a well-told moral tale, was a tract. It perhaps overcame the moral dangers of novel reading in America.[43] Solid, considered advances were to safeguard tradition in the new order. Self-interest led to virtue, to prudence, temperance and fortitude: the Scottish Common Sense philosophy.[44]

The solution was a variation on the old Calvinism: an informed moral elite should govern. Like the old American Puritanism, the family, the church, the commonwealth were part of the ordered relationship with God.[45] The godly were undoubtedly in the minority. If providence was absent, then Robertson foresaw difficulties: 'to discard voluntarily from the supreme to a subordinate station, and to relinquish the possession of power in order to attain the enjoyment of happiness, seems to be an effort too great for the human mind'.[46] Selfishness and self-importance proved human frailty and inadequacy before the true Protestant god. The histories are moral tales, sermons in favour of virtue and morality. He was restating a more palatable, secularised, Enlightened version of the coming of the Kingdom.[47] It was a comfortable view.[48] Intelligence and morality must not truckle to the ignorant mob.[49] A minister, Moderate or otherwise, whatever his formal academic role, could hardly do otherwise.

The Protestant work ethic was endorsed: 'The labour and operations of man not only improve and embellish the earth, but render it more wholesome and friendly to life'.[50] Given Robertson's own strict upbringing and his initial resistance even to playing whist, his outlook is understandable. He did not look back to a rural idyll: rather he saw progress in city life. He would endorse Simon N. Patten:

> Rationalism fails in a complex society because there are no necessary principles nor is there any general utilitarian calculus. The seemingly general principles, are not after all, universal . . . The victories of religion are in complex societies. The great religions of man emphasise the impulses of men and thus unite men on the issues where progress is possible. The standpoint of partial adjustment can do nothing to placate struggle and conflict between classes and races. Only in the ideals and impulses of complete adjustment does harmony exist . . . A common environment and common desires create a united race and a rational basis of action.[51]

As Frederic Harrison, his Comtean contemporary, said: 'religion consists, not in answering questions but in making men of a certain quality'.[52]

Robertson did appreciate the environment more readily than most. The climate and resources of America were vast and boundless: 'Nature seems here to have carried on her operations with a bolder hand, and to have distinguished the features of this country by a peculiar magnificence'.[53] Professor John Nichol of Glasgow wrote the first *History of American Literature* (Edinburgh, 1882) with a similar awareness. Both long foreshadowed David Potter's *People of Plenty* (1954). He saw the natural abundance with but few people in a land filled with animals of prey but devoid of domesticated beasts made for a different form of rude society.[54] That condition meant hard physical labour and produced robust people. Unfortunately little improvement came to themselves or their lands. Torture and death held few terrors for their hardened beings. It also meant 'rude notions'.[55] Lithe, comely figures of men aborted or murdered the weak or deformed.[56] They practised euthanasia.[57] The opposites of European propriety, they gave few hostages to fortune, were rootless and a threat to Robertson's sense of a stable order.[58] Far from being an inherent racial characteristic, their cultural behaviour demonstrated the need for superior moral training and discipline.[59] They were part of degenerate world.[60] Although having some redeeming features, they remained essentially barbarians. It was a view the rationalist feminist Frances Wright, perhaps surprisingly, endorsed.[61]

A mobile, hunting lifestyle meant that they did not acquire property. They therefore became listless, inattentive and weak. Lack of property meant the end of social distinction.[62] Their apathy thanks to the climate and easy means of survival did little to improve them. Their lack of culture meant they showed 'improvident indolence' and 'the thoughtless levity of children or the improvident instinct of animals'.[63] Equally they sought vengeance in raids and massacres executed by stealth: 'they resembled beasts of prey rather than animals formed for labour'.[64] Some contemporaries claimed Robertson was too superficial and harsh on savage weaknesses. A sophisticated settled society alone improved primitive behaviour: in Peru, religion built up a complex social order. Duty and service prevailed.[65]

Industry was a major test. Many nations clearly did not manifest the desired 'Protestant' characteristics. Portugal was 'a nation, naturally slow and dilatory in forming all resolutions'.[66] Robertson had a misplaced confidence in inevitable progress: 'the necessary arts of life, when once they have been introduced among any people are never lost'.[67] Jefferson and others were sceptical. Indians showed few moral scruples. Insensitive to beauty and love, they showed little respect for chastity 'to which he is a stranger'.[68] Marriage was not a norm: permanent unions were unusual.[69] Similarly they were unaccustomed to subordination and discipline 'like all unpolished nations'.[70] They gambled and drank excessively, particularly during lengthy festivals. Similarly Bryce found an ominous fatalism in 'the dead weight of ignorance' among Central, Southern and Eastern European migrants to America, while 'childishness and lack of self control' marked Afro-Americans[71]

The pioneering Scottish clergyman Rev Dr. John Dunmore Lang shared similar attitudes in Australia. He could combine ferocious anti-Chinese sentiment with the conviction 'we are here to advance the best interests of our common humanity – we are here to promote the grand and glorious objects of our common Christianity'.[72] Not surprisingly Dr. Robert Knox produced the scientific apology for American Southern slavery in 1855. As one critic has claimed, the Scottish Enlightenment had a distinctly nativist tinge.[73] Scotland for some was 'the most priest-ridden nation in Europe' who 'tries her church, her clergy, her school, her opinions . . . by no standard but her own cherished prepossessions; and she finds them perfect'.[74]

Autocratic regimes were invariably 'illiberal fanatics'.[75] Such governments invariably led to stagnation in trade, commerce and intellectual life. A flourishing trading world meant peace.[76] The masses, inevitably, would 'always be [prevented] in every country, from entering upon any speculative inquiry by the various occupations of active and laborious life'.[77] Only the elite would have the necessary affluence, leisure and education to reflect and to act. The elite therefore had responsibilities to the lower orders. Most people conformed from habit, inertia, ignorance or sloth. Reform, amelioration or improvement came from external forces: men and societies did not change from within.[78] Even so, Robertson welcomed those primitives 'who conscious of their dignity and capable of the greatest efforts in asserting it, aspire to independence'.[79] Many barriers remained. The intelligentsia, the moral, intellectual and social superiors had to be up and doing. A freer Scotland might have been more creative and useful but liberated men of talents should be active.

These notions of the lower orders and races coloured Robertson's view of the early English settlements. When Captain John Smith left Jamestown, 'profligate or desperate' colonists proved 'little capable of the regular subordination, the strict economy, and the persevering industry that their situation required'.[80] Similarly in Virginia, colonists devoid of principle and humanity sought to exterminate the Indians.[81] Religious and social extremists like the Brownists and 'the levelling genius of fanaticism', apprehensive for their own survival, migrated to America. English colonists were 'not animated with such liberal sentiments, either concerning their own personal and political rights, as have become familiar in the more and improved state of their constitution'. The superior discipline of Europeans was vital. Like the British in India, Alexander needed a few European officers to direct some 30,000 Asians.

Not dissimilar notions colour James Bryce's writings. He lamented the dangerous classes of twentieth century cities. They had little contact with nature: segregated classes, disease and other pressures destroyed morality.[82] In particular he worried that

> That scum which the westward moving wave of emigration carries on its crest is here stopped because it can go no further. It accumulates in San Francisco and forms a dangerous constituent in the population of

> that great and growing city – a population perhaps more mixed than one finds anywhere else in America for Frenchmen, Italians, Portuguese, Greeks and the children of Australian convicts abound there, side by side with negroes, Germans and Irish.[83]

Indeed he attributed much to Robertson and Scottish influences upon previous American developments. Newer migrants were devoid of 'fundamental ideas and ingrained traditions of the New Englander and Virginian of the old stock for those ideas and sentiments do not go with the language and the right to vote'.[84] Public opinion, as expressed by Robertson's Edinburgh Protestants in 1780, was enforcing its 'own qualities of orderliness, good sense and a willingness to bow to the will of the majority'.[85] Bryce even saw humanity in the lynch mob giving whisky to its victim just as Robertson had considered British executions humane.[86] It was a view reminiscent of the Southern demagogue who welcomed lynching as showing the sense of justice was alive and well among the people.

Bryce indeed went further. He discussed Afro-Americans whose enslaved condition did not greatly disturb Robertson in his *History*. He sharply criticised the enfranchisement of freed slaves after the Civil War. In particular their 'childishness and lack of self control which belongs to primitive peoples' appalled him.[87] Emancipation had come too fast: 'Rights which the agricultural labourers of England did not obtain until 1885 were in 1867 foist upon those whose highest form of pleasure had hitherto been to caper to the strains of the banjo'.[88] Clearly he would have disfranchised most of today's youth! More seriously, Afro-Americans were not schooled in puritan earnestness: they were unable to see their real interests, or what a white elite deemed to be their interest.

If Robertson tolerated Catholicism, he retained a negative image. In so far as it demonstrated 'Protestant' qualities it was acceptable. He applauded the Catholic opposition of Las Casas and the Dominicans to slavery.[89] Similarly Isabella's humanity and Columbus's concern for Indians as human beings 'reduced by a common calamity to the same condition as ourselves' won approval. An unusual priest 'displayed a moderation as well as a gentleness . . . rare among persons trained up in the solitude and austerity of monastic life'.[90] In Edinburgh he initially favoured some legal relief for Catholics but immediately public opinion appeared in mob outrage, Robertson saw the time as inopportune. Social development had not so far evolved. Equally he desired that Catholics secure only the rights of a man rather than full citizenship. A lower level of intellect, they needed education.[91] Popery however was reactionary: pre-Reformation failings hung heavily still around Catholicism.[92] However ridiculous the popular prejudices, the parliament should recognise them as real. In his own writings the

Scottish Reformation was more a popular than a theological movement. Yet in preaching he refused to preach what pleased people rather than for their edification. He may have been an astute politique or social scientist but there remains the trimming opportunist.[93]

Bryce in turn remained uneasy about Catholicism. He worried at the Irish character of Boston, clerical political opportunism and excessive servility: 'Obedience is to most sweeter than independence; the Roman Catholic Church inspires in its children a stronger affection than any form of Protestantism for she takes their souls in charge and assures them that, with obedience, all will be well'.[94] He was somewhat more restrained than the more evangelical Scot, Rev Dr. William Arnot, who found Catholicism 'as stupid and sinful as the idol worship of the Hindus'.[95] As a delegate of the General Assembly of the Church of Scotland he found his American trip reinforced his attitudes. Others found Catholics were responsible for the urban ills of New York.[96] In short the Scottish consensus was they were a different breed.

Robertson was the human face of the old Presbyterian order. He envisaged a social hierarchy based on property and talent, setting the agenda for a godly commonwealth. The education of the masses inculcating basic literacy and morality was a first step. Sustaining the family as the bastion of morality, stability and industry served God and Man. If the poor became more disciplined, sober, industrious and thrifty, they would be saved here and in the hereafter. Voluntary moral endeavour was vital. The role of the state was suspect. In America through his friend, Benjamin Franklin, an acceptable moral social order seemed to be evolving through constitutional means. A traditional moral community offered security in a fluctuating world. A vibrant locality depended on a morally gerrymandered constituency: the right environment produced more humane citizens. On occasion cosmopolitan religious insights could reinvigorate a province. Ideologues were unwelcome: sober, industrious, intelligent men must prevail. As John Galt's *Lawrie Todd* said: 'I have seen many [Scottish] self-conceited emigrants, who . . . not being able to make England like America come here and their first work is to make America like England'.[97] Otherwise they became single-minded materialists.[98] To a degree American experience reinforced Toryism or at least Whiggery: the novelist and traveller, Thomas Hamilton, believed the cure for British radicalism was to spend a year in America.[99] Even exceptionally prosperous Scottish migrants retained misgivings about American democracy: it smacked of unprincipled mobocracy.[100] The locality and centre must flourish and interact to the advantage of both. What could be more appropriate in the United States?

Thomas Chalmers took these notions further. While more Whiggish and more evangelical, he shared many attitudes with Robertson: he earnestly desired to eliminate dependency and regenerate sturdy independent individuals. Personal contact, aid and inspirational example from his largely middle class elders would overcome pauperism.[101] These ideas were exported to and retailed in America through the nineteenth and early twentieth centuries: Benjamin Tuckerman of Boston, for example, came to learn and returned to disseminate Chalmers' strategy.[102] Through his preaching and writings, Chalmers encouraged a sense of social service. At the same time the social order remained unaltered: only the individual changed. Scottish schools, as Henry Barnard saw, provided an invaluable 'reformatory and preservative power, a system of common schools'.[103] Scottish visitors to America had seen earlier the benefits of Scottish education as advocated by Robertson: 'combining the highest degree of industrious habits with the highest degree of moral habits'.[104]

The early nineteenth century saw education as a practical necessity, a social insurance and a form of secularised piety: 'schools and schoolmasters the cheapest defence, the best treasures and the highest glory of nations'.[105] Moral nurture, family and church ensured liberty prevailed over equality. Benevolence was born of fear of anarchy. Crevecouer foresaw the absence of tradition meant an absence of God and morality.[106] William Russell, a Glasgow graduate, was pre-eminent in the development of school teaching as a profession in America. Rigorous and disciplined, he impressed Bronson Alcott as 'the most orderly mind he ever' met.[107] Like his contemporary Robert Cunningham, an Edinburgh graduate, who established the first professional teacher training institutes in Pennsylvania and Britain, he promoted the Robertson tradition. They sought to demonstrate the validity of Scottish Common Sense philosophy in educational practice. Pestalozzian ideas brought forward the virtues in every human being. The schools were 'the nursery of the Church'.[108]

The basis of rational responsible government was education. As Lord Bryce, in his *American Commonwealth*, said:

> Education ought, no doubt, to enlighten a man; but the educated classes, speaking generally, are the property owning classes, and the possession of property does more to make a man more timid than education does to make him hopeful. He is apt to underrate the power as well as the worth of sentiment; he overvalues the restraints which existing institutions impose; he has a faint appreciation of the curative power of freedom, and of the tendency which brings things right when men have been left to their own devices and have learnt from failure how to attain success. In the less-educated man a certain simplicity and openness of mind go some way to compensate for the lack of knowledge. He is more apt to be influenced by the authority of leaders; but as,

> at least in England and America, he is generally shrewd enough to discern between a great man and a demagogue, this is more a gain than a loss.[109]

With Albert Shaw and several other Progressives he shared misgivings about the enfranchisement of all citizens as a right. The vote was to be earned. Like Robertson he believed the moral authority of the governor or leader more important than democratic forms. Like the 1775 pastoral of the New York Presbyterian Synod, Robertson and Bryce saw guarantees of traditional civil rights as the basis for reconciliation. Informed citizenship was a prerequisite.[110]

Teachers were to play a providential pastoral role, to open *'the inner world of conscious intellectual being'* and its inference of the deity.[111] Teachers, as John Dewey said, were engaged, not simply training individuals forming the proper social life: 'in this way the teacher is always a prophet of the true God and the usherer in of the true Kingdom of God'.[112] Children in shared common school experiences would become aware of their own internal moral code: 'The real problem was to educate the democracy to be their own masters'.[113] As T.H. Green, friend and inspirer of later Scottish intellectuals and thinkers, said:

> There is a great difference between feeling that a certain line of conduct is expected of me and conceiving it as a form of universal duty. So long as the requirements of an established morality are felt in that way, they present themselves to the man as imposed from without.[114]

Natural science would coincide with the moral Christian order: Enlightenment and Christianity were a partnership. Altruism was 'the product of cohesive society'.[115] Individual inherent moral sense would be liberated: self-regulating moral mechanisms voluntarily observed on a small scale would be the foundation for the larger society.[116] The local was part of the universal: 'universal culture then – unlimited education – is the only adequate means of general happiness'.[117] As William Russell wrote:

> A narrow feeling of exclusive preference for home scenes and mere local information is no proper fruit of education. But an early and enlightened attachment to local associations, while it forms a distinctive basis of social character, in communities is, in no respect, incompatible with that enlarged and liberal regard to the national interest and relations which should ever distinguish the citizens of the United States. Local preferences may be justly cherished without increasing the faults of local prejudice.[118]

Naturally these codes coincided with the traditional 'Protestant' work ethic, as endorsed by Robertson: with thrift, industry and sobriety. In a developing urban and commercial society, education was a guarantee of patience and stability: education was 'coextensive with citizenship and allegiance'.[119] Mankind empowered by education and inspired by religious ideals would sustain a self-disciplined democracy: the inner-directed man would work for the common good.[120] By the late nineteenth century that notion was becoming increasingly secularised. For example Johns Hopkins University determined to 'produce leaders capable of recognising the true ideals and of intelligently directing the nation's energies to their accomplishments'.[121] Such lofty notions, perhaps more whistling in the agnostic dark, came from Professor R.M.Wenley of Michigan, a Glasgow pupil of Edward Caird, who believed life 'an imperative summons to immediate participation in the complete ideal'.[122]

Another transatlantic figure, Jacob A. Riis, endorsed Robertson's belief in the necessity of a stable, propertied basis for social and moral advance. A race of mobile people perishes: 'The home feeling can never grow where people do not stay long enough to feel at home anymore than a plant can which a child is pulling up every two or three days to 'see if it has roots''.[123] The Progressive reformers, Sophia P. Breckinridge and Henry A. Moskowitz, similarly endorsed that view: 'without rootage there is no moral advance'.[124]

The locality remained the key battleground in this tradition. External forces might inject dynamism into a locality. Thomas Chalmers in his social concerns saw the local personal contact as decisive. The external charge generated new local dynamism. Benjamin Tuckerman, an American follower, likewise espoused that view in his work in Boston. Later, Stanton Coit, an American ethical culturist in Britain, believed the locality was the key for general social amelioration.[125] Josiah Royce, the philosopher, rejoiced in creative provincialism.[126] The ethos, derived from Robertson, was a mixture of Whiggish and evangelical concern for a free but disciplined mass society.

Every individual in every home had to be liberated from moral and intellectual failings and from dependency on the state. The *élan vital* of each individual and area must be set free. Canon W.H. Fremantle believed a truly Christian nation would call forth dynamic gifts from localities and individuals and in turn reflect the strength of local Christian life in national life.[127] John Bascom, president of the University of Wisconsin, saw 'each lesser finding leads to a higher'.[128] As Simon N. Patten claimed:

> In each locality, a class, a group of desires in harmony with the local environment must displace or modify the old desires upon which the existing tradition is based. There will then develop a new moral code, local in character and practical enough to induce large bodies of men to accept . . . The local, class and sectional forces making for unity are

> moral: the general forces are impulses and ideals formulated as rights. It is not therefore from a theory of distribution that a solution to the present difficulties will come but from a better formulation of the moral code and from a clearer perception of the common rights that the new impulses and ideals evoke.[129]

Unity, then, was the end. In a fragmenting and divided society, these reasonable views were very appealing: 'A community of purpose . . . is more effective than tradition because it pervades the whole of man'.[130] It would realise the Kingdom on earth, the Theophany.[131] It was the continuation of Robertson's inclusive community.

Model municipal government was one response. The town council should 'present the theocratic idea – i.e. government by the highest good'.[132] The Civic Church was another response. W.T. Stead, following his visit to Chicago, returned to Britain. He idealised Glasgow as a 'moral caucus'.[133] The Civic Church would 'energise all the institutions which make for righteousness'.[134] Local insight and local initiative would contribute to national progress:

> As the Civic Church is in advance of the State, so the individual reformer is ever in advance of the Civic Church. The heretic always leads the van. What the Civic Church can do is to generalise for the benefit of all the advantages which hitherto have been confined to the few.[135]

Robert A. Woods, the Boston social settlement minister, endorsed that view following a visit to Glasgow: 'the state has its being in the village sense of the people who pass their days in spontaneous neighbourhood relationships which they have learned to direct to effective ends'.[136]

Jane Addams, influenced by Scottish ideals, aspired to a dynamic practical faith: 'the doctrine must be understood through the deed. It is the only possible way, not only to stir others to action but to give the message itself a sense of reality'.[137] She demanded a 'cathedral of humanity' that was 'capacious enough to have a fellowship of common purpose . . . beauutiful enough to persuade men to hold fast to the vision of human solidarity'.[138]

At the same time the emphasis upon neighbourhood allowed for continuity. Robertson and Chalmers, both alike suspicious of bureaucracy, found a soulmate in John Bascom, the president of the University of Wisconsin and one of Robert Lafollette's mentors: 'Religion must be a free elastic, progressive, versatile life, ever-embodying itself in new forms as the ages unfold. The moment it stiffens into organisation and settles into final statements, the ages begin to struggle with it, to shake it off and leave it behind'.[139] Like Robertson, these later transatlantic faithful believed 'The

Further Evolution must go on, the Higher Kingdom come'.[140] For 'A God who was nearer to Man in the past than he is at present could not be the God of the future'.[141] Robertson and his Scottish and American successors accepted a God derived from their Presbyterian Christian faith: He was part of a largely unquestioned cultural package. Theology was the history of God's dealings with man. History, then, particularly in the transatlantic world, was the ultimate revelation of Christian godliness. Local understanding made for universal comprehension. As all such interim statements, it was flawed.

By the later nineteenth century, the Civil War and subsequent disenchantment, industrial and urban growth changed America. The massive changing migrant ethnic population made the Common Sense philosophy less generally acceptable. The holocaust of idealism in the First World War meant its demise. The erosion of religion by affluence and the scientific innovations further discredited its hold. If Common Sense was the philosophy of the provinces, then consolidation and centralisation were its increasingly powerful enemies. In the wake of the Great Crash in 1929, the New Deal and its social welfare bureaucracies displaced moralising rhetoric. New forms of mass media, radio, film and television, challenged local opinion makers. It struggled manfully but the pressures were overwhelming.

Within education, the retiral of McCosh from Princeton and the emergence of the new dynamic research-based Johns Hopkins University were symptomatic of the shift. Clergymen were a fast diminishing band of university principals while acceptance of any Biblical faith came increasingly under attack. Quality control demanded ever more rigorous primary research. More critical and cynical historians like the Marxists and Beard undercut idealist historical rhetoric: they exposed the class basis of idealism. The anthropological work of Franz Boas and others challenged the merchants of superior culture and imperialism. More democratic critics questioned patronising moralists: Prohibition was enough. As state intervention increased in the transatlantic world, so voluntarism became outmoded. Affluence and abundance made self-discipline appear outdated. Robertson's dream of commercial camaraderie evaporated.

Common Sense philosophy with its emphasis on duty, deeds and a guarantee of spiritual and economic success had travelled some distance from faith. It believed in man rather than in God.

To end as I began with a quote, but this time by a Scot about the English:

> I am indeed quite ready to admit that there is nothing more disgustingly intolerant than a gang of Englishmen sallying forth into the world, full of his own ignorance and John Bullism – judging of mankind by his own

> petty and narrow notions of fitness and propriety – a mighty observer of effort and disregarder of causes, and transversing continents and oceans at once blinded and shackled by the bigotry and prejudice of his own limited and imbecile intellect.[142]

Maybe we are all in that limited condition but the historians of the past seem more obviously so. As Humboldt said of Robertson and his fellow historians,

> These authors regard as barbaric any state of mind that differs from the notion of culture that they have formulated for themselves with their systematized ideas. We cannot accept these sharp distinctions into barbaric and civilised nations.[143]

Today we more readily accept diversity, complexity or social responsibility. We are more humble in the wake of empire and economic decline. Our ideas of Scottish and American identities have moved on since his day. We are or should be more inclusive. Nevertheless we should not forget the debt we owe pioneers of scientific method like the redoubtable William Robertson.

REFERENCES

1. Marquis of Lansdowne to Richard Price, 29 November 1786, quoted in *Proceedings of Massachusetts Historical Society,* May 1903, p.359. For similar comments see F. Bowditch Dexter (ed.), *Literary Diary of Ezra Stiles, D.D., LL.D., President of Yale College* (New York, 1901) p.184.
2. J.R. Saul, *Voltaire's Bastards: The Dictatorship of Reason in the West* (New York, 1993 ed.), p.120. The book is a blast against the Enlightenment and the evils which allegedly flowed from it. The background to these opening paragraphs will be found in Anand Chitnis, 'Agricultural improvement, political management and civic virtue in Enlightened Scotland: an historical critique', *Studies on Voltaire and the Eighteenth Century,* v 245 (1986) pp.475–88; R.A. Houston, *Social Change in the Age of Enlightenment: Edinburgh 1660–1760* (Oxford, 1994); Colin Kidd, *Scottish Whig Historians and the Creation of an Anglo-British Identity* (Cambridge, 1993), and his 'North Britishness and the nature of eighteenth century British patriotisms', *Historical Journal,* 39 (1996), pp.361–82; A. Hook and R. Sher (eds.), *The Glasgow Enlightenment* (East Linton, 1993), and Samuel Clark, *State and Status: The Rise of the State and Aristocratic Power in Western Europe* (Cardiff, 1995). On Robertson as a mixture of ambition, dominant conversationalist, puritan and creative thinker see Alexander Carlyle, *Autobiography* (Edinburgh, 1861, third ed.), pp.285–91. For further indications that the Scottish Enlightenment was not confined to Edinburgh see Jennifer J. Carter and John H. Pittock, *Aberdeen and the Enlightenment* (Aberdeen, 1987) and Paul B. Wood, *The Aberdeen Enlightenment: The Arts Curriculum in the Eighteenth Century* (Aberdeen, 1993).
3. Quoted in *History of Scotland,* 2 vols. (London, 1827), liii. On the background see Dalphy I. Fagerstrom, 'Scottish Opinion and the American Revolution', *William and Mary Quarterly,* 3rd series, v 11 (1954), pp.252–275.
4. See William Smith, Jr., *The History of the Province of New York,* 2 vols. (New York, 1972 ed.), xliii; Peter J. Diamond, 'Witherspoon, William Smith and the Scottish Philosophy in Revolutionary America,' in Richard B. Sher and Jeffrey J. Smitten (eds.), *Scotland and America in the Age of Enlightenment* (Edinburgh and Princeton, 1990), pp.115–32; N. Phillipson, 'The Scottish Enlightenment', in Roy Porter and Mikulos Teich (eds.), *The*

Enlightenment in National Context (Cambridge, 1981), pp.12–40; Anand Chitnis, *The Scottish Enlightenment: A Social History* (London, 1976); Harvey Wish, *The American Historian. A Social-Intellectual History of the Writing of the American Past* (New York, 1960), pp.34–5; Hugh Trevor Roper, 'The Scottish Enlightenment', in *Studies on Voltaire and the Eighteenth Century,* v 58 (1967), pp.1635–58; Andrew Skinner, 'Economics and History-The Scottish Enlightenment', *Scottish Journal of Political Economy,* 12 (1965), pp.1–22;

5. See Holden Furber with P.J. Marshall (eds.), *The Correspondence of Edmund Burke, 1782–89,* v 5 (Oxford, 1965), pp.221–22.
6. Sir William Hamilton (ed.), *The Collected Works of Dugald Stewart* (Edinburgh, 1858) VI, 'An Account of the Life of William Robertson, D.D.', pp.101–242, 161; and Aylwin Clark, *An Enlightened Scot: Hugh Cleghorn, 1752–1837* (Duns, 1992), p.9. The Scottish critical spirit affected Catholicism too: Mark Goldie, 'Common Sense Philosophy and Catholic Theology in the Enlightenment', *Studies on Voltaire and the Eighteenth Century,* v 3002 (1992), pp.282–320.
7. William B. Willcox (ed.), *The Papers of Benjamin Franklin* (1962–73), v.13 12, 80–1,98–9, 165–6; v.14 218–20; v.15 290; v.19 50; J.Bennett Nolan, *Benjamin Franklin in Scotland and Ireland, 1759 and 1771* (Philadelphia, 1938) and Andrew Hook, *Scotland and America, 1750–1835* (Glasgow, 1975) p.26; Jeremy J. Cater, 'The Making of Principal Robertson', *Scottish Historical Review,* 49 (1970), pp.60–69. Robert A. Ferguson, *The American Enlightenment, 1750–1820* (Cambridge, Mass., 1997) ignores Robertson.
8. *The Letters of Thomas Jefferson,* v.8.175; v.9., 441; v.11, 11, 18; v.16 384, 481.
9. John Adams, *Diary* (Cambridge, Mass., 1962) I. 113, 13 Mar 1782; II. 398 [1779]; [1968] III. 226, 12 July 1796; *Diaries of John Adams,* 4 vols.(Cambridge, Mass, 1968) III 208 15 April 1830.
10. L.H. Butterfield (ed.), *Letters of Benjamin Rush,* 2 vols. (Princeton, 1951) v.I. 538–39 and George W. Corner (ed.), *The Aubiography of Benjamin Rush* (Princeton, 1948), p.50.
11. N.A. Carter, *Letters from Europe, comprising the journal of a tour through Ireland, England, Scotland, France and Italy in 1825, 1826 and 1829,* 2 vols. (New York, 1829) VI, p.237.
12. *North American Review,* 1831. See critical citations in *Analectic Magazine,* 6 (August 1815) 92; *Monthly Anthology* 2 (Oct 1805) pp.538–41; *American Review,*1 (Jan 1810) pp.1–16 in George H. Callcutt, *History in the United States,* 1800–60 (Baltimore, 1970) p.20.
13. W.H. Gilman et al (eds.), *Journals and Notebooks of R.W. Emerson,* 1819–22 (Cambridge Mass.,1960) v.II. 108. Also v.I, 55–6.
14. Wayne R. Kime and Andrew B. Myer (eds.), *The Works of Washington Irving* (Boston, 1984) v. 4. 359. Also Sue Field Ross (ed.), v.5. 231.
15. H.J.C. Grierson (ed.), *The Letters of Sir Walter Scott,* 12 vols. (Edinburgh, 1935) v. 3, 166, 188–89, 223; v.5., 180, 450; v. 8. 244; v. 10. 440. On Robertson's contribution to Romanticism see Owen Dudley Edwards' forthcoming essay and A.Leslie Wilson, *A Mythical Image: The Idea of India in German Romanticism* (Durham, N.C., 1964) For a recent analysis see Karen O'Brien, 'Enlightenment History in Scotland: The Case of William Robertson', *Studies on Voltaire and the Eighteenth Century,* v, 303 (1992) pp.467–85.
16. John Nichol, *American Literature: An Historical Sketch* (Edinburgh, 1882). p11.
17. See Reginald Horsman, *Race and Manifest Destiny* (Cambridge, Mass., 1981) pp.182–84; Thomas F. Gossett, *Race: The History of an Idea in America* (Dallas, 1953), pp.182–84; C. Harvey Gardiner (ed.), *The Papers of William Hickling Prescott* (Urbana, 1964) p.41; George Ticknor, *Life of W.H. Prescott* (London, 1864) p.50.
18. See Union Catalogue. I am also grateful to Barbara Turner, Bowdoin College for her assistance.
19. See Emma Willard, *Journals and Letters from France and Great Britain* (Troy, New York, 1833) p.365; S.E. Ahlstrom, 'The Scottish Philosophy and American Theology', *Church History,* 24 (1955) pp.257–72; David Lundberg and Henry F. May, 'The Enlightened Reader in America', *American Quarterly,* 28 (1976) pp.262–84, and his *The Enlightenment in America,* (New York, 1976); D.H. Mayer, *The Instructed Conscience: The Shaping of the American National Ethic* (Philadelphia, 1972); Douglas Sloan, *The Scottish Enlightenment and the*

American College (New York, 1971} and Garry Wills, *Inventing America: Jefferson's Declaration of Independence* (New York, 1979); T.M. Devine, *The Tobacco Lords* (Edinburgh, 1975); William R. Brock, *Scotus-Americanus* (Edinburgh 1982); my own, *Portable Utopia: Glasgow and the United States,* 1820–1920 (Aberdeen, 1984); Ned Landsman, *Scotland and Its First American Colony,* 1683–1750 (Princeton, 1985); R.B. Sher and Jeffrey R. Smitten (eds.), *Scotland and America*; Reginald Horsman, *Race and Manifest Destiny: The Origins of American Racial Anglo-Saxonism* (Cambridge Mass.,1981); Emory Elliott, *Revolutionary Writers: Literature and Authority in the New Republic,* 1795–1810 (New York, 1982); D.T. Bailey, *Shadow on the Church: Southern Evangelical Religion and the Issue of Slavery,* 1733–1860 (Ithaca, 1985); Marilyn J. Westerkamp, *Triumph of the Laity: Scots-Irish Piety and the Great Awakening,* 1625–1760 (New York, 1988). Leigh Eric Schmidt, *Holy Fairs: Scottish Communions and American Revivals in the Early Modern Period* (Princeton, 1989); Robert D. Amer,' Thomas Dobson's American Edition of the Encyclopaedia Brittanica in Baltimore', *Studies on Voltaire and the Eighteenth Century,* v 315 (1994) pp.201–54.

20. For the first American history see Peter Dobkin Hall, *The Organisation of American Culture,* 1700–1900: Private Institutions, Elites and the Origins of American Nationality (New York, 1982). For the second see Garry Wills above and R.A. Humphreys, *William Robertson and His History of America* (London, 1954).
21. See his sermon 'The Dominion of Providence over the Passions of Men', *Works* (Edinburgh 1804), v 5, 176–216, especially p.203 and his appended 'Address to the Natives of Scotland Residing in America', pp.217–36. See the essays by Ned C. Landsman, Richard B. Sher and Peter J. Diamond in R.B. Sher and Jeffrey J. Smitten, *Scotland and America.* The standard life remains Varnum L. Collins, *President Witherspoon,* 2 vols. (Princeton, 1925).
22. H.L. Mencken,*The American Language* (New York, 1962 ed.) p.5. and *Supplement* II, 19.
23. *Ibid.*, p.160.
24. Simon N. Patten, *The Theory of Prosperity* (New York, 1902) p.206. See also Colin Kidd, *Remembering Scotland's Past: Scottish Writing of History and the Creation of an Anglo-British Identity,* 1689–1830, chapter 8.
25. E.g. Robert and Robert Dale Owen and the notorious Frances Wright, *Views of Society and Manners in America* (1821) (Cambridge Mass., 1963.)
26. A.D. Bache, *Report on Education in Europe* (Philadelphia, 1839), p.32. On the background see Andrew Hook, *Scotland and America,* 1750–1835 (Glasgow, 1975); my *Portable Utopia* . . . and Christopher Mulvey, *Anglo-American Landscapes: A Study of Nineteenth Century Anglo-American Travel Literature* (Cambridge, 1983).
27. John Nichol, *American Literature,* p.446.
28. Sir George Campbell, *White and Black: The Outcome of a Visit to the United States* (London, 1879) p.30.
29. See his *Home and Abroad,* (Glasgow 1871); *Among the Darkies and Other Papers* (Glasgow, 1876); *The Americans at Home* (Glasgow, 1885 ed.) and *America Revisited and Men I Have Known* (Glasgow, 1908).
30. *The Development of English Thought: A Study in the Economic Interpretation of History* (New York, 1899) p.391.
31. Cf. Michael Kammen, *The Transformation of Culture in American Culture* (New York, 1991 ed.); Philip Gleason, *Speaking of Diversity: Language and Ethnicity in Twentieth Century America* (Baltimore, 1992); John Bodnar, *Remaking America* (Princeton, 1992).
32. Orville Dewey, *Works* (London, 1844) p.617 from his *Old World and the New* (1833). Also see the former Ayrshire schoolmaster, John Regan, *The Emigrants' Guide to the Western States of America* (Edinburgh, 1853) pp.234–42; Wilbur Fisk, *Travels in Europe* (New York, 1838), pp.644, 686; Francis Wayland, *Thoughts on the Present Collegiate System in the United States* (Boston, 1842) p.126; William Oliver, *Eight Months in Illinois* (Newcastle-on-Tyne, 1843) p.54; John Price Durbin, *Observations in Europe principally in France and Great Britain* (2 vols., New York, 1844) II.173–75; E.K.Washington, *Echoes of Europe* (Philadelphia, 1860) p.219; E.C. Benedict, *A Run Through Europe* (New York, 1860) p.526.

33. J.N. Larned (ed.), *Letters, Poems and Selected Writings of David Gray* (Buffalo,1888) p.32.
34. W.E. Channing, *Letter on Elevation of the Labouring Portion of the Community* (Boston, 1840) p.69.
35. Horace Bushnell, *Barbarism, The First Danger: A Discourse for Home Missions* (New York, 1847) pp.6–7. See Frances Wright d'Arusmont, *Life, Letters and Lectures* (New York, 1972 ed.) pp.101–16, 140–5 and R.D. Owen, *Popular Tracts* (New York, 1830) pp.4–5.
36. Letter of Gilbert Elliott to W. Robertson, 3 March 1771 cited in M. A. Stewart (ed.), *Studies in the Philosophy of the Scottish Enlightenment* (Oxford, 1990), p.125. Also see pp.91, 114–5. Concern for control is clear in Roger L. Emerson, 'The Social Composition of Enlightened Scotland: The Select Society of Edinburgh, 1754–64', *Studies on Voltaire,* v.114 (1973) pp. 291–329.
37. Frances Wright, *View.,* pp.63–65, 215, 225.
38. E.g. Robert Scott, *Scotland Through American Eyes* (Edinburgh, 1928), p.47. Scott, a Scot spent some 40 years in America.
39. Cf. Peter Neilson, *Recollections of A Six Years Residence in the United States of America* (Glasgow, 1830) pp.110–11; J.D. Borthwick, *Three Years in California* (Edinburgh, 1857) pp.49, 56, 66–9 He also shared some of the anti-Semitic, anti-Chinese feelings of his contemporaries, pp.54, 116, 118, 143
40. George M. Marsden, *The Evangelical Mind and the New School Presbyterian Experience: A Case Study of Thought and Theology in Nineteenth Century America* (New Haven, 1970) p.48.
41. W.M. Sloane, *Life of James McCosh* (Edinburgh, 1896) p.35. Also J. David Hoeveler, *James McCosh and the Scottish Intellectual Tradition* (Princeton, 1981).
42. Simon N. Patten, *The New Basis of Civilisation* (New York, 1907) p.169.
43. Herbert Ross Brown, *The Sentimental Novel in America,* 1789–1860 (Durham, North Carolina, 1940) p.6 where Witherspoon attacks the novel.
44. S. A. Grave, *The Scottish Philosophy of Common Sense* (Oxford, 1960).
45. Cf. E.S. Morgan, *The Puritan Family* (New York, 1966) and Leon Poliakov, *The Anjan Myth* (New York, 1996 ed.), p.177 quoting Lord Kames.
46. *History of Charles V,* v.5. p.270.
47. Cf. Henry F. May, *The Enlightenment in America* (New York, 1975) pp.154, 342.
48. Cf Ian D. Clark, 'From Protest to Reaction: The Moderate Regime in the Church of Scotland, 1752–1905' in N.T. Phillipson and R. Mitchison (eds.), *Scotland in the Age of Improvement* (Edinburgh, 1970) pp.200–24.
49. Thomas Hamilton, *Men and Manners in America* (Edinburgh, 1843 ed.,) p.xvii.
50. *Works,* 6, p.245.
51. Simon N. Patten, *The Theory of Prosperity* (New York, 1902) p.207. Also Sir George Campbell, *White and Black,* pp.70, 97–105.
52. F. Harrison, *The Philosophy of Common Sense* (London, 1907) p.350.
53. Robertson's *America* quoted in Antonello Gerbi, *The Dispute of the New World: The History of a Polemic,* 1750–1900 (Pittsburgh,1973 ed.), p.159. Professor John Nichol of Glasgow wrote the first *History of American Literature* (Edinburgh, 1882) with a similar awareness.
54. *Works,* 6, pp.247, 251, 257,276–77. See also Charles Camic, *Experience and Enlightenment: Socialisation for Cultural Change in Eighteenth Century Scotland* (Chicago, 1983) p.57.
55. *Works,* 6, pp.281, 284, 340, 342, 349.
56. *Works,* 6, p.284.
57. *Works,* 6, p.383.
58. *Works,* 6, pp. 394–95.
59. *Works,* 6, p.398.
60. Cf. Anthony Pagden in Nicholas Canny and Anthony Pagden (eds.), *Colonial Identity in the Atlantic World,* 1500–1800 (Princeton, 1987) pp.76, 81.
61. *Views,* pp.106–112.
62. *Works,* 6, p.323.
63. *Works,* 6, pp.302 and 295 , see also p.296.

64. *History of America* quoted A. Gerbi, *The Dispute*, p.168. Also pp.235, 261, 268, 314
65. *Works*, 7, p.292.
66. *History of America, Works*, pp.6, 68.
67. *Works*, 6, p.257.
68. *Works*, 6, p.278. Also 6, p.340.
69. *Works*, 6, p.302.
70. *Works*, 7, p.37.
71. *American Commonwealth*, II, pp.310, 352 and 516.
72. J.D. Lang, *Queensland, Australia: A Highly Eligible Field for Emigration and the Future Cotton Fields of Great Britain* (London, 1861) pp.233, 235.
73. James D. Young, *The Rousing of the Scottish Working Class* (London, 1979) p.140.
74. George Combe, *Notes on the United States of North America during a Phrenological Visit in 1838, 1839, 1840*, 3 vols. (Edinburgh, 1841) III. 32, also 33.
75. *An Historical Disquisition Concerning the Knowledge which the Ancients had of India and the Progresss of Trade with That Country*, in *Works*, v 8, pp.288, 292.
76. *History of Charles V, Works*, 5, p.21.
77. *Works*, 8, p.346.
78. *Works*, 5, p.140; 8, p.293.
79. Quoted in C. Camic, *Experience and Enlightenment: Socialisation for Cultural Change in Eighteenth Century Scotland* (Chicago, 1983) p.57.
80. *Works*, 8, p.46.
81. *Works*, 8, p.60.
82. James Bryce, *The Menace of Great Cities* (New York, 1913) p.12.
83. James Bryce, *The American Commonwealth*, 2 vols. (New York, 1916 ed.) II. p.429.
84. *Ibid.*, II, p.484.
85. *Ibid.*, II, p.370.
86. *Ibid.*, II, p.526.
87. *Ibid.*, p.517.
88. *Ibid.*, p.516.
89. *Works*, 6, p. 205.
90. *Works*, 6, p.212.
91. Sir William Hamilton, *Works of Stewart*, 1, pp.187–89
92. Robertson, *Works*, 5, pp.140, 152–55.
93. *Stewart*, 1, p.191.
94. *American Commonwealth*, II 355 Also pp.303–04, 474.
95. *Autobiography* (London, 1877) p.176.
96. Sir George Campbell, *White . . ,* p. 404.
97. John Galt, *Lawrie Todd*, 3 vols. (London, 1830) II. p. 239.
98. See Richard Weston, Edinburgh bookseller, quoted in W.S. Shepperson, *Emigration and Disenchantment* (Norman, Oklahoma, 1965), pp.84–5
99. T. Hamilton, *Men and Manners in America* (Edinburgh, 1843 ed.) p. xix.
100. G. Lewis, *Impressions of America and the American Churches* (Edinburgh, 1845) pp.34–5.
101. Cf. Jay Brown, *Thomas Chalmers and The Godly Commonwealth* (Oxford, 1982).
102. Daniel T. McColgan, *Joseph Tuckerman: Pioneer in Social Work* (Washington D.C., 1949), pp.93–116.
103. H. Barnard, *Papers on Preventive, Correctional and Reformatory Institutions and Agencies in Different Countries* (Hartford, Conn., 1857) p.343.
104. P. Shireff, *A Tour Through North America* (Edinburgh, 1855) p.55.
105. J.E. Alexander, *Transatlantic Sketches*, 2 vols. (London,1833) p.305.
106. See J. Merton, England, 'The Democratic Faith in American Schoolbooks, 1783–1860', *American Quarterly*, 15 (1963) pp.191–99; J.L. Thomas, 'Romantic Reform in America, 1815–1865', *American Quarterly*, 17 (1965) pp.679–95; David Tyack, 'The Kingdom of God and the Common School: Protestant Ministers and the Educational Awakening in the West' *Education Review*, 36 (1966) pp.447–69; Stanley K. Schultz, *The Culture Factory:*

Boston Public Schools, 1789–1820 (New York, 1973) p 22 et seq.; Clive Bush, *The Dream of Reason: American Consciousness and Cultural Achievement from Independence to the Civil War* (London, 1977); David Nasau, *Schooled to Order: A Social History of Schools in the United States* (New York, 1979); Cynthia M. Koch's 'Teaching Patriotism: Private Virtue for the Public Good in the early Republic', in John Bodnar (ed.), *Bonds of Affection: Americans Define their Patriotism* (Princeton, 1996), pp.19–52 appeared after this paper was given.

107. Odell Shepard, *Pedlar's Progress: A Life of Bronson Alcott* (London, 1908) p.145.
108. R. Cunningham, *Thoughts on the Question whether the normal seminaries ought to be district establishments or ingrafted on Colleges? Being an inaugural address on his inauguration as professor of ancient languages in Lafayette College, Easton, Pa., January* 1 1838 (Philadelphia, 1838) p.5.
109. James Bryce, *The American Commonwealth*, II, pp.255–56.
110. Cf. Sir George Campbell, *White . . ,* p.48.
111. W. Russell, *Address at the Dedication and Opening of the New England Normal Institute at Lancaster, Mass., Wednesday May* 11th 1853 (Boston, 1853) p.13.
112. quoted in Lawrence A. Cremin, *The Transformation of the School: Progressivism in American Education* (New York, 1962) p.100.
113. John MacCunn, *Liverpool Addresses on the Ethics of Social Work* (Liverpool, 1911) p.27.
114. T.H. Green, *Lectures on the Principles of Political Obligation* (London, 1941 ed.) p.25.
115. Simon N. Patten, *The Theory of Prosperity* (New York, 1902) p.169.
116. E.g. J. McCosh, *The Method of Divine Government, Physical and Moral* (Edinburgh, 1855 ed.) passim.
117. W. Russell, *On Associations of Teachers, An Address* (Boston, 1830) p.12.
118. W. Russell, *Harper's New York Class Book* (New York n.d.) introduction.
119. Thomas Wyse, *Education Reform* (London, 1836) pp.459 and 386.See George M. Marsden, *The Evangelical Mind and the New School Presbyterian Experience: A Case Study of Thought and Theology in Ninetenth Century America'* (New Haven, 1970) especially p.48.
120. See T.H.Green, *Lectures on the Principles of Political Obligation* (London, 1941 ed.), p.25; J. MacCunn, *Liverpool Addresses on the Ethics of Social Work* (Liverpool, 1911); W.R. Hutchison, *The Modernist Impulse in American Protestantism* (Harvard, 1976) esp. p.158.
121. Hugh Hawkins, *Pioneer: A History of the Johns Hopkins University*, 1874–89 (Ithaca New York, 1960).
122. *Modern Thought and the Crisis of Belief* (New York, 1909) p.289.
123. *The Battle With the Slum* (New York, 1902) p.130 and his *The Peril And Preservation of the Home* (London 1909) pp.18–9.
124. See her edited book, *The Child and the City* (London, 1912) especially Moskowitz on p.268.
125. Jay Brown, *Thomas Chalmers . . ,* for example pp.79,104; T. Chalmers, *The Christian and Civic Economy of Large Towns*, 3 vols. (London, 1819–26); Stanton Coit, *Neighbourhood Guilds: An Instrument of Social Reform* (London, 1892); Edward T. Devine, *Progressive Social Action* (New York, 1923) pp. 7–9, 204. Also Professor A.B. Bruce, *The Providential Order of the World* (London, 1897) esp. p.293 and Jane Hume Clapperton, *Scientific Meliorism* (London, 1885) p.427.
126. See his essays 'Provincialism' and 'The Philosophy of Loyalty' in John J. McDermott (ed.), *The Basic Writings of Josiah Royce*, 2 vols. (Chicago 1969) II, pp.952–53 and 1067–88.
127. W.H. Fremantle, *The World As Subject of Redemption* (London, 1885) p.349.
128. J. Bascom, *Evolution and Religion* (New York, 1897) p.167.
129. S.N. Patten, *The Theory of Prosperity*, pp.213–14. Also see pp.222–23.
130. Hugo Munsterberg, *The Americans* (London, 1905) p.5.
131. Mary P. Follett, *The New State*, p.161.
132. Elizabeth Blackwell, 'On the decay of municipal govenment', in her *Essays on Medical Sociology*, (2 vols. London, 1902) I 176–210, 181. Also see her *The Religion of Health* (Edinburgh,1888) and Mary P. Follett, *The New State* (London, 1918, 1934 ed.) p.161.
133. *Review of Reviews*, October 1893 and January 1893.

134. *Review of Reviews*, September 1893, p.314.
135. *Review of Reviews*, September 1893, p.315.
136. R.A. Woods to Rev. Mr. Wragge, 22 June 1891, *Woods Papers*. Woods wrote a series of articles in the Glasgow *Modern Church*, 9 April, 2 May, 16 July, 10 Sept., 19 Nov 1891 and 3 March 1892.
137. Jane Addams, *Democracy and Social Ethics* (Cambridge Mass.,1964, ed.) pp. xii, 7, 14.
138. Quoted in C. Lasch (ed.), *The Social Thought of Jane Addams* (Indianapolis, 1965) p.24. Cf. Walter Rauschenbusch, *Theology of the Social Gospel*, p.13.
139. J. Bascom, Sociology (New York, 1887), p.179
140. Henry Drummond, *The Ascent of Man* (London, 1894), p. 444.
141. Edward Caird, *The Social Philosophy and Religion of Comte* (Glasgow, 1885), p.11.
142. Thomas Hamilton, *Cyril Thornton* (Edinburgh, 1856 ed.) p.205. Washington Irving wrote of the Engishman: 'However I might be disposed to trust his probity I dare not trust his prejudices.' J. Nichol, *American Literature*, p.8. Also G.K. Chesterton's devastating indictment in his introduction to Arnold's Essays:

    'Matthew Arnold found the window of the English soul opaque with its own purple. The Englishman had painted his own image on the pane so gorgeously that it was practically impossible: a dead panel; it had no opening to the world outside. He could not see the most obvious and enormous objects outside his own door. The Englishman could not see (for instance) that the French Revolution was a far-reaching, fundamental, and most practical and successful change in the whole structure of Europe. He really thought that it was a bloody and futile episode, in weak imitation of an English General Election. The Englishman could not see that the Catholic Church was (at the very least) an immense and enduring Latin civilisation, linking us to the lost civilisations of the Mediterranean. He really thought it was a sort of sect. The Englishman could not see that the Franco-Prussian War was the entrance of a new and menacing military age, a terror to England and to all. He really thought it was a little lesson to Louis Napoleon for not reading *The Times*. The most enormous catastrophe was only some kind of symbolic compliment to England. If the sun fell from heaven it only showed how wise England was in not having much sunshine. If the waters were turned to blood it was only an advertisement of Bass's Ale or Fry's Cocoa. Such was the weak pride of the English then. One cannot say it wholly undiscoverable now.' quoted in *Irish Ecclesiastical Record* 23 (1908) , pp. 390–91.
143. Quoted A. Gerbi, *The Dispute*, p.415.

Eleven

Urbanization in Eighteenth-Century Scotland

IAN D. WHYTE

Introduction

'URBANIZATION' IS ONE of those terms which is often used loosely without being properly defined. It involves the increasing concentration of population in urban areas with a growth in the size of towns and cities and a rise in the proportion of the population of a country or region living in towns. But urbanization is something more than merely urban growth. It involves changes in society as people adopt urban economies and social and cultural patterns. It is an important indicator of changes in society and, at the same time, it is an agent of change. Along with industrialization, it has been seen as a key element of modernisation. Particularly significant in a British context was the shift, between the mid-eighteenth and mid-nineteenth centuries, from the relatively low levels of urbanization which characterised the pre-industrial world to the high levels associated with full industrialization and the change to a modern society. In this contribution to the seminar series on eighteenth-century Scotland I have been asked to consider urbanization. I want to look first at how we can measure it before going on to look at patterns of urbanization in eighteenth-century Scotland. I will then assess these in relation to what was happening elsewhere in Britain and Europe. Finally, and most importantly, I want to consider the significance of urbanization in a Scottish context and the nature of the underlying forces which produced the trend towards a much more urbanized society.

Sources of Data for Eighteenth-Century Urbanization

The standard measure of urbanization is the percentage of the total population living in towns and cities over a given minimum size. The level at which that threshold is drawn depends, in part, on the scale of analysis and the quality of the data available. De Vries, in his classic study of European urbanization, used a lower limit of 10,000 inhabitants because of the difficulty of getting comparable and reasonably accurate data for smaller towns at a continental scale.[1] However, for selected areas he was able to use thresholds of 5,000 and even 2,000.

The calculation of the percentage of the Scottish population living in towns of various sizes at particular times during the eighteenth century may seem simple enough. In practice there are difficulties relating to the nature of the source material. Four sets of data are available for calculating Scottish urban populations in this period. These are the hearth tax returns of 1691, supplemented by some poll tax lists from the mid 1690s. Then there is Webster's census of 1755, the population information given in the *Old Statistical Account* (OSA), and the first official census of 1801. Unfortunately none of these sources is unambiguous when it comes to calculating urban populations and none is strictly comparable with any of the others. The hearth tax returns provide data for most Scottish towns but calculations of urban populations, and indeed the total population of Scotland, depend on using a multiplier for mean household size on data which may not be complete or accurate in the first place. Our initial baseline figures, then, are somewhat dubious. Although my calculations agree well with those of Tyson,[2] Langton has recently suggested that my calculations of Scottish urban populations from the hearth tax returns are, compared with his for England, if anything over-estimates. If this is indeed the case then it is possible that the rate of urban growth between 1691 and 1755 was greater than the figures I will discuss presently suggest. Webster's census has been considered reasonably accurate but it gives the populations of parishes, not those of towns within parishes. This is an important distinction in Scotland – particularly in the case of many middle-rank towns situated in large parishes with extensive landward areas. Brechin, Dunfermline, Haddington, Inverness and Jedburgh are examples where 'urban' populations are swelled, at parish level, by many rural dwellers. The same problem applies to the 1801 census. Calculations based on these sources will inflate urban populations, particularly of the middle- and lower-rank towns.

The *Old Statistical Account* gives detailed populations, not only for towns but also for villages, within each parish but the accuracy of the figures for some of the larger settlements is suspect and there has clearly been some estimation and rounding. A general appendix to the *OSA* provides a table listing the population of 'towns' with 300 inhabitants and upwards. However, many of the smaller settlements, especially those with populations under 500, are described in the individual parish accounts as 'villages', while the list also omits a number of settlements, some described as towns. Nevertheless, despite these caveats, the data from the *OSA* do provide our best picture of the Scottish urban system towards the end of our period.

Patterns of Urbanization

Table 1 shows the proportions of the populations in Scottish towns of different sizes based on these four sources. Remember that the figures for 1755 and 1801 are inflated against those for 1691 and 1790 because of the inclusion of some rural dwellers. The first problem is to decide where the threshold between urban and rural lies. For England at this time it has been placed as high as 2,500 by Corfield.[3] However, Stobart's recent study of urbanization in eighteenth-century Lancashire identifies as market towns centres with populations of under 1,000 in 1801, under 600 in the 1770s and as low as 300 in the 1660s.[4] Studies of market towns in Cumbria and Yorkshire over the same period have used comparable thresholds.[5] It is difficult to believe that in Scotland urban thresholds would have been higher. In my work on late seventeenth century Scottish urban occupational structures I have suggested that a lower threshold for towns, based on occupational diversity, occurred at around 450–500 people. The *OSA* lists settlements as small as 300 as 'towns'. However, there is considerable variability in settlement nomenclature in the accounts of individual ministers. Places as large as Tranent and Stromness with 1,300–1,400 inhabitants are described as villages, others as small as Dornoch with 500 as towns, while places as small as Anstruther Wester with a population of only 324, clung tenaciously to their ancient burghal status. There is clearly some overlap. Biggar, with just under 600 inhabitants was, on the basis of the occupational structure given, clearly a town while Stonehouse, with a similar population, was just as clearly a weaving village. The dividing line between rural and urban lay somewhere between 500 and 800 by this date.

It is not meaningful, however, to attempt calculations of populations for Scottish towns below c2,000 from the 1755 and 1801 data for reasons I have already mentioned. The information from the *OSA* is sufficiently detailed and accurate to allow calculations to be made for all towns, however small. The population of some, but not all, small centres can also be worked out from the hearth tax returns. However, the hearth tax data are far more dubious in quality than the later sources. For broad comparisons, it seems safest to stick to settlements with c2,000 inhabitants and above, although we shall consider small towns later on. This is, in any case, a useful threshold. Urbanization is essentially concerned with the growth of population in larger towns and cities. Almost all settlements with populations over 2,000, even at the end of the eighteenth century, had urban characteristics and functions. So did many places with fewer than 2,000 inhabitants including Thurso, Strathaven and Langholm, but this threshold at least allows us to omit places like Catrine and New Lanark which were clearly factory villages, as well as planned estate villages like New Keith.

TABLE I: PERCENTAGE OF THE TOTAL SCOTTISH POPULATION IN TOWNS

	1691	1775	1790	1801
Edinburgh	3.9	4.5	5.6	5.1
Other towns 10,000 & over	2.7	4.4	10.8	12.8
5,000–9,999	1.6	3.2	3.2	8.9
2,000–4,999	3.1	4.2	6.4	9.3
1,000–1,999	3.5	?	6.3	?
500–999	?	?	3.4	?
Total over 10,000	6.6	8.9	16.4	17.9
Total over 5,000	8.2	12.1	19.6	26.8
Total over 2,000	11.1	16.3	26.0	36.2

What the table shows is the tremendous growth in the proportion of Scotland's population living in towns during the eighteenth century. While the Scottish population, on Tyson's estimate, grew by a mere 2.5% between the early 1691 and 1755,[6] there was slow, but nevertheless significant growth in towns of all sizes. The population of towns with over 10,000 rose 6.6–8.9%. The percentage in towns with between 5,000 and 10,000 doubled from 1.6% to 3.2%, and that in towns with between 2,000 and 5,000 rose from 3.1% to 4.2%. As parish populations have been used for the hearth tax returns the scale of increase to 1755 should be approximately correct.

During the second half of the eighteenth century, while the population of Scotland grew by 27.1%, urban growth was much more marked, and rather more even than in the first half of the century. The percentage of the population in towns with over 2,000 inhabitants more than doubled. By 1801, allowing for some population inflation due to the use of parish data, around a quarter of Scotland's population was living in towns with over 5,000 inhabitants and over a third in towns with over 2,000. Though this level of urbanization was modest compared with what was to be achieved by the middle of the nineteenth century, it represents a dramatic shift from the position in the 1690s and even 1755.

The figures appear all the more remarkable when compared with England (Table 2). At the start of the eighteenth century there was a marked contrast between the two countries. England had 13.3% of her population in towns with over 10,000 compared with 5.3% for Scotland. By 1801 the figure for England had risen to 20.3% but that for Scotland had more than trebled to 17.3%. By 1801 Scotland was rapidly catching up in levels of urbanization. Urban expansion began later in Scotland and occurred at a much more rapid rate than south of the Border.

TABLE 2: COMPARATIVE LEVELS OF URBANIZATION IN SCOTLAND AND ENGLAND

	Scotland 1691	England 1700	Scotland 1801	England 1801
Capital	3.9	10.6	5.1	9.4
Other Towns Over 10,000	2.7	2.6	12.8	10.9
Total over 10,000	6.6	13.2	17.9	20.3
5,000–9,999	1.6	2.7	8.9	4.6
2,000–4,999	3.1	2.2 +	9.3	5.2 +

+ = figures relate to towns with over 2,500 inhabitants.

The pace of change in Scotland is even more remarkable when set in a broader European context (Table 3). From being one of the least urbanized countries in Europe in 1500, 1600 and even 1700, Scotland was, by de Vries' measure of people living in centres with over 10,000 inhabitants, fourth in Europe after England, the Netherlands and Belgium.[7] By 1801 the percentage of the population in towns with between 5,000 and 9,999 inhabitants was also markedly greater than in other parts of Europe where population figures at this level are available, including England. The proportion of the population in smaller centres with 2,000–4,999 was also higher in Scotland than in England and most parts of Europe.

TABLE 3: SCOTTISH URBANIZATION IN A EUROPEAN CONTEXT

	Scotland 1691	Ireland 1680s	Denmark 1672
Capital	4.5	3.5	8.8
Other Towns over 10,000	2.7	3.8	0
5,000–9,999	1.6	2.3	0
2,000–4,999	3.1	3.1	4.7

	% in Towns over 10,000	% in Towns 5,000–9,000	% in Towns OVER 5,000
Scotland 1801	17.9	8.9	26.8
England 1801	20.3	4.6	24.9
Germany 1792	6.5	2.9	9.4
France 1806	9.1	3.4	12.5
Switzerland 1800	3.7	2.3	6.0
Netherlands 1795	28.8	6.2	35.0
Scandinavia 1800	4.6	1.3	5.9
Belgium 1792	18.9	8.2	27.1

Source: de Vries (1984)

The development of the Scottish urban hierarchy can be considered by examining the rank/size distribution of towns. Geographers have shown that in a modern industrialized society, the distribution of the rank order of towns in an urban system, graphed against their size on a double logarithmic scale, corresponds closely to a straight-line plot.[8] Pre-industrial urban systems have rank-size distributions which are characteristically concave – dominated by over-large primate cities in the way that London dominated seventeenth-century England, or flat-topped and convex, where several regional centres were prominent.[9] Scotland's rank/size plot in the early seventeenth century was slightly convex suggesting an urban system which was not yet fully integrated with a number of distinct urban regions (Graph 1). By the later seventeenth century this had shifted to a more concave plot as the result of growth in the largest towns, particularly Edinburgh and Glasgow, confirming Gibson and Smout's assessment, based on regional variations in grain prices, that a high degree of market integration existed in the Lowlands by the later seventeenth century.[10] By the end of the eighteenth century, however, the Scottish rank/size plot was closer to a straight line with Glasgow rather larger, Dundee and Aberdeen a little smaller than a perfect straight line relationship would have predicted. In 1801 England's rank-size distribution was still concave, arguably less mature than the Scottish one in some respects with London's primacy only partly challenged by a bulge in the middle of the graph representing rapidly growing northern industrial centres.

We can identify further distinctive features of Scottish urbanization by enlarging our scale of focus. An important feature of the first half of the eighteenth century is the occurrence of significant urban growth at a time when, between 1691 and 1755, Scotland's total population grew by only 2.5%. There are problems in measuring the scale of urban growth because of variations in the quality of the hearth tax data and lack of direct comparability with the 1755 census. There is also the difficulty that, a few years after the heath tax lists were compiled, urban populations were affected by the famines of the later 1690s. So urban growth rates from c1700 were probably in many cases higher than indicated here. In the case of Aberdeen the growth rate from 1695 to 1755, calculated by Tyson from the poll tax lists which were drawn up after the city had been affected by famine conditions, was 51%, not the 27% which I have calculated using the 1691 hearth tax.[11]

Nevertheless, if the hearth tax data are calculated for urban parishes it is possible, with some caution, to relate them to Webster's data, at least for the larger towns. The population of the four largest towns grew by 32% between 1691 and 1755. Glasgow increased its population by around 75%, Edinburgh by only about 18%, Aberdeen by 27% and Dundee by around 25%. Smaller towns between 2,000 and 5,000 grew by 26% overall. However, the experience of smaller towns was more varied than for the larger ones with some growing markedly, some stagnating and others registering a drop in population. Some of these trends may reflect problems of comparability between the two data sets. However, there is a broad fit between the trends

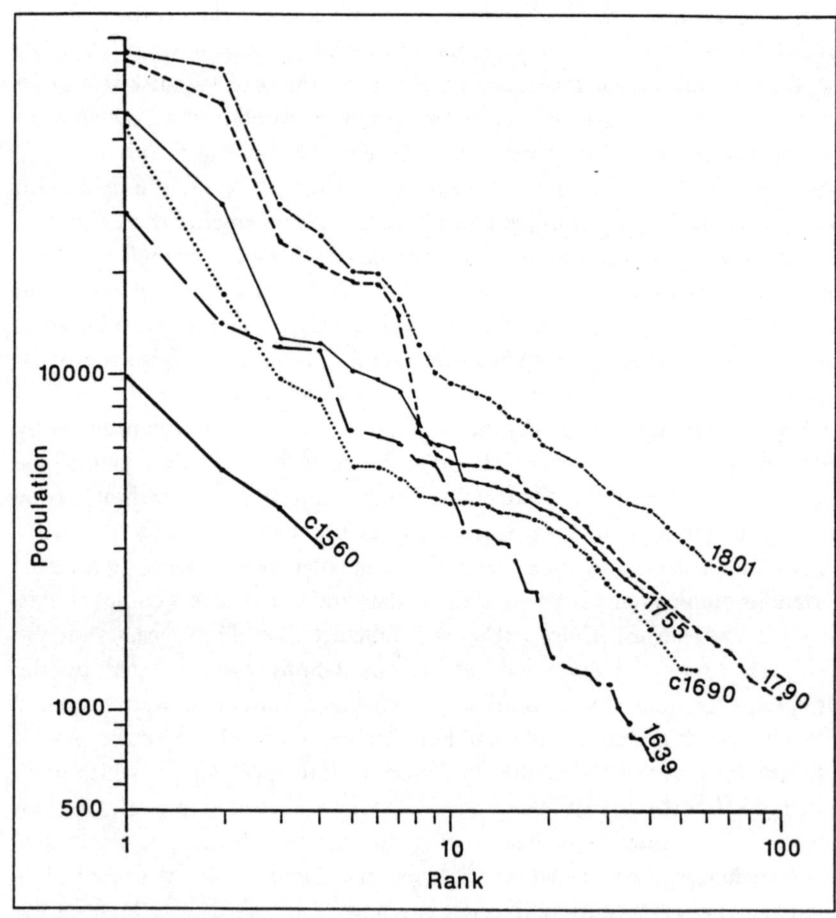

Figure 1 Rank/Size distributions of Scottish towns c. 1560–1801

of individual towns and changes in county populations calculated by Tyson. Thus in the Lothians, which outside Edinburgh, according to Tyson, lost population between 1691 and 1755, Haddington and Linlithgow declined while Musselburgh stagnated.[12] The growth of population which Tyson establishes for Lanarkshire seems to have been accounted almost entirely by the growth of Glasgow.[13] Otherwise urban expansion in west-central Scotland seems to have been modest.

The influences behind urban growth at this time are not entirely clear. Nor, in turn, is the effect of urban growth. In the case of Aberdeen, what changes in the relationship between the town and its hinterland were associated with the 51% rise of population between 1695 and 1755 yet a fall of population of 7.7% within its hinterland?

In the second half of the century it was towns with over 10,000 people, apart from Edinburgh, which were growing fastest, along with smaller centres, while many middle-rank towns seem to have grown more modestly or even stagnated. In part this can be seen as the result of a few towns: Greenock, Paisley, and Perth, crossing the 10,000 threshold without enough smaller centres rising above 5,000 inhabitants to compensate. It can also be argued, however, that this represents a continuation of a long-established trend in the Scottish urban hierarchy – noted by Michael Lynch for the late fifteenth and sixteenth centuries – of a weakness in the middle ranks of the Scottish urban system which was dominated by Edinburgh and large regional foci like Aberdeen, Dundee and Glasgow, to the detriment of middling sheriffdom centres.[14]

Between 1755 and 1801 the number of Scots living in towns with over 2,000 inhabitants increased by more than 200,000. This represented an increase of c64% against that for the total Scottish population of 27.1%. Average growth rate 1755–1801 for the seven largest towns in 1801 was 222%, for the next seven 66% and the next 10 62%. The rate of growth for the top 15 was 138%, for the middle 15 54% and the bottom 15 46%. 51% of this growth was concentrated in the four largest cities, Edinburgh, Glasgow, Dundee and Aberdeen. If satellites of Edinburgh and Glasgow, including Dalkeith, Musselburgh, Greenock and Paisley, are added the figure rises to 68%. This emphasises the degree to which growth was concentrated in existing entres, and highlights the underlying stability of the Scottish urban hierarchy. Of the 12 largest towns between 1755 and 1801 only Edinburgh and Dumfries grew at a slower rate than the overall average of 64%. The start of a distinct shift in the pattern of urban growth towards west-central Scotland is evident, with 46% of urban growth being concentrated in the shires of Lanark, Renfrew and Ayr. However, urban growth was also prominent in some eastern areas with 21% located in Fife and Angus.

The stability of the Scottish urban hierarchy between the end of the seventeenth century and 1801 contrasts with England where, below London, there was much greater change in the rank ordering of towns. In England, of the 32 leading towns in 1700, only 7 retained their place in the top half of an equivalent ranking in 1801.[15] Stability is also evident in towns lower down the urban hierarchy. From the populations given in the *OSA* it is clear that old urban foundations – royal burghs and baronial burghs established before 1500 – dominated even the lower levels of the urban hierarchy. With only a couple of exceptions, like Greenock and Kilmarnock, baronial burghs founded in the sixteenth and seventeenth centuries only secured footholds at the bottom of the hierarchy.[16] The continuing vitality of the four main regional centres helps to explain the modest growth or even decline of many middle-ranking towns. Those which did grow substantially – such as Dumfries and Lanark – were relatively distant from large regional centres.

Another feature of Scottish urbanization in the later eighteenth century was its marked geographical concentration, anticipating the even stronger trends of the nineteenth century. A belt of country 100km long, between Greenock and Arbroath, only 40km wide, held 76% of the urban growth between 1755 and 1801 – a much more concentrated pattern than in England, where there was a major shift in the balance of distribution of urban population from London towards the Midlands and North in the later eighteenth century.

Considering individual towns, Glasgow grew most rapidly between 1755 and 1801 among those at the top of the hierarchy – x2.7 1755–1801 but Dundee, x2.1 and Aberdeen x1.8 were both well ahead of Edinburgh (x1.4). Among other towns which more than doubled their populations, Greenock (x8.9) and Paisley (x4) were especially striking but Arbroath, Forfar and Cupar also doubled in size, emphasising the importance of the textile industries. Other textile centres and ports which almost doubled their populations included Kilmarnock, Ayr, Port Glasgow and Montrose. Some sheriffdom centres like Dumfries and Perth grew by more than 50% but others, like Linlithgow and Haddington, barely increased at all. Some towns even lost population, including St. Andrews, though in the case of Jedburgh and Elgin the loss may have been due to population changes within their extensive landward parish areas rather than in the town itself.

De Vries has characterised the seveenteenth century and the first half of the eighteenth throughout Europe as a period when urban growth was highly concentrated in large cities, linked to the development of government and overseas trade.[17] From the mid eighteenth century into the mid nineteenth, however, large cities only grew at approximately the same rate as total population growth. During this period it was the smaller urban centres whose growth was particularly marked. De Vries' model fits Scotland in some respects, though not in others. Much of the growth of Edinburgh in the late seventeenth/early eighteenth century related to the development of the city's administrative, social and service functions, much of Glasgow's to the development of trade. In the second half of the eighteenth century Edinburgh's growth was relatively modest and, although there was still strong growth in other large towns, the start of rapid industrial-related growth centres in smaller towns is clearly evident.

Implications and Background

What were the influences fuelling this urban growth and what were its effects on Scottish social and economic development? The question is easy to put but difficult to answer because of the complex nature of the interlocking and inter-related variables involved. Urbanization and industrialization in eighteenth-century Britain are clearly linked – but the direction of the linkage is not clear; did industrialization encourage urbanization or vice versa? In England the tendency to draw out the chronology of the Industrial Revolution by seeking earlier origins for it has led to the view that urbanization was the dependent variable.[18] However, recent studies at a regional scale for areas including north west England have shown that marked urban growth was a feature of the first half of the eighteenth century, preceding the start of the classic Industrial Revolution in the 1760s.[19] In Scotland too, urban growth was clearly important well before the onset of full-scale industrialization from the 1760s. Although the reasons behind this growth are not fully understood some of the implications are clear.

It is curious that we know less about changes in the society and economies of Scottish towns in the period between the Union of 1707 and the onset of industrialization than we do for the seventeenth or even the later sixteenth centuries. In particular, apart from a few studies, like Devine's work on Glasgow, and Houston on Enlightenment Edinburgh, we have only a vague idea of how Scottish towns, especially the middling and smaller ones, changed during the first half of the eighteenth century.[20] Themes which would repay more detailed study for this period include patterns of urban in-migration, the economic and social role of small towns, the impact of the Union on urban economies, the growth of functional specialization within the urban system and changing patterns of urban occupations as measures of economic and social change.

Some of the economic linkages between town and countryside which encouraged urban growth during the first 60 years of the eighteenth century can be readily identified, if not precisely evaluated. The textile industries formed one key sector. The development of putting out systems for the spinning of linen yarn and the weaving of cloth controlled by urban merchants had a similar effect. By the 1790s linen spinners in the central

Highlands and even north of the Great Glen were tied into urban production.[21] By this time, however, production was starting to switch to a factory-based system which, in time, would act powerfully to promote the concentration of people in towns.

Links between agricultural improvement, transport and urban markets are also evident. From the 1720s Glasgow's rapid population growth began to outstrip the capacity of local farmers to supply the city.[22] Devine has shown how the expansion of the city's trade and of Glasgow's population, had a major impact in encouraging agricultural improvement within the city's immediate hinterland.[23] The construction of the Forth and Clyde canal, which reached the outskirts of Glasgow in 1777, was partly aimed at facilitating the transport of grain to Glasgow from the eastern Lowlands.[24]

The rapidly growing urban population generated demand for fuel as well as grain. The Monklands Canal, completed in 1792, was specifically conceived to improve Glasgow's coal supply.[25] Domestic consumption of coal, mainly in the towns of the Central Lowlands, accounted for up to two thirds of Scottish coal production at the start of the eighteenth century.[26] The expansion of domestic demand during the first 60 years of the eighteenth century must have been one of the most important factors in encouraging the rapid increase in coal production during this period. Demand for coal stimulated the development of infrastructure including turnpikes, waggonways and the use of steam engines. The improvement of communications in the second half of the eighteenth century – especially the construction of turnpikes and bridges but also the building of harbours – united towns into a real urban system and brought them closer to the countryside.

Social and cultural developments in Scottish towns should not be neglected. Education, for example, was another major urbanising influence as more and more children from rural backgrounds went to burgh grammar schools and even to university. The role of Edinburgh as an educational centre has been highlighted by Houston, but the provision of educational facilities in smaller towns, especially the sheriffdom centres, merits more attention.[27]

Urban In-migration

Urban growth in eighteenth-century Scotland was sustained, and in turn encouraged, by in-migration. The factors which encouraged people into the towns have been discussed by Devine, who emphasises the positive pull of higher wages rather than the negative push off the land resulting from agricultural restructuring.[28] Available sources of information do not allow us to categorise the nature of rural-urban movement with any clarity – though there is plenty of scope for further research. Much of the movement was probably a stepwise continuum with people moving initially from the countryside to a planned estate village or small town and then, possibly, moving on to a larger urban settlement. Movement within the urban hierarchy, from smaller to larger towns, is also likely to have been considerable but direct movement from rural areas to the larger towns is also likely.

Using the methodology established by Wrigley for London between 1650 and 1750 it is possible to make rough calculations of numbers of immigrants into the four largest Scottish towns.[29] In the early eighteenth century these towns would have required net migration of around 1,300 a year to maintain population and allow for growth at the rates which have been shown. By the end of the eighteenth century this may have risen to c4,500, or c6,500 into the seven largest towns with over 10,000 inhabitants. These are net figures – if one allows a significant element of return migration from town to countryside then the real figures for in-migration would have been higher. It is interesting to compare the figure for the early eighteenth century with the estimate of 2,000 emigrants a year leaving Scotland for much of the seventeenth century.[30] Emigration was reduced in the first half of the eighteenth century and it is possible that it was balanced, in part, by the attractiveness of the larger towns generating larger internal migration flows.[31]

Town and country in eighteenth-century Scotland were closely linked. Tidswell's work on migration shows that it is a mistake to consider rural and urban populations as separate entities, with people moving irrevocably from the countryside to the town.[32] There is evidence of a lively two-way interchange between town and country in later eighteenth century Scotland. The autobiography of Alexander Somerville, although referring to the early nineteenth century, shows how a man might move from country to town and back again more than once, demonstrating considerable occupational as well as geographical mobility.[33] The wide range of skills in industry, particularly in textiles, which many Lowland rural areas possessed, especially with the rapid growth of linen manufacture from the mid eighteenth century, would have provided a valuable preparation for urban work.[34] Most migration from the countryside to the towns appears to have operated over short distances. Rural dwellers in the Lowlands must have been familiar with local towns, large as well as small, through the marketing of agricultural produce, attending hiring fairs, selling webs of cloth, undertaking legal and financial business and participating in leisure activities. Even longer-distance migrants, from the Highlands, must often already have had knowledge of urban life from previous temporary migration. Shearers moving south for the Lothian harvest, congregating in Edinburgh for the hiring markets, would already have had some experience of city life. Many would also have had contacts in the towns. As Withers has shown, there were distinct Highland communities in most major Scottish towns from the end of the seventeenth century.[35]

Small Towns

For much of this seminar I have been considering the larger towns, partly because of their demographic importance. Scotland's small towns should not be ignored, though. In the 1790s settlements with between 500 and 2,000 people accounted for a similar proportion of the population as towns with between 2,000 and 10,000. Scotland was, in many ways, a country of small towns. In the 1790s there were 16 towns with over 5,000 inhabitants, and 33 with between 2,000–5,000. On the other hand there were 70 centres with 1,000–2,000 and a similar number with between 500–1,000, many of which had urban attributes. As in England, small towns have received far less attention so far from urban historians. Their importance, numerically, economically and socially may have been increasing rather than otherwise. With the concentration of craft and artisan activities which had formerly been spread throughout the countryside into villages and small towns, and a shift from individual artisans towards small businesses, their local importance may have been enhanced rather than diminished. They formed many people's first experience of urban life, channeling migration towards the main towns. In England the role of such centres in news dissemination, education, and leisure activities not just for minor gentry but for ordinary people has been explored but little comparable work has yet been done for Scotland.

We need to look at diffusion of various functions and activities down through the urban hierarchy to determine how far down they reached at different periods. During the eighteenth century, especially the second half, functional specialization became a much more prominent feature of the Scottish urban system. While some centres retained and expanded their traditional roles as legal, mercantile and social centres for surrounding rural hinterlands, others developed along more specialist lines. This is demonstrated, especially for smaller centres, from the *OSA* accounts. For example, Portpatrick's employment structure was dominated by its role as a communication centre.[36] Moffat was prospering as a spa centre, attracting visitors from a wide area.[37] An increasing number of small towns, especially in west-central Scotland, were becoming specialised textile manufacturing centres. In the small baronial burgh of Stonehouse three quarters of the tradesmen were textile workers.[38]

Industrial centres like these were mostly characterised by very limited provision of higher level services. Other towns retained a more diversified role as regional centres providing social activities for the surrounding gentry and trading facilities for their tenants. Industries in Dumfries seem to have been geared more to the finishing of manufactures produced in the town's hinterland. Its importance as a regional centre is demonstrated by the strength of the legal and medical professions within the town. It was the seat of Sheriff, Justiciary and Commissary courts, of the JPs Quarter Sessions and of both presbytery and synod. Its functions as a social centre are highlighted by its activities in printing and the production of a weekly newspaper, by its wide range of schools, its infirmary, by its three banks and its coffee house as well as inns, taverns and a quite amazing number of alehouses.[39] On a smaller scale, and in remoter settings, small towns like Inveraray performed similar roles.[40] Population growth was relatively modest in these towns compared with some of the rapidly growing textile towns. However, lack of growth does not necessarily mean lack of prosperity. We badly need detailed studies of how the society and economy of such towns changes during the eighteenth century.

The Impact of the Union

The question of the effects of the Union on Scottish towns has hardly been raised. The positive response of Glasgow's merchant community has received detailed study but how did other towns adapt to, or fail to cope with, the problems and opportunities which the Union created? We know in general terms that economic growth was slow to materialise but to what extent did the ways in which individual towns cope with the new post-1707 trading system help to determine their success later in the century? Some towns, like Jedburgh which prior to 1707 had been a centre for trans-Border smuggling, clearly suffered and declined.[41] More generally there is plenty of evidence which, superficially, suggests widespread urban decline in the early eighteenth century, something which fits in with the demographic experience of a number of towns between 1691 and 1755. In the case of some towns this was related to a specific industry, such as the decline in exports of plaiding from Aberdeen, or the drop in exports of coal, salt and ironware from Culross.[42] Sometimes sources such as the records of the Convention refer merely to a 'general decay of trade'. Local rather than national factors may lie behind such declines though. The demise of the ironware industry in Culross was largely due to competition from neighbouring unfree manufacturers in Valleyfield.[43] This suggests a change in the pattern rather than the volume of trade. The trade of some small royal and baronial burghs seems to have depended on the presence of a single merchant family. The decision of Thomas Mathie to move from Prestonpans to Cockenzie seems to have drastically curtailed the foreign trade of the former town.[44]

Some apparent evidence of decline should be treated with caution. Decaying harbours may have been due to storm damage rather than a long-term decline in trade. The decay of public buildings may have indicated a crisis in burghal finances but this did not necessarily mean that the inhabitants were impoverished. While the volume of legitimate trade passing through a port may have been declining many inhabitants may have benefited from smuggling, which assumed large proportions during this period.

The royal burgh tax rankings down to 1737 show relatively little change overall, suggesting stability within the urban hierarchy, confirming the demographic evidence. Changes in tax rankings broadly confirm the trends of population. Glasgow, not surprisingly, showed the greatest increase in its proportion of burghal taxation. Arbroath, Dumfries, and Kirkwall also seemed to be in a favourable position. Of the burghs which had their percentages of the tax contribution reduced the most important group was in Fife; St Andrews, Burntisland, Crail, Culross, Cupar, Dysart, Inverkeithing and Kirkcaldy, though Dunfermline improved its position. This trend may reflect a continuation of the decline noted by Lynch at an earlier period. Elsewhere Ayr, Dumbarton. Elgin, Peebles and Selkirk also registered substantial falls in their proportional tax contributions.[45]

With regard to these regional centres an important aspect of their development was the diffusion down the urban hierarchy of various innovations which enhanced their role. Some innovations related to communications: the development of stagecoach and carrier services, the establishment of newspapers and postal services. Others were linked to their social and business role – coffee houses, inns, banks, libraries, specialist shops. A knowledge of the timing of the spread of such innovations to different sized towns within the urban hierarchy would be valuable in showing how they responded to changes in the economy at national and regional levels. By the end of the eighteenth century even small centres like Biggar had medical and legal services while remote ones like Inveraray had a range of shops.[46]

Urban Occupations

The ministers who contributed to the *OSA* produced a wide range of occupational breakdowns but there is little chance of consistency between such a range of observers, or of accuracy beyond the smallest towns. Trade directories begin to make their appearance in the later eighteenth century, first for Edinburgh then for other centres, but directories, despite the interesting information they contain, fail to provide occupational profiles extending right down the social scale. One source which has been little exploited for occupational data is marriage registers.

The marriage registers for Edinburgh (Table 4) suggest that there was little overall change in the occupational profile of the city during the first half of the eighteenth century.[47] The percentages of the male workforce in the professions, the service sector and manufacturing remain virtually unchanged. There are, however, some interesting differences in detail within these categorties. A fall in the proportion of people in the legal profession and a rise in people connected with city and government administration is evident. Within the manufacturing sector there was a rise in the importance of building and construction, probably linked to the first phase of the city's expansion beyond its medieval limits. During the second half of the eighteenth century changes were more far-reaching. The percentage of the workforce in the professions remained unchanged but the legal profession continued to lose ground while posts in administration and business proliferated with the rise of activities like banking and insurance. The most marked change was a substantial decline in manufacturing and a rise in service activities. Part of this may have been related to the spread of manufacturing into the city's outer suburbs. Apart from the building trades, whose growth must have been linked to the development of the New Town, most areas of manufacturing registered a decline. The variety of occupations within the manufacturing sector was much greater, however, in the 1790s than the 1750s, reflecting a more specialised and diverse industrial base. Within the service sector the proportion engaged in transport and communication rose sharply. Edinburgh was noted as a manufacturing centre even in the sixteenth century when many of the city's industrial activities were finishing trades adding value to basic commodities produced elsewhere. In the eighteenth century the city's role as a service sector seems to have grown in conjunction with its importance as a social and cultural centre.

A comparison of occupational data from the marriage registers of Edinburgh and Glasgow in the 1750s highlights the contrasts between these cities.[48] In Glasgow the professions formed a much smaller proportion of the workforce than in Edinburgh. The merchant community and service sector were also smaller. Several of Glasgow's trades, including clothing and construction, were proportionally smaller than in Edinburgh but the overwhelming contrast was the size of Glasgow's textile industry which accounted for 38% of the listed occupations against 7% for Edinburgh. By the 1790s there was little change in the proportion of professional occupations in Glasgow but the category of 'manufacturers', very small in Edinburgh, was far more important in Glasgow. The principal change was a fall in the overall importance of manufacturing and a corresponding rise in service activities.

TABLE 4: OCCUPATIONAL STRUCTURES FROM MARRIAGE REGISTERS.

	Edinburgh 1701–10	Edinburgh 1740–49	Edinburgh 1790–99	Glasgow 1756–59	Glasgow 1790–94
Law	9.1	6.5	4.5	0.7	0.6
Medicine	1.6	1.5	1.9	0.4	0.5
Church	0.7	1.4	0.5	0.1	0.1
Education	0.5	1.1	0.8	0.7	0.3
Admin	0.7	1.3	2.8	0.2	1.2
Army 38; Navy	0.9	0.4	2.1	0.1	0.1
All Professions	13.5	12.2	12.5	2.2	4.7
Trade	11.5	11.5	7.7	8.5	7.0
Textiles	6.1	6.8	4.2	35.7	26.4
Clothing	13.4	12.3	3.9	8.4	6.6
Leather	10.5	9.5	6.3	9.7	6.5
Wood	4.7	9.3	6.6	5.0	9.6
Metal	5.2	4.5	4.1	5.1	4.5
Construc	3.3	4.3	4.8	2.8	4.2
Food and Drink	8.5	6.5	2.8	5.2	4.0
Misc.	1.7	2.9	3.5	2.1	2.8
Labourers	0.0	0.8	7.6	4.0	6.1
All Manu.	53.4	56.9	43.8	78.0	70.7
Transport & Communication	1.7	3.3	8.6	2.1	4.6
Books, Printing	0.9	2.5	1.4	0.6	0.7
Hairdressers	0.8	0.7	1.4	1.3	0.9
Misc Services	1.4	1.8	3.8	3.9	1.5
Servants	14.3	9.2	12.6	0.1	2.1
All Services	19.1	17.5	27.8	8.0	9.8
Soldiers	2.4	2.4	8.1	5.5	7.6

Conclusion

In this chapter I have tried to present some quantitative measures of the rise of urbanization in eighteenth-century Scotland. Many of the individual figures are open to question but I believe that the broad outlines are reasonably valid. One important theme is the scale, and reasons for, urban development in the first half of the eighteenth century at a time when population growth was very slow. In recent years one or two stray pieces of evidence including Whatley's study of the coal industry and Devine's work on the tobacco trade suggests that economic growth in Scotland during the first half of the eighteenth century, though modest compared with the second half, was greater and more significant than has sometimes been accepted.[49] I have shown here that urban growth in the period before the Industrial Revolution has also been underestimated. Rather than industrialization causing urbanization the process was a more complex and interactive one.

Numerically, and in terms of its economic and social effects, urbanization in the later eighteenth century was more significant and is better understood.

Yet, as I have tried to show, there are still many major unanswered questions regarding this period of urban growth and there is plenty of scope for new research. By 1800 Scotland was still a long way from becoming an urban society. However, the rate at which urban population was growing was the fastest in Europe. The balance between rural and urban had begun to shift decisively in favour of the towns – and Scottish society was increasingly influenced by urban lifestyles, values, consumer goods and services. The nature of Scottish society had been decisively changed – but the nature of these changes requires much further study.

REFERENCES

1. J. de Vries, *European Urbanization* 1500–1800 (London, 1984).
2. R.E. Tyson, 'Contrasting regimes: population growth in Ireland and Scotland during the eighteenth century' S.J. Connolly, R.A. Houston and R.J. Moris (eds.), *Conflict, Identity and Economic Development. Ireland and Scotland, 1600–1939* (Preston, 1995), pp64–76.
3. P.J. Corfield, *The Impact of English Towns* 1700–1800 (Oxford, 1982), p.6.
4. J. Stobart, 'An eighteenth-century revolution? Investigating urban growth in north west England 1664–1801', *Urban History* 23 (1996), pp.26–41.
5. J.D. Marshall, 'The rise and transformation of the small Cumbrian market town', *Northern History* 19 (1983), pp.128–209;. R.A. Unwin, 'Tradition and transition: market towns in the Vale of York', *Northern History* 17 (1981), pp.72–116; M. Noble, 'Growth and development in a regional urban system: the country towns of eastern Yorkshire, 1700–1850', *Urban History Yearbook* (1987), pp.1–21.
6. Tyson, 'Contrasting Regimes', pp.65 6.
7. de Vries, *European Urbanization*, p.39.
8. *Ibid.*, pp.85–120.
9. *Ibid.*
10. A.J.S. Gibson and T.C. Smout 'Regional prices and market regions: the evolution of the early modern Scottish grain market', *Economic History Review* 48 (1995), pp.258–82.
11. D. Adamson (ed.), *West Lothian Hearth Tax, 1691* (Scottish Record Society, Edinburgh, 1981).
12. Tyson, 'Contrasting Regimes', p.65.
13. *Ibid.*
14. M. Lynch, 'The social and economic structure of the larger towns, 1450–1600, in M. Lynch, M. Spearman and G. Stell (eds.), *The Scottish Medieval Town* (Edinburgh, 1988), pp.279–80.
15. R. Lawton and C.G. Pooley, *Britain* 1740–1950. An Historical Geography (London, 1992), pp.90–92.
16. I.D. Whyte, 'The function and social structure of Scottish burghs of barony in the seventeenth and eighteenth centuries' in A. Maczak and T.C. Smout (eds.), *Grundung und Bedeutung Kleinerer Stadte im Nordlichen Europa der Fruhen Neuzeit* (Wolfenbuttel. 1991), pp.11–31.
17. de Vries, *European Urbanisation*, pp.255–60.
18. Stobart 'Eighteenth Century Revolution', p.26.
19. *Ibid.*
20. T.M. Devine, 'The golden age of tobacco' in T.M. Devine and G. Jackson (eds.), *Glasgow. Volume I: Beginnings to* 1830 (Manchester, 1995), pp.139–83; R.A. Houston, *Social Change in the Age of Enlightenment: Edinburgh 1660–1760* (Oxford, 1994).
21. A. Durie, *The Scottish Linen Industry in the Eighteenth Century* (Edinburgh, 1979), pp38–42.
22. Gibson and Smout, 'Regional Prices', p.279.

23. Devine, 'Golden Age', pp.139–183.
24. I.D. Whyte and K.A. Whyte, *Scotland's Changing Landscape* 1500–1800 (London, 1991), pp.195–6.
25. C.A. Whatley, 'New light on Nef's numbers: coal mining and the first phase of Scottish industrialization c1700-c1830' in A.J.G. Cummings and T.M. Devine (eds.), Industry, *Business and Society in Scotland since* 1700 (Edinburgh, 1994), p.16.
26. *Ibid.*, p.5
27. R.A. Houston, 'Literature, education and the culture of print in Enlightenment Edinburgh', *History,* 78 (1993), pp373–92.
28. T.M. Devine, 'Urbanisation' in T.M. Devine and R. Mitchison (eds.), *People and Society in Scotland. Vol.* 1 *1760–1830* (Edinburgh, 1988), pp.27–52.
29. E.A. Wrigley, 'A simple model of London's importance in changing English society and economy 1650–1750' in E.A. Wrigley, *People, Cities and Wealth* (Oxford, 1987), pp133–56.
30. T.C. Smout, N. Landsman and T.M. Devine, 'Scottish emigration in the seventeenth and eighteenth centuries' in N. Canny (ed.), *Europeans on the* Move: Studies on European Migration 1500–1800 (Oxford, 1994), pp.85–90.
31. *Ibid.*, pp.90–100.
32. D. Tidswell, Geographical mobility, occupational change and family relationships in nineteenth-century Scotland with particular reference to the precognitions of the Lord Advocate's Department 1812–21 (Unpublished Ph.D thesis, University of Edinburgh, 1994).
33. A. Somerville, *The Autobiography of a Working Man* (London, 1948).
34. T.M. Devine, 'Urbanisation', pp.44–45.
35. C.W. Withers, 'Highland migration to Dundee, Perth and Stirling 1753–1891', *Journal of Historical Geography* 11 (1985), pp.395–418.
36. Sir John Sinclair (ed.), *Statistical Account of Scotland,* Vol 1 pp.39–43.
37. *Ibid.*, Vol 2. p.293
38. *Ibid.*, Vol 2. p.226.
39. *Ibid.*, Vol 5. p.135.
40. *Ibid.*, Vol 5. p.293
41. *Ibid.*, Vol 1. p.6
42. J.D. Marwick (ed.), *Extracts from the Records of the Convention of the Royal Burghs of Scotland.* 1711–35 (Edinburgh, 1885), pp. 8 38; 124.
43. *Ibid.*, p.146.
44. *Ibid.*, p.242.
45. *Ibid.*
46. Sinclair, (ed.), *Statistical Account,* Vol 1. p.335.
47. Scottish Record Office. Old Parish Registers OPR 644/23–29, Glasgow.
48. H Paton (ed.), The Register of Marriages for the City of Edinburgh 1700–1750. Scottish Record Office, Edinburgh, 1908; F.J. Grant (ed.), Register of Marriages of the City of Edinburgh, 1751–1800. Scottish Record Society, Edinburgh, 1922.
49. Whatley, 'New Light on Nef's Numbers'; Devine, 'Golden Age'.

Twelve

Demographic Change

ROBERT E. TYSON

It is now over twenty years since the publication of *Scottish population history from the seventeenth century to the* 1930s. Part 4, which was written by Mitchison, covered the eighteenth century and despite subsequent research (much of it by Mitchison herself) is still the starting point for any discussion of that period.[1] It appeared only four years before Wrigley and Schofield's monumental *The Population History of England* 1541–1841: *A reconstruction* transformed the study of the subject.[2] Although the sources available for the study of Scottish population history improve considerably after 1700, the deficiencies of the Old Parish Registers make it impossible to employ the techniques of family reconstitution and aggregate back – projection (except in a very limited way in the case of the former) which provided Wrigley and Schofield with such a wealth of statistical data.[3] Nonetheless, it is now clear that demographic change in eighteenth century Scotland differed from that of England in a number of ways and that within Scotland there were considerable regional variations.

The first reliable population estimate that we have for Scotland is the 1,234, 575 in Webster's census of 1755.[4] However, if we assume that the population rose by 18 per cent between 1700 and 1755, as was the case in Aberdeenshire, there were 1,072,000 people at the beginning of the eighteenth century, a figure, incidentally, which falls neatly between George Chalmer's estimate of 1,093,000 and Sir John Sinclair's one of 1,048,000.[5] This means that Scottish population growth between 1700 and 1755 averaged only 0.3 per cent a year, about the same as in England and fairly typical of Europe in the first half of the eighteenth century. It is only in the second half that Scotland's growth began to diverge from rates in England and a number of other countries, including Ireland.[6] Between 1755 and 1801, when the first government census revealed a population of 1,608,420, there was an increase of 27 per cent or 0.5 per cent a year but in England the annual growth rate was 0.8 per cent and in Ireland 1.3 – 1.6 (which may have been matched by Finland).[7]

The growth rate for Scotland as a whole, however, concealed considerable variations at regional and county level which to a large extent were the result of internal migration. Population mobility was high when compared with, for example, France and perhaps even England but most of it was over relatively short distances. Houston's analysis of 6,817 testimonials from a sample of Lowland parishes between 1652 and 1817 reveals that a fifth of those moving were single, with a sex ratio similar to that of the population at large, that 70 per cent had stayed less than three years in the parish granting the certificates, that a similar percentage had moved less than 10 miles, and that where occupations were given, the great majority were farm and domestic servants[8] Before agricultural improvement there was also considerable movement of tenants and sub-tenants, again over short distances. Whyte and Whyte have shown that 45 per cent of completed tenures on four contiguous Angus baronies between 1650 and 1714 lasted for five or fewer years and that the average distance moved to take up new tenancies was only 3.7 miles.[9] Apprentices moving to towns travelled longer distances but for those going to Aberdeen in the first quarter of the eighteenth century the mean distance was still only 18 miles, and in the case of Edinburgh, which recruited nation-wide, 31.[10] Before 1750 the most numerous long-distance migrants were probably unskilled young men seeking work and relief in towns. Movement by whole families was unusual except in years of severe dearth such as 1740–41 when there was an influx of paupers into Edinburgh and other towns, including many from the Highlands.[11]

From about the middle of the eighteenth century, however, there appears to have been an increase in long-distance migration though in the case of apprentices to Edinburgh there was a shrinking of their catchment area as a result of competition from Glasgow and other towns. The result was a marked disparity in regional and county rates of growth. Between 1755 and 1801, the population of the West of Scotland grew by 82.7 per cent, three times the rate for Scotland, compared with 9.0 per cent in the Eastern Borders and 3.1 in the North-East. Of the 31 counties in the same period four – Banff, Moray, Peebles and Roxburgh – actually experienced a decline and a further 14 had rates below the national average but Lanarkshire grew by 80.7 per cent and Renfrewshire by a staggering 194.6.[12] Such variations were the result of profound economic and social changes. The West of Scotland in particular was experiencing rapid industrialisation and urbanisation while the first stage of agricultural improvement involved the creation of larger farms with longer leases, the removal of sub-tenants (who in some counties were half or more of the rural population), and a greater reliance on farm servants. The last continued to move short distances, usually less than 10 miles, and some dispossessed tenants and sub-tenants were able to go into nearby towns and villages.[13] Others, however, were forced to find employment outside their region, especially the North-East where the population of Aberdeenshire, for example, fell by 10,000 between 1783 and 1801, and the southern and eastern Highlands.[14] The Highland-born population of Greenock rose from c. 410 in 1755 to 5,100 in 1801, when it was 29 per cent of the total.[15] Such was the movement to towns, both short and long distance, that no less than 45 per cent of Scottish population growth in this period took place in towns with more than 10,000 inhabitants in 1801 whereas between 1700 and 1755, when the increase in population was considerably smaller, the comparable figure was 16 per cent.[16]

While such migration played a major role in determining differences in regional and county growth rates, its impact on the country as a whole, mainly by subjecting migrants to the towns to higher mortality rates, was probably modest. This was certainly not the case with emigration though the numbers involved were lower than in either the seventeenth or nineteenth centuries. The most recent estimates suggest that fewer than 23,000 left for North America in the first sixty years of the eighteenth century, all but 3,000 from the Lowlands. Between 1760 and 1775, however, 30,000 went from the Lowlands and 15,000 from the Highlands. This outflow was checked by the War of Independence and although it was renewed with the return of peace, only a further 3,000–5,000 left between then and 1800. Thus over the whole century something like 80,000 Scots went to North America, two-thirds of them from the Lowlands. To these must be added those Scots who left for the Continent and the remainder of the British Isles, particularly London and the industrial towns of the north.[17]

Landsman has put the total number of emigrants at less than 100,000, against which must be offset an unknown but small number of immigrants, mainly skilled workers from England together with Irish immigrants from the 1780s onwards.[18] Emigrants are traditionally assumed to be predominantly males aged between 14 and 30 years which resulted in unbalanced sex ratios and a reduction in fertility in the areas from which they departed. Bailyn, however, found that 25 per cent of emigrants leaving Scotland in 1773–76 were children compared with 6 per cent from England and that 40 per cent were female as against 16 per cent from south of the Border.[19] The imbalance and therefore impact on fertility was much greater in the case of temporary migrants who consisted overwhelmingly of young men. Large numbers of Scots, for example, served in the Royal Navy and merchant marine, and in the Newfoundland, Greenland and whale fisheries. Others were employed in the service of the East India and Hudson Bay companies – one minister writing in the *Old Statistical Account* reckoned that there were always between 400 and 500 Scots living in the Hudson Bay settlements, most of them from Orkney.[20] Even greater numbers joined the Army which in the last quarter of the eighteenth century usually took between a quarter and a third of its recruits from Scotland.[21] Many of these temporary emigrants failed to return home and became a permanent loss. Just how important this could be can be seen by examining the statistics of English emigration.

Canny has suggested that 80,000 English emigrated to the North American mainland, the West Indies and Ireland between 1700 and 1780, proportionally far fewer than left Scotland.[22] Wrigley and Schofield, however, estimated that over the whole century English net migration, which included soldiers who died abroad and the surprisingly large number of sailors lost at sea, was 518,676 or 12.6 per cent of the natural increase.[23] If we assume that the latter in Scotland was 0.5 per cent a year over the eighteenth century, as opposed to an actual increase of 0.4 per cent, net migration from Scotland would have been just under 150,000. This figure may actually be on the low side but if accepted, it means that in the absence of such net migration, the population of Scotland in 1801 would have been 9.3 per cent larger. Although by no means insignificant, particularly when compared with England and probably most other countries, the impact of net migration on the Scottish population was clearly much less than that of fertility and mortality.

Any discussion of these before civil registration in 1855 is bedevilled by the problems of obtaining reliable statistics. The solution is to compare the age-structures of Scotland's population derived from Webster's Census of 1755 and the *Old Statistical Account* of the 1790s with the model populations in Coale and Demeny's Princeton life tables. The first attempt was made by Hollingsworth in *Scottish population history*. He assumed that when Webster divided the population in 1755 into 0–10, 11–20, 21–30 etc. age groupings, he really meant 0–9, 10–19, 20–29 etc., resulting in 25.48 per cent under the age of 10 (0–9) and 44.11 under 20 (0–19). On the further assumption that the natural rate of increase was 3.75 per 1,000, the result was a demographic regime with extremely high levels of fertility and mortality (see table 1).[24] Mitchison subsequently argued that Webster did indeed mean what he wrote which meant 23.59 per cent of the population were under 10 and 42.32 under 20. She also used the estimates of population of a large number of parishes in the Church of Scotland's petition for the augmentation of stipends – the so-called Augmentation Returns – to calculate an annual rate of growth of 4.73 between 1748 (when the figures were probably collected) and 1755 which she then reduced to 4.0. At North level 6, these produced considerably lower vital rates. However, there seem no good reasons for reducing the original growth rate for 1748–55 and as some allowance needs to be made for net migration, a natural increase of 5.0 per 1,000 is more plausible. At North level, such a rate in conjunction with Mitchison's revised age groupings gives more or less the same crude birth rate as she calculated but somewhat lower mortality (see table 1). The only comparable Scottish figures are for the Kincardineshire coastal parish of Benholm where the minister kept a note of all births, marriages and deaths between 1753 and 1777, together with annual totals of population. The crude birth rate in 1753–57 was 35.6 and the crude death rate 28.8, surprisingly similar figures.[25]

TABLE 1: POPULATION INDICES CALCULATED FROM WEBSTERS AGE-STRUCTURE OF SCOTLANDS POPULATION, 1755

	Hollingsworth (1977)	Mitchison (1989)	Tyson (1997)
Crude birth rate	41.8	34.7	34.6
Crude death rate	38.0	30.7	29.6
Life expectancy at birth	26.6	31.6	33.5
Infant Mortality	239	222	195

Sources: M. Flinn et al., *Scottish Population History* (Cambridge, 1977), p.259; R. Mitchison, 'Webster Revisited: A Re-examination of the 1755 "Census of Scotland" ', in T.M. Devine (ed.), *Improvement and Enlightenment* (Edinburgh, 1989), p.31.

These latest figures for 1755 may be compared with those for the 1790s which Mitchison produced for *Scottish population history*. These gave a crude birth rate of 35.1, only slightly higher than in 1755, but the crude death rate had fallen from 29.6 to 24.1 and expectation of life at birth had risen from 33.5 years to 39.4 years (see table 1).[26] Thus the natural increase in Scotland's population in the second half of the eighteenth century was almost certainly the result of a fall in mortality, but one much less dramatic than in Hollingsworth's original estimate. This is in stark contrast to England where mortality was unchanged but the crude birth rate rose from 32.8 in 1754–58 to 38.7 forty years later. If comparisons are made with those European countries that have similar data, it is clear that there were a number of demographic regimes, with Scotland much more like Sweden than England, whose reliance upon fertility for nearly all its growth was unique (see table 2).

TABLE 2: POPULATION INDICES OF SCOTLAND, ENGLAND, FRANCE, FINLAND, NORWAY AND SWEDEN: 1750S AND 1790S

	1750s	CBR	CDR	1790s	CBR	CDR
Scotland	1755	34.6	29.6	1790	35.1	24.1
England	1754–58	32.8	25.9	1794–98	38.7	26.7
France	1755–59	41.0	35.3	1795–99	36.6	29.5
Finland	1755–59	44.6	32.3	1795–99	40.1	23.4
Norway	1755–59	33.0	24.5	1795–99	32.4	22.1
Sweden	1755–59	34.6	28.7	1795–99	33.4	24.9

Sources: Flinn, *Scottish Population History*, p.270; E.A. Wrigley and R.S. Schofield, *The Population History of England* 1541–1871: A reconstruction (London, 1981), p.529; J. Dupâquier, *La Population Francaise aux XVIIe et XVIIIe sièctes* (Paris, 1979), p.98; B.R. Mitchell, *European Historical Statistics* (London, 1981), p.114; M. Drake, *Population and Society in Norway* 1735–1865 (Cambridge, 1969), pp.164–175.

Flinn believed that in the long run population growth depended upon a reduction in the frequency, severity and ubiquity of mortality crises caused by war, famines and above all epidemics of disease.[27] In the case of England, Wrigley and Schofield defined a national mortality crisis as a 10 per cent or more deviation in the annual crude death rate from a centred 25 year moving average. There were 45 such years of high mortality in England between 1541 and 1871 of which eleven were three-star crises when the crude death rate was 30 per cent above trend. Three of these occurred in the harvest years 1727, 1728 and 1729 and the final one was in 1741. The last two-star crisis (20–30 per cent above trend) was in 1763 and although one-star crises (10–20 per cent above trend) continued throughout the century, they were less frequent than before 1700. Wrigley and Schofield concluded that the marked decline of what Flinn called the instability of mortality began in the third quarter of the seventeenth century and was due to the decline and eventual disappearance of two- and three-star crises.[28] However, in no 25 year period between 1541 and 1871 was crisis mortality responsible for as much as ten per cent of all deaths and even if crisis mortality is factored out, the remaining 'normal' mortality was well above that before 1700. As in France, any eventual fall in mortality was largely achieved by a reduction in 'normal' or non-crisis mortality.[29]

In order to carry out a similar analysis of Scottish mortality crises, we have to relay on Flinn's index of mortality from 1615–1854 which he constructed from the best surviving parish registers, the great majority of which were from the Lowlands. Despite many weaknesses, it reveals a long-term trend similar to that in England although the chronology of crises were different. The last three-star crisis was in the calendar year 1699 and in the eighteenth century there were only two-star crises in 1740, 1770 and 1788. One-star crises continued to be common but after 1750 the prevailing level of mortality was much lower and any crises were modest when compared with earlier periods. Indeed, it is likely that some went unnoticed by contemporaries (see table 3).[30]

TABLE 3: DECENNIAL INDICES OF MORTALITY IN SCOTLAND: 1650–1799 (1790–99 — 100)

1650–59	125	1700–09	146	1750–59	154
1660–69	162	1710–19	165	1760–69	140
1670–79	171	1720–29	171	1770–79	137
1680–89	175	1730–39	161	1780–89	126
1690–99	198	1740–49	174	1790–99	100

Source: Calculated from Flinn, *Scottish Population History* (1977), pp.483–88.

Mortality in the year immediately after the famine of 1695–99, which was a much more serious crisis than anything experienced in England, appears to have been low though this was probably because so many children and old people had died during the famine rather than because there was an improvement in life expectancy. Flinn's index indicates high levels of mortality in the 1720s and 1730s, so much so that the population may have fallen for a time, though there appears to have been nothing comparable with the English crisis of 1727–31 which reduced the population of England by four per cent.[31] The famine of 1695–99 was the last nationwide subsistence crisis in Scotland and although there was some upward movement of prices in the 1720s and 1730s which was accompanied by an increase in price volatility and a temporary falling away in the synchronisation of fiar prices, there was no serious dearth until 1740–41. The harvest of 1739 was a light one and was followed by exceptionally cold weather which killed large numbers of cattle and sheep and delayed the spring sowing. Unusually for Scotland this was followed by a summer drought and a poor harvest which led to grain prices twice as high as those in the harvest year 1738. There were food riots in Edinburgh and other towns and probably localised famines in the Highlands, where the heavy loss of livestock had reduced the ability to purchase grain from the Lowlands, but nothing comparable to the heavy mortality in countries as far apart as Ireland, Norway, Sweden and Austria. One explanation is that in Scotland there were only two successive years of high prices compared with four on the Continent. Local authorities and heritors also made great efforts to import food and sell it at cost price. Some deaths were undoubtedly from diseases associated with death, such as dysentery, measles and typhus but smallpox was also widespread and there may also have been an increase in mortality as a result of the exceptionally cold weather in the winter of 1739–40.[32]

The first forty years were characterised by numerous localised epidemics which though less serious than the great mortality crises of the sixteenth and seventeenth centuries occurred at more frequent intervals and, as in England, may have increased the crude death rate. Many were described in the bills of mortality simply as 'fevers' and only measles, chin cough (whooping cough) and smallpox can be accepted as meaningful terms. The most serious of all was smallpox (*variola major*) which following the disappearance of bubonic plague after 1650 became the most feared disease. Although the case – fatality rate of c.17 per cent was much lower than that of bubonic plague, because it was an airborne disease, it was much more contagious – indeed it has been described as the most contagious disease known to man – and unlike plague was found in the countryside as well as towns. By 1700 the pool of susceptibles (infants, young children and migrants from the countryside) was large enough for the disease to become endemic in Edinburgh by 1700 and in Glasgow by 1750 though there were still epidemics every two or three years. In other towns the disease was probably still epidemic, with outbreaks every four or five years. In the countryside the interval depended upon the risk of exposure. Thus parishes on trade routes were more vulnerable than more isolated areas, especially in the Highlands and Islands, though the longer the interval between epidemics, the higher mortality tended to be.[33]

In the towns, smallpox was primarily a disease of infants and young children between six months and two years. In Kilmarnock between 1728 and 1763, for example, the mean age of these dying from the disease was 2.6 years and only 8.2 per cent of victims were above four years. Any adults who died were likely to have been new arrivals from the countryside who had not previously contracted the disease and therefore had no immunity. Bad harvests may have been followed by an increase in migration to the towns, thus increasing the size of the population at risk. This probably explains the prevalence of smallpox in a number of towns in 1740–41, including Edinburgh, where it was responsible for 16.9 per cent of all deaths in those two years compared with a mean of 10 per cent in 1744–67 (though in that 20 year period only in 1752 was a poor harvest followed by a smallpox epidemic). In other communities which have bills of mortality, smallpox was responsible for one in six of all deaths, somewhat higher than in Edinburgh.[34]

It is much more difficult to estimate the impact of smallpox in the countryside. In Benholm, which as a coastal parish with a small port had a higher frequency rate than many inland parishes, there were three epidemics between 1778 and 1788 which were responsible for 9.6 per cent of all deaths in that period compared with 14.5 per cent attributed to fevers. In the Dumfriesshire parish of Torthorwald, however, only 5 per cent of all deaths between 1764 and 1790 were from the disease and some were attributed to the consequences of smallpox inoculation.[35] The most spectacular loss of life occurred in the Northern and Western Isles. One visitor to Shetland in the summer of 1700 later wrote that shortly after he had left, an epidemic of the disease killed a third of the population on some islands and two-thirds on Fair Isle. The worst hit of all appears to have been St. Kilda which only had two visitations of the disease. The first in 1726 is said to have reduced the population, which Martin at the end of the seventeenth century estimated to be 180, to four adults and twenty-six children and the island had to be repopulated with settlers from Harris.[36]

Despite its importance, it is difficult to find evidence about 'normal' mortality, particularly when smallpox is not the cause of death. One clue is provided by the age structure of mortality. Infant mortality in 1755 was 195 per 1,000, slightly lower than in Sweden though well above that of England which had very low levels. This works out at 22.8 per cent of all burials of which nearly half were probably in the first four weeks after birth during which babies have a natural immunity to disease. Most such infant deaths in this period, therefore, were endogenous i.e. the result of birth defects and the trauma associated with birth. After a month mortality was increasingly exogenous as babies became susceptible to the dangers of the surrounding environment. Intestinal diseases, for example, were common among infants who had been weaned and reached their peak between August and October. Heavy mortality, mainly from infectious disease, continued throughout early childhood, especially in towns. In Edinburgh in 1740–41 35.1 per cent of all deaths were of those aged under two years and a further 16.4 were of children between two and four years.[37]

For adults, whose mortality tended to peak in winter when respiratory diseases were most common, the only reliable figures that we have are for advocates and Writers to the Signet. Between 1650–99 and 1700–49 expectation of life at thirty rose from 23.3 to 31.7 years for Writers to the Signet and from 27.4 to 33.9 years for the more exalted advocates. Such a dramatic decrease in adult mortality before the demographic revolution was found among other elite groups in Europe but in the case of Scottish lawyers, who lived predominantly in Edinburgh, it is not easy to find any environmental improvements which could explain it.[38] It may have been a consequence of the transition from epidemic to endemic disease, above all smallpox, which while improving adult life expectancy reduced that of infants and children, as was the case in England.

Unlike the population at large, there was no improvement in the life expectancy of lawyers in the second half of the eighteenth century in spite of the building of Edinburgh New Town and a falling urban death rate. Where mortality figures for specific age groups exist for other countries, they all reveal that the fall in mortality was largely among infants and children under the age of ten. In Scotland, infant mortality fell from 195 to 175 between 1755 and the 1790s (when it was lower than in England) but this explained only 11 per cent of the decline in the crude death rate, which was likely to have been most marked among young children (1–4 years).[39]

The most obvious explanation for the fall in mortality among this age-group is smallpox inoculation. A recent discussion of this subject in Scotland, however, concludes that it was too little practised to fulfil its potential for controlling the disease except in Galloway and the Highlands and Islands. Overall, therefore, it made only a minor contribution to the decline in mortality and it was only with the introduction of vaccination after 1800 that smallpox ceased to be a major killer.[40] Nor is there any evidence to suggest that many Scots suffered from malnutrition before 1750 except in years of exceptional dearth – indeed measured by intake of calories and by height they appear to have been relatively well fed – or that there was an improvement in per capita food consumption in the second half of the eighteenth century. This was a period that saw a long-term upward movement in food prices (which was accompanied by serious food riots) while the appalling harvest of 1782 caused acute distress throughout the north of Scotland. Other possible explanations such as an improvement in medical services and better sanitation are not convincing though there may have been some improvement in rural housing and in private hygiene.[41]

In recent years there has been considerable emphasis on the role of an increase in the duration of breast feeding in bringing about a reduction in infant mortality. Mitchison found that in the predominantly urban parish of Kilmarnock the interval between births fell from 26.9 months in 1741–53 to 24.4 in 1770–95, a decrease of 76 days.[42] This suggests that women breast fed their babies for about a year in the first period but only for nine or ten months in the second, perhaps because there was an increase in the demand for female labour. In the Banffshire rural parish of Rothiemay the birth interval between 1750 and 1799 was 31.5 months, slightly higher than the 30.4 months for England between 1600 and 1799. This probably means that infant feeding lasted for 14–18 months.[43] What evidence there is, and it is very thin, suggests no increase in the length of time that women breast fed their babies; indeed, in the towns and perhaps those rural areas of the Lowlands where agricultural improvement was well under way before the end of the century, a decrease seems more probable.

The improvement of six years in expectation of life at birth in Scotland between 1755 and the 1790s is a conundrum that as yet has no satisfactory explanation. Perhaps the most likely, as Fridlizius has argued for Sweden, is the emergence of a new balance between invading micro-organisms and the human host, either as a result of changes in viruses and bacteria or, more plausibly, because human beings were developing a growing immunity to some diseases.[44]

We are on firmer ground with fertility though the only measurements available for Scotland are the crude birth rates for 1755 and the 1790s which are almost identical. Mitchison, however, found considerable regional variations in the 1790s, ranging from 40.3 in the Highlands and Islands to 28.2 in the North-East. There were also variations in illegitimacy with its highest rate in the Western Borders, though that for Scotland as a whole in the 1760s was relatively low at 3.6 per cent of all births.[45] Most children were born in wedlock and before the widespread adoption of family limitation from the end of the nineteenth century onwards, fertility levels were determined primarily by the age at which women married and the proportion who did so during their fertile years.

Houston found that the mean age of first marriage by age 50 in a sample of female deponents in the High Court of Justiciary between 1660 and 1770 was 26.6 years.[46] There is no evidence that this increased, at least before 1820, whereas in England the age of first marriage fell from 25.3 years for women born c.1716 to 22.6 for those born in 1791.[47] Houston also found that 20 – 25 per cent of women in a sample of Lowland burial registers died unmarried between 1740 and 1790, a figure supported by evidence from the *Old*

Statistical Account. For England, however, the comparable figure was only 10 per cent.[48]

There are a number of possible explanations for these striking differences between Lowland Scotland and England but the most likely are the composition of their respective agricultural labour forces and, perhaps more importantly differing levels of poor relief. In Scotland, unlike England, agricultural improvement brought an even greater reliance on unmarried farm servants who, as farms were enlarged and sub-tenancies disappeared, found it difficult to obtain a holding or even a cottage and therefore to marry since couples were expected to establish their own households. Poor relief was less generous than in England and there was no equivalent of the payments to agricultural labourers, including child allowances, which undoubtedly encouraged early marriage. When such payments were eventually reduced in England, the age of marriage rose.[49]

Women in Scotland probably married earlier in the towns than in the countryside though levels of celibacy may have been high. In Kilmarnock between 1732 and 1753 the mean age of marriage of those living in the urban part of the parish was three years lower than in the remainder but 26 per cent of females dying over the age of 50 were spinsters.[50] Although proto-industrialisation was widespread, with an estimated 80 per cent of Scottish women doing some spinning, there is no evidence that it had much impact on the age of marriage. Indeed, the minister of Liff and Bervie in Angus, which had a considerable linen industry commented that many men married older women whose earnings allowed them to begin married life in some comfort 'which must be a hindrance to population'. He attributed the substantial increase in population size primarily to immigration.[51]

The most striking differences in nuptuality occurred in the Highlands and Islands where the old order was replaced by two distinct economic and social systems. In South Argyll, Central and Eastern Inverness, Easter Ross and Caithness there was a consolidation of land similar to that in the Lowlands which not only led to an increase in migration but eventually to an increase in the age of marriage and in the percentage of women never marrying. Along the western seaboard of the mainland and in the Northern and Western Isles, however, there was a movement towards crofters and cottars living in coastal townships. The small size of the holdings made some employment essential even when potatoes were increasingly grown and it was this which determined nuptuality. The production of kelp in particular was very labour intensive and the landowners who controlled the industry were prepared to allow the subdivision of holdings in order to build up a large labour force. The result was a close correlation between kelp output and population growth in the Western Isles.[52] The relationship was less marked in Orkney where landlords found it more difficult to prevent their people from migrating.[53] The impact of increasing sub-division on nuptuality was especially marked in the case of Shetland where in the seventeenth and early eighteenth century a local law had prohibited anyone marrying without sufficient property or an occupation to live by. The rise from c.1720 of a large commercial fishing industry controlled by merchant–lairds resulted in the law being ignored. The labour force consisted of small farmers who paid their rent in fish and in order to increase their numbers, the merchant-lairds sub-divided farms and encouraged early marriage. It was reckoned that a young man started to fish at the age of 18 or 19 and was considered adult and therefore ready for marriage after one season.[54]

It is not clear how low the age of marriage and celibacy in the Western Isles and adjacent areas of the mainland were before the creation of crofting though Martin Martin claimed in the 1690s that on St. Kilda women married at about thirteen or fourteen.[55] Pennant, more plausibly, gave the age of marriage on Canna when he visited in 1771 as 20 for women and 27 for men while the minister for Tiree wrote that men married at 19 or 20.[56] A figure can also be estimated from the list of inhabitants on the Duke of Argyll's estates on the Argyll mainland and Tiree in 1779. This gives the ages of all men, women and children and though there is a tendency for age heaping or a concentration of ages at particular numbers (usually 20, 30, 40 etc) it is possible to obtain a rough age of marriage by subtracting the ages of eldest children from those of their mothers and adding a year for the interval between marriage and the birth of the first child. On mainland Argyll the mean age of 62 mothers who in 1779 were under the age of 40 was 23 and of 139 similarly aged women in Tiree 22.[57] This low age of marriage is supported by a number of Western Isles ministers writing in *the Old Statistical Account* while in four Argyll parishes in the 1790s just over 10 per cent of women aged 45 and over were unmarried.[58] The result was that on Tiree in 1779 43 per cent of the population were under 15 years and on Mull 44 per cent compared with 35 per cent in England at that time and 33 per cent in Scotland in 1755.[59]

There is still much that we do not know about the demography of Scotland in the eighteenth century but it is much easier to discern the main trends than it was in 1977 when *Scottish Population History* was published. The revised vital rates for 1755 in particular have revealed a demographic regime no longer like that of France, with its very high levels of mortality and fertility, and much closer to that of Sweden. The similarity of economic and social change in England and Scotland as opposed to Sweden raises fundamental questions about the supposed relationship of such changes and the causes of population growth. There is clearly some relationship in the case of fertility but it is not easy to see one in that of mortality, especially in the absence of famine or even widespread malnutrition.

REFERENCES

1. M. Flinn et al., *Scottish Population History from the seventeenth century to the 1930s* (Cambridge 1977), pp.203–97.
2. E.A. Wrigley & R.S. Schofield, *The Population History of England 1541–1871: A reconstruction* (London, 1981).
3. For Scottish population sources see Flinn, *Scottish Population History*, pp.45–97 and 203–09.
4. For a discussion of Webster's census see R. Mitchison, 'Webster Revisited: A Re-examination of the 1755 Census of Scotland' in T.M. Devine (ed.), *Improvement and Enlightenment* (Edinburgh, 1989), pp.62–77.
5. R.E. Tyson, 'Famine in Aberdeenshire 1695–99: Anatomy of a Crisis', in D. Stevenson (ed.), *From Lairds to Louns,* (Aberdeen 1986), pp.49–50: Flinn, *Scottish Population History,* p.241.
6. J. de Vries, *European Urbanisation 1500–1800* (London, 1984), pp.36–37.
7. J.G. Kyd, *Scottish Population Statistics* (Scottish History Society, Edinburgh, 1952) p.82; R.S. Schofield, 'British population change, 1700–1871', in *The Economic History of Britain since 1700, Vol. 1, 1700–1860*, in R. Floud and D. McCloskey (eds.) (Cambridge, 1994) p.93.
8. R.A. Houston, 'Geographical Mobility in Scotland, 1652–1811', *Journal of Historical Geography,* ii (1985), pp.379–94, I.D. Whyte, 'Population Mobility in Early Modern Scotland', in R.A. Houston and I.D. Whyte (eds.), *Scottish Society, 1500–1800* (Cambridge, 1989), pp.37–58.
9. I.D. Whyte and K.A. Whyte, 'Continuity and Change in a Seventeenth Century Farming Community', *Agricultural History Review,* 32 (1984), pp.159–69; I.D. Whyte and K.A. Whyte, 'Geographical Mobility in a Seventeenth Century Rural Community', *Local Population Studies,* 32 (1984), pp.45–53.
10. A.A. Lovett, I.D. Whyte and K.A. Whyte, 'Poisson regression analysis and migration fields: The example of the apprenticeship records of Edinburgh in the seventeenth and eighteenth centuries', *Transactions of the Institute of Britain Geographers.* n.s. 10 (1985), pp. 317–332, I.D. Whyte and K.A. Whyte, 'Patterns of migration of apprentices to Aberdeen and Inverness during the seventeenth and eighteenth centuries', *Scottish Geographical Magazine,* 102 (1986) pp.81–91.
11. I.D. Whyte, *Scotland before the Industrial Revolution* (London, 1995), p.131.
12. Calculated from J.G. Kyd, *Scottish Population Statistics.* For regions see Flinn, *Scottish Population History,* pp.xxii-xiii.
13. T.M. Devine, *The Transformation of Rural Scotland* (Edinburgh, 1994), pp.111–64.
14. M. Gray, 'Scottish Emigration: The Social Impact of Agrarian Change in the Rural Lowlands, 1775–1875' *Perspectives in American History,* 7 (1974) pp.95–174; W. Kennedy, *Annals of Aberdeen,* Vol 1 (London, 1818), p.313.
15. Flinn, *Scottish Population History,* p.475.
16. Calculated from Kyd, *Scottish Population Statistics.*
17. T.C. Smout, N.C. Landsman and T.M. Devine, 'Scottish Emigration in the Seventeenth and Eighteenth Centuries, in N. Canny (ed.), *Europeans on the Move: Studies in European Migration, 1500–1800,* (Oxford, 1994), pp.90–112
18. Smout, Landsman and Devine, 'Scottish Emigration in the Seventeenth and Eighteenth Centuries', pp.97–98.
19. B. Bailyn, *Voyagers to the West: A Passage in the Peopling of America on the Eve of Revolution* (New York, 1986), pp.126–203; N. Canny, 'English Migration into and across the Atlantic during the Seventeenth and Eighteenth Centuries', in Canny, *Europeans on the Move,* p.52.
20. Sir John Sinclair, *The Statistical Account of Scotland, 1791–95* [hereafter *OSA*] (new ed., Wakefield, 1975–83), vol. XIX pp.246–50.
21. R. Floud, R. Wachter and A. Gregory, *Height, Health and History: nutritional status in the United Kingdom, 1750–1980* (Cambridge, 1990), p.89.
22. Canny, 'English Migration', p.64.
23. Wrigley and Schofield, *English Population History,* pp.219–21.
24. Flinn, *Scottish Population History,* pp.250–60.

25. Mitchison, 'Webster Revisited' pp.62–77; A.J. Coale and P. Demeny, *Regional Model Life Tables and Stable Populations* (Princeton N.J., 1966), *OSA,* XIV, pp.38–9.
26. Flinn, *Scottish Population History*, pp.260–70.
27. Flinn, *Scottish Population History*, pp.100–01.
28. Wrigley and Schofield, *Population History of England*, pp.332–35.
29. R.W. Fogel, 'Second Thoughts and the European Escape from Hunger: Famine, Chronic Malnutrition and Mortality Rates' in S.R. Osmani (ed.), *Nutrition and Poverty* (Oxford, 1992), p.247; R.W. Fogel, 'New Sources and Techniques for the Study of Nutritional Status, Health, Mortality and the Process of Ageing', *Nutritional Methods*, 26 (1993), pp.5–6
30. For Flinn's mortality indices see Flinn, *Scottish Population History* pp.98–104 and 483–88.
31. Flinn, *Scottish Population History* pp.485–86; Wrigley and Schofield, *Population History of England*, p.533.
32. Flinn, *Scottish Population History*, pp.209–23; A. J. Gibson and T.C. Smout, *Prices, Food and Wages in Scotland* 1550–1780 (Cambridge, 1995) pp.172–73; J.D. Post, *Food Shortage, Climatic Variability and Epidemic Disease in Pre-industrial Europe* (Ithica and London, 1988), pp.30–50.
33. J.R. Smith, *The Speckled Monster* (Chelmsford, 1987), pp.15–6; A. Mercer, Disease, *Mortality and Population in Transition* (Leicester 1990), pp.22–23, 57–59; S.R. Duncan, S. Scott and C.J. Duncan, 'Smallpox Epidemics in Cities in Britain', *Journal of Interdisciplinary History.* 25 (1994), pp.255–71.
34. C. Creighton, *A History of Epidemics in Britain*, Vol. 2 (London, 1965), pp.522, 526–27; Flinn, *Scottish Population History*, pp.292–93.
35. OSA, XIV p.40; OSA, IV, pp.508–09.
36. Flinn, *Scottish Population History* P.185; Martin Martin, *A Description of the Western Isles of Scotland Circ.* 1695 (Edinburgh, 1994 ed.), pp.93, 144.
37. For recent discussion of endogenous and exogenous infant mortality and seasonal fluctuations in mortality see J. Landers, *Death and the Metropolis: Studies in the demographic history of London* 1670–1830 (Cambridge, 1993), pp.139–41 and 203–41.
38. R.A. Houston, 'Mortality in early modern Scotland: The life expectancy of advocates', *Continuity and Change* (1992), pp.47–69; R.A. Houston, 'Writers to the Signet: Estimates of Adult Mortality in Scotland from the Seventeenth to the Nineteenth Century', *Social History of Medicine*, VII (1995), pp.37–53.
39. Wrigley and Schofield, *Population History of England*, p.249; A. Perrenoud, 'Mortality decline in its secular setting' in T. Bengtsson, G. Fridlizius and R. Ohlsson (eds.), *Pre-Industrial Population Change* (Stockholm, 1984), pp.50–55.
40. D. Brunton, 'Smallpox inoculation and demographic trends in eighteenth-century Scotland', *Medical History*, 36 (1992) pp.403–29.
41. Gibson and Smout, *Prices, Food and Wages in Scotland*, pp.173, 225–60; Flinn, *Scottish Population History*, pp.233–39.
42. I am grateful to Professor Mitchison for allowing me to use her unpublished work on birth intervals in Kilmarnock. See also Flinn, *Scottish Population History*, p.287.
43. A. Blaikie *Illegitimacy, Sex and Society: North-East Scotland* 1750–1950 (Oxford, 1993), p.107; C. Wilson, 'The Proximate Determinants of Marital Fertility in England 1600–1900' in L. Bonfield, R.M. Smith and K. Wrightson (eds.), *The World We Have Gained* (Oxford, 1986), pp.222–23.
44. G. Fridlizius 'Mortality Decline in the First Phase of the Demographic Transition': Swedish Experiences' in Bengtsson, Fridlizius and Ohlsson, *Pre-Industrial Population Change*, pp.81–109.
45. R. Mitchison and L. Leneman, *Sexuality and Social Control: Scotland* 1660–1780 (Oxford, 1989), p.156.
46. R.A. Houston, 'Age and Marriage of Scottish Women', circa 1660–1770, *Local Population Studies*, 43 (1989), pp.63–66.
47. R.S. Schofield, 'English marriage patterns revisited', *Journal of Family History*, x (1985), pp.2–20.
48. R.A. Houston, 'The Demographic Regime' in T.M. Devine and R. Mitchison eds *People*

and Society in Scotland Vol. 1 1760–1830 (Edinburgh, 1988), p.20; Schofield, '*English marriage patterns revisited*, pp.2–20; Flinn, *Scottish Population History*, pp.280–282.

49. Devine, *The Transformation of Rural Scotland*, pp.34–78; Gray. 'Scottish Emigration: The Social Impact of Agrarian Change in the Rural Lowlands, 1775–1875,' pp.107–111; R. Mitchison, 'The Poor Law' in *People and Society in Scotland* pp.252–67; G. R. Boyer, Malthus was right after all: Poor Relief and Birth Rates in South-eastern England', *Journal of Political Economy*, 97 (1989) pp.92–114.
50. Flinn, *Scottish Population History*, pp.276–77, 280.
51. I.D. Whyte, 'Proto-industrialisation in Scotland', P. Hudson ed., *Regions and Industries* (Cambridge, 1989), pp.240–41; R.E. Tyson, 'The Rise and Fall of Manufacturing in Rural Aberdeen', J.S. Smith and D. Stevenson (eds.), *Farmfolk and Fisherfolk* (Aberdeen, 1989), pp.63–82; OSA XIII, pp.394–95.
52. T.M. Devine, *The Great Highland Famine* (Edinburgh, 1988), pp. 1–11; M. Gray, *The Highland Economy, 1750–1850* (Edinburgh, 1957), pp.57–104, 124–38.
53. W.P.L. Thomson, *Kelp-Making in Orkney* (Stromness, 1983), pp.97–100; G. Schrank, 'Crossroads of the North: Proto-Industrialisation in the Orkney Islands; *Journal of European Economic History*, 21 (1992) pp.378–88.
54. B. Smith, 'Adam Smith's Rents From the Sea: Maritime Sharecropping in Shetland' in T.C. Smout (ed.), *Scotland and the Sea* (Edinburgh, 1992), pp.94–113; T. Gifford, *Historical Description of the Shetland Isles in the Year 1733* (Edinburgh, 1879), pp.76, 84–85.
55. Martin, *A Description of the Western Islands*, p.438.
56. T. Pennant, *A Tour in Scotland and Voyage to the Hebrides Vol 2* (London, 1780), p.314; *OSA*, XII, p.266.
57. Calculated from E.E.R. Cregeen (ed.), *Inhabitants of the Argyll Estate* (Scottish Record Society, 1963), pp. 4–21, 26–65.
58. Flinn, *Scottish Population History*, pp.279, 282.
59. Calculated from Cregeen, *Inhabitants of the Argyll Estate*, pp.26–65, 70,–115; Wrigley and Schofield *Population History of England*, p.529; P. Laslett (ed.), *Household and Family in Past Time* (Cambridge, 1972) pp. 80–82.

Thirteen

The Improvers and the Scottish Environment: Soils, Bogs and Woods

T. C. SMOUT

By the first half of the eighteenth century, Scotland had been suffering from several thousand years of slow environmental degradation without any effective actions having been taken to reverse it, and from at least two centuries of declining and stagnant living standards, which flight and famine on a rare scale had failed to relieve. That did not make her exceptional among north-west European countries, except perhaps in the determination of so many of her inhabitants to seek their fortunes elsewhere by emigrating. In the course of the succeeding century, in the rural Lowlands, though perhaps not in the Highlands, environmental degradation had been counteracted, and the living standards of the population in the rural Lowlands, though evidently not in the Highlands, had improved. That fact, too was not unique in north-west European countries, though Scotland and Denmark probably vied for having made most progress. The economic, social and political leaders of the countryside in this dramatic century were the Improvers, once much praised as enlightened patriots, now more subject to historical deflation. By the term Improver is to be understood those landowners of the period 1720–1820, assisted by their land stewards and large tenants, who, in their own districts, deliberately broke with the agricultural traditions of the past. One of the questions to be considered is whether their attitudes and actions contributed significantly to the turnaround. Did they address what, for his country, the Danish historian Thorkild Kjærgaard describes as an ecological crisis overcome by a green biotechnological revolution?[1] Or were they irrelevant?

My opening began with sweeping generalisations which demand some justification. A declining standard of living? Surely so, when most people's incomes consisted of food, and the most obvious change over the years 1500–1750 was from a country famous for eating animal produce to one famous for eating oatmeal – certainly plentiful and highly nutritious, yet Dr. Johnson's snide observation about oats being horse-feed in England and human food in Scotland struck home.[2] The reason is clear enough: 500,000 people could live in Scotland enjoying an animal-based diet supplemented by meal, but

1,250,000 could not. When Rev. Dr. Walker toured the Hebrides in the 1760s, he found the old-fashioned diet only on Jura, and partly on Rum, both with a high land-to person ratio: his own calculations estimated the inhabitants of Jura as one per 246 acres ('a most melancholy Proportion'), of Rum one per 53 acres, against a Hebridean average of one per 30. On Jura, the people lived on milk, butter, cheese, fish, mutton, venison and very little vegetable food, and were 'in general a long lived people'. On Rum, he told of an old man who died aged 103 without having tasted bread until he was 50:

> This old man used frequently to remind the younger People of the simple and hardy Fare of former Times [i.e. animal food, fish and milk] . . . and judged it unmanly in them to toil like Slaves with their Spades, for the Production of such an unnecessary Piece of Luxury [as bread].

The old man's perspective was entirely realistic, but Dr. Walker was keener on high population than high standard of living.[3]

If you prefer to this culinary fare some admittedly shaky statistics, some published recently indicate that in Edinburgh, wages, measured against oatmeal prices, fell by 25% for masons and 17% for labourers, between the mid-sixteenth century and the mid-seventeenth, and did not obviously improve again for another hundred years or more: this was in marked contrast to the situation after 1650 in England.[4] As for flight and famine on a rare scale failing to relieve the situation, such estimates as we have for emigration suggest that (taking together the flight to Ulster, Poland and the mercenary armies) in the first half of the seventeenth century a fifth of the marriageable males may have left the country, and that overall for the whole century the emigration rate was probably the highest in Europe.[5] Such data as we have on famine suggests that in the 1690s the population of Scotland might have fallen by 13%, though not only by mortality.[6] Neither set of events was followed by a rise in real wages or a clear improvement in the standard of living, suggesting that the marginal productivity of labour remained close to zero. The only time that wage rates showed a jump and English standards seemed within reach was, ephemerally, in the Cromwellian 1650s, at the end of the disruption, bloodletting and plague of civil war: but those good days for survivors ebbed within a decade.[7] Revisionist historians and others who seek to put the brightening days of Scottish economic history decisively back to the seventeenth century need to come up with a better supported case.

How about the alarming generalisation about those thousands of years of environmental degradation accompanied by inaction? This hinges on the long-term availability of plant nutrients in the face of change induced by a combination of natural and anthropogenic forces. When the glaciers of the last Ice Age disappeared 10,000 years ago, they ground the rocks into a highly nutritious mineral mix, and in due course the face of most of Scotland became clothed with forest. For farmers, the crucial element is nitrogen in a form available to plants, a chemical element particularly liable to diffusion into the atmosphere, but which forests are good at capturing. The main source of fertility available to Neolithic, bronze-age and iron-age farmers was the high quality nitrogenous humus on cleared forest land. Most of the woods on cultivable land had probably been cleared at least once before the Roman invasion (remember they can regrow, on a slash-and-burn regime common in parts of France or Finland into the eighteenth or even early nineteenth centuries). Although the extent of woodland cover ebbed and flowed subsequently, in response to population fluctuation and climatic change, the trend was always downwards. Archaeologists will probably never completely satisfy themselves about the relative contributions of human activity and climatic change in the downfall of the primal woods and the increase of bogs, but from earliest times they must have been mutually reinforcing. The Scottish Lowlands at least were finally, largely, though never totally, denuded of wood by the end of the thirteenth century, a decline in woodland cover from possibly a prehistoric maximum of 80 per cent to, at most, 5%. The situation in the Highlands, if better, left only two or three times as much woodland cover, and that is very uncertain. One would have expected woodland recovery in the century and a half following the demographic catastrophe of the Black Death and associated events, but it is hard to find, possibly because increased cold and wet discouraged it, possibly because extensive grazing did the same, probably because of a fell combination of the two. These were the centuries of maximum complaint about wolves – fewer people, lots of sheep, cattle and horses, a lupine paradise.[8]

The gradual and fluctuating trend of the woodland decline over a period of 5000 years does not detract from its serious character or its fatally debilitating nature. The removal of forest cover starts a chain reaction. More water is released into streams and rivers, because the ability of the trees to return it to the atmosphere through their leaves, or to delay its course through the soil by their roots, disappears. From this follows erosion, more rapid leaching of mineral nutrients left by the grinding glaciers, more rapid dissipation of nitrogen, acidification of the soil, formation of podsols and other alterations of soil structure associated with water logging, floods, bog formation, and so forth. Such deterioration, especially rising water levels, is likely to kill other existing woods, and to press farmers on to partially elevated lands, the slopes of the valleys, where inputs of nitrogen and other nutrients through manure are likely to wash out even more rapidly. As the Englishman Thomas Morer put it in 1689: 'they have many fine vallies . . . almost useless, on the account of frequent bogs and waters in such places . . .

[yet] 'tis almost incredible how much of the mountains they plough, where the declensions, I had almost said the precipices, are such, that to our thinking, it puts 'em to a greater difficulty and charge to carry on their work, than they need be at in draining the vallies'.[9] Morer's solution showed little understanding of the problems of drainage in Scotland, but there are many independent witnesses to his vision of fertile ground under water and marginal land in cultivation.

Environmental change may be almost imperceptible from one generation to another, but it is change nevertheless. Enhanced rainfall, from whatever cause, steadily lowers the pH value of the soil as it washes out the natural lime: if the pH level falls from 7 to 4, this inhibits the growth of nearly all agricultural plants, and, even more seriously perhaps, stops the growth of wild clover and other leguminous plants with nitrogen-fixing powers. Once the forest humus is gone (and its initial nitrogen returns to the atmosphere relatively quickly), a problem arises. The other main sources for nitrogen before the agrarian changes of the eighteenth century were manures, mainly dung, locally seaweed or turf, and the atmosphere itself. Calculations concerning eighteenth-century Denmark suggest that farmers could contribute to cultivated ground about 30 kilogrammes of nitrogen per hectare per year from the middens, equivalent to only 10–15% of the nitrogen supplement given on Danish farms in the 1980s: and that on uncultivated grazing ground about 20 kilogrammes fell from the atmosphere or was produced by wild plants. This was the basis of contemporary low yields.[10]

But – here is the gist of the matter – nitrogen levels were not only low, but by the logic of rainfall's eternal leaching of minerals, yields were prone imperceptibly to fall forever unless an increasing input of manure could somehow be provided by ever-increasing human effort in the manufacturing of soils. From the thirteenth century onwards the construction of deepened soils spread throughout north-west Europe, the so-called plaggen soils of the Netherlands, Germany and Ireland, which have also been identified in Scotland. They were made by transporting volumes of turf from the hill to the inbye land, impoverishing the hill and enriching the inbye, an enormously labour intensive task which, after 800 years, provided a topsoil of 80 cms. depth at Papa Stour in Shetland. Such labour constructed phosphorous-rich soils, but the nitrogen bonus from them was short lived and depended on constant laborious replenishment from new turf.[11]

The great cornucopia of nature, in fact, had a slow leak. It is no wonder that the archaeologists at Skara Brae, excavating a Neolithic farming and hunter-gathering community at the very start of this process, marvel at the plentiful resources and apparently easy life enjoyed by prehistoric man, compared to his early modern counterpart.

Seventeenth-century Scots (like seventeenth-century Danes) had no response to this conundrum. Little that was done by way of agrarian initiative then addressed these problems: consolidation of holdings and longer leases probably made the mobilisation of labour easier, to hold the problem at bay for a moment, but did not address the root cause of the matter. The slow and partial introduction of liming, especially to the Lothians, was more relevant, as where it was practised it visibly increased yields by changing the pH level. Perhaps the only widely popular and effective Scottish response was to go to Ulster. The coincidence is striking of the prosperous century for the farmers there compared to the dismal years just over the Irish sea, especially in the 1690s. It cannot conceivably be due to any difference in climate. Was it because Ulster, when invaded, was among the most forested parts of Ireland, and the settlers found a nitrogenous humus-bonus just as the English did in North America? And was the subsequent migration of the Scots Irish, in the decades hinging on the 1720s to Pennsylvania and the Carolinas, related to the search for another humus bonus as the Ulster one became exhausted? It merits investigation.

* * *

So at last we come to the Improvers. Did they have remedies for the ecological degradation we have described? The question does not demand that they understood the scientific reasons behind the problems; plainly in a pre-scientific age they could not. Nor does it demand that their remedies, if they had any, should be immediately adopted by the entire farming community. Nor does it demand that they should make a profit from their ideas, or even avoid bankruptcy in their efforts to carry them out. But it does demand that they had, from empirical observation, some correct notion that their ideas would transform the productive capacity of the land, and it also demands that, ultimately, someone, not necessarily themselves, should carry them forward. Let us examine these questions by looking firstly at soils, secondly at bogs, and thirdly at woods.

The Improvers' attitudes to soils should have concentrated upon two things: legumes and lime. Red clover was the best of the legumes, a family of plants which almost alone could call down nitrogen from the air and fix it in the soil. Peas, beans, sanfoin and wild white clover belonged to this family, and could do the same as red clover to a more limited extent: of these, peas and beans had been widely cultivated in the Lowlands since the Middle Ages. A range of historians, but especially C.P.H. Chorley, have, however, singled out the introduction of clover as overwhelmingly the most important cause of the increase in agricultural productivity between 1750 and 1850, by which time Peruvian guano and later Chilean nitrates were coming to the aid of the nitrogen deficit.[12] In the Scottish context, enthusiasm for clover is usually disguised under a general enthusiasm for sown grasses and rotations that alternated 'green' crops with 'white' – i.e. legumes with corn. Characteristically, in East Lothian, this entailed a six-course rotation of wheat; peas and beans mixed; barley; sown grass; oats; fallow. By sown grasses was generally understood clover and rye grass. The key figure here was the sixth Earl of Haddington, whose *Short Treatise on Forest Trees, Aquatics, Evergreens, Fences and Grass Seeds* (Edinburgh, 1735), concludes with a discussion on the relative 'utility of sowing bread clover, small white clover, mixtures of clover and rye grass, or rye grass by itself, sanfoin and lucerne'.[13] There is little doubt of the importance attached to sown grasses, or the speed with which clover spread in the decades before 1790. In East Lothian, the minister of Whittinghame in the *Statistical Account* said 'a trifling quantity of clover and rye grass seeds might be sown, upwards of 50 years ago; but it will not exceed 37 years, since it became the universal practice among farmers'. He added that 'turnips and grass crops are certainly among the greatest and most valuable improvements, which have been made in agriculture', a comment echoed by his colleague at Athelstaneford, who listed the Earl of Haddington's introduction of clover among 'the first, and will probably prove to be the most important and permanent, of all improvements in modern husbandry'.[14] The purist will correctly want to object that Haddington may not deserve his reputation for being the first to introduce clover, and to point out that it may have been grown earlier on other estates. But the prestige and success of his example undoubtedly helped to push it on its way. By the 1790s, 46 per cent of parishes in Lanarkshire, 62 per cent in Fife and 71 per cent in Angus were using sown grass rotations.[15]

But if the Improvers were keen on clover, they were no less keen on liming, either through the application of marl dug from calcareous deposits, or through the distribution of lime made from limestone in kilns throughout the country. Here one could certainly not award eighteeenth-century Improvers the priority of discovery or introduction: lime was well known in the seventeenth-century as the usual way of improving land in the Lothians, and had been used on grass in Ayrshire since at least the 1590s.[16] But the area using lime before 1700 appears to have been restricted, and the Improvers universalised its use across Lowland Scotland. The most remarkable example of this was the Earl of Elgin's £14,000 investment at Charlestown in Fife in 1777 and 1778: he built nine large draw-kilns, a harbour, waggon-ways and a village for the 200 employees who quarried the 80–90,000 tons of limestone and loaded the slaked lime onto 1300 separate cargoes a year, with a total annual value of over £10,000. The concern burnt some 12,000 tons of coal a year, and the lime was distributed throughout the Forth and the Tay, and as far as the North of Scotland, with 30–50 ships queuing in summer at Charlestown to load their cargoes.[17] In other areas – for example in

Dumfriesshire, and near Roscobie Loch in Angus – the digging of shell marl provided similar benefits. These were instantly recognised, though not understood, when they changed the pH of acid ground. Thus Robertson's account of south Perthshire agriculture in 1794:

> There is nothing more common, and perhaps few things more difficult to be accounted for, than, when lime is spread on short heath, or other barren ground, which has a dry bottom, to see white clover, and daisies, rising spontaneously and plentifully, the second or third spring thereafer, where not a vestige of either, nor even a blade of grass, was to be seen before.[18]

There was a third novelty of improving agriculture, which we do not propose discussing, as its main impact came in the nineteenth century, beyond the purview of this volume: this is the introduction of turnip husbandry. Before 1800 it had made relatively minor progress beyond Fife, Angus and East Lothian, though where it had been introduced it also greatly helped the nitrogen crisis by allowing more of those dung-producing machines, cattle and sheep, to be kept through the winter. The fourth novelty of great importance was the potato, so immediately accepted that the Improvers are usually overlooked as those who urged its adoption in the first place. We shall not deal with that here, as it was more of a crop novelty than something that had an impact on soil as such. But of course, in a Boserupian way, it provided an effective response to the conundrum of rising population in a still deteriorating Highland environment.

In other ways the Improvers' attitude to soil was much more conservative; the emphasis on legumes and lime was genuinely innovative, but much of the Improvers' effort went into the old, uphill task of manufacturing soil with muck and turf. It was not entirely futile, though some of the effort was questionable. The use of human dung on the fields within about five miles of Edinburgh enabled large increases in production of grain, especially of wheat, and similar benefits resulted near other towns. Price movements indicated the growing appreciation of town ordure: according to the minister of Duddingston, the price of a cart load of the offals of the streets of Edinburgh had risen from 2d. to as high as 1s. 6d. between 1730 and the 1790s. It normally went free on the toll road, though an attempt by the turnpike operators round Edinburgh to charge for it led in 1787 to a boycott – 'no farmer would purchase it, so that the good town had to collect the fulzie itself for several weeks, till the husbandmen came into better temper'.[19]

That, however, was quite local, and there were many other local solutions to the nitrogen problem, mostly either opportunistic, or involving large labour inputs to provide short-term benefits, in the same way as the age-old manufacture of plaggan soils. It did not need Improvers to teach the use of kelp-spreading on the field, within reach of the coast: in some places mussels were similarly used as manure by the local people. More illustrative of the restless innovation and opportunism of the Improvers was the activity of John Auldjo, a merchant of Aberdeen, who manured his ground with a mixture of horse dung, spent tan bark and composted dogfish bought in quantity after their livers had been extracted for the oil from the local merchants: in Ayrshire, farmers used soap waste, in Clydesdale they mixed midden refuse with horn shavings, soot, woollen rags, parings of leather, peat and coal, and in Aberdeenshire in 1811 they used whale blubber from the Greenland fleet, which raised 'a very rich crop for the first year, and a tolerable one for the second'.[20]

If it is difficult to imagine a sustainable improvement in agricultural productivity based on such hand-to-mouth resources as dogfish waste and whale blubber, an even bigger question mark hung over the publicised techniques of paring and burning turf. In a way, this was plaggan extended. The aforementioned Auldjo of Aberdeen, for example, had his own recipe: he took a large quantity of turf from the moss, set it alight, added a layer of clay, another of turf, another of clay until the pile was as high as a man could reach, getting 1000 cart-loads at a single burning. According to Alexander Wight, 60 loads on an acre of oats or peas did wonders, and 30–40 loads as a top dressing for grass 'never fail to mend the crop'.[21]

Most commentators in the period of the *General Views of Agriculture*, 1794–1814, were against the practise of burning, however: as was said of Ayrshire, 'by burning moss you may raise one great and one moderate crop, but the moss will never produce another of much value', and in Roxburghshire 'it reduces to ashes some of the best soil, and has hurt ten acres for every one it has benefited'. Others were not so negative, recommending paring and burning to bring into cultivation the wide wastes of Inverness-shire, or as the best method of improving deep, peaty land in Perthshire. Yet advocacy of this technique scarcely shows the Improvers in a very progressive light. Paring and burning was, firstly, very labour intensive; secondly, provided ephemeral benefits in respect of the nitrogen deficit; thirdly, actually impoverished the moor and accentuated the difference between inbye and outbye.[22] In popularising clover and greatly extending liming, the Improvers provided things qualitatively new and critical: in other directions they were often drawing experimental blanks or trying to breathe new life into ancient desperate remedies.

* * *

The question of bogs illustrates something rather different: the ability of the Improvers to take a completely new look at a natural resource. As T.M.

Devine has recently put it:

> The rationalism of the Enlightenment helped to change man's relationship to his environment. No longer was nature accepted as given and pre-ordained; instead it could be altered for the better by rational, systematic and planned intervention.[23]

A reading of *Macfarlane's Geographical Collections*, mainly composed of observations between about 1630 and 1730, gives an overwhelming impression of nature as given and preordained, and often appreciatively described. Bogs were seen as a useful resource and a blessing to the community: thus at Keith in Aberdeenshire there was 'great plenty of fir under ground, which the people thereabouts dig up some two fathoms deep, and by this they are served with winter light and timber for their houses. In this hill is a large peat bank about six or seven foot deep and near two miles long'; at Fetteresso in Kincardineshire the parish was said to be supplied with 'inexhaustible mosses, wherein are digged the best of peats', supplying not only the inhabitants but also neighbouring communities of Dunnottar, Inverbervie and Stonehaven, and even Aberdeen some fifteen miles away. Conversely, a parish without such resources was cursed: of Cushnie it was said 'it is a poor countrey both for Corn and Pasture, and exceeding scarce of Fewel'.[24]

By the age of the Improvers, however, bogs had become both scandalous wastes and opportunities for a human response to the challenge. Thus Andrew Steele, in the opening to a treatise on peat moss in 1826, spoke of the bogs as 'immense deserts . . . a blot upon the beauty, and a derision to the agriculture of the British Isles', and Robert Rennie in 1807 of 'the innumerable millions of acres [that] lie as a useless waste, nay, a nuisance to these nations. The benefits that might accrue to Europe by a slight attention to this subject, are above all calculation. It is impossible for numbers to express, or the imagination to conceive, correctly, the extent of these'.[25] Those who had got to grips with the bogs were heroes and patriots, like Lord Kames whose conquest of Blairdrummond Moss so fired the contemporary imagination. William Aiton in 1811 compared Lord Kames with David Dale, entirely to the advantage of the former. Both had employed displaced Highlanders, but whereas at Blairdrummond 'the moss colony remain healthy and happy, delighting in their situations, warmly attached to their patron, and to the Government, ready to extend their brawny arms, in the cultivation of the dreary wastes, or to repel their country's foes', those at New Lanark 'became discontented with their situation and soon abandoned it'. That 'several hundreds of ignorant and indolent Highlanders', he continued, 'were converted into active, industrious and virtuous cultivators, and many hundreds of acres of the least possible value rendered equal to the best land in Scotland are matters of the highest national interest, to which I can discover no parallel in the cotton mill colony'.[26]

There is no doubt that reclamation of bogs, large and small, ultimately provided many hundreds of thousands, perhaps millions, of acres for agriculture, and in one sense rolled back the consequences of millennia of environmental impoverishment of a natural or anthropogenic character, until late in the present century people began to worry if any of the characteristic biodiversity of the peatlands would remain and consequently put the brakes on the process. Probably even more important, however, was the general boost that the reclamation campaign gave to field and land drainage, culminating in the 1830s in the enthusiasm for subsoil ploughing and tile drainage, above all associated with Smith of Deanston, innovations which were able to 'turn sour, waterlogged soil into high quality, productive land . . . [so that] the change must have seemed nearly miraculous'.[27] Whereas in the past, in the words of the minister of the Aberdeenshire parish of Tarves, 'the stagnation of water on the low ground utterly precluded tillage, while the arable lands were . . . chilled from November to May by innumerable land springs'[28], now high water levels that had persisted, perhaps, in millennia since deforestation, dropped. Consequently, minerals in soils previously unavailable to crops on account of the 'slow biological turnover' became part of the farmers' resource.[29]

Drainage schemes were all expensive, and early pioneers often overreached themselves. But when Thomas Hope of Rankeillor, President of 'The Honourable the Society of Improvers' from 1723, drained Straiton's Loch on what became the Meadows of the north side of Edinburgh, to demonstrate to his fellow landowners what could be done with boggy land, he was also demonstrating the mind-set of the Enlightenment in respect to the possibility of altering the inherited environment.[30] There is a tower of effort, stone patiently added upon stone by trial and error, between the tentative experimental optimism of Hope of Rankeillor and the well-grounded opinions of Smith of Deanston a century later. That so many of the early Improvers, like Hope, lost money, no more shows the futility of their efforts than the financial problems of Sir Clive Sinclair shows that he should not have been inventing calculators or electric cars.

* * *

Our third examination is into Improvers and woods. Probably because of their unusual combination of beauty and utility, tree planting programmes around the policies of landowners were already well-established in the seventeenth century, but it took the Improvers to begin planting on a large scale and away from the immediate surroundings of the great house. Some of the great eighteenth-century names – Grant of Monymusk, the Earl of Haddington, the Duke of Atholl – planted millions of trees in their lifetimes, some on new sites, like Haddington's Binning Wood on a sandy waste near Tynninghame, some on old sites, like the Earl of Moray's replanting with beech and other trees the site of the ancient Forest of Darnaway.[31] Frequently trees were planted as windbreaks on the field margins to create a more favourable micro-climate: the upland edges of Lothian and the Borders are full of lines and spinneys of beech and sycamore planted to improve the chances of crops and sown grasses higher up the hill. For the first time deliberate anthropogenic reforestation was replacing deforestation, not because Improvers had a detailed knowledge of ecological science but because, first, wood was the source of several essential raw materials in diminishing supply in an expanding economy, secondly, trees were ornamental and prestigious (a well-planted estate was considered well-cared-for) and thirdly, it was perceived by empirical observation that they protected and 'warmed' the land. In absolute terms the Improvers cannot have added much to the tree cover of Scotland – probably less than one per cent of the land surface was re-afforested by them in the eighteenth century. But they made a start.

The Improvers, on balance, also introduced very much better standards of care for the semi-natural woods, which were the precious descendants of the original forest cover.[32] Certainly the situation varied from place to place and from time to time, and few lairds who found themselves suddenly assailed by financial hardship could resist making depredations on their woods as a way of trying to meet them – this was true of families as various as the Dukes of Queensberry and the Grants of Rothiemurchus. On the other hand the damage done by such forays could be restored – as at Drumlanrig and at Rothiemurchus – by good stewardship in the next generation, so that clear felling by no means necessarily meant the demise of a wood.

To some extent what happened to the pine woods may have depended on which side of Scotland they stood. Quite severe felling episodes in the Spey woods (Abernethy and Rothiemurchus), or those along the Dee (Glentanar) or Carron (Amat) in eastern Scotland were generally followed by regeneration, but in the west, felling at Glen Orchy, Glen Coe and Ardgour led largely to extinction. There is possibly a climatic element at work – in the west, heavy moss cover may have made regeneration impossible after felling in the eighteenth century, due to climatic alteration over the period since the standing generation of trees were seedlings, up to 300 years earlier. Improving noblemen like the Earls of Breadalbane and the Dukes of Argyle presided over this destruction, which Breadalbane at least noticed in retrospect with dismay, but they had no remedies. Enclosure of the pine woods to keep out peasant stock was apparently introduced as a novel tool in pinewood management by the Committee for Annexed Estates; it may have had some effect at the Black Wood of Rannoch, but was not always persisted in for long enough to make a difference.[33] Other improving landowners, especially the Earls of Fife in the Forest of Mar, effectively prevented regeneration in the woods (despite their commercial value) by encouraging deer for sporting purposes at the end of the eighteenth century. The parlous state of the upper Deeside Caledonian pine at present is the result of 200 years or more of systematic misuse, inaugurated mainly by the Fife family.[34]

Nevertheless, the Improvers must be credited with having done a great deal to halt the decline of broad-leafed woodland, especially the natural oaks of the west coast and Perthshire, when the market for charcoal and tanbark dramatically improved from the middle of the eighteenth century. It is true that some of the earliest iron masters may have inflicted damage where landowners failed to check them and when grazing of the regeneration was allowed to follow cutting – this is suspected, for example, around Loch Maree and in Glen Kinglas. But from the 1750s, when the Lorn Furnace Company arrived in Argyll, ironmaster and landowner alike co-operated to improve the care of the woods, led by the Duke of Argyle. They did this by fencing, systematic use of coppice, and exclusion of peasant stock, especially by banning the keeping of goats.[35] Tanbark by 1800 was providing a better reason for good woodmanship than charcoal manufacture, even in the west: and in Perthshire and Menteith it had always been tanbark that was the most important woodland product. The owners of tanbark woods, like the Dukes of Montrose along Loch Lomondside and in the Trossachs, the Dukes of Atholl at Dunkeld and elsewhere, and many others, similarly enclosed, coppiced, and excluded the peasants' animals. They also sowed a great many acorns, often on previously arable land, and weeded out less valuable trees like birch, alder and willow to try to create a virtual monoculture of oak.[36]

All this was good practice unless you happened to be a tenant of one of these Improvers and relied on the woods to shelter your animals in winter. Their exclusion might occasion great hardship, and further trouble was occasioned by shortage of accessible wood for peasant use in the midst of natural plenty. In southern Argyll, for example, where farm houses had been bigger than average because of the abundance of oak, tenants were by 1798 having to import Norwegian softwood for their homes, as the woods were closed to them by the landowners.[37] Sometimes enclosure led to temporary rent reductions. More often, the lack of any consideration that tenants might need to be compensated for losses of this kind appears as characteristically high-handed behaviour by the Improvers, and compares badly with the situation in Denmark where a statute of 1805 established the right and duty of landowners to enclose the woods, but awarded tenants an equivalent area of grazing for the value of the rights they had lost by enclosure.[38] The penalty was seen later in the nineteenth century, when the value of tanbark and charcoal collapsed, lasting equivalent uses for oak were not found, the enclosures tumbled down and the woods reverted to grazing. As far as the farmers were concerned, that was all they were good for. Any lingering tradition of peasant care for the wood had evaporated, especially as there was less need for native wood as a raw material with the coming of cheap iron and steel for tools and the availability of foreign softwood for construction, thanks to free trade, steam ships and the railways.

To be fair to the landowners, it is nevertheless rather questionable how deep a tradition of peasant care for the woods there had ever been in Scotland. Perhaps this was because, however freely the tenants had helped themselves to supplies of bark and of building and tool timber in the past, it had always been clear in Scots law (in contrast, say, to Norwegian law) that the woods and the trees in them belonged to the landlords, not to the tenants, so they had no special incentive to treat them well.

Stories of the decay of the native woods, and serious economic and ecological consequences following, come in the late eighteenth and early nineteenth centuries from Sutherland and Wester Ross, where much of the wood was birch of little commercial worth, and where the reach of the market to enhance values for such oak as there was, was less significant than further south. Here one hears of straths becoming deforested for causes that baffled contemporaries, but which are less puzzling when one learns that local farmers kept up to 80 goats apiece, as well as cows and horses. One consequence of the decay of the woods was the need to keep cattle indoors for three or four extra months in the year, with greater mortality among the animals: also bracken and heather took over the good grass sward that had grown beneath the trees, so the land was less able to support stock, though it was alleged that sheep could thrive on such degraded ground better than cattle. The reporter used this evidence of ecological decay (which was independently corroborated by a local minister by no means sympathetic to the policy of clearance) as a justification for replacing cattle by sheep in the straths.[39]

Attention has been drawn before to ecological degradation thought to have been brought about by the impact of these post-clearance sheep on the uplands of the far north by about 1870: it is interesting to find that such degradation was apparently beginning to be noticeable well before the clearances.[40] The arch-clearer Patrick Sellar did attempt to preserve from misuse such of the birch woods of Strathnavar and places thereabouts that he considered possible to save, perhaps with a better sense of their fragility.[41] In a short time the sheer weight of numbers of sheep nevertheless overwhelmed his tentative efforts in that direction, and the uncontrollable flocks of the capitalist accentuated the process that the peasants' own stock had begun.

* * *

So where does all this leave us? The Improvers were not people with particularly original minds, and all too often not people of a practical bent, as their frequent bankruptcy shows. They could never have improved Scotland unless price movements had rewarded their efforts after 1760, and particularly after 1790, so the demand side was critical. All they did was to help force the pace. Growing clover was already common in parts of England and the Netherlands, reclaiming land especially common in the Netherlands, good forest practice common in England and France and perhaps also in parts of Lowland Scotland. But the cumulative effect of their stimulus, perhaps especially in soil treatment, was, indeed, Improvement of an environment heavily stressed by long misuse. It would be nice if we could be sure that we were doing as well at the close of the twentieth century as they were doing at the close of the eighteenth.

REFERENCES

1. T. Kjærgaard, *The Danish Revolution, 1500–1800: An Ecohistorical Interpretation* (Cambridge, 1994).
2. A.J.S. Gibson and T.C. Smout, 'Scottish food and Scottish history, 1500–1800', in R.A. Houston and I. Whyte (eds.), *Scottish Society, 1500–1800*, (Cambridge, 1989)pp.59–84.
3. M.M. McKay (ed.), *The Rev. Dr. John Walker's Report on the Hebrides of 1764 and 1771*, (Edinburgh, 1980) pp.115, 196.
4. A.J.S. Gibson and T.C. Smout, *Prices, Food and Wages in Scotland, 1550–1780* (Cambridge, 1995), chapters 8 and 9.
5. T.C. Smout, N.C. Landsman and T.M. Devine, 'Scottish emigration in the seventeenth and eighteenth centuries', in N. Canny (ed.), *Europeans on the Move: Studies in European Migration, 1500–1800*, (Oxford, 1994) pp.76–90.
6. R.E. Tyson, 'Contrasting régimes: population growth in Ireland and Scotland during the eighteenth century', in S.H. Connolly, R.A. Houston and R.J. Morris (eds.), *Conflict, Identity and Economic Development: Ireland and Scotland, 1600–1939* (Preston, 1995), p.67.
7. Gibson and Smout, *Prices*, pp.275–6.
8. For Scottish woodland history, see, for the prehistoric, R. Tipping, 'The form and fate of Scotland's woodlands'. *Proceedings of the Society of Antiquaries of Scotland*, Vol. 124 (1994), pp.1–54: for the Middle Ages, there is an indication in J.M. Gilbert, *Hunting and Hunting Reserves in Medieval Scotland* (Edinburgh, 1979). The figures for woodland cover are my own crude estimates.
9. P.H. Brown, *Early Travellers in Scotland* (Edinburgh, 1891), pp.266–7.
10. Kjærgaard, *Danish Revolution*, p.22.
11. D.A. Davidson and I.A. Simpson, 'Soils and landscape history: case studies from the Northern Isles of Scotland', in S. Foster and T.C. Smout (eds.), *The History of Soils and Field Systems* (Aberdeen, 1994), pp.66–74.
12. C.P.H. Chorley, 'The agricultural revolution in Northern Europe, 1750–1880: nitrogen, legumes and crop productivity', *Economic History Review*, second series, Vol. 34 (1981), pp.71–93. See also Kjærgaard, *Danish Revolution*, pp.84–7.
13. J.E. Handley, *Scottish Farming in the Eighteenth Century* (London, 1953), pp.145–6.
14. *The Statistical Account of Scotland* (henceforth, *OSA*), (edn. Wakefield, 1972–83), Vol. 2, *Lothians*, pp.649, 452.
15. T.M. Devine, *The Transformation of Rural Scotland: Social Change and the Agrarian Economy, 1660–1814* (Edinburgh, 1994), p.54.

16. Ian Whyte, *Agriculture and Society in Seventeenth-Century Scotland* (Edinburgh, 1979), pp.198–208.
17. *OSA*, Vol. X, *Fife*, pp.308–9.
18. J. Robertson, *General View of the Agriculture in the Southern Districts of the County of Perth* (Edinburgh, 1794), p.26.
19. *OSA*, Vol. 2 (*Lothians*); G. Robertson, *General View of the Agriculture of the County of Midlothian* (Edinburgh, 1793), pp.48–9.
20. A. Wight, *Present State of Husbandry in Scotland* (Edinburgh, 1778–84), Vol. 3, pp.599–600; W. Fullarton, *General View of the Agriculture of the County of Ayr* (Edinburgh, 1794), p.52; G.S. Keith, *General View of the Agriculture of Aberdeenshire* (Edinburgh, 1811), p.432.
21. Wight, *Present State*, p.600.
22. W. Aiton, *General View of the Agriculture of the County of Ayr* (Edinburgh, 1811), p.374; R. Douglas, *General View of the Agriculture of the Counties of Roxburgh and Selkirk* (Edinburgh, 1798), p.132; J. Robertson, *General View of the Agriculture of the County of Inverness* (Edinburgh, 1808), p.231; J. Robertson, *General View of the Agriculture of the County of Perth* (Edinburgh, 1794), p.274.
23. Devine, *Transformation*, p.65.
24. A. Mitchell (ed.), *Geographical Collections Relating to Scotland, Made by Walter Macfarlane* (Scottish History Society, Edinburgh, 1906), Vol. 1, pp.31, 89, 248.
25. A. Steele, *The Natural and Agricultural History of Peat-moss or Turf-bog* (Edinburgh, 1826), p.1; R. Rennie, *Essays on the Natural History and Origin of Peat Moss* (Edinburgh, 1807).
26. W. Aiton, *A Treatise on the Origin, Qualities and Cultivation of Moss-Earth, with Directions for Converting it into Manure* (Ayr, 1811).
27. A. Fenton, *Scottish Country Life* (Edinburgh, 1976), pp.21–2.
28. Francis Knox, writing in the *New Statistical Account* (Edinburgh, 1842) and cited by W.A. Porter, *Tarves Lang Syne, the Story of a Scottish Parish* (York, 1996), p.36.
29. Kjærgaard, *Danish Revolution*, p.57.
30. J.A. Symon, *Scottish Farming Past and Present* (Edinburgh, 1959), p.302.
31. See M.L. Anderson, *A History of Scottish Forestry* (Edinburgh, 1967).
32. See T.C. Smout (ed.) *Scottish Woodland History* (Edinburgh, 1997), esp. Chapter 7.
33. J.M. Lindsay, 'The Use of Woodland in Argyleshire and Perthshire between 1650 and 1850' (unpublished University of Edinburgh Ph.D. thesis 1974), p.291.
34. A. Watson, 'Eighteenth century deer numbers and pine regeneration near Braemar, Scotland', *Biological Conservation*, Vol. 25 (1983), pp.289–305.
35. J.M. Lindsay, 'Charcoal iron smelting and its fuel supply: the example of Lorn furnace, Argyllshire, 1753–1876', *Journal of Historical Geography*, Vol. 1 (1975), pp.283–98.
36. J.M. Lindsay, *thesis, passim*; R.M. Tittensor, 'History of the Loch Lomond oakwoods', *Scottish Forestry*, Vol. 24 (1970), pp.100–18.
37. J. Smith, *General View of the Agriculture of the County of Argyle* (Edinburgh, 1798), p.132.
38. Kjærgaard, *Danish Revolution*, pp.111–2.
39. J. Henderson, *General View of the Agriculture of the County of Sutherland* (London, 1812), pp.83, 86, 106, 176–7.
40. J. Hunter, 'Sheep and deer: Highland sheep farming 1850–1900', *Northern Scotland*, Vol. 1 (1973), pp.199–222.
41. R.J. Adam (ed.), *Papers on Sutherland Estate Management, 1802–1816* (Scottish History Society, Edinburgh, 1972) e.g. Vol. 1, pp.187–8, 197; Vol. 2, pp.149–50.

Fourteen

A Conservative People? Scottish Gaeldom in the Age of Improvement

THOMAS M. DEVINE

By the middle decades of the nineteenth century it seemed that there were two radically different societies in Scotland. In the Lowlands a world class economic system had emerged based on productive farming, textile manufacture and heavy industry; in the Highlands there was a different world of poverty, heavy emigration and famine. The north and west seemed to have more in common with the poorer districts of Ireland than the rest of Scotland and the United Kingdom.

Victorian observers were troubled by this stark contrast, especially as the Highland population began to suffer acute distress when the potatoes failed in the 1840s. Their explanations for the underdevelopment of Gaeldom were many and varied but there was a single recurrent theme in several of the analyses. This was that the Highlander was fundamentally conservative, blindly attached to the customs and practices of the past and unwilling or unable to embrace the new ways which might have offered the possibility of material amelioration and an escape from the threat of destitution.[1] It was a persuasive critique which seemed to find compelling support in the plight of the Gaels in the 1840s. Their resources during the potato famine had become exhausted and as a result they were forced to depend for survival on the charity of benevolent Lowlanders.[2] Inevitably, this produced from some quarters the charge that the Highlanders were ultimately responsible for their own fate. Their inertia and indolence in the past now meant that they had to be supported by the 'industrious' population elsewhere in Scotland.[3]

It is in the eighteenth century, when the new social and economic order was beginning to take shape, that this criticism of the social conservatism of the Highland people can best be discussed. After the end of the Napoleonic Wars, and especially from 1820, the terms of trade were moving so relentlessly against the north west Highlands that only large-scale sheep farming, in which there was precious little opportunity for peasant enterprise, had any real economic viability. In the earlier period, however, in the transition from clanship to capitalism, there were indeed real possibilities. However, even before 1800, modern scholars have argued that, especially in relation to the Lowlands, Gaeldom lacked a real spirit of enterprise. Thus, it is asserted that a key difference between the two societies was that in the farming districts of the Lowlands, the population were prepared to work with the new agrarian regime.[4] They surrendered land with minimal protest. Some moved into the commercial farming class while the majority formed the skilled agricultural proletariat. In the north and west, however, it was much more a story of truculent opposition to and even alienation from the new order. T.C. Smout argues that this response reflected the innately conservative outlook of the people.[5] Similarly, in his study of the Highland economy, Malcolm Gray draws a clear distinction between the dynamic nature of social change in the late eighteenth century Lowlands and what he terms 'an area of settled archaic nonconformity' in north west Scotland.[6] An image is conveyed of relative stagnation in one part of the country and progressive change in the other. From this contrast developed the vastly different regional social experiences of the nineteenth century.

In addition, the evidence of the large-scale emigrations of tacksmen and tenants from the 1760s is employed to further support the point about the intrinsic conservatism of Gaeldom. The argument goes that as commercialisation intensified in the last quarter of the eighteenth century the people of entire areas in the Highlands deserted the country in large numbers in order to protect an ancient way of life now under pressure from rising rents, expanding markets and the threat of eviction.[7] Since many of the migrant groups were led by clan gentlemen seeking to protect their old status in the new world the exodus seemed to lend credence to the view that the Gael could not adjust to the new challenging economic realities. Permanent exile across the Atlantic and the recreation of traditionalism was a more appealing alternative.

This analysis in turn was also related to an assessment of the Highlands before 1760 and, in particular, before the '45. It is argued by scholars such as A.J. Youngson in his *After the '45* that the Highlands were socially and culturally unprepared for market capitalism because before the final Jacobite rebellion they were locked into a system of clanship which gave ultimate priority to the militaristic values of courage, loyalty, obedience and communal cohesion rather than personal acquisitiveness, competition and individualism. Clanship and commerce in this view were incompatible.[8] The shock to the entire social system of Gaeldom brought about by the Jacobite defeat at Culloden and the military and legal repression in its aftermath resulted in disorientation and an inevitable failure to respond in vigorous fashion to the market opportunities of the later eighteenth century. Indeed, contemporary developments seemed to lend support to such an interpretation. The establishment of the Commission for Annexed Forfeited Estates and later the British Fisheries Society to 'improve' the

Highlands was partly founded on the Whig premise that the 'primitive' Gaels lacked the initiative to exploit land reform and industrial development by themselves.[9]

Over the last decade or so, however, the continued development of Scottish historiography has produced a variety of works which allow the conventional notion of a conservative, rigid and hidebound Highland society to be reviewed, challenged and in some cases qualified. New interpretations have emerged which give fresh perspectives on the response of the Gaels to the dramatic eighteenth century changes in land use and the expansion of the market economy. The argument which follows, based on this research, is that the traditional historiography has significantly underestimated the capacity for enterprise, self-help and resourcefulness of the Highlanders and has uncritically accepted some of the unproven assumptions made by improving Enlightenment and Victorian writers about the inadequacies of Highland society.

Before the '45

Commerce was an integral part of Highland society long before the eighteenth century. Indeed, the very sparsity of resources and the meagre areas of arable land in the north west had long compelled the people of the region to rely on better endowed localities to the south to make ends meet.[10] The main exports in return for meal and other necessities consisted of skins, fish and live cattle. It was in this last sector, the droving trade, that the 'primitive' Highlands most effectively demonstrated a capacity to respond vigorously to commercial opportunity. The decline of militarism in Gaeldom, the growth of large Scottish towns such as Edinburgh and Glasgow and, above all, the voracious demands from the vast London market and the Royal Navy provided the context for a massive increase in the exportation of live cattle from the Highlands.[11] By the early 1720s as many as 30,000 cattle a year were being driven south to the great fair at Crieff and elsewhere. It is even more remarkable that this sector, which depended mainly on Highland producers, was probably the only part of the Scottish economy which responded rapidly in the short-term to the market opportunities derived from the Anglo-Scottish Union of 1707. Linen and tobacco, the two other leading sectors, did not forge ahead in similar fashion for over a decade or more later.[12] The ability to market many more beasts than before demonstrates the capacity of the old Highlands to increase production for its primary export through cattle-rearing rather than stock-fattening.

The dynamism of the droving trade is also a telling illustration of peasantry's ability to respond to the new material demands of the clan chiefs. The clan elite's money needs significantly increased in the later seventeenth and early eighteenth centuries as consumer tastes expanded, absenteeism became more common and indebtedness intensified.[13] In essence the chiefs and leading clan gentry were forcing their clansmen to shift from the payment of food rents and payments in kind to money dues in order to provide the income stream to support the new consumerism of the elite.[14] For this reason the peasantry adopted a strategy of selling more livestock and at the same time became accustomed to a new rental regime which was directly responsive through money payments to the nature of the market. Evidence of this transformation and its implications for the commercialisation of relationships within clanship are abundant and only a few illustrations need be given here.

On the Macleod estates in Harris and Skye rents were mainly paid in kind until the 1640s. By the 1680s, however, money rents made up half the value of the total and in the 1740s over three-quarters.[15] The Campbells of Glenorchy shifted to cash rents even earlier and the process of conversion was virtually completed by the end of the seventeenth century. R.A. Dodgshon's survey of rental data illustrates that this trend was underway throughout most of the western Highlands and Islands in the decades before and after the Union of 1707.[16]

The expansion in the cattle business was a striking example of the Highland economy's exploitation of regional comparative advantage. Very few districts in the north and west had a regular surplus of grain. The exceptions were Glen Urquhart, parts of Speyside and Kilmuir in Skye.[17] It made economic sense, therefore, to specialise in pastoralism and augment indigenous grain supplies with imports from more favoured lands to the south and east. Ironically, therefore, far from being insulated from the market, much of Gaeldom was forced into strong commercial relationships with the Lowlands. Thomas Pennant's evidence in the 1770s that whole areas of the central and western Highlands were able to subsist only by large imports of meal was also true of the early eighteenth century.[18] This experience of commercial exchange is in contrast with the position elsewhere in much of rural Scotland. Outside the Lothians area of the south east and the Borders most Lowland localities were dominated in the early eighteenth century by smaller farms geared mainly to subsistence production.[19] In the later seventeenth century rentals in kind were common and only began to disappear rapidly in subsequent decades. Feudal obligations, especially thirlage, remained in force.

The droving trade was the most notable example of a dynamic commercial response in Scottish Gaeldom in the first half of the eighteenth century but it was not unique. Allan Macinnes has drawn attention to the entrepreneurial activities of the House of Argyll and the cadet branches of the Clan Campbell throughout the southern and parts of the Central Highlands.

This involved tenurial change, including the abolition of the role of tacksmen, rent increases, timber, lime slate and coal exploitation and investment in fisheries along the Clyde coast and in Loch Fyne.[20] There is always the possibility, of course, that the Campbell empire, dominant throughout most of Argyll and the Breadalbane lands in Perthshire, may not be representative of the policies of the Highland elite as a whole. Only further systematic research on other landed estate archives elsewhere can confirm or refute this. It is already clear, however, that many Highland chiefs were much more than the patriarchal tribal leaders of Jacobite legend and romance and had a keen eye for business opportunity. George Pratt Insh put forward the thesis that the Jacobite rebellions should be seen as an ideological struggle between clanship and capitalism.[21] The archaic tribal society of Gaeldom was confronted by the dynamic mercantile world of the Lowlands in a long-drawn-out conflict which only ended in the final triumph of Hanoverianism and capitalism in the aftermath of the '45. One difficulty with this interpretation is that commercial values were already widely developed among those Highland chiefs who supported the Jacobite cause. The clan elite of Clan Cameron had interests in American land, timber exportation, the Edinburgh money market and Caribbean plantations. MacDonnell of Glengarry was heavily involved in the provision of timber for charcoal for the production of iron. The Duke of Perth had interests in agricultural improvement and the Robertsons of Struan ran an extensive commercial forestry operation. Deals produced from local timber around Loch Rannoch were floated down the rivers Tummel and Tay and from there to lowland markets.[22]

The evidence presented in this section does not therefore suggest the Highlands were locked within a rigid system of social conservatism. Landed enterprise did occur. Clanship and commerce were not necessarily incompatible. The huge expansion in the cattle trade reflected the ability of the peasantry to adjust to new demands. Market connections between Highlands and Lowlands in the meat, fish, timber and slate trades were flourishing. The familiar image of an archaic pre-Culloden Highlands lacking the capacity to adjust to a changing world requires substantial modification if not complete rejection.

The Regional Factor

It is now a well established fact that generalisation about Scottish Gaeldom is not easy because of the pronounced differences in land, climate and agricultural possibilities in the region. Both contemporary and later critics of the Gaels' response to economic change tend to focus their attention on crofting society, which includes parts of the central Highlands, the north west coastlands from Ardnamurchan to Cape Wrath and the inner and outer Hebrides. Less attention is usually given to the southern and eastern frontier lands of the Highlands. There were, however, Gaelic-speaking areas of settlement throughout this zone, in particular in southern Argyll, eastern Inverness, northern Perthshire and the mountainous fringes of the countries of Cathness, Cromarty, Aberdeen, Banff, Nairn, Kincardine, Angus, Dumbarton and Stirling.

This is a considerable territory and when its historical evolution is examined for the decades after c.1760 it becomes apparent that these areas of Gaeldom, far from being committed to the defence of traditional values, displayed remarkable levels of innovation. By the early nineteenth century a new social and economic system had begun to emerge which unlike that to the north and west was viable and enduring in material terms. Moreover, this was the result of indigenous enterprise and owed little to external influences. The experience of this region clearly indicated that 'improvement' ideology and the values of Gaelic culture were not necessarily in conflict. Indeed, in a number of ways this regional system reflected the key features of the new agricultural regime in the Lowlands so highly praised by commentators in the nineteenth century and later. Society in this area had several characteristics which, though not equally uniform in all parts, served to differentiate the south and east from the rest of the Highlands.[23]

First, there was consolidation of tenancies with some members of the old land-holding peasantry extending their holdings while others became more dependent as full-time or part-time workers on the new farms or as crofters or cottars. This followed the pattern in general terms which was being established throughout lowland Scotland at this time. Yet there was little large-scale consolidation on the Lothians model. In southern Argyll and Highland Perthshire it was the 'family' sized holding of 40 to 60 acres which was more common by the early nineteenth century than the big farm of several hundred acres,[24] a teneurial pattern similar to parts of the south west and north east Lowlands. But even these relatively modest concentrations represented the enterprise of a small number of families from within the older peasant class who were prospering within the new economic order.

Second, along the eastern Highlands, arable and mixed agricultural areas were to be found on a considerable scale. This meant a heavy demand for labour during the busy seasons and the emerging farming class recruited this from full-time servants but also from crofting and cottar families who provided an invaluable source of short-term assistance. This added to the overall social stability of the system by ensuring that the enhanced income stream from improved agriculture percolated widely throughout the community.[25] Thirdly, non-agricultural employment was available and enduring well into the nineteenth century. The herring fishery in the Lochs of

Argyllshire and in parts of the north east was so successful that it encouraged the development of communities of specialist fishermen. Elsewhere, for instance, in Highland Perthshire the linen manufacture was a vital source of alternative employment.[26]

In many ways this regional society with its modest levels of prosperity, overall economic stability and a close relationship between the supply and demand for labour was a model for what might have been achieved in the north and west. But that did not happen, not because the people of the rest of the Highlands lacked the human resources of those elsewhere but more probably because the geological and climatic contexts of the two regions were dramatically different. The key factor was that the south and east had enough arable land to allow for the development of medium-sized mixed farms which formed the economic backbone of the area. Elsewhere, Sir John Sinclair estimated in 1800 that the proportion of cultivated to uncultivated land was between 9 and 15 per cent.[27] On one typical north west estate, that of Barrisdale in Invernesshire, only 80 out of 13,000 acres were used as arable in the 1750s. This fundamental distinction meant that the small-scale farming structure of central and southern Argyll and Highland Perthshire, combining indigenous enterprise and labour, was never a serious option for most of the inhabitants of the north west.

The Issue of Crofting

The revolutionary nature and impact of the development of crofting has not always been recognised. Unlike the changes already surveyed for the south and east region it did not produce the 'landless' population favoured by the improving propagandists. Indeed, because it preserved the traditional peasant access to land, crofting seems to suggest continuity with the old order and, as a remnant from a past era, a further reflection of the conservatism and social inertia of Gaeldom. This is unconvincing. In fact, when the development of crofting is examined carefully it becomes apparent that the system was as radical an innovation as the consolidated farms and the new rotations of the Lowlands. There is one obvious parallel between the systems in terms of time: both were adopted mainly from the last quarter of the eighteenth century. In the middle decades of the century the joint tenancy was still the dominant social formation in the western Highlands with land cultivated in runrig, pasture held in common and strong communal traditions associated with the tasks of herding, harvesting, peat-cutting and repair. Over less than three generations the joint farms were removed and replaced by a structure of separate smallholdings or crofts.

There was a second similarity between the north west Highlands and the Lowlands. The development of the croft had nothing to do with tradition and everything to do with the same improving ideology which was transforming the landscape elsewhere in Scotland in the later eighteenth century. Publicists for the new order such as John Knox and James Anderson concluded that the future of the Highlands lay in a dual economy: the interior straths and glens would become sheep runs and the people should then be relocated in crofts on the coast and earn their living primarily by fishing, kelping and other bi-employments.[28] The pastoral emphasis of their life had to change in favour of one where 'industrial' employment became dominant. The radical nature of this planned transition has to be stressed. Sir John Sinclair, possibly the most influential improving propagandist of the day, reckoned that a crofter had to obtain at least 200 days additional work outside his holding in order to escape destitution.[29] It was an explicit strategy on the part of the land surveyors responsible for the planning of the new crofts to reduce them to the size required to ensure that the occupants would need to look for other jobs. An additional and very acute pressure was that on many estates the new smallholdings were carved out of very poor land.[30] Crofting had revolutionary implications for traditional patterns of settlement, economy, labour and cultivation.

Studies of peasant societies in Europe have demonstrated that peasant families whose holdings did not directly yield enough for subsistence – as was inevitable in the new crofting regime – were likely to adopt several possible strategies.[31] One was to secure the subsistence minimum by using their limited land more intensively. In the Highland context the most remarkable example of this response was the rapid adoption of the potato. Over a few decades many crofting townships changed their main subsistence crop from grain to potatoes. This was a considerable departure for any peasant society where, if returns are insecure because of climate, the main aim is usually to maintain traditional cropping practices which guarantees at least enough in most years. In the 1750s cultivation of the potato was still rare but by 1811 James Macdonald, in his survey of Hebridean agriculture, claimed that potatoes already constituted much of the food intake of the Hebridean population.[32] Moreover, from the former conventional strip farming in the runrig system crofters developed the lazy-bed method in which sandwiches of soil well-fertilised with seaweed produced huge yields of the new crop even from marginal lands. This enabled settlement to expand on to formerly uncultivated land and mosses. As one contemporary put it, 'It is by the potato crop that all the wild land has hitherto been reclaimed'.[33]

A second strategy open to the crofting population was to supplement income from non-agricultural labour: '. . . households whose land-labour ratio was very unfavourable because of the small size of their holdings turned to industrial commodity production which was labour-intensive in contrast to land-intensive agricultural production. As the marginal product of their agricultural labour was rapidly approaching zero, they shifted part of their labour power to more productive activities, and rural industry provided them with an opportunity to do so'.[34] It is in this context of the inherent rationality of the peasant response that the expansion in subsidiary employment among the Highland population at this time is to be seen. Not simply was there a need to adjust to the new demands of crofting but also to the steep increase in rents and rise of population which began from the middle decades of the eighteenth century. Thus there was a veritable boom in the numbers employed in kelp, fishing, the army and navy, quarrying, temporary labour in the Lowlands and illicit whisky-making.

A third possible response was emigration. Current estimates suggest around 23–25,000 Highlanders emigrated for North America between 1700 and 1815 with the vast majority leaving after c.1760.[35] Bernard Bailyn's analysis of all British emigrants to North America in the years 1773–6 reveals that Highlanders contributed disproportionately to this outward flow. Indeed, the supposedly 'remote' and isolated Highlands of Scotland produced per head of population more emigrants at this time than any other part of mainland Britain.[36] The region accounted for 18 per cent of all emigrants in these two years.[37] Controversy still exists on the reasons for this large-scale exodus. Rising rents, the threat of the new crofting system to the traditional social structure, the early phases of sheep clearances, together with the prospect of available and cheap land free from arbitrary landlord interference have all been suggested as possible influences. However, the reasons for the movement are not so much the main concern here as its implications and what the successive waves of emigration tell about the issues under discussion in this chapter.

In this respect several conclusions emerge. First, the organisation of the whole process of emigration from areas of Scotland distant from the main shipping lanes reflected considerable initiative and organisational skills. The much maligned clan gentry or tacksman class were to the fore in this and displayed entrepreneurial abilities in handling everything from arrangement of transport to final settlement across the Atlantic.[38] Landlord assistance was not forthcoming and Highland emigration in this period took place in the face of implacable elite opposition. Secondly, the vast majority of those who made up the emigrant parties were middle-rank tenant families who could afford the journey and resettlement costs.[39] They were the economic backbone of the peasant communities of Western Highlands, the lynchpin of the system of cattle breeding and trading which had sustained the society throughout the eighteenth century. As such they had long experience of and involvement in commercial activity. In the later eighteenth century, therefore, this was not the flight of those who felt threatened by the market economy. Rather, as the author of a detailed study of emigration from western Invernesshire to Upper Canada makes clear, the decision to move signalled a radical departure from the past with the hope of a better life in the future: 'the emigrants were not refusing to participate in a commercial economy, they had increasingly done so in the eighteenth century and would, of course, do so again in Canada. What they objected to was the role which landlords assigned to them in the new order, as payers of rapidly escalating rents, or as crofters and labourers with little or no land to farm. The clansmen rightly assessed their situation as one of declining status and comfort and knew that the prospects of resistance were nil. Rather than be exploited they left, the actions, of a proud and self-reliant people.'[40]

Third, the daunting challenge of settlement in Canada after a sea journey which at this time meant permanent exile for the vast majority of emigrants should not be underestimated. Upper Canada was covered with great virgin forests which formed a formidable obstacle to cultivation. Land had to be cleared and log cabins built. There was a huge initial demand for labour to fell trees and dig out and clear roots before regular cultivation could take place. That new, prosperous settlements were eventually developed was a testimony to the determination, skills and endurance of these early Highland emigrants.[41]

Conclusion

Between c.1760 and 1815, and especially during the Napoleonic Wars, the way of life of the Gael was transformed through the full impact of market forces emanating from outside the Highlands. Southern demand for kelp, whisky, labour, fish, timber and grain and cattle and other commodities now conditioned the fate of the Highland population. In the same way that commercialisation had changed the lowland world forever so it also brought the old society in the Highlands to an end. During this Age of Improvement the people developed forms of enterprise and innovation which belie the traditional image of a conservative society and which would deserve more attention from scholars than they have received in the past.

REFERENCES

1. *Scotsman*, 10 February, 21 July, 1 September, 1847; J Bruce, *Letters in the Present Condition of the Highlands and Islands of Scotland* (Edinburgh, 1841); Scottish Record Office (SRO), HD6/2, Treasury Correspondence, Sir J. McNeill to Charles Trevelyan, 15 March 1847; SRO, HD6/2, Charles Trevelyan to Charles Baird, 19 March 1847.
2. T.M. Devine, *The Great Highland Famine: Hunger, Emigration and the Scottish Highlands in the Nineteenth Century* (Edinburgh, 1988, repr. 1991).
3. A Fullarton and C.R. Baird, *Remarks on the Evils at Present affecting the Highlands and Islands of Scotland* (Glasgow, 1838).
4. T.C. Smout, *A History of the Scottish People*, 1560–1830 (London, 1969), pp.308–331. See also R. Mitchison, 'The Highland Clearances' *Scottish Economic and Social History I* (1981), pp.4–24.

5. *Ibid*, p.358.
6. M.Gray, *The Highland Economy*, 1750–1850 (Edinburgh, 1957), p.80.
7. J. M Bumsted, *The People's Clearance: Highland Emigration to British North America 1770–1815* (Edinburgh, 1982).
8. Gray, *Highland Economy*, p.29. Gray notes that in the old Highlands 'a rigid class structure inhibited any real agricultural emulation' and quotes with approval the contemporary assessment by an improving writer that the great majority of farmers remained 'like that cast among the Hindoos who never think of rising above the rank which their fathers held in society'.
9. A.M. Smith, *Jacobite Estates of the Forty-Five* (Edinburgh, 1982); J. Dunlop, *The British Fisheries Society, 1786–1893* (Edinburgh, 1978).
10. E. Richards, *A History of the Highland Clearances* (London, 1982), Vol. I, pp.41–73.
11. A.I. Macinnes, 'Scottish Gaeldom: the First Phase of Clearance' in T.M. Devine and R. Mitchison (eds.), *People and Society in Scotland, Volume I, 1760–1830* (Edinburgh, 1988), p.71.
12. T.M. Devine, 'The Union of 1707 and Scottish Development', *Scottish Economic and Social History* 5 (1985); C.A. Whatley, 'Economic Causes and Consequences of the Union of 1707', *Scottish Historical Review*, (1989), p.68.
13. F.J. Shaw, *The Northern and Western Islands of Scotland: Their Economy and Society in the Seventeenth Century* (Edinburgh, 1980); A.I. Macinnes, *Clanship, Commerce and the House of Stuart, 1603–1788* (East Linton, 1996), pp.71–3.
14. R.A. Dodgshon, ' "Pretense of blude" and "place of their dwelling" the nature of Highland clans, 1500–1745', in R.A. Houston and I.D. Whyte, *Scottish Society, 1500–1800* (Cambridge, 1989), pp.193–5. Professor Dodgshon's valuable book, *Frmo Chiefs to Landlords* (Edinburgh, 1998) appeared too late to be incorporated in this analysis.
15. T.M. Devine, *Clanship to Crofters' War: the Social Transformation of the Scottish Highlands* (Manchester, 1994), p.15.
16. Dodgshon, 'Pretense of Blude', pp.193–4.
17. Gray, *Highland Economy*, p.43.
18. Thomas Pennant, *Tour in Scotland and Voyage to the Hebrides* (London, 1774), I, p.211; II, pp.177, 228, 278.
19. The points below summarise T.M. Devine, *The Transformation of Rural Scotland: Social Change and the Agrarian Economy, 1660–1815* (Edinburgh 1994), pp.1–35.
20. Macinnes, *Clanship, Commerce and the House of Stuart*, pp.145–6.
21. G.P. Insh, *The Scottish Jacobite Movement* (Edinburgh, 1952).
22. Devine, *Clanship to Crofters' War*, p.26.
23. The region was first examined in detail in Gray, *Highland Economy*, pp.223–238. The most accessible source is the *New Statistical Account of Scotland*, 15 vols. (Edinburgh, 1834–45).
24. Recent work on the Lowlands has shown that farms below 100 acres were by far the most common in most regions within the new agricultural system. See T.M. Devine, 'The Making of A Farming Elite? Lowland Scotland, 1750–1850' in T.M. Devine ed. *Scottish Elites* (Edinburgh, 1994). pp 62–76
25. R. Somers, *Letters from the Highlands* (London, 1848).
26. Gray, *Highland Economy*, pp.141–154.
27. Sir John Sinclair, *General Report of the Agricultural State and Political Circumstances of Scotland* (Edinburgh, 1814), IV, p.92.
28. Gray, *Highland Economy*, p.6.
29. James Anderson, *An Account of the Present State of the Hebrides and Western Coasts of Scotland* (Edinburgh, 1785); John Knox, *A View of the British Empire, especially Scotland* (London, 1785), 2 vols.
30. Devine, *Clanship to Crofters' War*, pp.47–8.
31. James Macdonald, *General View of the Agriculture of the Hebrides* (Edinburgh, 1811), p.236.
32. P. Kriedte, H. Medick and J. Schlumbohm, *Industrialisation before Industrialisation* (Cambridge, 1977), pp.16–17.
33. Macdonald, *General View*, p.232.

34. Quoted in Devine, *Great Highland Famine*, p.15.
35. Kriedte, Medick and Schlumbohm, *Industrialisation*, p.16.
36. T.C. Smout, N.C Landsman and T.M. Devine, 'Scottish Emigration in the Seventeenth and Eighteenth Centuries' in N. Canny (ed.), *Europeans on the Move: Studies on European Migration, 1500–1800* (Oxford, 1994), pp.100–12.
37. B. Bailyn, *Voyagers to the West: A Passage in the Peopling of America on the Eve of the Revolution* (New York, 1986).
38. M. McLean, *The People of Glengarry: Highlanders in Transition, 1745–1820* (Toronto, 1991), pp.78–167; Bumsted, *The People's Clearance*, passim; Ibid, 'Scottish Emigration to the Maritimes, 1770–1815', *Acadiensis*, 10 (1981).
39. *Ibid.*
40. McLean, *The People of Glengarry*, p.208.
41. G. Craig, *Upper Canada: the Formative Years* (Toronto, 1963), pp.7–11.

Fifteen

Highland Estate Change and Tenant Emigration

ANDREW MACKILLOP

THE THEME OF mass emigration from the Scottish Highlands in the last half of the eighteenth century has remained a somewhat differentiated and distinct branch within the broader subject of population movement from the region.[1] This distinctiveness is at least partly explained by certain characteristics and features which appear to structurally and fundamentally separate the eighteenth century emigrations from the larger exodus of people during the nineteenth century. Nowhere are these differences more apparent than in the broad economic backdrop. When compared with the onset of recession and collapse in the ancillary activities that supported the crofting north west in the years after 1815, conditions in the last half of the eighteenth century appear far more incongruous.[2] Generally, the years from the 1760s until 1815 were characterised by economic expansion and development. Enhanced profitability in established commercial enterprises, such as the black cattle trade, gave estate populations the ability to pay increased levels of rent, while the emergence of kelping, fishing, distilling, recruiting, spinning and weaving was supplemented by the burgeoning opportunities for seasonal employment in the Lowlands.[3] Population loss under such apparently positive economic conditions suggests that the experience of the Highlands during the last half of the eighteenth century mirrors a wider paradox in Scottish emigration highlighted in recent studies on the subject.[4]

Moreover, it is not merely the contrast in economic circumstances that distinguishes the question of eighteenth century population loss. Across a whole range of themes, from the impact of sheepfarming and tenant poverty to the role of the tacksman and the balance between voluntary and involuntary emigration, conditions in the earlier period appear to have differed radically from what was evident later. It has been a well established argument, for instance, that from the 1760s until perhaps as late as 1815 traditionally perceived forces of dispossession such as sheepfarming and evicting landlords were in fact conspicuously absent in the Highlands. With the lack of a broadly hostile economic climate, as well as these specific 'push' factors, attempts have been made to clarify the motivation behind Highland emigration. As a result, the movement of population in the eighteenth century has been portrayed as a 'People's Clearance', as a conscious response to the modernising 'improvement' strategies of landlords. Organised and led by tacksmen, who were by no means poverty stricken, emigration was seen, essentially, as a matter of choice and as a voluntary rejection of the new practices that threatened traditional lifestyles. Far from being driven by Malthusian pressure, emigration was in fact nothing less than a wholesale flight from the emerging commercial ethos and an attempt at the reconstruction of the Highland rural order in the North American colonies.[5]

The idea of a 'People's Clearance' and the themes raised by it remain a matter of considerable debate. Detailed study of the estate of the MacDonnells of Glengarry, for instance, has argued convincingly that sheep were in fact an active element in the conspicuous and large-scale emigrations from Knoydart in the mid and late 1780s.[6] In a broader sense, the whole dislocatory impact of landlord policy in the last half of the century has been re-emphasised and notions of 'voluntary' emigration undermined. While outright eviction was not a pronounced feature of the period, it has been argued that the rent increases that preceded the emergence of sheepfarming were, nevertheless, a substantial attack upon the often meagre profit margins of the smaller tenant groups.[7]

However, while debate surrounding the 'People's Clearance' has clarified some of the main issues, several neglected themes remain to be investigated within the question of Highland emigration during the first phase of clearance. Not least amongst these is the fact that many instances of high profile emigration took place in the north west, precisely in the area where landlords were actively encouraging the accommodation and settlement of populations. Despite the fact that loss of land through eviction forms the central theme of much of post-Culloden Highland history, it is in fact the apparent rejection by tenantry of at least some form of landholding that forms one of the central and most complex characteristics of emigration during this period. Estate settlement, however, was largely the experience of the islands of the north west and mainland seaboard. Given the radically different pattern of population development in the southern, eastern and central Highlands, it is clear that the latter lay under a distinct set of economic and estate management conditions.[8] This suggests that these two regions offer a useful area for comparison, especially in light of the complex and contentious problem of understanding the expulsive forces that operated during this period.

The irony of emigration during a period of ongoing access to land is mirrored in the attitude of proprietors towards their tenantry. The extent of elite opposition to population loss forms a central strand in the notion of a people's clearance and stands in stark contrast to the emigrationist policies of many nineteenth century landlords.[9] Given that their pro-population approach hardly fits the traditional perception of Highland landlords, it is surprising that it has remained a curiously understated and indeed neglected aspect of study. While the political campaigns of the elite against population loss have received attention, this perspective hardly encompasses the sphere of estate management where, of course, the leverage and influence of the landlord was at its greatest. Indeed, it is ironic that in order to gain a fuller understanding of eighteenth century emigration, landlord policies of accommodation and estate settlement must be examined in greater detail. This chapter, therefore, seeks to explore the differing estate conditions underpinning the departure of emigrants and how landlords correspondingly adapted or altered their policies in response to threatened and actual emigration.

Ironically, the landlords' effort to retain tenantry took place against the backdrop of their own determined and extremely successful strategy of rent increase. Table 1 demonstrates that augmentations were a generalised phenomenon across the Highlands.

TABLE 1: RENTS ON HIGHLAND ESTATES IN THE LAST HALF OF THE EIGHTEENTH CENTURY[10]

Estate	Year & Rent	Year/Rent & % Increase	Year/Rent & % increase	Year/Rent & % Increase	Year/Rent & % Increase	Y/R & % Increase	Total %
Lewis	(1750s)	(1766)	(1775)	(1787)	(1799)	(1803)	
	£1,200	£2,125	£2,290	£2,528	£4,488	£5,106	
		(77%)	(6.5%)	(10.3%)	(77.5%)	(13.7%)	325%
Urquhart	(1753)	(1761)	(1770)	(1783)	(1791)	(1804)	
(LochNess)	£370	£498	£1,168	£1,170	£1,635	£2,608	
	(34.5%)	(134%)	(0.7%)	(39.7%)	(59%)	604%	
Strathspey	(1755)	(1763)	(1773)	(1782)	(1792)	(1804)	
	£1,629	£1,695	£3,116	£3,919	£4,255	£7,022	
		(4.0%)	(83.3%)	(25.7%)	(8.5%)	(65%)	331%
Badenoch	(1751)	(1762)	(1773)	(1785)	(1795)	(1800)	
	£493	£674	£1,302	£1,512	£1,766	£2,463	
		(36.7%)	(93.1%)	(16.1%)	(16.7%)	(39.4%)	399%
Lochaber	(1754)	(1762)	(1772)	(1784)	(1795)	(1800)	
	£392	£553	£1,213	£1,338	£1,585	£2,960	
		(41%)	(119.3%)	(10.3%)	(18.4%)	(86.7%)	655%
Breadalbane	(1752)	(1766)	(1776)	(1785)	(1796)	(1800)	
	£2,118	£3,039	£4,599	£5,477	£8,895	£11,314	
		(43.4%)	(51.3%)	(19%)	(62.4%)	(27%)	434%

Sources: S.R.O. Gillanders of Highfield Papers, GD 427/9/1; GD 427/11/1; S.R.O., Seaforth Muniments, GD 46/17/4; GD 46/20/4/1/16; S.R.O., Seafield Muniments, GD 248/247/6/4; GD 248/533/1/8; GD 248/2802; GD 248/67/1/6; GD 248/49/4/20; GD 248/246/Unnumbered Strathspey factory accounts, 1782; GD 248/248/66; GD 248/2894 38; 2900; S.R.O., Gordon Castle Muniments, GD 44/27/4/54; GD 44/27/11/111; GD 44/51/732; GD 44/51/743/4–20; GD 44/25/2/28; GD 44/256/17; S.R.O., Breadalbane Muniments, GD 112/12/9/49–50; GD 112/9/2/2/3; GD 112/9/53, 64.

In roughly a generation, it appears that rentals had at the very least tripled; indeed, the examples of the Duke of Gordon's lands in Lochaber and Grant of Grant's Urquhart property suggest that five and even seven fold increases were not uncommon.

However, while rents are important in demonstrating the severe pressure that landlords exerted upon their tenantry, especially in the long term, they should not be relied upon to wholly explain cases of mass population loss. For instance, while rents in areas such as Lochaber and Urquhart increased substantially during the 1760s, it was not until the 1770s that emigration emerged strongly in these areas.[11] In 1765 the rental of Lewis was increased by 77% yet it was not until 1772 that large scale emigration began on the island.[12] Even on the Glengarry estate, the tacksmen and tenant reaction to initial rent increases was not one of immediate and intense hostility. In 1768 they agreed to a voluntary redemption of wadsets and a substantial increase in rent. Only in 1772, when another series of increases were imposed at a time of heavy cattle loss, did mass emigration begin upon the estate.[13]

This suggests that a deterministic linking of rent and emigration should be treated with caution, and that the relationship between tenantry and revenue demand was in fact more opaque, complex and multifaceted. Within the context of charting reaction to estate change there has undoubtedly been a tendency in Highland history to see the region's tenantry as somehow 'homogeneous', as sharing common concerns and agendas and acting together when faced with threatening landlord initiatives. A natural extension of this simplifying of internal hierarchies is the notion of communal responses to estate re-orientation. This particular argument has emerged strongly within the whole eighteenth century debate. The series of departures from Glengarry and Knoydart through the 1770s to the 1790s have been described as 'remarkably homogeneous' and indicative of the 'community emigrations' of the last half of the century.[14] This of course dovetails with ideas that 'the people' as a whole collectively reacted against estate change. Analysis of emigration lists for the years preceding the American war give support to this argument and reveal the familial character of emigrant parties and the extent to which Highlanders departed in extended family groups.[15] The pivotal role of the tacksmen class has also allowed emigration to be portrayed as the maintenance of traditional relationships between separate tenant groups. Thus in February 1771, Macleod of Macleod's Skye factor commented on the emigration being organised by neighbouring Macdonald tacksmen. He noted that the emigrants 'propose to go all in a body to North Carolina and buy lands and settle near each other'. He added that ten substantial tacksmen had drawn up;

> . . . a bond of unity and friendship for subscribing for a capital to purchase lands in America and settle a colony of their own, every subscriber having a share in proportion to his subscription money – No subscriber admitted under the sum of £20 . . . The smaller tenants are engaging with the subscribers as fast as they could wish.[16]

However, the particular argument that stresses the collective response of tenantry should not be accepted uncritically, if only because of its over reliance on examples from the north west such as Skye and Glengarry. It also faces more fundamental problems in that it fails to take account of the 'heterogeneous' nature of rural populations and the hierarchical structure of Highland society. After all, historians have emphasised the diversity of the social groups evident within estates and argued that these internal distinctions represent one of the defining characteristics of Scottish rural society.[17] Each was linked to the other by means of specialised functions and employment, and it is highly unlikely that these arrangements could have survived the processes of rapid change intact. New awareness of this diversity within rural society offers an alternative perspective beyond the conventional image of downward landlord pressure onto a monolithic and largely unresponsive tenantry. There is certainly a case for arguing that if the new forces of rental increase redefined relationships between Highland tenantry and the landlord, they also reconfigured the links between the various tenant groups.[18]

TABLE 2: SUBTENURE ON THE ESTATES OF URQUHART, LOVAT, THE BARONY OF COIGACH[19]

Estate/Year	Tacksmen	Subtenants
Urquhart/1761	10	52
Lovat/1763	25	83
Coigach/1763	11	44

Source: S.R.O., Seafield Muniments, GD 248/533/1/8; S.R.O. F.E.P., E 787/23/3(1); E 787/25/3(2).

The social structure on Highland estates underlines the importance of understanding any change in the links between tenant groups. Table 2 demonstrates that in the decade when sustained emigration became increasingly apparent in the region, there were often as many as three to five subtenant families residing beneath the superior tenant. Adjustment by either the landlord or leading tenants was thus bound to have an impact on a substantial number of people. Table 2 also shows how the failure of tacksmen to adapt to the new commercial regime cannot, in itself, satisfactorily explain the large numbers involved in Highland emigration for the simple reason that they constituted only a small minority upon any given estate – a point emphasised by studies detailing how emigrants consisted, in the main, of the middle and smaller tenants.[20] Further, the figures in Table 2 only reveal the number of recognised possessors and not the large imbalance between relatively secure tenants and the mass of the population. Military censuses show that, during the 1770s, a mere five Lochaber tacksmen had 159 men between 16 and 60 residing on their farms. The numbers in a military list compiled on North Uist in 1799 are even higher. Farms held by only ten tacksmen nevertheless sustained 380 men capable of military service.[21] This not only emphasises how the vast majority of the population had little or no formal connections to the land, but how understanding of mass emigration must involve charting the changing relationship between tacksmen and their lower tenantry.

Examination of estate conditions in the years immediately prior to the outbreak of mass emigration reveal a picture that is seriously at odds with the perception of entire populations responding as a collective whole to the forces of commercialism. Tenant petitions and reports for the estates of Lewis, Coigach, Lovat and Gordon's lands in Lochaber and Badenoch, show the extent to which inter-tenantry strain had emerged as a major characteristic of late eighteenth century Highland society.

TABLE 3: INTER-TENANTRY DISPUTE AND THREATENED EMIGRATION ON HIGHLAND ESTATES, 1763–1775[22]

Estate/years	No of Farms	Farms affected by tenant dispute & % of total estate rent	Farms affected by threat of emigration (actual migration)	% of rent affected by threatened (and actual emigration).
Lewis/1770–75	87	26 (31.5)	13 (11)	15.6 (14.6)
Coigach/1766–75	30	18 (79.3)	13 (13)	45.3 (8.4)
Lovat/1763–73	110	35 (42.7)	50 (No figure)	44 (N/f)
Lochaber/1765–75	46	11 (34.4)	7 (9)	23.7 (18.9)
Badenoch/1765–75	49	20 (35.6)	5 (No figure)	12.7 (N/f)

Source: S.R.O., Gillanders of Highfield Papers, GD 427/11/17; GD 427/163–65; GD 427/201–206; S.R.O., F.E.P., E 721/19; E 746/72,75–6,79,113,152,158; E 769/43,71,79,81,91; E 787/9; S.R.O., Gordon Castle Muniments, GD 44/25/2,4–6; GD 44/27/10–11; GD 44/28/20,34.

Table 3 shows that divisive disputes between the larger, middle and lower tenantry over land-use and estate resources were a common and, indeed, widespread phenomenon in the region. It is the scale of this internal friction that is immediately striking. The average on these properties over a ten year period was above one farm in three; and even large estates like Lewis could, in the relatively short space of five years, experience wide scale and intense conflict that affected well over one farm in four. The existence of these disputes show that commercialisation and improvement could divide estate populations as much as unite. They also call into question the whole concept of 'a People's Clearance'. Was such a collective response possible under these circumstances of bitter and ongoing dissension between tenant groups?

At the core of this inter-tenantry friction lay differing reactions to the pressures of rental increase. At the top of the tenant pyramid stood the tacksman who, in many areas, was the first to experience aggravated revenue demands. This, in turn, has been seen as a primary cause of mass population movement from the region in this period. [23] However, there are several problems relating to this particular interpretation. Given the transformation in our understanding of the tacksman it should not be at all surprising that, rather than the extreme and commercially risky option of emigration, others sought efficient and specialised practices that assisted the payment of rents. Far from being the ineffective farmer of eighteenth century improving literature, the tacksman has been recast not only as the manager and organiser of arable and pastoral resources, but also as the main entrepreneurial link in the region's droving trade. [24] Reassessment of the wider role and skills of this class calls into question the argument that they 'simply could not adjust to the situation created by the establishment of commercial landlordism'.[25]

By the early 1750s and 1760s, many tacksmen saw an increase in the productivity of their holdings, rather than emigration, as the natural way forward. In order to achieve this the larger tenants in south eastern and north western areas sought to secure and entrench their rights of management and regulation over subtenants and cottars. The flexibility this freedom allowed could, in turn, facilitate the revaluation of land use practices and the development of new strategies to meet the challenge presented to them. Leading tenants would then be able to extract additional income from the lower social groups or focus more clearly on the production of cattle or sheep.[26] Thus, in August 1772, leading Assynt tacksmen wrote that; 'We expect that they [the tutors of the Countess of Sutherland] shall leave these small tenants and the grounds on which they are, to be managed by us at pleasure, in the way and manner that may seem best to us consistent with equity, without control or check from any superintendent'.[27]

The ability to manage landed resources in a flexible and rational way was thus becoming more and more important as rental increases put pressure on tenant incomes. Moreover, where tacksmen and leading tenants successfully retained their holdings, many followed the example of their landlords and subordinated the interests of the populations beneath them in favour of the specialised pursuit of profit. This, in turn, produced substantially different patterns of development within the Highlands. It is clear from the emergence of relatively compact cattle and sheep farms that, in southern and eastern districts, many of the tenants constructed reasonably effective responses to the pressures of market forces.[28] Indeed, a report on the fourth Duke of Gordon's Lochaber estate in 1769 highlights how the first reaction to rental increase was not emigration but adaptation. It noted that 'the gentlemen and richer tenants will only mind their cattle, the management of them being attended with less expense'.[29] South eastern areas began to witness a pronounced transfer of outfield arable land and its supporting pasture into concentrated use for cattle and, increasingly, from 1775, sheep production. The impact of this strategy on estate populations is more than evident in the comments of James Grant, tacksman on Sir James Grant of Grant's estate in the parish of Duthill. In 1787 he highlighted 'the convenience of having the command of uninterrupted pasture and what disadvantage it is to have pasture eaten up as mine is by the people'.[30]

Such strategies, however, dramatically undermined the traditional grazing and cropping regimes used by the smaller tenantry. Faced with rising population levels, lower tenant groups constructed and perfected patterns of grazing and manuring designed to maximise arable production. The maintenance of large numbers of plough horses or the excessive use of potential winter fodder while securing manure for the arable in-field were particular strategies that assisted crop production at the obvious cost of specialised grazing regimes for cattle.[31]

Inter-tenant conflict thus arose from the clash between two different regimes of land-use, and it was the successful or attempted appropriation of pasture by commercialising tenants that sparked much of the disputes registered in Table 3. The pressure on grazing induced by such specialisation was an important element in the general 'oppression' suffered by the 107 people that emigrated from Glenorchy in 1774–75.[32] Facilitated by closer links to southern markets, the loss of small tenant grazing had intensified across Highland Perthshire and Argyll by the early 1790s. In 1791, on the fourth Earl of Breadalbane's lands in Glenlochy, consolidation of high sheiling land for local graziers meant that, while the landlord remained explicitly committed to the retention of population, over 200 people were involved in threats to drop their possessions.[33] Subsequent rearrangement of grazing in 1797–8 witnessed overcrowding in arable areas of Lochtayside and the recorded emigration of 18 families.[34]

It is important to clarify that the real impact of these developments did not lie in outright eviction, but in the destruction of traditional methods whereby the population maintained its arable base. Moreover, while much of the debate on eighteenth century emigration has centred on the arrival and impact of sheep, it is important to stress that the effect of specialised black cattle droving was similar to that of sheepfarming. In 1796, a report into Breadalbane's Argyllshire lands noted that; 'the hills in Nether Lorne are occupied by black cattle and mostly along the whole coast of Argyll even in the Braes of Lorne where gentlemen farmers have pretty good slices of hill farms where they prefer black cattle'. It was pointed out that while the earl had consciously sought to maintain population and had rarely removed tenants from arable infield areas, loss of grazing had made the maintenance of small holdings increasingly difficult, especially in light of inadequate manuring, overcrowding and excessive subdivision. Thus, despite the fact that it was cattle, not sheep, that had emerged as Nether Lorne's dominant commercial activity, the report concluded that 'the people are rather upon the decline than thriving in point of circumstance'.[35]

Comprehensive curtailing of the small tenantry's traditional means of support by developments in Argyll reinforces the assertion that while outright eviction was largely absent, concepts of 'voluntary' emigration are nevertheless largely meaningless.[36] Events on Gordon's estate in Lochaber not only underline this, but also show how specialisation in the supposedly benign black cattle trade not only sparked a breakdown in traditional inter-tenantry links but also how it has been seriously underestimated as a 'push' factor in Highland emigration. By 1771, Alexander Cameron of Glenevis, himself petitioning for the removal of his subtenants, summarised the effect of specialised grazing practices on the lower tenantry.

> The best grange farms thirled to the mill are turned waste under grass viz. Blarmacfildich which formerly keeped [sic] twelve families at least, and Mr Butter has laid waste Drummberban which supported six families – Mr Gray has laid waste more than a third of the farm of Torlundy for grazing of fat cattle for slaughter and John Mitchell by removing the tenants of Auchindaul reduces its corn growth to one half of the usual produce.[37]

What is particularly striking about these developments in Lochaber is that they reveal the expulsive nature of the economic regime that emerged in the southern and eastern Highlands. While removal or partial dispossession of grazing coupled to the retention of population on intensively farmed plots remained a common estate strategy, the Lochaber example suggests that outright eviction has been underestimated in this period. Moreover, the intensity and relatively early timescale is surprising. Conflict between social groups and subsequent removal of subtenantry became apparent on over 15% of holdings in the short period from 1769–1773.[38] The weakened position of the lower tenantry was underlined in a report of 1772 which noted that 'many of their [the tacksmen] subtenants have already left the country, and hundreds of them are carried off by a feverish disorder which rages violently through that country at present'.[39] This not only confirms that sheepfarming did not need to be present for population loss to occur, but that constraint and removal of subtenancy in many areas of the southern and eastern Highlands was in fact the direct result of tacksmen modernising and specialising in the black cattle trade.

Alternatively, in many areas of the Highlands, but especially in the north west, many tacksmen saw their subtenantry as a resource which could be increasingly exploited.[40] Thus, while suffering comprehensive vilification at the hands of those who viewed subtenancy as evidence of the larger tenants' inability or unwillingness to improve, the reality was that it was often deployed as a logical and cost effective response to new rental pressures.[41] Attempts by Assynt tacksmen in the mid 1760s to tighten the management and sale of the smaller tenants' cattle, and their increasing reluctance to stand caution for the rent of the lower social orders show that, under the pressure of estate re-orientation, traditional relationships of support and mutual assistance were being steadily eroded.[42] Moreover, elements of Gaelic oral tradition, as much as the figures in Table 3, reveal how this increasingly stringent use of lower populations produced inter-tenantry strain.[43]

In kelping and fishing areas, tacksmen regulated the settlement of additional small tenants which had the effect of undermining the arable resources of established middle tenantry. Thus, in 1786 and 1790, a tenant in Lewis complained of the arrival of six new subtenants and added that he 'needed and require to my own family almost all the arable grounds'.[44] That settlement and subsequent destruction of middle sized holdings formed a vital element in emigration from the north west can be seen from the fact that it was the relatively well endowed arable parish of Barvas that supplied a disproportionate 58% of the 478 emigrants from Lewis in 1772–73.[45] Likewise, emigrants from Reay in 1774 pointed out that the accommodation of new tenants undermined the viability of their holdings.[46] In Skye and North Uist, throughout 1801–3, the settlement of additional populations, often to satisfy promises made during the levying of men for the army or to maximise profits from kelping, saw middle tenantry vigorously object to the destruction of established holdings.[47]

Ironically, the accommodation of populations, by generating such subdivision, effectively meant that middle tenantry in both the south east and north west faced similar forces of constraint. Moreover, it has been highlighted how the social response of this numerous middle tenantry was conditioned by their strong aversion to loss of status and by the fact that they possessed lower reserves of capital and a limited ability to sustain even the partial loss of material resources.[48] Not surprisingly, therefore, the granting of new holdings, as much as the loss of grazing, could spark the internal disputes that characterised estate conditions immediately prior to emigration.

This background of competing tenant interests and objectives represents a vital dimension in eighteenth century population movement if only because it formed one of the main dynamics underpinning rental increase. By the 1750s and early 1760s landlords in areas as far apart as Badenoch and North Uist saw that, alongside policies of wadset redemption, direct access to the profit margins of the middle tenantry could produce large rent increases.[49] Implemented by means of competitive bidding, the policy of stressing the different tenant groups on estates brought unprecedented dividends to the landlords. In 1768 Macleod of Macleod ordered a new sett upon his estate. His adviser, Colonel John Macleod of Talisker, noted regarding any increase;

> . . . there are a very great number of small tenants on Macleod's estate, who are cottars to such as have larger tacks, and who tho' they possess but small shirts of the worst land are burdened with the whole rents . . . and if narrowly and properly enquired into, they might even be of great use in the present emergency.[50]

In light of the strain between social groups this strategy of actively encouraging inter-tenantry competition was always likely to be a tremendous success. The Laird envisaged that the total increase would bring the revenues from his six baronies to £3,749. Instead, after receiving the individual proposals of the tacksmen and smaller tenantry, managers found that the rental totalled £4,282 –14.2% above what Macleod had ordered. Exactly the same scenario was evident in Lochaber. Not untypical were the subtenants on the farm of Blarmacfildich who attempted to outbid their tacksman (an Argyll drover) with the result that the rent jumped from £30 in 1766 to £50 three years later. The defeated subtenants subsequently found the only way the tacksman could answer the rent was to evict them and shift over completely to grass.[51] It was against this backdrop that, in 1769, Gordon sought an additional £591 to bring the rent up to £1,030. This amount was in fact surpassed with the estate eventually setting for £1,234 – 19.8% higher than expected.[52]

These two examples clearly show how rents were often driven up by the social expectation of subtenants attempting to remove themselves from the influence of larger, modernising tenants. Thus, while rental increase has traditionally been seen as a matter of landlord dictate engendering subsequent mass emigration, such augmentations were often more immediately centred upon the deep divisions between tenant groups. This underlines how any attempt to view estate populations as collectively allied against the landlord should be treated with caution.

Competitive bidding, however, did produce severe instability in the longer term. Throughout the 1760s to the 1790s, commentators confidently predicted that a fall in cattle prices in the aftermath of inflated estate setts would inevitably produce emigration.[53] Indeed, it is ironic to note that many Highlanders in the last half of the century emigrated, not after eviction, but after recent social advancement and estate settlement. The observations of John Campbell, factor on Breadalbane's Argyll estate in 1800 not only show how internal friction drove up rents but how, ironically, the very act of securing access to land undermined tenantry and made emigration a likely possibility:

> You cannot conceive the inveterate feuds and animosities which these competitions produce in a district. The estate of Ardkinglass is a striking instance of this. Tenants without scruple hazarding their own ruin to injure others – and the parish church deserted by some families, who considered the minister a party in these feuds. I have myself seen innumerable instances of tenants offering more for lands than they could possible pay, owing partly to the influence of local attachments, and to the spirit of contention and revenge, which is excited when the tenants of a district are set to bid against each other. The effect of this on several estates in Argyllshire, has been universal bankruptcy and sequestrations. I have no hesitation in predicting, that two or three years of a fall in the markets will produce a total revolution among the tenants in that country.[54]

Moreover, this suggests that part of the structural problem underlying the periodic upsurges in emigration lay less in the population's passivity and lack of commercialised attitudes, as in their over-optimistic reliance on the largely profitable and upbeat cattle market. Amongst several of the tenants that emigrated from Lochaber in 1774 was one Archibald MacDonnell from the farm of Terindreish who, the factor noted, had until 1769 been a subtenant on the estate. He had subsequently advanced his status by offering large and, it appeared, unsustainable rents on the basis of high cattle prices.[55]

Both the evidence of inter-tenantry dispute and the intensity of competitive bidding show how the middle tenantry had increasingly found it in their best interest to become an active element in the erosion of tenurial hierarchies. Indeed, contrary to the perception of a conservative population unwilling to consider any real innovation, it is clear that many small tenants, having declined materially under the new management regimes of the tacksman, proved willing to countenance substantial social change. However, once removed from the cushion of the tacksman's protection, many smaller tenants found themselves increasingly vulnerable. Ironically, eighteenth century emigration did not necessarily centre around attempts to preserve traditional lifestyles or social hierarchies, but, in fact, often sprang from a sense of failed or constrained social advancement. Thus, in 1772, it was noted regarding conditions on the Strathspey estate of the Grant of Grant family:

> The people of six davochs . . . determined to go in a body to America if they did not get the proper deduction . . . As these people were formerly subtenants of one or other of the gentlemen and are only

> sett at liberty a few years ago, the truth is that these poor people were so elated at the thought of getting free of the tyranny of their former masters, that they agreed to pay more than the real value.[56]

Seen from the perspective of the middle tenantry, the immediate response to new commercial pressures was not emigration but an attempt at the re-definition of their place within the estate. When this failed the secondary reaction was emigration. Moreover, this attempt at re-adjustment helps to explain the instances of time delay between rent increases and population movement.

These shifts and progressive alterations in the status of tenantry not only underlay departures from the Highlands but also formed part of the response by landlords to threatened or actual population loss. In 1775, 1786 and again in 1801–3, proprietors organised and led sophisticated political campaigns against emigration. Indeed, the elite were so alarmed during 1774–75 that they requested the forcible repatriation of emigrants by means of troop ships returning from the reinforcement of America.[57] However, emphasis on the opposition of landlords should not be taken too far. Evidence of high profile campaigns should not detract from the fact that in many parts of the region depopulation had become more than evident by the end of the century. While the western seaboard from Morvern to northern Sutherland together with the Western Isles experienced population growth of more than 25% in 74% of its parishes between 1755 and the 1790s, 60.2% of the parishes in the south east Highlands failed to register any increase.[58] In light of these figures it is surely questionable whether all landlords adopted a generic approach to emigration. Instead, they suggest that proprietors in the south east either failed in their efforts to keep their tenantry or felt sufficiently unconcerned to mount a sustained effort at retention. Indeed, in many areas landlords and tacksmen often had clinical and dispassionate views on emigration. As early as 1774, an Assynt tacksman advocated emigration in a manner that presaged nineteenth century rhetoric when he called for the removal of the 'burden' of excessive population.[59] Even on the estate ClanRanald, dominated as it was by kelping concerns, an acceptance of emigration under poor economic conditions was evident in the 1770s. Thus Colin Macdonald of Boisdale noted that; 'I believe the country would greatly be the better if a third of the peoples being away, since their [sic] was no publick way of employing many of them'.[60]

Even conspicuously pro-population landlords like Breadalbane felt that, by the early 1790s, the region's ability to compete against the Lowlands in the manufacturing sector was all but gone.[61] Not unsurprisingly, he was prepared, albeit in a limited way, to allow the piecemeal departure of tenantry.[62] Indeed, just prior to the campaign for the Passenger Act, John

Campbell, fifth Duke of Argyll, a leading light in the push for legislation, was tacitly condoning the departure of small tenantry from Tiree.[63] Removed from the hyperbole of political lobbying, landlord opposition to emigration in the last half of the century appears neither as comprehensive nor as inveterate.

Much of the elite response was in fact conditioned by the specific nature of any given estate emigration. It is certainly the case that '. . . most of the observable and objectionable emigration came from the coastal region of the western Highlands and Islands', while movement in southern and eastern areas was largely accomplished through internal migration to Lowland Scotland.[64] This contrast between the dramatic and convulsive departures of the north west and the more steady drift from the south and east belies the fact that it was in the latter area that real overall de-population occurred. In south-eastern areas, the piecemeal shift into grazing and relatively consolidated farms was characterised by its slow if steady nature. While Sir James Grant's letter of appeal to Dundas when faced with the loss of over 100 people from his Strathspey lands in 1775 is highlighted as typical of elite attitudes, his approach should in fact be seen at two levels.[65] On his Strathspey estate the number of tenancies actually fell by 7% from 191 in 1763 to 177 by 1800. However, this relatively small overall decline disguised areas of intense consolidation. Thus, in the same period, the number of holdings within the parish of Cromdale fell from 106 to 86, a drop of just under 20%. However, a gradual overall approach towards re-orientation was facilitated by the fact that tacks on the estate had staggered expiry dates. In 1763 only 16% of holdings were without a tack, while the remainder of the leases expired at varying annual rates over a period of twenty years.[66] This suggests that where landlords could control the drift of population and match any vacant possessions to substantial tenants a certain amount of emigration or migration was acceptable, and hostile reaction largely confined to instances of uncontrolled population loss.[67]

The steady regime in Strathspey stands in stark contrast to conditions in the north west, where both rapid expansion in settlement and the structure of estate setts worked to facilitate a more convulsive approach. As late as 1792 the entire estate of Harris was held, apart from twenty three small tenants, by eight tacksmen. At the turn of the century the landlord broke up these large tacks and brought 185 subtenants onto his rental – a 496% increase in holdings.[68] Moreover, as landlords sought to increase rents by competitive bidding, entire estates were re-structured in order that their leases expired simultaneously. The comprehensive sense of insecurity and competition sparked by this form of management was highlighted by contemporaries as a factor in the instances of alarming mass emigration that particularly characterised departures from the north west.[69]

The instability of the Highland economy and its over-reliance on one or two particular commercial activities was highlighted in the early 1770s, in 1782–3 and again in 1793 and 1799. The numbers involved in these periodic upsurges of emigration are well known, and Table 3 suggests that landlords could face the loss of tenantry responsible for one quarter to one third of estate income.[70] The most obvious remedy was, of course, rent abatement. Table 4 demonstrates that when faced with the heavy loss of tenantry many landlords sanctioned substantial rent reductions.

TABLE 4:- RENT REDUCTION 1765–1774

Estate	Rents	Reduction	%
Rogart (Sutherland)	£81 (1765)	£21 (1773)	26%
Harris, Skye Glenelg	£4,280 (1769)	£917 (1774)	21.9%
Urquhart	£1,127 (1770)	£120 (1773)	10.6%
Lochaber	£1,234 (1770)	£382 (1773)	30.9%
Badenoch	£1,302 (1770)	£164 (1774)	12.5%

Source: N.L.S., Sutherland Papers, Dep. 313/2119; Dep. 313/1103/Unnumbered letter 15 June 1773; Dep. 313/1104/ Unnumbered letter 23 July 1773; Dep. 313/1106/Unnumbered letter 10 July 1773; D.C.M., 1/381/15; 2/105/1–2; 2/488/15; S.R.O., Seafield Muniments, GD 248/1035, 1889; S.R.O., Gordon Castle Muniments, GD 44/27/11/111; GD 44/25/6/17.

This affected small estates such as Rogart, where rent reduction was compounded by the settlement of tenants in preference to cattle grazing, as well as large properties held by first rank landlords. Forced to follow the example of Grant of Glenmoriston and the Chisholm family, Sir James Grant, by 1775, had lowered rent levels on 85% of his 330 holdings in Strathspey.[71] Moreover, while intended as a short term measure to ease immediate concerns, some rentals in fact took from fifteen to twenty years to recover. Income on the Lochaber estate did not return to 1769 levels until 1784. On the Macleod estate in Skye several farms took nearly a generation to reach their old rents and most of the substantial reductions in the aftermath of 1769 were not recovered until 1792 – almost 25 years later.[72]

The surprising scale of rent reductions notwithstanding, tenantry often refused to retain holdings and emigrated regardless, aware, no doubt, that the fundamental shift in landlord objectives made a return to high rents inevitable. Despite substantial reductions, Lochaber and Strathspey both witnessed subsequent emigration. In Glenelg, during the early 1770s, a 20% drop in rents failed to persuade fifteen of the estate's 73 tenants to remain, though the overall effect on Macleod's Skye baronies was undoubtedly the prevention of small tenant and particularly tacksman loss on the scale suffered by the neighbouring Macdonald estate.[73] Facilitated by a growing web of trans-Atlantic kin connections, many tenants adopted emigration as a long term objective and actually eschewed landlord offers of tacks; instead, they sought advantageous short term conditions in order to build up reserves of capital for a future departure.[74] Increasing prices and the growing pressures of population in the later years of the century prevented the need for further comprehensive rent reductions, though sporadic cases on individual farms continued to occur, as did the general freezing of rents to avoid emigration from Breadalbane in 1792 and Urquhart in 1784.[75]

A more effective strategy than rental reduction was the settlement of tenants upon conditions designed to lessen the likelihood of emigration. Many, though by no means all, landlords proved adept at negotiating and compromising with their tenantry and manipulating sentiments of kinship and local identity to secure their populations. In Badenoch during 1773, the Duke of Gordon eased concerns amongst his tacksmen by noting how he was 'much disposed to accommodate the Messr's MacDonnell because of their attachment to his family and upon account of their connection with many of his friends'.[76] In Skye, Talisker deliberated forced the new young chief to move amongst his tenants and live at Dunvegan. Moreover, at the height of an emigration scare in 1773, the Colonel emotionally blackmailed tacksmen and tenants by painting an image of their chief imprisoned in an English jail as a result of a collapse in his income.[77]

However, such tactics could only succeed in the short term. In order to secure their populations in the longer term proprietors sought to divide their tenantry and appeal to specific or individual interests. Landlords were advised to 'talk to the emigrants, bestow your eloquence among them severally but never in general meetings or convocations'.[78] In contrast, mass declarations of intended, as opposed to actual, emigration were tactics used by the tenantry to lever concessions from landlords, who responded by seeking fault lines in the collective body of the estate population. Given the level of disputes between tenantry over issues of grazing and changes in conditions of subtenancy, this tactic was often surprisingly successful. Faced with threatened emigration to secure a reduction in rent, Sir Alexander Macdonald of Sleat called his tacksmens' bluff and ordered his factor to begin the settlement of small tenants. Interestingly, the Laird of Macleod's factor argued that it was this attack on traditional hierarchy and tenurial structure, not the rental increase, that finally convinced leading tenants to depart.[79]

Exactly this policy was practised by Macleod of Talisker on his chief's Skye estate. His sentiments after meeting with tacksmen and tenants in February 1773 show how the internal distinctions within estate hierarchies formed one of the main weapons in the elite's fight against population loss.

> I thought it was right to appoint that second meeting among themselves as they will be a check on one another . . . the deductions should be given without feud or favour to anyone and should some principal

tacksmen throw up their leases I have not in the least fear of their lands being waste, or of your not getting the highest rent for them. [80]

This shows that in contrast to conditions in the south east, the landlord approach in the north west was the settlement of smaller tenantry at the expense of tacksmen. Indeed, landlords had already begun, in the 1750s and 1760s, to seek increased control over their profitable populations. While consolidation of grazing by larger tenants occurred in the south, limitations on the amount of land held by tacksmen became a favoured estate strategy in the north west. Many found their management of subtenure severely curtailed, and a crucial social consequence of mass emigration was that it expedited this process.[81] By 1769, the tutors of the Countess of Sutherland began to limit tacksmen to individual farms; and the instances of leading tenants seeking increased profits from the lower groups or assisting their emigration in order to consolidate holdings only helped to focus these anti-tacksmen trends in west Highland estate management. By 1774, half of Assynt was sett to small tenants so there could be 'no apprehension of emigration from that county . . . now that their leases are out, the poor sort of people are much pleased that they are to have no tacksmen over them'.[82]

The departure of Donald MacNeil, tacksman of the Park of Lewis, in the early 1770s saw the systematic settlement of smaller tenantry to prevent them following suit; moreover, contrary to perceptions of community emigration, such groups took full advantage of the situation to actively attack the established tenurial structure. It is ironic to note that by threatening emigration to the extent that the word 'Americans' became part of estate vocabulary, many subtenants, in the midst of population departure, secured new conditions of accommodation. Thus John Morrison, tacksman in Lewis, noted regarding his subtenants;

[I] neither received obedience nor dues from them and now since some of them resolves for America, and that such as resolves to stay went to your Honour and by the encouragement they got, the Americans and they agree about setting the lands as they please . . . My tenants told me this morning they had got a promise of my tack.[83]

A review of estate conditions immediately prior to emigration, as well as some of the tactics adopted by proprietors, shows that Highland society in the eighteenth century should not be viewed as a simple breakdown between landlords on the one hand and a monolithic bloc of 'tenantry' on the other. While the tacksman in this period has been primarily portrayed as the leader of west coast emigration, it is also clear that from 1750–1800 black cattle and modernising tacksmen emerged along with sheepfarming and landlordism as significant factors underpinning the drift of south eastern populations in particular. This not only underlines the sharp divergence between the different districts of the Highlands, but also shows how commercial reorientation presented varying opportunities to the distinct groups within estate structures. In the south and east, new commercial pressures produced the development of a relatively consolidated tenantry while in the north west they underwrote a spate of estate settlement that generated a negative response within much of the established middle tenantry. Ironically, both these radically different patterns of commercial development produced emigration. While population loss from the north west has generally received more attention, it is ironic to note that the constraint and removal of smaller tenantry in southern and eastern areas during the eighteenth century involved a greater element of expulsion and dispossession than contemporary developments in emerging crofting districts. In the north west, it was the settlement of additional populations that provided the destabilising factor. Landlords keen to retain valuable labour found that it was best accomplished through the active destruction of older tenant hierarchies. Ironically, this suggests that while crofting history has been dominated by the removal of its nineteenth century populations, the system itself was in fact born on the back of eighteenth century dispossession and emigration.

REFERENCES

1. E. Richards, *A History of the Highland Clearances, vol. 2: Emigration, Protest, Reasons* (London, 1985), chapter 7.
2. For description of this period see M. Gray, *The Highland Economy, 1750–1850* (London, 1957) pp.181–190; T.M. Devine, *The Great Highland Famine: Hunger, Emigration and the Scottish Highlands in the Nineteenth Century* (Edinburgh, 1988) pp.18–19, 37–39; J. Hunter, *The Making of the Crofting Community* (Edinburgh, 1976), pp.73–74, 77–81.
3. For a general summary on the labour intensive nature of the developing Highland economy see A.I. Macinnes, 'Scottish Gaeldom: The First Phase of Clearance', in T.M. Devine and R. Mitchison (eds.), *People & Society in Scotland, 1760–1830*, vol. 1 (Edinburgh, 1988), p.78.
4. T.M. Devine, 'The Paradox of Scottish Emigration' in T.M. Devine (ed.), *Scottish Emigration and Scottish Society (Edinburgh,* 1992), pp.2 and 6.
5. M.I. Adam, 'The Highland Emigration of 1770' *Scottish Historical Review*, xvi (1919), pp.282–83; 'The Causes of the Highland Emigrations of 1783–1803' *Scottish Historical Review*, xvii (1920), pp.74, 81–83. Gray, *Highland Economy*, p.99; M.W. Flinn, 'Malthus, Emigration and Potatoes in the Scottish North West' in L.M. Cullen and T.C. Smout (eds.), *Comparative Aspects of Scottish and Irish Economic and Social History, 1600–1900* (Edinburgh, 1977), pp.50–52; J.M. Bumsted, *The People's Clearance: Highland Emigration to British North America, 1770–1815* (Edinburgh, 1982), pp.29, 46 and 63.
6. M. McLean, *The People of Glengarry: Highlanders in Transition, 1745–1820* (London, 1991), pp.5, 67–69, 100, 108, 111 and 115.
7. A.I. Macinnes, 'Scottish Gaeldom', pp.74 and 86; T.M. Devine, 'Landlordism 38; Highland Emigration' in Devine (ed.), *Scottish Emigration and Scottish Society*, pp.85, 99–100. While more receptive to the role played by the broader demographic, social and economic

forces impacting upon the region such revisionist arguments support, in several key respects, the conclusions of historians who see the proprietor in his or her more traditional evicting role.

8. For a summary on the development of population in both the north west and south east see M. Gray, *Highland Economy*, pp.63–65.
9. J.M. Bumsted, *People's Clearance*, xi-xv.
10. Scottish Record Office (SRO), Seafield Muniments, GD 248/49/2/16.
11. S.R.O., Gordon Castle Muniments, GD 44/25/4/34; GD 44/51/734/4 and 8; GD 44/27/5/54. p. 7.
12. M. McLean, *People of Glengarry*, pp.65–66 and 86.
13. No fully extant rental for Lewis survives for the mid 1750s. However, before the new sett in 1765 the Reverend John Walker noted that the rent of Lewis was £1,200 in the early 1760s. This can be taken as generally indicative of rents for the last years of the 1750s.
14. McLean, *People of Glengarry*, pp.125–126. For other comments on the communal nature of emigration see Richards, *Highland Clearances*, p. 195; Macinnes, 'Scottish Gaeldom', p.79.
15. B. Bailyn, *Voyagers to the West: Emigration from Britain to America on the Eve of the Revolution* (London, 1987), p.95.
16. Dunvegan Castle Muniments (DCM), 4/113 38; 114.
17. M. Gray, 'The Social Impact of Agrarian Change in the Rural Lowlands' in T.M. Devine & R. Mitchison (eds.), *People and Society in Scotland, 1760–1830*, vol. 1 (Edinburgh, 1988), p.54; T.M. Devine, *The Transformation of Rural Scotland: Social Change and the Agrarian Economy, 1660–1815* (Edinburgh, 1994), pp.9–13.
18. N.L.S., Sutherland Papers, Dep. 313/725:- Minutes of Tutors 1767–1782: Meetings dated 20 July 1769 and 11 March 1773; S.R.O., Gillanders of Highfield Papers, GD 427/156/1.
19. The figures only include the number of subtenants upon farms held by tacksmen. Multiple tenant numbers on each estate are not shown, nor indeed are the subtenants or cottars holding from this particular middle tenant group.
20. Bailyn, *Voyagers to the West*, pp.98–103; McLean, *People of Glengarry*, pp.81–82.
21. S.R.O., Forfeited Estate Papers (FEP), E 769/91/102(1); S.R.O., Gordon Castle Muniments, GD 44/25/2/55; Clan Donald Trust Library (CDTL), GD 221/4388.
22. 'Tenant dispute' can be summarised as one of the following. Removal or attempted removal of subtenantry by larger tenants. Disputes between separate farms over grazing rights or internally upon a farm over particular land use. Requests by lower tenantry for settlement upon tacksmen farms or appeal by the same group for change in status to direct holding from the landlord.
23. R. Brown, *Strictures and Remarks on the Earl of Selkirk's Observations on the Present State of the Highlands* (Edinburgh, 1806), pp.36–39.
24. A. Mackerral, 'The Tacksman and his holding in the south west Highlands', *Scottish History Review*, vol. 26 (1947), pp.11–21; E.R. Cregeen, 'The Tacksmen and their successors: a study of tenurial reorganisation in Mull, Morvern and Tiree in the early eighteenth century', *Scottish Studies*, vol. 13 (1969), p.100; R.A. Dodgshon, *Land and Society in early Scotland* (Oxford, 1981), p.281.
25. Hunter, *Crofting Community*, p.14.
26. For examples of how important this control was to large tenants see S.R.O., Seafield Muniments, GD 248/508/1/77; GD 248/509/1/28–29x; N.L.S., Sutherland Papers, Dep. 313/1103/Unnumbered letter dated 29 May 1772; S.R.O., Gillanders of Highfield Papers, GD 427/208/4.
27. S.R.O., Gillanders of Highfield Papers, GD 427/205/28; N.L.S. Mackenzie of Delvine Papers, Ms 1161, f. 190a.
28. Gray, *Highland Economy*, pp.93–94.
29. S.R.O., Gordon Castle Muniments, GD 44/28/34/40 and 99x; S.R.O., Seafield Muniments, GD 248/49/2/16–17; GD 248/51/2/114.
30. For examples from Lochaber, Badenoch, Strathspey and Highland Perthshire, see S.R.O., Gordon Castle Muniments, GD 44/25/2/30; GD 44/27/10/68, 131, 197; GD 44/28/34/58;

S.R.O. Seafield Muniments, GD 248/44/4/22; GD 248/533/3/19; GD 248/227/2/68; GD 248/347/1/8; S.R.O., Breadalbane Muniments, GD 112/11/1/4/42 and 64; GD 112/16/7/1/12.

31. R.A. Dodgshon, 'Strategies of farming in the Western Highlands and Islands of Scotland prior to Crofting the Clearances', *Economic History Review*, vol. 46 (1993), pp.691–695.
32. S.R.O., Breadalbane Muniments, GD 112/14/12/7/8; P.R.O., T 42/12, ff. 48 119–20.
33. S.R.O., Gordon Castle Muniments, GD 44/43/143/1. For evidence on the appropriation of holdings and sporadic emigration from Breadalbane's Perthshire estate in the 1780s and early 1790s see S.R.O., Breadalbane Muniments, GD 112/11/1/4/63; GD 112/14/12/7/13; GD 112/16/5/5/17, 20–22, 31 and 35; GD 112/16/31, n 29.
34. S.R.O., Breadalbane Muniments, GD 112/16/5/2/7; GD 112/12/1/2.
35. S.R.O., Breadalbane Muniments, Robert Robertson's Report on Nether Lorne 1796, R.H.P. 972/5.
36. A. Macinnes, 'Scottish Gaeldom', p.86.
37. S.R.O., Gordon Castle Muniments, GD 44/25/2/41(1–2); GD 44/25/4/5–8.
38. This trend of subtenant dispossession is drawn from the section of Lochaber correspondence. See S.R.O., GD 44/25/2, pp.4–6.
39. S.R.O., Gordon Castle Muniments, GD 44/27/11/38x.
40. S.R.O., F.E.P. E769/79/3; E 769/91/106–8; E769/91/140(1–5). For evidence from Lewis and central Highland areas see S.R.O., Gillanders of Highfield Papers, GD 427/11/7; GD 427/232/1 and 2; S.R.O., Gordon Castle Muniments, GD 44/26/9/26.
41. A.J. Youngson, *After the '45* (Edinburgh, 1973), pp.12–14; M. Gray, Highland Economy, p.26. For contemporary condemnation of the tacksmen see A. Irvine, loc. cit. pp.50 38; 69; R. Brown, *Strictures and Remarks on the Earl of Selkirk's Observations on the Present State of the Highlands* (Edinburgh, 1806), pp.36–39; D.C.M., 2/95 and 4/310; S.R.O., Seafield Muniments, GD 248/201/2/1; N.L.S., Mackenzie of Delvine, Ms 1485, f. 97; S.R.O. F.E.P., E 787/9/119.
42. N.L.S., Sutherland Papers, Dep. 313/1101/15; Dep. 313/725: Meeting of Tutors 2 March 1772; Dep. 313/3126/1; S.R.O., F.E.P., E 746/152/2(1)3,4(6); P.R.O., T. 47/12, f. 29.
43. For evidence on the Gael's dislike of subtenure see Hunter, *Crofting Community*, p.13.
44. S.R.O., Seaforth Muniments, GD 46/1/268.
45. *Public Record Office* (PRO), State Papers 54/45, f.164.
46. P.R.O. T. 47/12, f. 29.
47. A. Mackillop, 'Military Recruiting in the Scottish Highlands, 1739–1815: The Political, Social and Economic Context, unpublished Ph.D. thesis, University of Glasgow, 1996, pp.348–9; C.D.T.L., GD 221/674/2; GD 221/737.
48. Devine, 'Landlordism and Highland Emigration'. pp.93–4.
49. S.R.O., Gordon Castle Muniments, GD 44/28/34/34; N.L.S., Mackenzie of Delvine Papers, Ms 1309, f.241. For examples of wadset redemption as a means of increasing rents see D.C.M., 2/25; S.R.O., Seafield Muniments, GD 248/49/2/16–17x.
50. D.C.M., 4/294.
51. S.R.O., Gordon Castle Muniments, GD 44/25/4/5–6, 11 and 31.
52. D.C.M., 2/485/35/1 38; 1/381/15; S.R.O. Gordon Castle Muniments, GD 44/25/2/50 38; GD 44/ 25/4/31.
53. McLean, *People of Glengarry*, pp.101–2; D.C.M., 1/866/1; S.R.O., Gordon Castle Muniments, GD 44/28/34/90.
54. S.R.O., Breadalbane Muniments, GD 112/41/5, pp-25–33.
55. S.R.O., Gordon Castle Muniments, GD 44/25/5/20.
56. S.R.O., Gordon Castle Muniments, GD 44/27/11/17x.
57. For evidence on the various campaigns against emigration see S.R.O., Seaforth Muniments, GD 46/17/1/Unnumbered letter dated London, 28 January 1773; S.R.O., Seafield Muniments, GD 248/244/4/2; *Caledonian Mercury*, N 10,059: 1 March 1786; S.R.O., Highland Society Sederent Book, 1795–1803, RH 4/188, pp. 441, 543 38; 487; P.R.O., S.P. 54/45, ff. 165 38; 172a.

58. Gray, *Highland Economy*, p. 59.
59. For examples of either ambivalence towards, or espousal of, emigration, see S.R.O., Seafield Muniments, GD 248/49/2/57; GD 248/49/3/1; GD 248/349/3/8; GD 248/508/1/77; GD 248/509/1; S.R.O., Gillanders of Highfield Papers, GD 427/206/7 and 15; GD 427/214/24 and 27; N.L.S., Sutherland Papers, Dep. 313/1102/4; Dep. 313/1103/Unnumbered letter dated 26 June 1772; Dep. 313/725: Letter to Tutors, 17 February 1772; Dep. 313/1107/Unnumbered letter dated 18 February 1774.
60. S.R.O., ClanRanald Muniments, GD 201/5/1232/1/6.
61. S.R.O., Breadalbane Muniments, GD 112/41/4/6 and Unnumbered letter 15 February 1792; GD 112/74/254/138;7.
62. S.R.O., Breadalbane Muniments, GD 112/41/4/3; GD 112/74/254/3, 7 and 23.
63. E.R. Cregeen (ed.), *Argyll Estate Instructions: Mull, Morvern and Tiree 1771–1805*, (Edinburgh, 1964), pp.63, 66, 72–72.
64. Bumsted, *People's Clearance*, p.29; T.M. Devine, 'Highland Emigration to Lowland Scotland, 1760–1860', *Scottish Historical Review*, lxii (1983), pp.135–138; Richards, *Highland Clearances*, pp.180–81.
65. S.R.O., Seafield Muniments, GD 248/244/4/2; P.R.O., T.47/12, f. 26.
66. The figures are drawn from a comparison of rentals from 1763 and 1800. The break-up of several large tacks in Abernethy and Inverallen through this period in fact make the overall number of holdings larger in 1800 than forty years previously. However, as the numbers of tenants holding from these tacksmen is not known, only a direct contrast with tenancies shown in both rentals is recorded. S.R.O., Seafield Muniments, GD 248/248/6 and 8; GD 248/458/5.
67. S.R.O., Seafield Muniments, GD 248/52/2/40.
68. R. Brown, *Strictures and Remarks on the Earl of Selkirk's Observations on the Present State of the Highlands* (Edinburgh, 1806), pp.45–46.
69. For examples of landlords ensuring the simultaneous expiry of tacks in order to heighten rental see D.C.M. 4/227; S.R.O., Seafield Muniments, GD 248/227/1/2; GD 248/229/6/16–17x. For the general connection with emigration see T.M. Devine, 'Social responses to Agrarian "Improvement": The Highland and Lowland Clearances in Scotland', in R.A. Houston and I.D. Whyte (eds.), *Scottish Society, 1500–1800* (Cambridge, 1989), p.165; D.J. Withrington and I.R. Grant (eds.), *The Statistical Account of Scotland*, vol. 20, (Wakefield 1983), pp.71–72n
70. One of the most detailed studies of the scale and pattern of eighteenth century emigration suggests that Highlanders made up a round 15% of total British emigrants in the period 1773–1776. After the American War of Independence it is widely believed that emigration ran at only 33% of pre war levels and did not return to pre 1775 levels until the turn of the nineteenth century. See Bailyn, *Voyages to the West*, pp.111–112. For a description of the course and scale of emigration from the region after 1783 until the turn of the century see McLean, *People of Glengarry*, pp.97–100, 134.
71. N.L.S., Sutherland Papers, Dep. 313/1103/Unnumbered letter 15 June 1773; S.R.O, Gordon Castle Muniments, GD 44/25/5/43; GD 44/27/11/90x; S.R.O., Seafield Muniments, GD 248/349/3/8; GD 248/244/4/7x; S.R.O., GD 248/248/32; GD 248/242. For a general description on rental reduction see S.R.O., Gillanders of Highfield Papers, GD 427/205/25(2).
72. S.R.O., Gordon Castle Muniments, GD 44/27/11/81; D.C.M., 1/381/15; 2/485/44, 56, 66 and 69; 2/484/397; 4/397.
73. S.R.O., Gordon Castle Muniments, GD 44/27/11/24x, 38x, 91x. P.R.O., T. 47/12, f. 26; D.C.M., 2/105/1–2
74. In 1774 a survey of Sutherland emigrants found that 8 of the 31 interviewed already had close relations in America. Another 12 noted a rather more vague connection and stated simply that they had 'friends' in the colonies. See P.R.O., T. 47/12, f. 29. For tenants refusing long leases in order to have the flexibility to emigrate and plan in advance see S.R.O., Seafield Muniments, GD 248/227/2/17; S.R.O., Gordon Castle Muniments, GD

44/27/11/90x.

75. C.D.T.L., GD 221/771/2; S.R.O., Breadalbane Muniments, GD 112/16/31, n 29; S.R.O., Seafield Muniments, GD 248/229/6/16–17x, GD 248/534/6/4 38; 8.
76. S.R.O., Gordon Castle Muniments, GD 44/27/11/8. For a less successful attempt at using traditional means see S.R.O., Gillanders of Highfield Papers, GD 427/205/8, 26 38; 34; GD 427/214/24 and 28; GD 427/215/2, 4 and 17.
77. D.C.M., 4/387; 4/392/1; 4/397.
78. D.C.M., 4/392/1.
79. S.R.O., Seafield Muniments, GD 248/226/4/50x; D.C.M., 4/113–14.
80. D.C.M., 4/397.
81. For tack stipulations that constrained larger tenants' control over subtenure see S.R.O., Seaforth Muniments, GD 46/1/212; S.R.O., Gillanders of Highfield Papers, GD 427/56/2; GD 427/150/1; D.C.M., 2/32/1; S.R.O., Sutherland Papers, Dep. 313 725/ Meeting of Tutors 20 July 1769.
82. N.L.S., Sutherland Papers, Dep. 313/1107/Unnumbered letter 14 July 1774. For emigration focusing on the tacksman in a hostile way in Skye see, D.C.M. 4/392/1.
83. S.R.O., Gillanders of Highfield Papers, GD 427/215/6; GD 427/205/26–28.

Sixteen

The Dark Side of the Enlightenment? Sorting Out Serfdom[1]

CHRISTOPHER A. WHATLEY

THE IMPOSITION OF a form of serfdom amongst the Scottish coal and salt workers has been perceived as the 'dark side' of the social history of Scotland during two centuries which saw in the eighteenth century the flourishing of the Scottish Enlightenment. Yet in spite of the appearance of a stream of revisionist publications over the past decade, an unwarrantably bleak image of the Scottish colliers and salters still lingers, perhaps because much of the new work has appeared in specialist outlets. This chapter summarises and emphasises the more significant aspects of recent research, but also points to some of the gaps in historians' knowledge of the topic which remain.[2] A second aim is to account for the tenaciousness of the older view. The final section of the chapter will re-examine prevailing explanations for the 'Emancipation' Act of 1775 and shed new light on it by suggesting that insufficient attention has been paid to the role of the economic ideology of the Scottish Enlightenment in the process which resulted in the ending of legal life-binding.

In the broader context of labour conditions and social relations in eighteenth-century Britain the picture of a degraded army of collier and salter serfs has had the effect of presenting Scotland as starkly different, feudal, brutal and backward in comparison to her southern neighbour.[3] Yet recent studies of social structure in the early eighteenth century suggest that after allowances have been made for local and regional variations and Scotland's relative poverty, Lowland Scotland and England had much in common, with differences being of degree rather than kind.[4] The labour market in England in the eighteenth century has recently been described as being 'in a state of suspension' between feudal servitude and the free contractual system of the following century.[5] Points of convergence in the work-related and social experience of coal and salt workers on both sides of the border have been identified too. Thus the year-long 'bonds' which were widespread on Tyneside in the eighteenth century (and which were commonplace in Scotland by the turn of the nineteenth century), along with indebtedness, are said to have made English coal workers 'only a degree less unfree' than the Scots.[6] On the other hand, while the law in Scotland stipulated that coal miners and salters should work six days a week, Scottish work patterns were virtually identical to those in English pits and pans. Water and bad air, thickness of seams, injuries and illness, individual and collective notions of what constituted a day's work and voluntary absenteeism were amongst the main determinants of collier attendance and output in both England and Scotland.

There are also grounds for exploring the observations made by contemporaries and some historians of the similarities of features of Scottish collier and salter serfdom with both the 'new serfdom' of Central and Eastern Europe and negro slavery in North America. Scottish collier and salter serfdom cannot be neatly categorised, but neither should we expect this: everywhere, what determined the character of serfdom 'were the circumstances in which it operated'.[7] Comparative analysis on a scale which is impossible in this short essay would greatly enhance historians' understanding of the labour process in pre-industrialised Scotland and place the actions of the state, the operation of the law and the policies of those Scottish landowners with coal-bearing estates who utilised the labour of life-bound workers, within the wider framework of the early modern European economic periphery. What seen through Anglophile eyes was an 'anachronistic system',[8] the Scottish variant of what was an extreme but not uncommon form of coerced labour can be located here too (that is as well as in a British context), even though unlike the peasant serfdom of Poland, Hungary and Bohemia, Scottish serfdom, confined to the coal and salt industries (as well as to some fisherfolk), impinged upon only a minority of the population.[9] However, like both medieval serfdom and the new serfdom of mainland Europe in the sixteenth and seventeenth centuries Scottish serfdom was designed to retain scarce labour, thereby to secure and increase the output of two valuable commodities both for the domestic market and for overseas sale. In Scotland as elsewhere the 'new serfdom' was introduced by the state in the interests of an increasingly commercially-motivated nobility, justified on mercantilist grounds.[10] The legal basis of the system was laid at the turn of the seventeenth century, as Scotland's population grew, as did the prosperous and coal-hungry larger burghs. There was potential for further expansion in the Scottish salt and coal trades as a result of the waging of intermittent economic war by Spain on the Low Countries. The most rigorous enforcement of the law, followed soon after by the first moves to eliminate serfdom in Scotland, appears to have occurred as demand for coal – and coal mining labour – sharpened in the 1760s and 1770s, a decade when demand for salt also experienced a modest upturn.[11] The deteriorating legal status of the coal and salt workers resulted from Court of Session judgements in 1762 and 1763 which argued that the Roman law concept of *adscriptii glebae*, which bound colliers to a particular coal was not appropriate, but rather that coal workers were bound to a master who was entitled to move them from pit to pit or even to another part of his estate. Further research is required however to ascertain more precisely how stringently the law was enforced over time.

Of the many pessimistic accounts of the nature and human consequences of Scottish collier and salter serfdom, perhaps the most eloquent was that of Tom Johnston, a future Labour Secretary of State for Scotland, who described the 'poor unfortunates' who were 'condemned to . . . servitude in the mines and salt works' as a 'race apart'. They were:

> buried in unconsecrated ground; some of them wore metal collars round their necks; they were bought and sold and gifted like cattle . . . they were wholly unlettered; they developed a jargon of their own, and were regarded with superstitious fear and terror by the majority of their own countrymen; they lived in colonies; and in every old mining district in Scotland local tradition still tells of how the 'brown yins' or the 'black folk' allowed no stranger near their habitations.[12]

This is a powerful indictment which has been developed over a century of historical writing. Serfdom has been held responsible for the employment underground of women, their continuing presence as late as the 1830s being explained by one commentator as the 'remnant of the slavery of a degraded age'; the lowly status of the 'dull-witted' coal and salt workers within the occupational and social hierarchies of pre-industrialised Scotland was confirmed with the depiction of their work as unskilled and easily supervised, appropriate employment therefore for vagabonds and beggars who were periodically rounded up and forced to endure a lifetime's servitude.[13]

On the face of it there are good grounds for adopting such a perspective, including the use which could be made by coal and salt masters of the Scottish Poor Laws of 1579 and 1597 to bind former vagrants for life, but primarily the legislation of the Scottish Parliament of 1606, 1641, 1647, 1661 and 1701 which was specifically directed at coal and salt workers and distinguished these groups of workers from the rest of the lower class. The core Act of 1606 did not create serfdom as such but it did allow masters to recover former workers who had left them without permission, provided the process to reclaim such individuals was made within a year and a day of the desertion. Nevertheless, subsequent rulings of the Privy Council and Court of Session ensured that 'the operation of a very real serfdom in practice was maintained'. The 1661 Act ratified those of 1606 and 1641, forbade poaching of labour with the offer of large bounties and insisted on a six-day working week.[14] There is unambiguous evidence that in spite of uncertainties about the legal basis of life binding, the practice did occur in many parts of the Scottish coalfield and in the saltworks, while absconders were brought back and sometimes incarcerated, fined and even subjected to corporal punishment.[15] That on several estates the children of coal workers were considered to be life bound too brings the Scottish experience within the margins of a slave system.

Yet the temptation to overstate the argument should be resisted. Key questions about numbers and the extent of serfdom have too rarely been asked, let alone answered. Thus whilst one of the coal industry's leading historians supposed that serfdom was 'very much the norm' in the Scottish coal industry, there are others who have suggested that the evidence of comparatively high wages mean that there must have been large numbers of 'free' men, perhaps as many as half of the total collier population in the west of Scotland. The reality is of enormous diversity in custom and practice which could vary from estate to estate, which is altogether overlooked in the confident, sweeping assertions about the nature of collier and salter servitude made by contemporary legal authorities such as Lord Bankton.[16] Until the painstaking task of searching systematically through collections of estate papers to determine the status of the Scottish colliery employees has been carried out, historians will not be in a position to make authoritative statements about what proportion of the workforce of some 5–6,000 colliers estimated to have been employed in the industry in the 1770s was life-bound. Such an exercise should pay attention too to the growing body of evidence which points to a significant degree of gender-differentiation in the labour market, with female coal bearers being in relatively short supply and in some cases being able to negotiate separate contracts from the male hewers for whom they worked. That females worked underground in some English coal mining districts raises doubts about the extent that their employment was due to their servile status, although they too could be life-bound: more likely explanatory factors are the tradition of household employment in the rural south-east of Scotland and the rapidity of the coal industry's growth, which may have led, as in Cumberland, to the recruitment of females.[17]

One generalisation is almost certainly justified however. Paradoxically, although the legal constraints on the movement of bound colliers were tightened by a series of Court of Session judgements during the 1760s and early 1770s, the numbers of free colliers, including several who were brought north from England, was also rising while one-year bonds were becoming more common, alongside life-binding. Colliery proprietors and lessees intent on increasing production had to bow to the dictates of what was a far from one-sided labour market in order to entice workers into new, deeper or extended mines. Although the overall numbers were small there are sufficient examples of males entering pits after having worked at other occupations – more often than not as unskilled 'workmen' – to suggest that the drawbacks of colliery employment (including the 'stigma' of serfdom) were less of a disincentive than most historians have assumed.[18]

'Voluntary slavery' was not unknown in societies where income levels were low; within what has been described as the 'chain of exploitation' serfs did not occupy the lowest places.[19] Thus in the economic circumstances of the first half of eighteenth-century Scotland, where the households of most rural labourers struggled to reach subsistence living standards and lengthy periods of under- and unemployment were commonplace, coal or salt workers who signed long contracts or who entered into agreements which bound not only themselves but also their unborn children to a particular master who then became his dependents, may well have been acting in an eminently rational economic manner.[20] Coal workers in Midlothian, at Bo'ness colliery and perhaps at a handful of Fife collieries did enlist in the movement to end life-binding. However it is not clear how widespread collier support was. Contemporaries recognised that there were significant numbers of colliers even in 1774 who were distinctly lukewarm about the prospect of obtaining their liberty, fearing that the abolition of serfdom might lead to a reduction in their earnings and a longer working week.[21]

Whatever quantitative conclusions are eventually drawn the picture will be further complicated by the substantial body of evidence which demonstrates – as Ashton and Sykes conceded as early as 1929 – that there was a considerable degree of mobility between collieries in Scotland, whether or not the colliers or bearers concerned were life-bound.[22] The requirements of many coalmasters for colliery labour during periods of expansion, either locally or nationally, generally tended to over-ride their respect for the relevant legislation and persuaded them that the principal way of securing additional supplies of the requisite quality of worker was to offer sizeable entry fees and shorter fixed-term contracts. For those masters whose collieries were working below expectation or had even been abandoned, there were considerable cost advantages in releasing workers and handing over the responsibility for their maintenance to someone else.

A list of coal hewers and bearers on the Rothes estate (Fife) for 1739 reveals that of twenty-one colliers working at Strathore pit only one was bound at Rothes. The rest had entered from other pits in Fife or travelled from even further afield, from the Lothians and Stirlingshire.[23] In this as in other instances the colliers had migrated from other pits in search of work, although most moved less often than domestic or agricultural servants, and not as regularly. Even so, annual bounties were paid and wage rates were frequently renegotiated – as they were in the serf-free north-east of England in the eighteenth century – regardless it appears of whether or not the colliers concerned were life-bound.[24] Coal hewers were more likely to remain at a colliery if regular employment was available on acceptable terms.

At Rothes in 1740 these included written contracts for a fixed period of years, a free house and yard, meal at an agreed price and support in ill-health and old age. Customary payments – in the form of ale at Martinmas, an ox at Christmas or drink money for Handsel Monday – were expected of and provided by the proprietors at Rothes, and in accordance with estate custom throughout virtually the whole of the Scottish coal region. Similar payments were common in England too. It was when work was unavailable, perhaps because a mine was flooded or the accessible coal was worked out, or because working conditions or the terms of employment or employer-employee relations were poor that workers 'deserted', either temporarily in the hope that collective action would bring about improvement, or permanently. A study of negro slavery in Maryland and Virginia has shown that it was skilled industrial slaves in particular who were able to damage the financial interests of uncompromising employers.[25]

Harsh punishment, meted out to absconding or unruly colliers and salters, was not confined to these occupational groups. The authority of baron courts as well as those of the grander courts of regality extended throughout an estate and could equally be used to punish offending farm tenants and cottars. It was not only employers of colliers and salters who, frequently with the connivance of the state, used a range of coercive devices to regulate and discipline their labour forces in their efforts first to kick-start the Scottish economy and then to maintain the industrialisation process. English workers too, notably those in manufacturing and mining, endured a rigorous extension of employment legislation as the economy modernised in the eighteenth century.[26] Accounts of the oppressiveness of the colliery and saltwork regimes have been grossly inflated. Indeed, contrasting with the image of the oppressed collier serf is the comment made by Sir Thomas Erskine of Alloa in 1760, after thirteen of his colliers had left him, that there had been 'thro' all Scotland much too little of the custom of punishing Coalliers'.[27] Many tried but most attempts at social engineering in the coal and salt industries failed abysmally. If anything and despite the general recognition now that the Scottish coal and salt workers were far from docile, the extent of combination and other instances of collective action on the part of the Scottish coal workers in defiance of their employers has been underestimated and on occasion overlooked by earlier generations of historians whose analysis of class relations was distinctly one-sided, and based on a pre-Thompsonian perception of the nature of paternalism. Thus the return of miners belonging to the Duke of Buccleuch to Sheriffhall, Midlothian, from a new colliery at Canonbie which they had been employed to open in 1768, was attributed to the decision of the men's 'humane employer', Buccleuch. Ignored however is the evidence that throughout their stay at Canonbie the Midlothian men continually attempted to renegotiate their terms of employment and had to be cajoled to work with a series of concessions, including drink money. They returned to Midlothian because they were dismissed from Canonbie as they were too expensive.[28] Not unlike the 'ungovernable' colliers of Kingswood in the first half of the eighteenth century, Scottish coal workers had clear ideas about the limits to the power and the responsibilities of their social superiors and were prepared to take direct action to defend their interests.[29] In what is a remarkable historiographical turnaround it now appears that Scottish coal workers formed combinations earlier than their counterparts in the great coalfield on the north east of England, while evidence of collective action from the Scottish coal industry has been used to demonstrate the extent to which labour consciousness had developed in Europe prior to the era of the Industrial Revolution.[30]

The claim that the coal and salt workers were a 'race apart' requires careful scrutiny. It is not only in Scotland that it has been challenged: historians of English coal workers have also taken earlier writers to task, arguing that the concept of a type of people who were physically and culturally separated from the rest of humankind is convincing only in relation to the location and nature of coal mining work and the structure of collier society. In Scotland there is a case for proposing a 'workplace-related sense of collective identity . . . but not to the exclusion of everything else'.[31] Collier communities in Lowland Scotland became increasingly distant geographically in the later eighteenth century and certainly in the nineteenth century, after Lanarkshire, the inland parts of Ayrshire and Fife had been opened up by the railway, but this was much less often the case earlier. Cartographic evidence suggests that prior to this most coal mines and saltworks were situated near to or even in coastal burghs such as Stevenston in Ayrshire or Dysart in Fife, that is within easy and cheap transport distance of either domestic consumers or harbours. Coal and salt workers formed 'communities within communities', with whose inhabitants they interacted economically and socially. There is now a sizeable body of evidence which shows the extent to which coal workers were involved in protesting crowds in defence of the 'moral economy' or to oppose the appointment of an unwanted minister of the kirk, or in other forms of communal activity such as fairs.

The presumption that colliery employees were outcast from the church, unbaptised and buried outside the grounds of Christian kirkyards can be contradicted by the most cursory glance at birth, marriage and burial records in coal mining parishes, and occasionally, surviving gravestones. A better indication of the attitudes of coal and salt workers to organised religion comes from Kincardine-on-Forth in the mid-seventeenth century, where the colliers and salters protested that the nearest church was too far distant and offered to contribute to the cost of a new building nearer to hand. In Ceres,

Fife, in 1769, colliers joined with sixteen other local inhabitants to break down newly-erected dykes in order to keep open the route they usually took to church. Literacy levels amongst the collier and salter populations have received only cursory attention. However the appearance of colliers amongst lists of subscribers to books and their signatures on documents contradicts the most damning claims about their intelligence and abilities, while the accusation by Tulliallan kirk session in 1684 that a collier there had encouraged his son to write 'disgraceful words in imperfect Latine and English' indicates that he was aware of the power of the written word.[32] Some fragments of collier verse have survived while both Allan Ramsay and Robert Burns wrote poems which pay tribute to the physical and other desirable qualities of the 'collier lassie'.

It has now been established beyond doubt that coal cutting and salt making required considerable skill. Indeed it is this which partly explains why the wages of both colliers and salters were relatively high; it explains too why in the first half of the eighteenth century, when mining engineers or 'viewers' were in short supply, some colliery proprietors periodically assembled their colliers to consult with them about future mining operations. In short the colliers' and salters' lowly legal status was incompatible with the realities of coal mining or supervising the operations of a saltpan – which required a lengthy period of training as well as skill and judgement. The idea that beggars and vagabonds should be taken underground and made to work in the highly-dangerous stoop and room coal cutting system where an error on the part of one man could be the ruin of them all loses credence in the face of the substantial evidence there is that most coal miners were descended from collier fathers, alongside whom many worked.

It remains to explain why, accepting the more pessimistic accounts of the coal and salt workers' experience are flawed, the older view has been so strongly rooted. This is a large-scale historiographical question to which justice cannot be done here, although some possible reasons may be suggested.

Sheer sensationalism may be one, with the image of the degraded collier serf over-stimulating the imaginations of some Scottish historians who until the 1970s tended to eschew comparison and to betray a marked Whiggishness in approach. As has been seen comparison demands greater care in the assessment of the nature of Scottish serfdom and discourages unmeasured claims of uniqueness. The alleged feudalism of the Scottish legal system, which included the heritable jurisdictions and entails, and the perceived economic and political failings of the self-interested Scottish landed class, were key ingredients of the Anglo-British whig critique of pre-Union Scotland which had the effect, compounded by the work of later historians, of placing seventeenth century Scotland into an historical dark age.[33] The institution of serfdom may well have its place in this cavern of misguided aristocratic endeavour although the moralising rhetoric of English observers of mining communities south of the border serves as a reminder that coal workers generally evinced feelings of apprehension on the part of outsiders.[34] However pity and the depiction of the coal and salt workers as victims predominates in most accounts, which betrays a distinctively Scottish form of historical whiggism, seen in the writings of influential working class historians or those of a left-wing or a liberal persuasion. Thus a connection between increased strike activity in the early 1770s and a clamour for an end to life-binding is implied (but not proven) and considerable satisfaction is derived from the perception of coal workers confronting the oppressive system of legal servitude. The struggle for liberation is presented as an important plank in the onward and upward march of organised labour, with, ultimately, the National Union of Mineworkers in the vanguard.[35]

Perhaps as a consequence structural flaws in the argument have gone unnoticed. The available evidence has often been read less critically than it should have been while the weight of interpretation which some of it has been asked to bear is too heavy. One example is the brass collars allegedly worn by collier serfs. In fact, although many reproductions were apparently made, only one brass collar has been discovered and this was not *necessarily* worn by a coal worker. All that is known is that the unfortunate wearer was a servant of Sir John Erskine of Alva, who did operate coal mines. The court's motive for this exercise in public humiliation in 1701 appears to have been to draw attention to the severity of the crime committed and the sentence passed, which declared those found guilty to be forever 'bondsmen and servants' to those to whom they were gifted. There was no specific mention of colliery or saltwork servitude.[36] A similar criticism can be applied to the oft-repeated evidence of a witness to the Royal Commission on Mines in 1842 who declared that he had been bound as a slave at Grange colliery when he was nine and that disobedient workers had been put in the jougs or made to run backwards all day at the horse gin. This however is the testimony of one man of 81 years, used without any questions being asked about either its reliability or its typicality.

Of more general significance is the case of Fife, which as far as labour conditions were concerned has been described as very much the worst of the Scottish counties, where the status of colliers was so low that they were unable to find burial plots in consecrated ground.[37] Yet the conclusions of more recent detailed work on the coal and salt industries in Fife are strongly optimistic.[38]

The explanation may partly lie in the credence which has been given to the work of A. S. Cunnningham, a prolific local historian who in the early twentieth century wrote a series of books about several of the Fife villages. Careful reading of Cunningham however reveals that his pessimistic depictions of the 'poor miners' in early modern Fife are based on what appear to be a handful of documentary sources. These however are considerably more ambiguous than Cunningham allows, and include evidence that Wemyss salt workers refused to work unless at prices they found acceptable and that 'Balbirny's coalliers' were 'nobody's property' and could therefore be easily hired (notwithstanding Cunningham's insistence that coal and salt workers were 'slaves'). Even so, while it is appropriate that Wemyss material should be used in his book on the parishes of Scoonie and Wemyss, less legitimate is Cunningham's use in subsequent work, on different localities, of the same evidence without any indication being given that it related to Wemyss and not the focus of his current enquiry.[39] The charge against Fife is not proven, which suggests that the contrast which is often made between conditions in the east and the west of Scotland should be reconsidered, with greater attention being paid to individual estate custom and practice and to the longevity of coal working in a particular locality.

Serfdom in Scotland was eliminated in two stages, following Acts of Parliament in 1775 and 1799. The 1775 measure has been variously explained. Suggestions that there may have been a humanitarian impulse have been replaced by much more cynical interpretations of the reformers' motives. Even here however there have been differences, some stressing pressure to reduce wages, another emphasising the coalmasters' concern to attract fresh labour into the industry by removing the 'stigma' of serfdom while more recently the present author has emphasised the anti-combination thrust of the Act. In fact these three positions are compatible and are in keeping with the available evidence.

What is lacking from previous accounts is any consideration of the extent to which Enlightenment ideas about political economy impinged on the thinking of at least some of those concerned to shape the 1775 Act. What is becoming clear from recent investigations into the causes of Scotland's rapid industrialisation process in the second half of the eighteenth century is that the importance of two contributory factors has been seriously underestimated. The first of these is the role of the state, the second, the impact of Enlightenment ideas and attitudes upon economic action.[40]

At first sight however it would appear that there were few links between the Enlightenment and the coal and salt workers. Scottish serfdom was not a major issue in Enlightenment circles. Nevertheless the Enlightenment as it manifested itself in Scotland was particularly (but not uniquely) pragmatic in its nature and often focused on real economic problems which confronted Scotland's patriotic landed and commercial classes.[41] Not directly so but ultimately of considerable relevance to the coal industry and the Scottish coal workers was the 'rich country-poor country' debate in which David Hume was a seminal participant.[42] Hume was convinced that a smaller poorer country like Scotland could close the gap with England and approach the 'opulence' of its southern neighbour. Scotland's relative economic backwardness and the advantages of wealth creation for the improvement of society were issues which exercised the minds of men like James Anderson, Sir James Steuart, Professor John Millar, as well as Adam Smith. The means of achieving economic success was a topic which was discussed at some length, with considerable passion if also without much sophistication, in clubs and debating societies in Scotland in the years leading up to 1774. Significantly, this was precisely when the employers' campaign to alter the laws affecting Scottish coal and salt workers began to take off.

Although there was considerable controversy about whether rich countries with their higher wage levels would inevitably decline owing to competition from those nations where production costs were lower, that low wages were a vital ingredient for poorer countries trying to emulate their more opulent rivals was hardly in dispute and was central to the prognostications of both Hume and Steuart. This is a consideration which features strongly in the correspondence of reforming coalmasters such as George Glasgow, in Irvine, Ayrshire, who was engaged in an ongoing competitive struggle with Cumberland pits to expand sales in the lucrative Irish market. Ayr coalmasters such as William Alexander and John Beaumont were amongst the instigators of the reform agitation.[43]

Yet the rhetoric of George Glasgow's contribution to the campaign was not simply that of concern about wages, nor was it confined to coal. What was at stake was the much bigger issue of Scottish economic development, in other words of how a poor, relatively underdeveloped country like Scotland might become a great manufacturing nation. Thus in a lengthy letter to Walter Scott, campaign co-ordinator, Glasgow provided a closely-observed and highly-perceptive analysis of England's current economic strengths. Unlike Adam Smith, whose *Wealth of Nations* which was published two years later gives little hint of the new industrial nation which Scotland was to become, Glasgow was clearly aware of the nature and significance of modern coal fuel-fired manufacturing industry. What he describes is the decay in England of rural manufacturing, which had formerly been situated in grain-growing regions. Manufactures had been relocated in 'barren and uncultivated' situations such as northern Lancashire and the North and West Riding, with the key locational factor not being the availability of low-cost corn but rather the proximity of coal.[44]

Earlier in the same letter the rich country-poor country issue is reported with direct reference to Scotland:

> Trade Manufactorys and Commerce keep shifting from Country to Country and from place to place and only become fixed and permanent

> in such situations as are fraught with the most Natural Advantages and Conveniencys of human life. The Firth of Forth and the Firth of Clyde with adjacent Countrys to each of them and that Interveaning by means of the Cannal that is at present carrying on to join the rivers Marks that district of Scotland as the only one adapted for Foreign trade and must be the principal Mart of all our Imports and Exports And from the Cheapness of fuel is the best adapted for increasing the old and Establishing New Manufactories.

Provided landowners and coalmasters did their duty and provided low cost fuel, the outcome would be the replacement by Scottish manufacturers of many goods 'that at present are brought from England and the Continent and constitute a great part of our Exports'.

It was at this point that the argument turned to wage levels – and the deleterious effect upon the last of collier combinations which with their 'villainous by Laws & Regulations' meant that 'one half of their [the colliers'] time is imployed in cheating their Master leavying fines from their Brethren to raise Drink' – to the ruin of their families. Yet even here the Enlightenment influence is clear, with moral improvement being central to the Scottish men of letters' agenda. Recourse was had to the wage data reported by John Millar in his *Observations concerning the Distinction of Ranks in Society* published in 1771, although this was supplemented by figures comparing colliers' wages in Ayrshire and Cumberland. Significantly in this case Ayrshire wages had fallen slightly (although they were still above those paid in Cumberland) following the Ayr Bank crash. Here again disputed economic theory – this time over the effects of increasing money supply within an economy – is applied to the coal industry, with Glasgow in this instance siding strongly with Hume who in his essay 'Of the Balance of Trade' had demonstrated that a rise in money supply raised prices and reduced competitiveness. 'Natural Causes produce natural Effects', wrote Glasgow, and if 'the medium by which Labour provisions & the raw materials of a kingdom is estimated is increased to an extraordinary degree it must have a fatal tendency on the Manufactorys of that Country by increasing the price of Labour & provisions'. Recent experience had demonstrated the truth of the hypothesis: both in Paisley where labour costs had been lower and attracted London manufacturers to Scotland, and in the shoe and saddle trades of Glasgow and Kilmarnock, success overseas had been due to the 'Diminution of Labour Compared to that of England', and in the case of the leather industry had given the Glasgow masters virtual control of the North American and West Indian markets.[45]

Laced with patriotic overtones this was an argument which had to be developed with care and could hardly be articulated without qualification at

Westminster. In the debate about the coal question as in the wider discussion of whether or not strongly emergent nations would eventually cause the downfall of the previously rich care had to be taken not to alarm the English and any suggestion that the Scots were intent on 'underworking' the coalhewers of England was strongly denied. Rather the stated aim was to 'come as near them as possible'. The reformers however could and did make use of the English connection where this served their purpose: in the light of the Mansfield decision which had outlawed negro slavery throughout Britain and not only in England, it was argued that the survival of a form of slavery in Scotland was inconsistent with a united kingdom.

The root cause of the problem for the coal trade however was not the over-issue of paper currency but the institution of a form of slavery in the Scottish coalfields. To this the reformers had two main objections: the first, following Millar, was that the system raised the price of labour as workers demanded an 'additional premium' in return for their bondage; the second was that the system was 'contrary to reason & common sense'. One aspect of this was the self-delusion of the coalmaster, 'pleased with the Sound that his Coalliers are his Slaves', but who failed to recognise that the 'Slaves dupe their Master & make him pay double & triple for such labour as may be performed by a free man'. More important, in practice the system of life-binding was absurd and contradictory, with little or no foundation in law. As has been noted above, legal constraints had become more onerous during the 1760s. The system was damaging not only to the interests of individual coalmasters but also to those of the community at large and to the 'Trade Commerce & Manufactories of the Country'.

The older idea that there was a humanitarian dimension to the legal changes of 1775 has been strongly denied. This conclusion may have to be modified. The language of liberty is to be found in the letters of some of the reformers who were certain that no matter how lukewarm the response to their proposals might be in Scotland, a British Parliament was likely to be much more sympathetic to that cause. How sincerely such sentiments were held is impossible to say and there was clearly an element of calculation in some cases. The most active campaigners for change were coalmasters who had few or no bound colliers of their own. It is easy however to be over-cynical. In the letters Walter Scott wrote canvassing support for reform he carefully tailored his appeals to each of the individuals he approached. Even so and despite the prominence of economic arguments there are grounds for believing that Scott's motives were at least partly humanitarian, with one letter for example referring unambiguously to a system of servitude which had been imposed 'upon a set of men, members of the community who have ane Equall right with ourselves to the benefits of living in a free Country'.[46]

The reformers did not achieve their objectives. Radical in its origins, ultimately the Act of 1775 was a conservative measure, a fudge. The coalmasters in Scotland were deeply divided on the issue. As commonly happened when slaves or serfs were emancipated attempts were made to regulate the work and behaviour of those freed, with Scottish colliers being required to train apprentices before they could apply for their freedom, itself a complicated legal procedure.[47] In practical terms little changed. The colliers too replaced one form of servitude for the 'debt slavery', into which many had been slipping beforehand anyway.[48] In the final analysis the reformers' pleas that the good of the community and the nation's commerce should be prime considerations were blunted by the demands of those coalmasters who had established legal rights over their workforces and of others too who were concerned that there would be a haemorrhage of labour out of the industry if the law was suddenly relaxed. It was not until 1799 that the system was finally brought to an end in an Act which was even more concerned than that of 1775 to outlaw collier combinations.

It has been argued that 1799 marked the beginning of the process of proletarianisation of the Scottish colliers. In fact this movement was well under way by the end of the century. However, together the two Acts which ended life-binding in the Scottish coal industry can be seen as marking an important transitional stage in Scotland's march towards modern industrialisation. The debate which began in the early 1770s represented a struggle between the monopolising landed proprietors of established coal mines and an emergent group of capitalist entrepreneurs whose leaders articulated the doctrine of a free labour market. Neither what its opponents called 'pretended Slavery' in Scotland's coal mines, nor the issues which surrounded it, should be considered as an historical side-show. The coal industry played a crucial role in Scottish industrialisation in the later eighteenth and nineteenth centuries. In turn that process owed much to low labour costs. The arguments over the coal workers represent in ideological terms one of the more important landmarks in production relations in Scotland, the physical manifestation of which was the series of employer-worker confrontations which punctuated the 1810s and 1820s and culminated in the defeat of the cotton spinners in 1837.

REFERENCES

1. The author wishes to thank Dr Colin Kidd and Professor W.H. Fraser for their helpful comments and suggestions made during the preparation of this paper.
2. The first of these was R. Houston, 'Coal, class and culture: labour relations in a Scottish mining community, 1650–1750', *Social History*, VIII (1983), pp.1–18.
3. Examples are T.S. Ashton and J. Sykes, *The Coal Industry of the Eighteenth Century* (Manchester, 1929), pp.70–83; R. Page Arnot, *A History of the Scottish Miners* (London, 1955), pp.3–7; M. W. Flinn, *The History of the British Coal Industry, Volume 2, 1700–1830* (Oxford, 1984), pp.358–61.
4. K. Wrightson, 'Kindred adjoining kingdoms: an English perspective on the social and

economic history of early modern Scotland' in R.A. Houston and I. Whyte (eds.), *Scottish Society 1500–1800* (Cambridge, 1989), pp.253–60.

5. P.K. O'Brien, 'Political Preconditions for the Industrial Revolution' in P.K. O'Brien and R. Quinault (eds.), *The Industrial Revolution and British Society* (Cambridge, 1993), pp.129–30.
6. S. Pollard, 'Labour in Great Britain', in P. Mathias and M.M. Postan (eds.), *The Cambridge Economic History of Europe, Vol VII, Part I* (Cambridge, 1978), p.136.
7. M. Bush, 'Introduction', in M.L. Bush (ed.), *Serfdom and Slavery: Studies in Legal Bondage* (London and New York, 1996), p.15.
8. Flinn, *British Coal*, p.358.
9. S.L. Engerman, 'Slavery, serfdom and other forms of coerced labour: similarities and differences', in *Serfdom and Slavery*, p.19; see too I. Wallerstein, *The Modern World-System II. Mercantilism and the Consolidation of the European World-Economy 1600–1750* (London and New York, 1980).
10. B.H. Slicher Van Bath, 'Agriculture in the Vital Revolution', *in Cambridge Economic History of Europe, V, The Economic Origins of Early Modern Europe*, E.E. Rich and C.H. Wilson (eds.) (Cambridge, 1977), p.121; *The Institutions of the Law of Scotland by James, Viscount of Stair, 1693*, D.M. Walker (ed.) (Edinburgh and Glasgow, 1981), p.1013; J.U. Nef, *The Rise of the British Coal Industry* (2 vols, London, 1932), II, pp.157–64.
11. C.A. Whatley, *The Scottish Salt Industry 1570–1850* (Aberdeen, 1987), pp.34–40, 50; Duckham, *Scottish Coal*, p.23.
12. T. Johnston, *A History of the Working Classes in Scotland* (Glasgow, 1929), pp.79–80.
13. H.G. Graham, *The Social Life of Scotland in the Eighteenth Century* (London, 1909 ed.), pp.530–33; T.C. Smout, *A History of the Scottish People, 1580–1830* (London and Glasgow, 1969), pp.182, 433.
14. B.F. Duckham, 'Serfdom in Eighteenth Century Scotland', *History*, LIV, 181 (1969), pp.178–81.
15. For a compelling account see Smout, *Scottish People*, pp.178–83, 430–40; a fuller, more recent study is B.F. Duckham, *A History of the Scottish Coal Industry Vol 1, 1700–1815* (Newton Abbot, 1970), pp.24–61; for saltpan workers see Whatley, *Scottish Salt Industry*, pp.100–101.
16. Whatley, 'New Light', p.11; A. McDouall (Lord Bankton), *An Institute of the Laws of Scotland* (4 vols, Edinburgh, 1751; Stair Society ed. 1993), I, pp.68–9.
17. Whatley, 'Scottish "collier serfs", British coal workers', p.72.
18. Whatley, 'New Light', pp.10–11.
19. Bush, 'Introduction', p.16; Engerman, 'Slavery', p.21. In Scottish saltworks it was the salter assistants, employed and paid by the master salters, who endured the most wretched conditions.
20. A.J.S. Gibson and T.C. Smout, *Prices, food and wages in Scotland 1550–1780* (Cambridge, 1995), pp.281–5, 347–8.
21. Duckham, *Scottish Coal*, p.298; Whatley, '"The fettering bonds of brotherhood": combination and labour relations in the Scottish coal mining industry c.1690–1775', *Social History*, 12, 2 (1987), p.152.
22. Ashton and Sykes, *Coal Industry*, p.77; C.A. Whatley, 'New Light on Nef's Numbers: Coal Mining and the First Phase of Scottish Industrialisation, c.1700–1830', in A.J.G. Cummings and T.M. Devine (eds.), *Industry, Business and Society in Scotland Since 1700* (Edinburgh, 1994), pp.8–9.
23. C.A. Whatley, 'Collier Serfdom in Mid-Eighteenth-Century Scotland: New Light from the Rothes MSS', *Archives*, XXII, 93 (1995), pp.29–30.
24. Whatley, 'The fettering bonds of brotherhood', pp.143–4; D. Levine and K. Wrightson, *The Making of an Industrial Society: Whickham, 1560–1765* (Oxford, 1991), p.398.
25. R.L. Lewis, *Coal, Iron and Slaves: Industrial Slavery in Maryland and Virginia, 1715–1865* (Westport and London, 1979), p.112.
26. For a recent overview see J. Rule, 'Employment and Authority: Masters and Men in

Eighteenth-Century Manufacturing' in P. Griffiths, A. Fox and S. Hindle (eds.), *The Experience of Authority in Early Modern England* (London, 1996), pp.286–94.

27. Scottish Record Office (SRO), Mar and Kellie MSS, GD 124/6/270/19, Thomas Erskine to John Syme, August 1760.
28. Duckham, *Scottish Coal*, pp.248–9; SRO, Buccleuch MSS, GD 224/240/6, Journal of Matthew Little. I am grateful to the Duke of Buccleuch and Queensberry for allowing me to use his papers.
29. R.W. Malcolmson, 'A set of ungovernable people': the Kingswood colliers in the eighteenth century', in J. Brewer and J. Styles (eds.), *An Ungovernable People: The English and Their Law in the Seventeenth and Eighteenth Centuries* (London, 1980), p.124.
30. J. Lucassan, 'The Other Proletarians: Seasonal Labourers, Mercenaries and Miners', *International Review of Social History*, 39, Supplement 2 (1994), pp.171–94.
31. Whatley, 'Scottish "collier serfs", British coal workers', pp.73–5.
32. P. Laslett, 'Scottish weavers, cobblers and miners who bought books in the 1750s', *Local Population Studies Magazine and Newsletter*, 3 (Autumn 1969), pp.7–15; D. Beveridge, *Culross and Tulliallan* (2 vols, Edinburgh and London, 1885), II, p.199.
33. C. Kidd, *Subverting Scotland's Past* (Cambridge, 1993), pp.129–84; D. Stevenson, 'Twilight before night or darkness before dawn? Interpreting seventeenth-century Scotland', in R. Mitchison (ed.), *Why Scottish History Matters?* (Edinburgh, 1991), pp.37–47.
34. Levine and Wrightson, *Industrial Society*, p.276.
35. See Page Arnot, *Scottish Miners*, v-viii, pp.425–7; A. Campbell, *The Lanarkshire Miners: A Social History of their Trade Unions, 1775–1874* (Edinburgh, 1979), pp.12–13.
36. Perth Museum and Art Gallery, Archive 1155, Act of Doom, 1701.
37. Smout, *Scottish People*, p.181.
38. C.A. Whatley, *"That Important and Necessary Article": The Salt Industry and its Trade in Fife and Tayside, c.1570–1850* (Dundee, 1984); R. Douglas, 'Coal-Mining in Fife in the Second Half of the Eighteenth Century', in G.W.S. Barrow (ed.), *The Scottish Tradition: Essays in Honour of R.G. Cant* (Edinburgh, 1974), p.221: 'From the evidence of the level of wages . . . no picture of exploitation emerges.'
39. A.S. Cunningham, *Rambles in the Parishes of Scoonie and Wemyss* (Leven, 1905), 144–7; *Markinch and its Environs* (Leven, 1907), pp.92–4.
40. C.A. Whatley, *The Industrial Revolution in Scotland* (Cambridge, 1997), pp.46–9.
41. D.J. Withrington, 'What was Distinctive about the Scottish Enlightenment?', in . J. Carter and J.H. Pittock (eds.), *Aberdeen and the Enlightenment* (Aberdeen, 1987); J. Robertson, 'The Scottish Enlightenment', *Revista Storica Italiana*, CVIII, II-III (1996), pp.808–29.
42. I. Hont, 'The "rich country-poor country" debate in Scottish classical political economy', in I. Hont and M. Ignatieff (eds.), *Wealth and Virtue: The Shaping of Political Economy in the Scottish Enlightenment* (Cambridge, 1983), pp.271–315.
43. Duckham, *Scottish Coal*, pp.298–9; C.A. Whatley, 'The Finest Place for a Lasting Colliery: Coal Mining Enterprise in Ayrshire, c.1600–1840', *Ayrshire Collections*, 14, 2 (1983), pp.86–9.
44. SRO, CS 238/S/10/9, Walter Scott v. James Dewar, 1781, George Glasgow to Walter Scott, 2 March 1774.
45. SRO, CS 238/S/10/9, Glasgow to Scott, 21 February 1774.
46. SRO, CS 238/S/10/9, Copy letter, Walter Scott to (?), 19 March 1774.
47. Engerman, 'Slavery', p.39; see too Duckham, *Scottish Coal*, p.301.
48. Campbell, *Lanarkshire Miners*, p.13.

Seventeen

Scottish Radicalism in the Later Eighteenth Century: 'The Social Thistle and Shamrock'[1]

ELAINE W. MCFARLAND

THE OUTWARD-LOOKING and internationalist spirit of radical political activity which was so much a poetic commonplace in the 1790s has traditionally been assigned a lower status in modern historical scholarship. Just as the dawn of international brotherhood was to be swamped by heightened national consciousness and, as Linda Colley has memorably argued, mass allegiance to a British national identity, political historians have too often adopted an introverted and isolationist stance on early democratic movements and insurrectionary threats. It has taken the pioneering work of, for example Arthur Goodwin and Marianne Elliott to place these movements in their full European context.[2] This chapter aims to extend a similar 'internationalist' paradigm to the case of Scotland. More specifically, it considers the alliance forged by Scottish and Irish radicals in the Society of United Irishmen in the closing decade of the eighteenth century.[3]

The project then is a 'revisionist' one. Indeed, it is doubly revisionist. It aims to reconstruct not only perceptions of the radical movement in Scotland, but also the nature of the Irish presence in Scottish political life. Whereas Irish migration has commonly been identified with the experiences of demographic disaster, poverty and famine among the Catholic population, this study introduces an earlier, political dimension to population movement and highlights the forced exile of both Catholics *and* Protestants; in the Scotland of the 1790s, Irishness was by no means coterminous with Catholicism. Nor can the contribution of these migrants to the development of progressive politics be read simply as the impact of an external agency on a pristine, native body of doctrine and practice What John McCaffrey has suggested for the 1830s and beyond perhaps holds best for the late eighteenth century: Irish issues and personnel were intrinsic to the formation of a new radical tradition in Scotland, amidst the emergence of similarly novel social, economic and political forces.[4]

Focusing on the intertwining of Irish and Scottish democratic politics also assists in re-assessing the nature of the radical challenge in Scotland. Both movements shared a similar dynamism, feeding on a volatile international situation which tested existing domestic mechanisms of political and military control. It was through the medium of their Irish alliance that the Scots were brought into the orbit of the wider European revolutionary movement and offered the entrancing prospect of external aid for their cause. This may explain why, after repeated reversals in fortune, a determined minority were prepared to persist in their struggle. It also renders more comprehensible the nervousness of Scotland's ruling elite.

Yet the Irish alliance can also be held as a mirror to the inherent limitations of Scottish radicalism. The self-confident sweep of the Irish movement was attractive to the Scots largely due to consciousness of their own weakness and the more restricted terrain for large scale democratic mobilisation in Scotland. The strategy of mutual assistance imposed its own costs, quickly engaging the attentions of the uniquely repressive Scottish legal system. Ultimately indeed, Irish inspiration was to prove problematic when sensitivity to Scottish conditions was lacking, with the dream of international brotherhood dissipating amid undignified squabbles over resources.

To explore these themes of stimulus and conflict, our starting point is the intellectual and political antecedents of the alliance. We will then trace its organisational expression from the era of constitutional protest to the emergence of a revolutionary underground in the later 1790s, concluding with a discussion of the impact of the 1798 United Irishmen's Rebellion on the development of Scottish radicalism.

Early Bridges

Far from pursuing separate, hermetically sealed pathways of development, the Irish and Scottish traditions of radical thought were from the outset historically rooted in complex patterns of reciprocal contact between the two countries. Already, the seventeenth century had seen the importation into Ulster of a radical Scottish Covenanting tradition which entwined religious and political dissent.[5] The potential for sustained intellectual exchange was further enhanced in the next century by the development of the educational and commercial network binding the north east of Ireland and west lowland Scotland, and by the expanding web of kin and friendship links between the two Presbyterian societies.

Above all, from the 1720s it was the Scottish Universities which were to provide the most formative and direct influence on Irish radicalism's intellectual development, schooling the Presbyterian middle classes who were to form the United Irishmen's leadership. Effectively barred from higher education in Ireland, Presbyterians were attracted to these institutions by their growing reputation for dispensing a 'useful' education. Here, amid the quickening intellectual climate of eighteenth century Scotland, they were exposed to a potent fusion of earlier radical Presbyterian ideas with the broader current of European Enlightenment thought.[6]

A pivotal figure in this process was Francis Hutcheson, Professor of Moral Philosophy at the University of Glasgow form 1729 to 1746.[7] Hutcheson's life, thirty years spent in Ireland and twenty two in Scotland was itself testament to the two societies' material and cultural interchange. His political thought also united Covenanting, Real Whig and 'New Light' Presbyterian themes and displayed a radicalism which greatly outweighed that of his academic successors Adam Smith and John Robertson.

Among Hutcheson's key convictions were the unalienable right of freedom of opinion and religious tolerance, and an insistence on the right to resistance against tyranny which developed the conception of the contractual relationship between ruler and ruled beyond Locke's original formulation. For Hutcheson this trust was broken if the potential 'utility' of civil society was not realised and government no longer served the public good. In these circumstances, political rebellion might be preferrable to continued subjection. These were ideas which maintained their vitality despite Hutcheson's early death, being passed down from one generation of thinkers and educationalists to the next. Their potency derived not only from the clarity of Hutcheson's own exposition, but from their applicability to real problems in a variety of contexts from colonial America to radical Ulster. In the case of Ulster Presbyterians, receptiveness was bolstered by their sense of apartness, as a distinct community excluded from the full range of political rights and civil liberties. Rapidly they embraced 'the Scotch ideas' and gave them their own distinct articulation in the form of 'the Belfast Principle', a liberal and rational brand of enlightened Presbyterianism.

The manner in which the Scottish intellectual legacy became welded to the Irish situation at once underlines the extent to which the two societies were marked by contrasts as well as correspondences. Between the two strands of this legacy, Presbyterianism and Enlightenment existed an essential contradiction. For running against the expansive universalism of Enlightenment thought was an older exclusiveness, rooted in Calvinism and displayed most trenchantly in opposition to Roman Catholicism.[8] In the case of Ulster this exclusivism had the potential to become a dynamic force. This was partly through the alienation of the Presbyterian community from the structures of authority, which cast them easily in the role of a persecuted elite, 'a people among the nations', but also drew on a senisitive sectarian balance, particularly in the border counties. The presence of a significant Catholic population thus gave anti-Popery the practical focus it lacked in eighteenth-century Scotland. In short, liberal ideals of tolerance and fears of Catholic domination could easily coexist within Irish radicalism, both tendencies drawing on Scottish intellectual legacy. This was a point which the United Irishmen struggled to grasp as they attempted to give their 'Brotherhood of Affection' a practical expression.

While 'the Scotch ideas' continued to flourish in Ireland, a decisive shift was also taking place in the relationship between radical thinkers in the two societies. Whereas for much of the eighteenth century it had been the Irish who had looked to Scotland for liberal inspiration, by the 1790s, it was increasingly Scottish democrats who now viewed 'the Sister Isle' as an encouraging example. The explanation for this is to be found in the immediate political antecedents of the radical alliance.

Essentially, the economic strains of Ireland's colonial status and the uncertainty of Anglo-Irish constitutional relations which were exposed in recurrent crises in the late eighteenth century meant that political protest activity in Ireland was more vigorous and mature than in Scotland, where the social and political hegemony of the landed elite carried more decisive weight. In the former case, both rural unrest and extra-parliamentary activity by the middle class had been steadily gaining momentum from mid-century. Already by the 1780s, amid the repercussions of the American War and the associated imperial crisis, traditional mechanisms of control were being tested as literate public opinion grew more estranged from existing parliamentary institutions.

The most tangible product of this process was the Volunteers movement. Formed in 1778, as an ad hoc response to the haphazard nature of Ireland's defence arrangements, their contribution to Irish politics far outweighed their military value. Within two years they had become a gentry-led mass movement, with a substantial Protestant middle class and artisan component. Their central aim was the restoration of legislative rights of the Irish parliament and to this end they employed a highly public campaign of reviews and assemblies. This pressure apparently achieved striking success as reform measures were rapidly put in motion. Even though the new parliament fell short of expectations, the Volunteers' political triumph had an electric effect on the psychology of the 'Protestant nation', building confidence in their ability to use peaceful mass mobilisation to outflank orthodox constitutional channels.

In contrast, the heady days of the 1780s had little equal in Scotland. Here, while movements for county and burgh reform, like the Volunteers, drew strength from the ambitions of the rising bourgeoisie, their aims and vision were altogether more limited and pragmatic. Absent were the great 'theoretical' or constitutional issues which had captured the popular imagination in Ireland. For absent too were the economic distortions caused by unequal linkage into the imperial system. Instead Scotland was increasingly enjoying the fruits of parliamentary union, her rulers' 'negotiated compromise' having sacrificed formal independence for practical power and material advance.

These differing circumstances were to structure the future of democratic politics in the two countries, and also conditioned attitudes towards the construction of a radical alliance. The experience of Volunteering, for example, was vital to the political education of a generation. Even when the movement was eventually forced into a humiliating climbdown over parliamentary reform, split over the issue of Roman Catholic emancipation, this merely illustrated for younger radicals the limits of open middle class protest and pointed the way to new ideas and methods.

Yet the very precocity of public protest in Ireland could also be problematic, breeding a sense of superiority over those, like the Scots, who could not boast such advanced positions as themselves.[9] Such condescension, however, overlooked the contradictions and longstanding sectarian tensions which still beset their own movement: Scottish democrats might have been less 'advanced', but they were also less prone to sectarian polarisation. There was a further risk attaching to boundless Irish confidence which was to be realised in the next decade at some cost to both movements. This was that the Irish would advocate actions, such as the linking of political radicalism with nascent nationalism which were more suitable to their own situation than to that of the Scots.

Building the Alliance: 1791–2

Notwithstanding its impeccable intellectual pedigree, the immediate context for the linkage of Scottish and Irish radicalism was formed by the international dislocation which followed the French Revolution. Throughout Europe, Carlyle's 'death-birth of a world' swelled the tide of progressive optimism as radicals put their faith in the power of reason to shake the old order. In Ireland and Scotland the impact of the Revolution was also shaped by their own unique historical situations. Irish enthusiasm, for example, must be set against the background of the previous decade's constitutional struggle and debate. With already heightened expectations, reformers now placed their efforts in the context of a European-wide conflict against tyranny and obscurantism. Believing that the French had already achieved their own ultimate goal of rationalising and modernising the political process, the Irish now firmly attached their movement, not simply to an enlightened ideal, but to the fortunes of a real and rapidly developing regime.[10]

In Scotland, however, the events of the Revolution were received in a nation where political debate remained relatively underdeveloped. Here the response of middle class democrats was warm, but restrained, with less active attempts to link native grievances to French achievements.[11] This caution, however, was ill-matched by the vigour and immediacy of popular protest. The new political overtones of the riots which hit Scottish towns during the early summer of 1792 convinced government representatives that the traditional displays of discontent, which had operated within a shared ideological framework, were fusing into something incomprehensible and threatening.[12] Already Scottish politics were becoming marked not only by bitter polarisation between reformers and supporters of the established order, but also by divergent hopes and aims amongst the broad spectrum of those favourable to change.

Bound up in the process of political polarisation was another by-product of the French Revolution: the channelling of discontent into the form of advanced reform clubs and societies. Of these the Scottish Friends of the People and the Society of United Irishmen were to be of the greatest historical significance for the development of democratic linkages between Ireland and Scotland. Reflecting the intellectual ferment of the times, both were rather amorphous groups. They shared a similar social and ideological profile as cross-class movements, more interested in the political dimensions of reform than the development of any meaningful social and economic blueprints. Yet, the detailed circumstances of their birth and their subsequent strategies and tactics again reflected specific local circumstances.

The origins of the United Irishmen lay in the impatience of Ulster Presbyterian radicals with the tameness and temporising of existing movements for reform. Amid a climate of drift during September 1791, advanced reformers William Drennan and Wolfe Tone evolved plans for a streamlined and committed fraternal association which would act as a focus for progressive opinion and a bridge for the reconciliation of Protestant and Catholic. The growing momentum of the United Irishmen as an intellectual and political powerhouse over the next year further reduced the need to conciliate more moderate reformers. Timid spirits thus stayed adrift from the new movement, which nevertheless proved adept at utilising existing channels of popular opinion, such as the Volunteers, for its own ends.

The Scottish Friends of the People could only envy the United Irishmen's status as a vanguard organisation. From the outset, their own modest aim was not to short-circuit established movements like the Burgh Reformers, but to bind them in a comprehensive national campaign for political rights. The vital effect of this national objective was that the new organisation was kept firmly on the path of self-conscious restraint, without actually achieving its goal, as the Burgh Reform movement continued to resist their advances. Meanwhile, the involvement of individual Whiggish reformers, like Lord Daer, meant a mutually abrasive alliance between moderates and radicals, united on the need to reform the existing political system, but at odds over the extent of reform required and the methods to be used to attain it.

For all these contrasts, it was hardly surprising that the paths of the United Irishmen and the Friends of the People were destined to cross. They shared after all an important first precept in the efficacy of enlightened public opinion brought constitutionally to bear on government. It was also testament to the small and intensely personal world of radical politics in the 1790s that contact between individual members of the societies began within weeks of the Scottish group's inception on 26 July 1792.[13] After the fashion of the day, these links were soon translated into formal 'correspondence'.[14]

For the authorities the logic of this process was clear from the outset. Radicals had engaged not only in a common cause, but a revolutionary conspiracy to destroy the existing constitution.[15] In fact, the alliance was never purely instrumental, but instead emerged from a confused mixture of idealistic *and* practical motives. The idealism drew strength from the new spirit of international fraternity which accompanied the Revolution in France. Typically, this was most pronounced in Irish radicals who had already reached out to reform movements on the mainland in the 1780s.[16] The older ideological and cultural exchange between Scotland and Ulster was also cited as high-minded rationale for a common front permitting the Belfast United Irishmen judiciously to invoke, 'the solemn ties of religion and blood [with] which many of us are connected with you'.[17]

More pragmatically, the establishment of an efficient and coordinated national movement was one of the characteristics of the 'ordering' of middle class protest in the late eighteenth century.[18] The extension of this principle to encompass reformers across the three British kingdoms was therefore not an aberration. Cross-border contact between radicals promoted an awareness that they were not campaigning in a vacuum, with the flood of solemn fraternal greetings, resolutions and correspondence playing an important psychological role in bolstering a shared sense of grievance and purpose. The radical press similarly promoted mutual awareness. Through the medium of newspapers like Belfast's *Northern Star* or Edinburgh's *Gazetteer* news of the progress of the other's cause became directly available. The latter's inaugural edition in November 1792, for example, featured a lengthy analysis of the Irish political situation in which Scottish readers were promised that the country, before a few months elapsed, might boast 'a free, not mercenary army of 10,000 volunteer citizens'.[19] Here, in the splendid public displays of the newly resurgent Volunteers is the most simple key to Irish radicalism's attraction, namely its reservoir of optimistic energy.

'A Civic Union': 1792–4

The first public contact between the United Irishmen and the Scottish Friends of the People came with an address 'To the Delegates Promoting a Reform in Scotland', sent to be read at the latter's first national convention in December 1792.[20] On the one hand, this is an excellent example of the Irish radicals providing fraternal assistance to the Scots who were struggling to consolidate their own fledgling organisation. Yet, the 'Scotch letter' also highlighted the tensions in the radical alliance which stemmed from gaps in the two movements' political experience.

Its author, the poet William Drennan, considered the address, which ran to almost 3000 words of flamboyant prose, as a literary exercise as much as a political statement. It began innocuously enough, hailing the Scottish reformers in a spirit of 'civic union' and recommending friendly competition to see who could be first to win a free constitution.[21] The difficulty stemmed, however, from the rest of its contents. First, its excitable 'nationalistic' tone, particularly evidenced in Drennan's trust of the regenerative powers of a union of the Irish people, seriously discomfited Whiggish delegates who considered that it contained 'high treason against the union betwixt England and Scotland'.[22] Although the United Irishmen were still far from republican nationalists, the constitutional uncertainty of the 1780s had made them readier to question existing constitutional arrangements than the Scots, whose literary patriotism had failed to kindle similar demands for the renegotiation of national rights. Second, moderates were concerned that the greater formal linkage between the Scottish and Irish reform campaigns which the Address advocated, might restrict freedom of action. This was reinforced by Drennan's references to sovereign assemblies of the people over-riding parliament, which seemed to confirm the United Irishmen's growing reputation for dangerous extremism.

Even more decisive for the fate of the address than accumulated levels of tactical and ideological development, were the current political situations of each country. While the United Irishmen hoped that the uplifting sentiments of the address would encourage the Scots to adopt bolder postitions, the piece was as much for an Irish audience.[23] In fact, it was one of several productions by a clique of Dublin-based radicals who wished the United Irishmen to function as an elite pressure group which would throw out public challenges to government. The difficulty in exporting this approach remained that, whereas Ireland was reaching a crescendo of optimism, in Scotland the situation for radicals in December 1792 was an extremely sensitive one.

For more restless spirits in the Scottish reform movement, such as Thomas Muir, the main promoter of the Irish Address in Scotland, the role of the first Friends of the People Convention was to electrify the process of reform, possibly learning from the example of the Irish Volunteers' assemblies.[24] For Whiggish moderates, the Convention was intended to produce a restrained and coordinated national policy. In the event, both interpretations were overtaken by external events. The radicalisation of the Revolution in France towards the end of the year, when coupled with continuing popular unrest at home prompted the Scottish authorities to harness the nervous energy of Scotland's propertied classes. To this end they employed the emergent arts of propaganda, including a flood of loyal addresses and a subsidised press.[25] This onslaught in turn seriously jeopardised any attempt to link up with the Burgh Reformers leaving the refutation of loyalist charges of treachery as the most pressing task for the Convention.

Accordingly, when the Irish Address was introduced to the assembly by Muir it provoked two days of bitter dispute among delegates whose internal divisions were becoming uncomfortably public. Despite a vocal minority, it was agreed that its content was too extreme for Scottish latitudes and the 'elegant piece of declaration' was returned to its author.[26] Yet, this was far from the end of its impact on the Scottish democratic movement, for the refusal of a public reading did nothing to stem the loyalist backlash. On the contrary, the offensive intensified with the outbreak of war with Revolutionary France in February 1793. The government proved as sensitive as the radicals to the tide of international events, as declarations of 'universal brotherhood' became synonymous with treasonable activity.

The gentlemen reformers presented tempting targets. Foremost among them, given his unabashed radicalism and organisational role in the Friends of the People, was Thomas Muir. His championing of the Irish Address also gave the authorities a perfect judicial weapon. Arrested after a peregrination through London, Paris and Dublin where he became personally acquainted with the United Irish leaders, he was tried in August 1793 for Sedition. Still glorying in Drennan's words and defending the the United Irishmen from the dock, he himself provided the collateral evidence for his prosecution. 'The Sidney of his Age' was sentenced to fourteen years transportation, ardently reassuring his new United Irish friends that 'the cause of truth and freedom derives strength from persecution'.[27]

Muir's trial was emblematic of the colder climate developing for radical politics in 1793. Ominous also was the government's determined passage in July of a Convention Bill for Ireland aimed at outlawing public assemblies and thus stopping the whole Irish tradition of extra-parliamentary protest in its tracks. Now the 'Just and Common Cause' between fellow radicals was no longer a pious article of internationalist faith, but a strategic necessity. After the failure of polite petitioning, more formal organisational links began to be forged not only with the Irish, but also with English radical societies. This latest phase of regrouping was assisted by the defection of the more circumspect radical leaders in Scotland. Now, both the broad example of Irish radical politics and the personal intervention of individual United Irishmen could flourish as defensive solidarity became accepted as a political necessity.

In the forefront of this new collective spirit was the British Convention, an assembly of delegates from the three kingdoms, projected for October 1793 to press home the full democratic agenda of universal suffrage and annual parliaments. Its proceedings were at once defiant and confrontationalist, signalled in the reading of a new 'Irish Address' from the Belfast United Irish societies, without the drama and debate which had surrounded its predecessor. More vigorous and assertive than even Drennan's piece, it trumpeted the United Irishmen's cosmopolitan vision, while hailing 'the vivid glow of patriotism which brightens the face of other nations'.[28]

A further fraternal gesture was the arrival of leading United Irishmen, Hamilton Rowan and Simon Butler in Edinburgh. In a bizarre episode Rowan had come to challenge the Lord Advocate, Robert Dundas to a duel over remarks made at Muir's trial. This was a very literal expression of the Dublin radicals' desire to provoke the authorities at every possible opportunity, and again it illustrated contrast in spirit and tone between the Irish and Scottish movements. Nevertheless, Irish intervention at this critical juncture had also a more positive impact. First, as the Convention reconvened in December with English delegates present, Rowan and Butler were able to present a chilling picture of the attack on democratic rights in Ireland by means of the Convention Act. This bolstered Scottish radicals in their conviction that their own assembly should function as a bulwark against any similar encroachments on the mainland. Second, perceptions of the united front of reaction which faced reformers again reinforced the need for closer correspondence and a concerted response. A committee was therefore established to draw up a plan of general union between the Scottish and English movements. The United Irishmen were also drawn in, as co-architects of the democratic alliance, and the Convention resolved that, 'all or any of the patriotic members of the United Irish Society of Dublin shall be admitted to speak and vote in this Convention'.[29]

The contrast with the timidity of the previous year was now complete. The United Irishmen, particularly their most radical elements, were heartened by the progress made since the First Friends of the People Convention, and moved quickly to consolidate this new closeness by making delegates of the British Convention and constituent assemblies full members of their own Society.[30]

Their high spirits were quashed almost immediately by a renewed government counter-offensive which embraced Britain and Ireland, and thus confirmed radical apprehensions of a coordinated government strike. Its effects were felt most severely in Scotland where the Convention was forcibly dispersed on 6 December. This reverse caused disagreement in United Irish ranks, but just as their leaders began to criticise the Scots for their pusillanimity, the official campaign turned against their own organisation. After a wave of arrests they were cowed and dispersed. The loss of direction which followed was described by Robert Emmet: 'The expectations of the reformers had been blasted. Their plans had been defeated . . . It therefore became necessary to wait on events, from which might be formed new plans'.[31]

The government had predictably failed to recognise the Scottish and Irish reformers' initial quest for order and legality, and by 1794 each side was fuelling the other's sense of crisis. Talk of the secret passage of material between Ulster and Scotland already hinted at what the radicals' 'new plans' might hold.[32] The future of their cause now lay in the hands of a developing revolutionary underground; the era of polite constitutional pressure had drawn to a close.

'Planting Irish Potatoes': 1795–8

While the personal champions of the radical alliance languished in exile or imprisonment by 1795, the alliance itself continued to advance. Not only had the experiences of the early part of the decade undermined deferential positions, they had also impressed upon democrats in the three kingdoms the need for a unified approach against a common enemy. Now this strategy gained a further practical impetus both from heightened government repression and from the French Republic's switch onto the military offensive from the end of 1794; the latter in turn implied the prospect of material assistance for their cause.

The connection between the Scottish and Irish movements was thus to be transformed by the parallel escalation of domestic and international crises as the decade progressed. Led by the Irish, both remodelled themselves in the form of oath-bound conspiracies, the burden of the new tactics being borne not by charismatic figures, such as Muir and Rowan, but by the anonymous 'disaffected'. As the social basis of radicalism shifted, so did the geographical axis of contact, Belfast-Glasgow replacing Dublin-Edinburgh. Even the language of association took on a less elegant turn, as 'civic union' gave way to the 'the planting of Irish potatoes', as the introduction of Irish underground methods was impudently known.[33]

The United Irishmen's links with Scotland were now only one part of a determined attempt to extend their new conspiratorial system and insurrectionary strategy throughout Ireland and onto the British mainland. The shift underground was probably a less dramatic and more uneven departure than was formerly believed, but took place with striking success once alternative options were finally closed off and the policy of official coercion became unambiguous.[34] This was in turn the product of the consolidation of loyalist opinion among the upper ranks of Irish Protestant society, a process accomplished later than in Scotland, but attended with much greater violence. By the early summer of 1795, the United Irishmen had established a vigorous new profile as a mass revolutionary movement, expanding numerically and geographically by means of an enthusiastic membership drive among the Protestant and Presbyterian lower orders and an alliance with the Defenders, an underground Catholic organisation.[35]

Very rapidly, Scotland was drawn into the United Irishmen's expansionary mission. After a false start in 1795, when the Belfast leadership drew back at the last moment from sending an undercover agent, missionising developed in two phases during 1796 and 1797, each fuelled by an escalation in government repression.[36] As an early object of concern, missionising efforts in Scotland were simultaneous with similar attempts in Connaught and Munster. This may reflect social as much as geographical proximity, with Scottish radicals forming a more familiar cultural and confessional reference point for the Belfast men than the Catholic Defender bands in the south of their own country. The old battlecry of radical solidarity was thus resurrected, and in July 1796 two Belfast delegates were despatched 'with new Irish constitutions for the inspection and approbation of the Scots'.[37] They returned in great enthusiasm, but subsequent deputations conveyed a more lukewarm and condescending impression of 'spirit', tempered by a poor numerical and organisational presence.[38]

By 1797 the context for missionising had further altered. A narrowly averted French landing at Bantry Bay at the end of the previous year led to a new government offensive; this concentrated on Ulster and withered the United Irish organisation there by arrests and forcible disarming. In these desperate circumstances, active missionising gave the Ulster committees an outlet for their restless energy which the passivity of the Dublin leadership denied them. Not only did external contact raise their morale during a period of enforced inactivity at home, it was also considered useful in negotiations for French support, if the prospect of a diversionary landing on the mainland could be held out.

In their discreet attempt to extend their system to Scotland the Ulster men had a number of advantages. They were, for example, well-versed in popular prosletysing work and were assisted by the fluid communications network between Ulster and Scotland. Regular migration flows of students and seasonal labour provided a cloak for the movement of agents.[39] The developing trend of permanent settlement in Scotland had also led to the growth of a number of Ulster migrant communities in centres such as Maybole which could serve as operational bases for underground activity.[40] Indeed the Irish authorities' policy of targeted coercion ensured that during 1797 the tide of migration became a flood.[41] Some of the new arrivals were motivated by the generally unsettled state of their home province and by economic imperatives, while for others these considerations were reinforced by the need to escape actual persecution. These developments were vital for the fortunes of the United system in Scotland. Now the Belfast committees were no longer reliant on financing agents to propagate their tactics, but also could draw on the spontaneous testimony of refugees who had witnessed the military offensive in Ulster at first hand.

The subversive potential of this population movement was firmly grasped by the Scottish authorities. Although they faced less of a domestic challenge than their Irish neighbours, fears of 'contagion' were to heavily influence their calculations. The security measures which resulted were tantamount to an ad hoc refugee policy, but still remained insufficient to counter the rate of arrivals; in areas such as Wigtown bodies of well over a hundred men could arrive daily, slipping away into the western counties.[42]

Irish missionising, however, was not directed at a completely barren landscape, for democratic aspirations had endured in a submerged form after the British Convention.[43] Indeed, Scottish radicalism was apparently well-placed in organisational terms to make the transition into an effective political underground. For all its weaknesses, the Scottish Association of the Friends of the People in Scotland had developed a centrally coordinated nationwide framework of clubs, which compared favourably with the diffuse pattern of metropolitan and provincial societies in England. In ideological terms, the common Presbyterian legacy of independent thought also suggested a closer approximation with conditions in Ulster.

Yet, these initial advantages did not guarantee success. Again the trajectories of Scottish and Irish radicalism were set to diverge – to an even greater extent than in the era of high-profile propagandising. A key feature was the slower shift to more desperate tactics in Scotland, but even more significant was the failure of the new covert tactics to secure for itself a mass social base. The shadowy new organisation of which government intelligence became slowly aware in the course of 1797 was the United Scotsmen. Roughly handled in subsequent historical debate, their strengths and weaknesses can best be grasped by treating them in their own terms and giving full attention to their external linkages.

The Irish contribution to the development of the United Scotsmen can be seen most clearly in the latter's formal structure. The Lord Advocate was correct when he stressed 'how exactly', down to the wording of tests and resolutions, they had copied United Irish proceedings.[44] Their efforts marked a conscious remoulding of Scottish radicalism in the Irish image, In ideological terms too, there was a fairly close correspondence. Much was made by United Scotsmen, like George Mealmaker, of the lawful right of resistance against an unjust regime, a constant in United Irish calculations, although contempt for parliamentary institutions and the pursuit of nationalist aims were less evident in the Scottish case.

More problematic is the extent of Irish involvement in the actual promotion of the United Scotsmen. Government sources on which the historian is forced to rely suggest that Irish involvement was considerable. The official account reveals a clear pattern of geographical diffusion: Glasgow and Ayrshire were the first strongholds by the Spring of 1797, from which the system was spread by 'emissaries' to Renfrew, Dumbarton, Fife and Perth during the Summer.[45] Distinctive Irish recruitment methods can also be identified. Radical principles, for example, were popularised through the medium of songs and ballads, and Freemasons' lodges employed as cover for underground activities.[46]

Yet, Scottish radical activity was never simply subsumed into the Irish organisation. In the first place, Irish missionising was not the sum total of external influences on the Scots, for independent links with the English societies had also survived from the days of the British Convention.[47] It would also seem that democratic politics in Scotland possessed a greater internal dynamic than elsewhere on the British mainland. The United Scotsmen drew on the same occupational groups who had formed the local rank and file of the Friends of the People.[48] Indeed, it has been suggested that the prime function of the new organisation was, 'to keep alive these groups' experience of political activity gained in the 1790s'.[49] If this was the case United Irish activity had its own galvanising role in the process, offering a systematic new method of organising radical activity and disseminating ideas. The local remnants of the Friends of the People societies were thus given a new direction and a sense of belonging to the wider world of radicalism.

Nor did this involve Irish agents 'inoculating' passive recipients with subversive ideas, as the authorities supposed. For these ideas to succeed they had to be credible to their intended audience. The advantage enjoyed by 'the emissaries of sedition' by 1797 was that popular experiences of economic crisis and a series of British military reverses were combining to create a receptive audience for the United message.[50] Yet it is here, in the interaction of the United Scotsmen with the broader dimensions of popular discontent and in their attempt to construct a mass movement on the Irish model, that the chronic limitations of the Scottish context become clear.

The most instructive comparison is the case of the Militia Riots. These had swept Ireland in 1793 and their outbreak in Scotland in 1797 appeared to give a direct boost to United Scottish activity. The contours of resistance to the imposition of a conscripted militia broadly corresponded in both countries. Protest was widespread and participants' grievances similar. The most dramatic contrast lay in the degree of violence which attended the protests. The Irish riots were distinguished by the brutal force used to suppress them and the willingness of mass formations of rioters to open fire in response. The casualties which resulted were five times greater that those incurred in the previous thirty years' agrarian disturbances, and indicative not only of the deep pre-existing fissures in Irish society, but also of the growing alienation between the lower class Catholics and the Irish ascendancy. Signifying the final bankruptcy of the Irish 'moral economy', the 1793 riots, Bartlett argues, 'helped create the atmosphere of fear and repression that made the 1798 Rebellion possible and some sort of '98 inevitable'.[51]

While for some of its representatives, government in Scotland was undergoing a similar crisis of hegemony, official nervousness should not divert attention from the greater resources of political stability and social and religious homogeneity at the authorities' disposal. This permitted a more subtle and effective strategy than in Ireland, in which military intervention was combined with active attempts to explain and win acceptance for the new militia provisions.[52]

For all the greater flexibility of power relationships in Scotland, the wave of popular unrest in 1797 did have a political dimension in certain areas and suggested a degree of frustration developing between ruler and ruled. This gave the United Scotsmen an entry point to integrate popular grievances into a wider political programme. These tactics may have helped the diffusion of the society into rural areas, but to put this in perspective, the United Scotsmen even at their height probably never attracted more than a few thousand members, active and nominal. For all activists' efforts, the participants in the Scottish militia riots were not an alienated and brutalised population, ready to rise, nor were the comparative leniency of official counter-measures ideal material for a new campaign of mass politicisation. By the end of the year, even those background factors which had favoured the United Scotsmen were dissipating and the government net closed in on Mealmaker and his comrades.

In short, while United Irish assistance could offer Scottish radicalism new organisational models, what it did not provide was a mass social base. More than this, as in the early 1790s, external linkages conferred problems as well as benefits.

The Scots were clearly still junior partners in the radical alliance, apparently without even the resources to send reciprocal delegates to Ireland.[53] Like the Friends of the People, the United Scotsmen looked to the greater political experience of the Irish and the inspiring example of a mass movement in the making. Evidence at Mealmaker's trial, for example, revealed that agents had imprudently carried with them copies of the government's own 1797 report on the United Irishmen, which revealed 100,000 men in the field in Ulster alone.[54] However, as repression in the province intensified, this identification could be problematic. With Scottish radicals already more isolated by their lack of numbers, news of the hanging of United Irish activists confirmed earlier worries over the shift to their new oath-bound format. Now, some members regretted ever becoming involved with 'the dangerous business, since matters were going on ill in Ireland and attended with bad consequences there'.[55]

The dilemma remained whether there was any real alternative to the secrecy of the United system, for as well as promoting a more cohesive structure, the Irish alliance also linked the Scots into an international revolutionary movement and even held out the promise of French military aid. This was fast becoming imperative, given the United Scotsmen's obvious failure to attract significant numbers at home, but it was also vital in encouraging a sense of mission which was to sustain the band of radicals in the years of adversity which lay ahead. As with the Irish alliance, however, the French strategy was also a qualified benefit.

One pressing worry was whether the United Scotsmen's weak numerical muscle was enough to raise French interest. Their response was to inflate their paper membership wildly and to increase genuine recruitment by dubious means, often regardless of whether these new members would melt away or turn informer at the first sign of government interest.[56] A second difficulty stemmed from a basic lack of information as to French intentions. It had already been demonstrated in Ireland that this could be enough to dispel the initial optimism raised by international linkages.[57] The position of the Scots was even more frustrating and debilitating, as they did not yet have their own representative to the French Directory, being forced to rely on scraps of second-hand intelligence via the underground network. Third and even more serious was the prospect that any French alliance would antagonise the same popular sentiments in Scotland which the United Scots hoped to mobilise. The French Revolution had boosted popular patriotism and loyalism as well as radicalism; in the Scottish case, patriotic volunteering had attracted higher participation from the population than in England.[58]

Domestic constraints aside, fundamental difficulties arose with the actual mechanics of attracting French support. Scottish radicals now discovered that when military aid was at stake, the United Irishmen's role as mediators between Scotland and France became plagued with contradictions as expediency outpaced international brotherhood. A Scottish dimension was still to be found in Wolfe Tone's early plans to gain French assistance in 1795, but as competition over scarce resources sharpened over the next few years, Tone shifted his position. He was highly sceptical, for example, of the imaginative scheme of the Dutch general Daendels in 1797 to make a direct attempt on Scotland, and approved when United Irish agents suggested that the Scottish patriots 'were not so far advanced' to assist such a hazardous attempt.[59] Admittedly, the position of emissaries like Tone was a delicate one following Ireland's failure to rise after the Bantry Bay expedition. When French interest did revive it became clear that any Irish venture was to be as a component in a general British invasion attempt. For Tone and his colleagues this meant that the *potential* for disaffection in England and Scotland was being given greater weight that the actual mass movement they had constructed in Ireland. They had also to accept that the whole missionising impetus of the Ulster committees might actually have damaged their own cause by directing French resources elsewhere.

Finally these conflicts were given a personal edge in November 1797, with the arrival of Thomas Muir in Paris after a thrilling escape from captivity. In a series of bombastic memorials to the French foreign ministry he attempted to claim leadership of the Scottish *and* Irish peoples for himself.[60] Above all, announced Muir, it was in Scotland that the cause of liberty had advanced and that any French invasion could expect the assistance of '50,000 Scottish Highlanders and 100,000 Scottish patriots in all'.[61]

Conclusion: 'Is Scotland Up?'

Muir's memorials had a woeful grasp of political reality. Like Muir himself, the politics of enthusiasm and bombast had become historical curiosities, overtaken by the quiet disciplined work of professional revolutionaries and by the momentum of popular unrest and government reaction.

As the Scots and Irish emigrés in Paris quarrelled, democrats at home were struggling to reconstruct the revolutionary alliance. The surviving strands of radicalism were to be bound together under a centralised executive and thus given a sense of direction previously lacking. Whether the Scots could be full participants in this project is unclear. They faced increasingly well-informed counter measures, while still struggling to attract mass support. Rumours of invasion had further stimulated popular patriotism and the Volunteers continued to spearhead a loyalist revival in the early months of 1798. Indeed, it is a credit to their dogged optimism that some cells in the old radical centres of Dundee and Perth persisted in their activities. Forced to wait on events, their determination was apparently rewarded by dramatic developments. By June, rebellion in Ireland had at last broken out.

In fact, the 1798 rebellion was to deliver a further deleterious blow to Scottish radicalism. The '98 was a spontaneous and bloody outbreak, far from the controlled contest against the authorities which the United Irishmen had originally envisaged.[62] Lacking in central direction, debilitating internal conflicts opened up over the direction of the coup. The rising thus broke out in an uncoordinated fashion and swiftly degenerated into chaotic sectarian slaughter, eloquent on the depth of the conflict between Catholic and Protestant which the United Irishmen had preferred to wish away. For all the reckless bravery of the rebels, the rebellion was a massive defeat for the United Irishmen. Although the movement and Irish popular disaffection outlived the attempt, the unique moment which had joined domestic pressures to the demands of French military strategy had passed and with it the United Irishmen's best chance of success.

Despite rumours that, 'the people of Scotland were as hostile to government as those in Ireland, and were up in great numbers', active Scottish participation in the '98 was not as radical brothers in arms, but as members of the crown forces engaged in extinguishing all manifestations of rebellion.[63] There is some evidence that a few Scottish democrats were encouraged by the United Irishmen's attempt, which for all its failures had brought thousands more men into the field than they could ever hope for in Scotland.[64] More commonly, however, the defeat in Ireland damaged the United Scotsmen's morale and credibility. Already conscious of their numerical weakness, the Irish rebellion brought home to them what 'revolution' might entail once it shifted from ideal to reality. One lesson was the failure of the French to provide anything beyond rudimentary aid, but even more sobering was the savagery of the conflict and the spectre of sectarian murder which sat uneasily with the messages of universal brotherhood delivered by their Irish allies over the past decade.

In the aftermath of the '98 Rebellion, the remnants of radicalism in Ireland and Scotland were in a confused state, holding even more firmly to that secrecy which had traditionally cloaked their activities.[65] Official links were now overshadowed by the efforts of individual 'enthusiasts', drawing strength from the ever-swelling Irish migration flow and contact thus became more sporadic and haphazard. Still, a leaven of democrats were determined to persist in pursuing the physical force option, no matter how unpromising the opportunities.

The new century, however, also brought significant changes for radicals in Scotland. At last, the extreme economic dislocation which followed the Napoleonic Wars allowed them to exploit increasingly their *own* resources of experience as they struggled to break out of their restricted power base and capture mass support. By no means did this signal the dearth of an outward-looking vision, nor the end of the Irish dimension in the building of a Scottish radical tradition. Both, in fact, were precisely part of that 'experience', accumulated during the previous decade. Although it is the continuing engagement with developments in England, which has understandably tended to absorb historians' attention, the legacy of contact with the Irish 'Sister Kingdom' was also maintained in various respects.[66]

First, the expressions of solidarity and common cause, which had so alarmed the Scottish administration in 1792, were now the common stock of radical activity. The first tangible evidence that links still existed between the disaffected in the two countries appeared in July 1807, when a set of 'Defender' documents, including an oath, constitution and a rambling history of the Society, were discovered in Kilmarnock, a centre for Irish migration from 1798.[67] While this group appear to have been a retrospective phenomenon, still clinging to faith in another French invasion, a more formidable challenge stemmed from the mainstream of Scotland's social and political development with a burst of trade union activity in 1809. In this year a combination had been formed among operative weavers in Glasgow who were in correspondence with different associations in England and Ireland.[68] The latter initiative was understandable, as Ulster was suffering from similar fluctuations in cotton manufactures with half of the factories in the Belfast area idle by 1814.[69] Personal contacts may also have been at work; the operative weavers in the west of Scotland included, in the Lord Advocate's view, 'a considerable body of Irishmen, disposed to riot and tumult', but fortunately kept quiet and peaceable by their native Scots colleagues.[70]

The government's handling of these industrial disputes, including their calculated use of the Combination Acts suggested the approaching end of the paternalism which had characterised Scottish workplace and community relations, and ushered in a new, more sharply antagonistic phase of social conflict. This was also translated into a new burst of sustained political protest in 1816–7, where a second aspect of the Irish legacy can be traced. For while open tactics of mass public meetings and parliamentary reform petitions were initially employed here, as the government remained implacable and economic distress intensified, underground insurrectionary tactics provided an alternative for some radicals. Here, the old United Irish system provided a convenient model, supplemented by a body of experienced personnel who lay ready to hand in the industrial communities of the west of Scotland.

In late 1816, the authorities discovered from their informer, the weaver Andrew Richmond, that secret committees were meeting in the west, drawing in 1812 activists and even survivors from the 1793 Societies.[71] 'The constitution of Masonry and Masonic signs' were employed as security devices, but the need was apparently felt for a more disciplined approach. Accordingly, when delegates from Manchester and Carlisle visited the Glasgow committee, 'copies of the arrangements of the Irish insurgents and of the traitors in Scotland in 1795' were compared, with the Irish blueprint emerging triumphant. Richmond originally reported that this was because it promised 'a regular and disciplined force' to allow the process of arming to commence in earnest, but later suggested that some of the Glasgow leaders also had personal familiarity with the United Irish system, using their prior knowledge to hammer out its detailed implementation.[72] This claim has substance as some of those involved in the new organisation were Ulster migrants; the committee met in the house of the weaver Hugh Dickson, who had left County Tyrone in 1800; his colleague Andrew McKinlay, another weaver, was a native of County Armagh, who had come to Scotland in 1799.[73] Yet, the sectarian dimension of the United Irishmen's Rebellion had left an obvious imprint. On this occasion the old oath was not to be an inclusive 'Bond of Union', for McKinlay decreed that Roman Catholics were not to be allowed into the association, 'because priests had preached against all interference in political matters and auricular confession made the associated afraid that Roman Catholics might be the means of betraying them'.[74]

The continuing involvement of Irish personnel in nascent Scottish political and industrial movements had a final negative effect which the original architects of the radical alliance could scarcely have conceived. This association confirmed earlier perceptions on the part of the host community that all Irishmen were disloyal by definition. For many ordinary Scots the '98 had been 'a real Popish rebellion', while for the authorities the very fact of a growing Irish population in the West of Scotland was considered inherently destabilising.[75] The Irish were thus to be treated as a security problem, whose activity was to be closely monitored, regardless of the diverse political and confession allegiances which, as the McKinlay outburst signalled, had increasingly opened up following the United Irishmen's Rebellion, and which had been transplanted as part of the migration process. Instead, a blanket association of Irish ethnicity with violence and rebelliousness was to persist for much of the century, which even the emergence of a strident Ulster loyalist community could not easily dispel.

REFERENCES

1. The title is taken from 'The Social Thistle and Shamrock', a poem by Henry Joy McCracken, in R.R. Madden, Literary Remains of the United Irishmen of 1798 (Dublin, 1887), p167.

   The Scotch and Irish friendly are,
   Their wishes are the same,
   The English nation envy us,
   And over us would reign.

2. A. Goodwin, *Friends of Liberty* (London, 1979), pp.30–1. For Marianne Elliott's work see, 'The "Despard Conspiracy" Reconsidered', *Past and Present*, 75 (1970), pp.46–61; 'The Origins and Transformation of Early Irish Republicanism', International Review of Social

History, 23, (1977), pp.405–28; *Partners in Revolution* (London, 1982); *Wolfe Tone* (London, 1979).

3. The relationship is examined at length in E.W. McFarland, *Ireland and Scotland in the Age of Revolution* (Edinburgh, 1994).
4. J. McCaffrey, 'Irish Issues in the Nineteenth and Twentieth Century: Radicalism in a Scottish Context?', in T.M. Devine (ed.), *Irish Immigrants in Scottish Society in the Nineteenth and Twentieth Centuries* (Edinburgh, 1990), pp.116–37.
5. A. Loughridge, *The Covenanters in Ireland* (Belfast, 1984).
6. I. Bishop, 'The Education of Scottish Students at Glasgow University during the Eighteenth Century' MA Thesis, The Queen's University of Belfast, 1987; C. Robbins, *The Eighteenth Century Commonwealthman* (New York, 1968), pp.167–266.
7. For a biographical sketch see W. Leechman, 'Some account of the life, writings and character of the author' prefixed to Hutcheson's posthumous, A System of Moral Philosophy (Glasgow, 1775); W.R. Scott, *Francis Hutcheson, his Life, Teaching and Position in the History of Philosophy* (Cambridge, 1900).
8. C. Camic, *Experience and Enlightenment: Socialisation for Cultural Change in Eighteenth-Century Scotland* (Edinburgh, 1983), pp.15–18.
9. As William Drennan commented of the Scottish political scene in the 1780s: 'They have made some attempts at Volunteers in this country, but they are rude and imperfect structures . . . time will show.': W. Drennan-M. M'Tier, September 1982, no.44, T.765, Public Records Office of Northern Ireland (PRONI).
10. R.B. McDowell, *Ireland in the Age of Imperialism and Revolution* (Oxford, 1979), pp.379–89.
11. For examples see, *Caledonian Mercury* 2 September 1790 and 16 July 1791.
12. W. Pitt to H. Dundas 4 July 1792, *Arniston Papers*, Scottish Records Office (SRO).
13. As a government spy reported, who had already ominously penetrated United Irish ranks, a member present reported he had private letters 'from some Scotch delegates lately assembled in Edinburgh who are determined to give up the idea of a partial reform of their burghs and join in demanding a *radical reform* of the whole *representation of the people* . . . . Rebellion Papers 620/19/97, National Archives of Ireland (NAI). It is possible that those who struck up the correspondence were Thomas Muir, Vice President of the Friends of the People Societies in and around Edinburgh and Hamilton Rowan, Secretary of the Dublin Society of United Irishmen: W.H. Drummond (ed.), *Autobiography of Archibald Hamilton Rowan Esquire* (Dublin, 1840), p.170.
14. *Rebellion Papers* 620/19/97, NAI. Contact was also intitiated with the London Friends of the People, *Rebellion Papers* 620/19/100 38; 104, NAI.
15. Report from the Committee of Secrecy of the House of Commons, 1799, p.11.
16. R. Foster, *Modern Ireland* 1600–1972 (Harmondsworth, 1987), p.255.
17. Copy in JC 26/280, SRO.
18. S. Nenadic, 'Political Reform and the 'Ordering ' of Middle Class Protest' in T.M. Devine (ed.), *Conflict and Stability in Scottish Society 1700–1850* (Edinburgh, 1990), pp.65–82.
19. *Edinburgh Gazetteer,* 16 November 1792.
20. Reprinted in *State Trials* xxi.154–60. It was also widely reported in the Irish press: see, *Dublin Evening Post*, 6 December 1792.
21. *Ibid.*
22. William Morthland's original protest to this effect against 'the Irish paper' is in JC26/280, SRO.
23. *Drennan Letters*, M. M'Tier-W. Drennan, 8 December 1792, no.356, T.765, PRONI.
24. J. Brims, 'The Scottish Democratic Movement in the Age of the French Revolution' (Ph.D Thesis, University of Edinburgh, 1983), p.269.
25. *Arniston MSS.* RH4/15/4, SRO.
26. McFarland, *Ireland and Scotland*, pp.87–8.
27. T. Muir-H.R. Rowan, (Second Letter) nd. [1793], *Memoirs*, pp.297–8, MS.24/ K.48, Royal Irish Academy.
28. JC 26/280, SRO.

29. Original of resolution in JC/26/289/31, SRO, see also coverage in *Edinburgh Gazetteer* 3 December 1793
30. *Rebellion Papers* 620/20/78, NAI
31. W. MacNeven, *Pieces of Irish History* (New York, 1807), p.70, quoted in Elliott, *Partners in Revolution* (1982), p.50.
32. *Rebellion Papers* 620/21/27, NAI
33. W. Scott-H.Dundas 22 July 1797,, Melville MSS. GD 51/5/29, SRO.
34. McFarland, *Ireland and Scotland*, pp.132–3.
35. Elliott, 'Early Irish Republicanism' (1977), pp.405–28.
36. The abortive expedition involved the polymath Scottish radical and balloon pioneer, James Tytler: McFarland, *Ireland and Scotland*, pp.405–28.
37. Newell's Report 21 July 1796, HO 100/62/141; *Frazier MSS*. II 23, NAI.
38. *Ibid*.
39. Rebellion Papers 620/35/130 for an example of the cover provided by Ulster students.
40. *Report into the Condition of the Poorer Classes in Ireland*, p.147.
41. Report of the Sheriff of Wigtown, 2 August 1797, RH2/4/80 ff.124 and 140, SRO. From April to June 1797 the Sheriff counted 83 vessels over and above normal traffic. On board were over a thousand passengers.
42. Lord Grenville to Lord Pelham 15 June 1797, *Pelham Papers* 15 June 1797; *Rebellion Papers* 620/31/96.
43. McFarland, *Ireland and Scotland*, p.130.
44. R. Dundas to Duke of Portland 13 January 1798, RH 2/4/83 f.21, SRO.
45. R. Dundas-Duke of Portland 13 January 1798, RH2/4/83 f.21, SRO.
46. W. Scott-H.Dundas 22 July 1797, *Melville MSS*. GD 51/2/29, SRO. For Freemasonry in Ayrshire see JC26/307.
47. R. Dundas-J. King 18 April 1798, RH2/4/83 f.179, SRO.
48. See, *Narrative of the Arrest, Examinaton and Imprisonment of George Mealmaker*, RH2/4/83 ff. 41–9, SRO.
49. C.M.Burns, 'Industrial Labour and Radical Movements in Scotland in the 1790s' (MSc Thesis, University of Strathclyde, 1971), p.205.
50. See *Edinburgh Advertiser* 6–9 June 1797.
51. T. Bartlett, 'An End to the Moral Economy: the Irish Militia Disturbances 1793', *Past and Present*, 99 (1983), p.58.
52. *Glasgow Courier* 24 August 1797.
53. T.W. Tone, *Life of Theobald Wolfe Tone*, vol. ii (Washington, 1826), p.432.
54. *State Trials* xxvi cols. 1147, 1159.
55. J. Kennedy declaration 11 April 1798, JC 26/298, SRO.
56. JC 26/295, SRO for an example of a 'somewhat intoxicated' recruit.
57. Elliott, *Partners in Revolution* (1982), pp.152–61.
58. Colley, *Britons*, pp.293–5.
59. Tone, *Wolfe Tone*, vol. ii (1812), p.132.
60. *Ibid*, p.462.
61. AAE Memoires et Documents (Angl.) II ff.153–72.
62. For a compelling narrative see, T. Pakenham, *The Year of Liberty* (London, 1972).
63. McFarland, *Ireland and Scotland*, p.194–5.
64. J. Brims, 'Scottish Democratic Movementment', vol. 2 (1983), p.573.
65. C. Hope -Lord Pelham 4 August 1803, RH2/4/88 f.231, SRO.
66. For a full discussion of relations with English reformers see W. Roach, 'Radical Reform Movements in Scotland' (PhD Thesis, University of Glasgow, 1970) and W.H. Fraser in *Conflict and Class: Scottish Workers 1700–1838* (Edinburgh, 1988), pp.108–10.
67. RH 2/4/92 ff.70–4, SRO.
68. *Glasgow Herald*, 15 March 1813.
69. *Glasgow Chronicle*, 13 February 1816.
70. A. Colquhoun to Lord Sidmouth 4 December 1812, RH 2/4/98 f.330, SRO.

71. A. Maconochie to Lord Sidmouth 25 December 1816, RH 2/4/112 f.729, SRO. The Spencean Philanthropists were also reported to have a Glasgow outpost: *Glasgow Chronicle* 22 December 1817; *Hansard* XXXV, cols. pp.411–18.
72. A.B. Richmond, *A Narrative of the Condition of the Manufacturing Population and the Proceeding of Government which lead to the State Trials in Scotland* (Glasgow, 1824), p.183.
73. AD 14/17/18, SRO.
74. A. Machonochie to Lord Sidmouth 26 December 1816, RH 2/4/112 f.722.
75. See *Glasgow Courier* 29 March and 29 May 1798. For an official view of the Irish see the Duke of Hamilton's remarks in *Glasgow Chronicle* 9 December 1819.

Index